European Agencies in between Institutions and Member States

EUROPEAN MONOGRAPHS

In the European Monographs series this book, *European Agencies in between Institutions and Member States*, is the eighty-fifth title. The titles published in this series are listed at the end of this volume.

European Agencies in between Institutions and Member States

Edited by

Michelle Everson
Cosimo Monda
Ellen Vos

Wolters Kluwer
Law & Business

Published by:
Kluwer Law International
PO Box 316
2400 AH Alphen aan den Rijn
The Netherlands
Website: www.kluwerlaw.com

Sold and distributed in North, Central and South America by:
Aspen Publishers, Inc.
7201 McKinney Circle
Frederick, MD 21704
United States of America
Email: customer.service@aspenpublishers.com

Sold and distributed in all other countries by:
Turpin Distribution Services Ltd
Stratton Business Park
Pegasus Drive, Biggleswade
Bedfordshire SG18 8TQ
United Kingdom
Email: kluwerlaw@turpin-distribution.com

Printed on acid-free paper.

ISBN 978-90-411-2843-0

© 2014 Kluwer Law International BV, The Netherlands

Printed and Bound by CPI Group (UK) Ltd, Croydon, CR0 4YY.

List of Editors and Contributors

Madalina Busuioc, Fellow in Risk and Regulation, London School of Economics and Political Science, UK

Florin Coman-Kund, PhD-Researcher, Faculty of Law, Maastricht University, the Netherlands

Michelle Everson, Professor of Law, Director of University International Diploma, Birkbeck, University of London, UK

Martijn Groenleer, Assistant Professor of Public Administration, Faculty of Technology, Policy and Management, Delft University, the Netherlands

Francis Jacobs, Head of Office, European Parliament Information Office Dublin, Ireland

Michael Kaeding, Professor and Jean Monnet Chair of European Integration and European Union Politics, University of Duisburg-Essen, Germany

Cosimo Monda, Senior Lecturer and Head of Information and Marketing Services, European Institute of Public Administration (EIPA), Maastricht, the Netherlands

Andrea Ott, Associate Professor and Jean Monnet Chair in EU Law, Maastricht University, the Netherlands

Annetje Ottow, Professor of Public Economic Law at the Europa Institute of Utrecht University, the Netherlands

Esther Versluis, Associate Professor of European Regulatory Governance, Maastricht University, the Netherlands

Ellen Vos, Professor of European Union Law, Law Faculty and co-director Maastricht Centre for European Law, Maastricht University, the Netherlands

Marco Zinzani, Associate, Studio Legale Padovan, Milano, Italy; academic coordinator Jean Monnet European Module, Tor Vergata University, Rome, Italy

Summary of Contents

List of Editors and Contributors   v

List of Abbreviations   xvii

Acknowledgements   xxi

PART I
Introduction   1

CHAPTER 1
European Agencies in between Institutions and Member States
Michelle Everson, Cosimo Monda & Ellen Vos   3

PART II
European Agencies and the EU's Institutional Balance of Powers   9

CHAPTER 2
European Agencies and the Composite EU Executive
Ellen Vos   11

CHAPTER 3
European Agencies: Barely Legal?
Michelle Everson   49

PART III
European Agencies: New, Old Roles and New Generations   71

CHAPTER 4
EU Agencies as a Solution to Pan-European Implementation Problems
Michael Kaeding & Esther Versluis   73

CHAPTER 5
European Agencies on the Global Scene: EU and International Law Perspectives
Andrea Ott, Ellen Vos & Florin Coman-Kund   87

CHAPTER 6
The New European Supervisory Architecture of the Financial Markets
Annetje Ottow   123

CHAPTER 7
Towards a New Agency Model? The Example of Telecommunications
Marco Zinzani   145

PART IV
Accountability and Democratic Control of European Agencies   173

CHAPTER 8
The Theory and Practice of EU Agency Autonomy and Accountability:
Early Day Expectations, Today's Realities and Future Perspectives
Madalina Busuioc & Martijn Groenleer   175

CHAPTER 9
EU Agencies and the European Parliament
Francis Jacobs   201

PART V
Conclusion   229

CHAPTER 10
What Is the Future of European Agencies?
Michelle Everson, Cosimo Monda & Ellen Vos   231

ANNEX I
Overview of European Agencies   241

ANNEX II
Joint Statement and Common Approach of the European Parliament,
the Council of the EU and the European Commission on Decentralized
Agencies of 19 July 2012   263

Table of Contents

List of Editors and Contributors   v

List of Abbreviations   xvii

Acknowledgements   xxi

PART I
Introduction   1

CHAPTER 1
European Agencies in between Institutions and Member States
Michelle Everson, Cosimo Monda & Ellen Vos   3

§1.01   EU Agencies at the Heart of European Integration   3
§1.02   From 'Ad hocery' to Common Approach   4
§1.03   European Agencies as 'Barely Legal' Hybrids   5
§1.04   EU Agencies: New, Old Roles and New Generations   6
§1.05   Accountability and Democratic Control of EU Agencies   7

PART II
European Agencies and the EU's Institutional Balance of Powers   9

CHAPTER 2
European Agencies and the Composite EU Executive
Ellen Vos   11

§2.01   Introduction   11
§2.02   The Upsurge of European Agencies in the Institutional Landscape
         of the EU   13

Table of Contents

§2.03   Definition and Taxonomy   17
        [A]   Functional Taxonomy   20
        [B]   Numerical Taxonomy   21
        [C]   Legal Taxonomy   21
§2.04   Hybrid Nature   23
§2.05   Sui Generis EU Agency Design   25
        [A]   Different but Similar Organizational Structure   25
        [B]   Less Is More?   25
        [C]   Member States on the Boards   26
        [D]   Conceptual Underpinning for Having Member States on
               the Boards   28
        [E]   Toothless Tigers?   30
        [F]   Towards a 'Ministerial' Responsibility?   31
§2.06   Agencies between Independence, Control, and Conflicting Interests 33
        [A]   Manifold Control and Accountability Mechanisms   33
        [B]   Independence and Conflicts of Interests   35
               [1]   European Parliament's Worries about Agencies'
                      Independence   35
               [2]   Independence as a Legal and Relative Concept   36
               [3]   Independence and European Agencies   38
§2.07   Delegation of Powers and *Meroni*   40
§2.08   Constitutional Recognition and Neglect   42
§2.09   Concluding Remarks   45

CHAPTER 3
European Agencies: Barely Legal?
Michelle Everson   49

§3.01   Institutional Balance: Between Constitutionality and the
        Rule of Law   49
§3.02   From 'Independent' Expertise to a Political Administration?   56
        [A]   Autonomy and Accountability in the Commission's Agency
               Model   56
        [B]   A Politicized Administration?   60
§3.03   Agencies in Action within the ESFS: A Tale of Unaccountable
        Inefficiency?   62
        [A]   Autonomy and Efficiency   65
        [B]   Accountability and Transparency   66
§3.04   A Complex European Executive with a Troubled Future?   68

PART III
European Agencies: New, Old Roles and New Generations   71

CHAPTER 4
EU Agencies as a Solution to Pan-European Implementation Problems
Michael Kaeding & Esther Versluis   73

§4.01	Introduction	73
§4.02	Implementation Tasks of EU Agencies	75
§4.03	EU Agencies as a Cure for EU Implementation Problems?	81
	[A] From Theoretical Expectations...	81
	[B] ...To the Latest Empirical Insights	82
§4.04	Concluding Discussion	84

CHAPTER 5
European Agencies on the Global Scene: EU and International Law Perspectives
Andrea Ott, Ellen Vos & Florin Coman-Kund 87

§5.01	Introduction	87
§5.02	Agencies' Actions in Light of International and EU Law	90
	[A] Defining an International Agreement	90
	[B] Inter-agency Agreements	91
	[C] International Agreements According to EU Law	94
	[1] Do Multiple International Legal Personalities Exist in the EU?	94
	[2] Institutional Balance in EU External Relations	94
§5.03	EU Agencies: Delegation and Typology in View of Their International Powers	98
	[A] Delegation	98
	[B] Disciplining the Reality: Typology	100
§5.04	EU Agencies' External Actions: Examples of Provisions and Practice	101
	[A] Category 1: Prior Approval by the Commission or Council	101
	[1] EASA	102
	[2] Europol	105
	[B] Category 2: Prior Consultation with the Commission	109
	[C] Category 3: General Mandate for International Action	112
§5.05	Agencies Global Activities: Overall Analysis	113
	[A] EU Law Perspective	114
	[B] International Law Perspective	115
§5.06	Conclusions	115
Annex		118

CHAPTER 6
The New European Supervisory Architecture of the Financial Markets
Annetje Ottow 123

§6.01	Introduction	123
§6.02	Europeanization: The New Trend	124
§6.03	The Original Starting Point: National Supervision ('Home State Control Model')	125
§6.04	Old Networks of National Regulatory Authorities and the Lamfalussy Process	127

§6.05   New Financial Authorities   129
     [A]   EBA, ESMA, and EIOPA   129
     [B]   A New Additional European Authority: ECB as European
         Prudential Supervisor   130
§6.06   Powers of the European Financial Supervisors   131
     [A]   European Systemic Risk Board   131
     [B]   European Supervisory Authorities   131
     [C]   The New Role of the ECB   132
§6.07   The New Institutional Structure   134
     [A]   Influence of the NRAs in the ESAs   134
     [B]   Influence of the Commission   135
     [C]   The Position of ECB: Embedding Its Independence   136
     [D]   *Meroni* Issues   137
§6.08   New Enforcement Powers: A Major Shift towards Europeanization   138
     [A]   The First Shift: Direct Interventions by the ESAs   139
     [B]   The Second Shift: Single Supervision by the ESMA on Credit
         Rating Agencies   140
     [C]   The Third Shift: Direct Enforcement by the ECB   142
§6.09   Challenges for the Future   142

CHAPTER 7
Towards a New Agency Model? The Example of Telecommunications
Marco Zinzani   145

§7.01   Introduction   145
§7.02   The Cooperation among European Telecom Regulators   148
     [A]   The Predecessors of the BEREC: The IRG as a Loose
         Network of Regulators   149
     [B]   The Predecessors of the BEREC: The IRG as an Enhanced
         Network of Regulators   150
§7.03   The BEREC and the Office   153
     [A]   Analysis of the BEREC   156
         [1]   Institutional Structure   156
         [2]   Powers   158
     [B]   Analysis of the Office   162
         [1]   Institutional Structure   162
         [2]   Powers   163
         [3]   Overall Compliance of the BEREC and the Office with
             the Principles of Good Governance   164
§7.04   Evaluation of the BEREC and the Office: New Model or Cosmetic
     Exercise?   168
§7.05   Conclusion   171

PART IV
Accountability and Democratic Control of European Agencies   173

CHAPTER 8
The Theory and Practice of EU Agency Autonomy and Accountability:
Early Day Expectations, Today's Realities and Future Perspectives
Madalina Busuioc & Martijn Groenleer   175

§8.01   Introduction: From Solution to Problem   175
§8.02   Early Day Expectations   177
         [A]   (Policy) Effectiveness through Independent Expertise   177
                [1]   Improving Policy Advice   177
                [2]   Enhancing the Enforcement of Policy Decisions   178
                [3]   Beyond Existing Institutional Solutions   179
                [4]   The Assumption of Independence   180
         [B]   Independent, Hence Unaccountable and Not (Democratically)
                Legitimate?   182
                [1]   Increasing Transparency, Visibility, and Accessibility   182
                [2]   'The Rise of the Unelected' and Its Risks   183
                [3]   Towards a 'Catch 22'   184
§8.03   Today's Realities   185
         [A]   Autonomy   185
                [1]   From Independence to Autonomy   185
                [2]   Limited Formal Autonomy upon Creation   185
                [3]   Institutionalization: Variation in Actual Autonomy across
                       Agencies and over Time   188
                [4]   Demonstrated Capacity   189
                [5]   Networks of Support   190
         [B]   Accountability   191
                [1]   From Control to Accountability   191
                [2]   Not Unaccountable: A Multiplicity of Accountability
                       Obligations   192
                [3]   A Lack of Tailored Accountability   195
                [4]   Ensuing Overloads   196
                [5]   Yet Still Deficits: Underuse of Formal Accountability   197
§8.04   Conclusion: From Problem to Solution?   199

CHAPTER 9
EU Agencies and the European Parliament
Francis Jacobs   201

§9.01   Introduction   201
§9.02   The European Parliament's Increasing Involvement with the
         Decentralized Agencies   202

§9.03   Formal Framework for European Parliament Involvement with the
         Agencies   205
         [A]   General References in the EU Treaties and in Inter-Institutional
               Agreements   205
         [B]   Specific References to the European Parliament in the Founding
               Regulations of the Agencies   205
         [C]   Appointment of Members of the Management Boards, the
               Executive Director and/or Other Organs   206
               [1]   Agencies Where the European Parliament Only Has
                     the Right to Nominate Members of the Management
                     Board   206
               [2]   Agencies with an European Parliament Role in the
                     Appointment of the Director but with No Nominees
                     on the Management Board   207
               [3]   Agencies Where European Parliament Has Both a Role
                     in the Appointment of the Director and Has Its Own
                     Nominees on the Management Board   208
               [4]   Re-appointment of Directors or Other Officeholders   208
               [5]   Dismissal of Directors or Other Officeholders   209
§9.04   Other References to the European Parliament   209
§9.05   The European Parliament and Agencies and the European
         Parliament: The Management of Mutual Relations   211
         [A]   Mechanisms for European Parliament Committee Engagement
               with the Agencies   211
               [1]   Delegation Visits to Agencies   213
               [2]   Committee Contact Persons and Standing Rapporteurs   214
               [3]   Dialogue with European Parliament Nominees on
                     Management Boards   215
               [4]   Exchange of Letters/Memoranda of Understanding
                     between European Parliament Committee Chairs and
                     Agency Directors   215
               [5]   The European Parliament and Agencies: Agencies as
                     Information Providers   215
               [6]   The Budgets and Budgetary Discharge Instruments   216
         [B]   Agency Mechanisms   217
§9.06   European Parliament's Position as Regards General Strategic
         Questions Concerning Agencies   218
         [A]   Need to Create an Agency   218
         [B]   Location   218
         [C]   Experience of the European Parliament Nominees on the
               Board, and Is Their Presence Justified?   219

[D]   Role of the European Parliament in the Appointment and
      Reappointment of Agency Directors   221
[E]   Budgetary Issues   222
§9.07   The Search for a General Framework   224
§9.08   Concluding Remarks   227

PART V
Conclusion   229

CHAPTER 10
What Is the Future of European Agencies?
Michelle Everson, Cosimo Monda & Ellen Vos   231

§10.01   The Extraordinary Agency Phenomenon   231
§10.02   Legitimating 'Politicized' Autonomy?   236
§10.03   A Future under Negotiation   238

ANNEX I
Overview of European Agencies   241

ANNEX II
Joint Statement and Common Approach of the European Parliament,
the Council of the EU and the European Commission on Decentralized
Agencies of 19 July 2012   263

List of Abbreviations

ACER	Agency for the Cooperation of Energy Regulators
AFCO	Constitutional Affairs Committee
AIDS	Acquired Immunodeficiency Dyndrome
Art.	Article
ASBL	Association Sans But Lucratif (non-profit organization under Belgian law)
BEREC	Body of European Regulators for Electronic Communications
BSE	Bovine Spongiform Encephalopathy
BTS	Binding Technical Standard
CdT	Translation Centre for the Bodies of the European Union
CEBS	Committee of European Banking Supervisors
CEDEFOP	European Centre for the Development of Vocational Training
CEIOPS	Committee of European Insurance and Occupational Pensions Supervisors
CEPOL	European Police College
CESR	Committee of European Securities Regulators
CFSP	Common Foreign and Security Policy
CJEU	Court of Justice of the European Union
COCOM	Communications Committee
CPVO	Community Plant Variety Office
DCAF	Democratic Control of Armed Forces
DG	Directorate General
DNB	Dutch National Bank
EACEA	Education, Audiovisual and Culture Executive Agency

EACI	Executive Agency for Competitiveness and Innovation
EAHC	Executive Agency for Health and Consumers
EASA	European Aviation Safety Agency
EASO	European Asylum Support Office
EBA	European Banking Authority
EC	European Commission
ECB	European Central Bank
ECDC	European Centre for Disease Prevention and Control
ECHA	European Chemicals Agency
ECJ	European Court of Justice
ECSC	European Coal and Steel Treaty
EDA	European Defence Agency
EEA	European Environment Agency
EEA	European Economic Area
EECMA	European Electronic Communications Market Authority
EFCA	European Fisheries Control Agency
EFSA	European Food Safety Authority
EFTA	European Free Trade Association
EIGE	European Institute for Gender Equality
EIOPA	European Insurance and Occupational Pensions Authority
EMA	European Medicines Agency
EMEA	European Medicines Agency
EMCDDA	European Monitoring Centre for Drugs and Drug Addiction
EMSA	European Maritime Safety Agency
ENISA	European Network and Information Security Agency
ENP	European Neighbourhood Policy
EP	European Parliament
ERA	European Railway Agency
ERCEA	European Research Council Executive Agency
ERG	European Regulators Group
ESA	European Supervisory Authority
ESFS	European System of Financial Supervisors
ESM	European Stability Mechanism
ESMA	European Securities and Markets Authority
ESRB	European Systemic Risk Board
ETF	European Training Foundation
EU	European Union
EUMC	European Monitoring Centre for Racism and Xenophobia

EU-OSHA	European Agency for Safety and Health at Work
EUROFOUND	European Foundation for the Improvement of Living and Working Conditions
EUROJUST	European Union's Judicial Cooperation Unit
EUROPOL	European Police Office
EUISS	European Union Institute for Security Studies
EUSC	European Union Satellite Centre
FRA	Fundamental Rights Agency
FRONTEX	European Agency for the Management of Operational Cooperation at the External Borders
GNSS	Global Navigation Satellite System
GSA	European GNSS Agency
HIV	Human Immunodeficiency Virus
IAC	Internal Audit Capacity
IAC	Interstate Aviation Committee
IAS	Internal Service Audit
ICMPD	International Center for Migration Policy Development
ILSI	International Life Sciences Institute Europe
IOM	International Organization for Migration
IRG	Independent Regulators Group
IT-Agency	European Agency for the operational management of large-scale IT systems in the area of freedom, security and justice
ITER	International Thermonuclear Experimental Reactor, the international fusion project
JAA	Joint Aviation Authority
MEP	Member of the European Parliament
MS	Member State
NCB	National Central Bank
NGA	Next Generation Access
NRA	National Regulatory Authority
NSA	National Supervisory Authority
OHIM	Office for the Harmonization in the Internal Market (Trade Marks and Designs)
OJ	Official Journal
OSHA	Organisation for Safety and Health at Work
PIB	Principles of Implementation and Best Practices
REA	Research Executive Agency
SSM	Single Supervisory Mechanism
TEN-T EA	Trans-European Transport Network Executive Agency
TEU	Treaty on European Union

TFEU	Treaty on the Functioning of the European Union
UK	United Kingdom
UNHCR	United Nations Commissioner of Refugees
UNODC	United Nations Office on Drug and Crime
US	United States
VCLT	Vienna Convention on the Law of Treaties
WHO	World Health Organization

Acknowledgements

This book was inspired by the many seminars that Cosimo Monda, Adriaan Schout and Ellen Vos organized in Maastricht between 2005 and 2010 under the title *Fashion or necessity? EU agencies in between EU institutions and Member States* on the basis of the collaboration between the European Institute of Public Administration (EIPA) and the Law Faculty of Maastricht University. Encouraged by the intense discussions between speakers and participants of these seminars, we embraced the idea of writing a book on the position of European agencies in the institutional landscape of the EU, operating in between the European Institutions and the Member States. This has resulted in the present volume.

The publication of this book would not have been possible without the help of a number of colleagues and friends. First and foremost we would like to express our thanks to all the contributors for their collaboration and commitment to the publication of this book. Special and sincere thanks go to Adriaan Schout with whom we had many discussions on the agency phenomenon and the elaboration of this book and who unfortunately, due to other commitments, could not contribute to this book. We would like to thank the speakers in our EIPA seminars who were a source of inspiration and information, in particular: Fabian Pereyra, Fabia Jones, Manuel Szapiro, Fernand Sauer and Mario Tenreiro: many thanks! We would also like to thank the participants of the expert meeting *Reflections on the Common Approach to Agencies* that we organised in October 2012.

Our dear colleague Marina Jodogne was incredibly competent in the formatting and editing of this book. She provided invaluable assistance through her able and patient work. She even came back from her holidays to help us out with the last bits of the manuscript. Without her, we would have been lost. We are enormously grateful to her for all her help. We would like to sincerely thank Carol Ní Ghiollarnáth for doing the language revision of the chapters so competently and promptly.

We would also like to express our gratitude to Giulia Giardi, Chiara Larghi and Anne-Sophie König for their help in drafting the overview table of all existing agencies, included as Annex 1 to this book. The friendly and co-operative attitude and patience of the colleagues of Kluwer Law Publishing, in particular Karel van der Linde and Lisa Zoltowska, were a constant encouragement to finish the publication of this volume.

Michelle Everson
Cosimo Monda
Ellen Vos
Maastricht, July 2013

PART I   Introduction

CHAPTER 1

European Agencies in between Institutions and Member States

Michelle Everson, Cosimo Monda & Ellen Vos

§1.01 EU AGENCIES AT THE HEART OF EUROPEAN INTEGRATION

The EU cannot be imagined without European agencies; it simply cannot function without them. European agencies perform a key role in the European integration process. These agencies, denoted recently by the Council, Commission, and Parliament as decentralized agencies,[1] deal with complex technical and scientific issues by providing expertise, they introduce more, and more flexible, administrative capacity and efficiency. They facilitate, coordinate, and strengthen cooperation between national authorities, (re)gain trust and credibility, improve implementation, supervision, and increase networking and participation of more actors, such as stakeholders and citizens. They adopt important decisions for both the European economy and its citizens, deciding about the registration of European trademarks, plant varieties, and certain chemical substances as well as about the airworthiness of airplanes. And, where they do not have binding decision-making powers, they do influence EU decision making to a great extent, for example, with their scientific opinions on the safety of foods and medicines, most of which are followed by the European Commission. Even agencies that merely collect data play a key role, as this data gathering guides the EU in its policy and decision-making.

EU agencies thus are critical for European integration, for the EU's economy and the well-being of its citizens. It is therefore no surprise that agencies, as 'non-majoritarian' creatures, were very much welcomed in the 1990s and especially in the 2000s and were seen as appropriate responses to various crises (e.g., BSE, oil tanker

---

1. For an overview of all agencies that exist in the EU's institutional landscape, see Annex 1 to this volume. This volume is foremost concerned with the decentralized agencies.

3

Erika) so as to overcome a lack of confidence in and credibility of EU decision-making. The enthusiasm of the EU for European agencies is understandable. Agencies have allowed the European Commission greater room to concentrate on its core tasks and policy priorities, as more specific administrative tasks were delegated to agencies. The creation of agencies has also responded to the need for more uniformity in the implementation of EU policies where harmonization appeared less attractive while upholding the EU's system of decentralized implementation.[2]

Many books and even more articles have been written about European agencies, offering comprehensive analyses of the agency phenomenon in the EU.[3] Our volume will therefore not repeat that. Instead it will focus on vital questions as to the role and powers of agencies in relation to their manifold 'principals', the EU institutions and the Member States, benefitting from both academic and practitioner insights from legal, political, and social sciences. It will address current queries about the position of EU agencies within the EU executive and the risk of fragmentation of powers and the kind of powers that should be conferred upon agencies, as well as their efficacy and accountability. It will therefore critically reflect on the position of agencies in the transformation of the EU executive. Key here is the question of what role agencies (should) have in the EU's institutional balance of powers and what kind of powers can be delegated to them. The book will therefore focus on the discussion of three new, old roles taken on by agencies that impact the interplay between agencies and the institutions and Member States, namely their roles as regards implementation and supervision and their role as a global actor. At the same time this book will investigate whether over time a new kind of agency has been developed based on former networks of national regulators in the telecoms sector and the supervisory authorities in the financial sector

§1.02   FROM 'AD HOCERY' TO COMMON APPROACH

While the first two agencies (EUROFOUND and CEDEFOP) were already created in 1975, it was only in the 1990s that other agencies were created. This was very much based on the need for more information (European Environment Agency) or scientific underpinning (European Medicines Agency) and not so much based on a general vision of the need for agencies in the EU setting. Yet, with the great enthusiasm for agencies at the end of the 1990s enabling confidence and credibility to be gained, also worries about the fragmentation of powers that delegation of powers to agencies entailed arose.[4] In 2002 therefore the European Commission called for a restructuring and rethinking of the role of European agencies in the institutional structure and proposed to set common framework for these agencies with defined structures and

---

2. R. Dehousse, 'Regulation by Networks in the European Community: The Role of European Agencies', *Journal of European Public Policy* 4, no. 2 (1997): 246–261.
3. See most recently, J. Trondal, M. Busuioc & M. Groenleer (eds.), *The Agency Phenomenon in the European Union* (Manchester: MUP, 2012).
4. See e.g., the speech by Romano Prodi, then President of the European Commission, before the European Parliament, 3 October 2002, SPEECH/00/352, < http://europa.eu.int/comm/commiss ioners/prodi/speeches/index_en.htm > .

responsibilities. The Council however systematically undermined these efforts, disagreeing with the Commission foremost on the form of the proposed framework (an interinstitutional agreement) and the proposed design (without Member States' representatives on the boards of agencies). After more than ten years of discussion on such a framework, the Council, Commission, and Parliament managed to adopt in 2012 a Joint Statement together with a Common Approach on decentralized agencies stipulating provisions on the organizational structure, powers, control, and accountability of agencies.[5] Importantly, the institutions confirmed the importance of agencies for the operation of the EU. While most of the provisions of the Common Approach do not come as a surprise and confirm the design, oversight, and accountability mechanisms of agencies currently in place, the Common Approach does bring some novelties. At the same time, the Common Approach has been received with criticism for not improving accountability and for putting into place weak monitoring mechanisms.[6] The Common Approach will be disparagingly discussed in the various contributions to this volume.

§1.03   EUROPEAN AGENCIES AS 'BARELY LEGAL' HYBRIDS

The second section of the book offers a discussion on the current challenges surrounding European agencies in terms of their hybrid nature, design, independence, delegation of powers, as well as the (dis)regard for agencies by the Lisbon Treaty. Ellen Vos examines the particular design of agencies in Chapter 2 and discusses how European agencies are modelled on the basis of networks, with national counterparts and/or stakeholders. It is this strong interplay with their national counterparts that typifies European agencies. They have been designed to operate as a kind of 'primus inter pares' with the national authorities, instead of being hierarchically placed above the national authorities, although in practice the agencies have a strong say and impact in the networks. She argues that European agencies based on network structures between national and European levels are in line with and part of the composite or shared administration of the EU in which agencies have become crucial amalgams between EU institutions and Member States. Agencification is thus part of the emerging European executive[7] within a system of integrated administration characterized by intense cooperation between the various executive levels.[8] Hereby the 'double-hatted' or 'triple-hatted' character of agencies seems at odds with requirements of independency. Ellen Vos moreover holds that the lack of the constitutional position of agencies with regard to the adoption of non-legislative acts may be problematic for a number of reasons.

---

5. See Annex 2 to this volume.
6. See *EU Institutions Fail to Improve Governance of EU Regulatory Agencies*, Statewatch News Online, August 2012, < http://database.statewatch.org/article.asp?aid=31729 > .
7. D. Curtin, *Executive Power of the European Union. Law, Practices and the Living Constitution* (Oxford: Oxford University Press, 2009).
8. See e.g., H.C.H. Hofmann & A. Turk (eds.), *EU Administrative Governance* (Cheltenham: Edward Elgar Publishing, 2006).

This question of the constitutionality of the position of European agencies within the EU's institutional balance of powers is further discussed by Michelle Everson in Chapter 3. Especially the question as to which powers may be delegated continues to be hotly debated, both in scholarly discussion and in daily practice. This is forcefully shown by the recent submission by the UK government arguing that delegation of powers to the European Securities and Markets Authority infringes the *Meroni* doctrine.[9] Michelle Everson therefore discusses the validity of the *Meroni*, 'anti-delegation' or better restrictive delegation of powers, doctrine and its application to the new kind of agencies, including the three supervisory agencies set up in the financial sector. These agencies challenge our accepted vision of the balance of powers as they have direct rule-making and supervisory competences that would clearly infringe the *Meroni* doctrine.

§1.04 EU AGENCIES: NEW, OLD ROLES AND NEW GENERATIONS

The Chapters in the third section of the book discuss new, old roles of agencies as well as new generations of agencies created in the field of the financial sector and telecommunications. Michael Keading and Esther Versluis consider in Chapter 4 the role of agencies to create more uniformity in the implementation of EU policies at the national level. While this 'implementation role' as such is not new, it is true that today agencies are increasingly considered to be a solution to the problematic implementation of EU law at the national level and powers are increasingly conferred to them related to ensuring that rules are implemented and enforced effectively and uniformly. They therefore investigate this new, old role of agencies and herewith the important interplay between European agencies and implementation at national level. They look at whether EU agencies truly can contribute to addressing the non-compliance of EU law by Member States and whether they can contribute to the improving of national implementation records by investigating the empirical reality.

A second new, old role of agencies is their role at the global plane. Also here this 'global role' of agencies is not really new as already the first two agencies EUROFOUND and CEDEFOP had a mandate to operate closely with partner bodies at the international level. Yet it is only recently that agencies have started to gain recognition as global actors and have become increasingly active at the international level, operating not only as EU agencies but also as EU agencies 'acting on behalf of the Member States'. Andrea Ott, Ellen Vos and Florin Coman-Kund examine in Chapter 5 the legal consequences of agencies' international activities. They categorize agencies in view of their external relations powers and discuss the legal nature of the acts of agencies and the impact on the EU's institutional balance of powers.

A third new, old role of agencies is a supervisory one, a role closely connected to the implementation role discussed in Chapter 4. Also this 'supervisory role' is not entirely new as a few agencies already had some kind of inspection tasks. However the implementation of this role with regard to the new supervisory authorities in the

---

9. Case C-270/12, *United Kingdom v. Council and Parliament*, OJ 2012, C273/2.

financial sector, following the economic and financial crises, is truly novel. Annetje Ottow explores these agencies within the new supervisory structure for the financial sectors in Chapter 6. She discusses the way in which powers are divided between European and national authorities and whether the agencies impact the implementation and application of EU measures at the national level. While these supervisory agencies are of interest for the new, old role that they fulfil, at the same time they are exemplary of the new generation of agencies created in the 2010s. These agencies largely rely on existing networks of national regulators that have been transformed into EU agencies. Marco Zinzani analyses such a new agency in the field of telecommunications, BEREC, in Chapter 7. He discusses the commonalities and differences between BEREC and the classic agencies.

§1.05   ACCOUNTABILITY AND DEMOCRATIC CONTROL OF EU AGENCIES

The hybrid character of agencies as part of the composite EU executive, and the fact that increasing powers are delegated to them, makes to need to pay attention to the efficacy and accountability of agencies ever more important. In Chapter 8 Madalina Busuioc and Martijn Groenleer therefore address the realities of the accountability mechanisms set in place currently; mechanisms that often test relations between agencies, the institutions and Member States. Here the perennial challenge underlying agency governance is to strike a balance between the autonomy of agencies, which is supposed to lead to more effective EU governance in the field in which agencies operate and the accountability they must render, which is to ensure their democratic legitimacy and that of the EU more generally. Democratic legitimacy and the role of the European Parliament vis-à-vis agencies are further elaborated on in the last chapter of the book. In Chapter 9 Francis Jacobs discusses the intricacies of the relationship between agencies and the European Parliament and investigates both formal and informal instruments and mechanisms set in place by the Parliament to get a better understanding on agencies.

Following the various contributions in this volume, challenges ahead and future perspectives on EU agencies are discussed by Michelle Everson, Cosimo Monda and Ellen Vos in Chapter 10.

PART II   European Agencies and the EU's Institutional Balance of Powers

CHAPTER 2

European Agencies and the Composite EU Executive

Ellen Vos

§2.01 INTRODUCTION

Today, almost forty years after the creation of the first two agencies in the EU's institutional structure, the European Foundation for the Improvement of Living and Working Conditions (EUROFOUND)[1] and the European Centre for the Development of Vocational Training (CEDEFOP),[2] the EU has over forty agencies that play an important role in the various policy areas.[3] This agencification is part of the emerging European executive[4] within a system of integrated administration characterized by intense cooperation between the various executive levels.[5] European agencies have been assigned a mixture of tasks in this, varying from provision of information to decision-making in various policy fields, such as food and air safety, medicines, environment, telecommunications, disease prevention, border control, trademarks, and banking. They make up part of a process of functional decentralization within the EU executive, with agencies being seated all over the EU from Helsinki to Crete, forming the 'long tentacles of Brussels'[6] in the Member States. As such they rely to a large extent on

---

1. Council Regulation (EEC) 1365/75 of 10 February 1975 establishing a European Centre for Development and Vocational Training [1975] OJ L39/1.
2. Council Regulation (EEC) 337/75 of 26 May 1975 on the creation of a European Foundation for the improvement of living and working conditions [1975] OJ L139/1.
3. See below and Annex 1 to this book.
4. D. Curtin, *Executive Power of the European Union. Law, Practices and the Living Constitution* (Oxford: Oxford University Press, 2009).
5. See H.C.H. Hofmann, 'Mapping the European Administrative Space', *West European Politics* 31 (2008): 671.
6. In the words of the title of an article on European agencies in a Dutch newspaper: 'De lange tentakels van Brussel', *NRC*, 25 September 2004.

networks, both inside and outside their formal institutional structure, with national authorities, experts, and/or stakeholders. Resorting to agencies has particularly been the EU's response to various crises, such as the BSE crisis, the oil tanker Erika crisis, and most recently the financial crisis, leading to a steep increase in the number of agencies in the 2000s.

Over the years these unforeseen and 'non-majoritarian'[7] actors have acquired an important place within the EU's institutional landscape and have become a true feature of European integration. Yet, the haphazard manner in which agencies have been created has led to queries as to the precise role and governance of agencies within the EU's institutional structure. Since the early 2000s the European Commission has attempted to set up a more coherent approach to agencies in the form of a general framework, stipulating provisions on the organizational structure, powers, control, and accountability. While the European Parliament largely sympathized with this initiative, the Council was particularly critical of it and did not see the need to set up such a framework.[8] The Commission however did not renounce its plans to have some kind of framework. After more than six years of cumbersome and unsuccessful negotiations on such a framework, it changed strategy and launched an interinstitutional dialogue between the Commission, the European Parliament and the Council in 2008 on the 'way forward' as regards European agencies.[9] In particular the role of Member States in agencies' management boards as well as the role of the European Parliament vis-à-vis the nomination of agency directors became problematic in the discussion. Finally on 12 June 2012, 'a genuine breakthrough for the good governance and the improved efficiency, effectiveness, transparency, and accountability of the EU's decentralized agencies'[10] was achieved by means of the adoption of a Joint Statement and a Common Approach, clarifying some of the challenging issues as regards the governance of EU agencies, and at last a common position on the composition of the agencies' management boards was taken.[11]

In that same year, two other developments were of importance for our discussion on agencies. First the accusations of the European Parliament in that year that the European Medicines Agency (EMA), the European Food Safety Authority (EFSA) as well as the European Environment Agency (EEA) could not properly guarantee the independence of their staff and external experts,[12] resulted in agencies' (lack of) independence now featuring highly on the political agenda. Moreover, in that year the

---

7. See G. Majone, 'The New European Agencies: Regulation by Information', *Journal of European Public Policy* 4, no. 2 (1997): 262–275. See in general G. Majone, *Regulating Europe* (London: Routledge, 1996).
8. Especially not in the form of an interinstitutional agreement. See F. Comte, '2008 Commission Communication "*European Agencies – The Way forward*": What is the Follow-up since then?', *Review of European Administrative Law* 3, no. 1 (2010): 69.
9. See COM(2008) 135.
10. Vice-President Maroš Šefčovič, Commissioner for Interinstitutional Relations and Administration, Press release European Commission of 13 June 2012, IP/12/604.
11. Joint Statement and Common Approach of the European Parliament, the Council of the EU and the European Commission on Decentralized Agencies of 19 July 2012, see Annex 2 to this book.
12. See 'EU Police College and Medicines Agency management not good enough, says Budgetary Control Committee' European Parliament News (Brussels 11 April 2011). See in more detail section §2.06[B][1].

British government decided to challenge the powers afforded to the European Market Security Authority (ESMA)[13] as they would violate the EU's institutional balance and the so-called *Meroni* doctrine.[14] This has revived the longstanding discussion on which kind of powers may be delegated to agencies in full glory. The debate surrounding the position of agencies and their powers has become even more relevant as the Lisbon Treaty overlooked agencies as possible receivers of delegated powers and provided for delegation of powers to the European Commission as the sole actor of executive powers that remain at the EU level.[15] This is all the more surprising as the Lisbon Treaty meaningfully squares agencies in the Treaties' provisions on transparency and judicial review.

This Chapter therefore will critically reflect on the position and role of European agencies in the EU's institutional setting post-Lisbon. It will address current challenges surrounding European agencies in terms of their hybrid nature (section §2.04), design (section §2.05), independence (section §2.06), delegation of powers (section §2.07) as well as the (dis)regard of agencies by the Lisbon Treaty (section §2.08). Before so doing, it will first give an account of the upsurge of agencies in the EU's institutional structure (section §2.02) and give a definition and taxonomy of agencies (section §2.03).

§2.02 THE UPSURGE OF EUROPEAN AGENCIES IN THE INSTITUTIONAL LANDSCAPE OF THE EU

The more than forty European agencies that currently exist (see below) have been created roughly in three waves.[16] After the initial set up of EUROFOUND and CEDEFOP, the early 1990s witnessed a second wave of resort to agencies with the

---

13. Case C-270/12, *United Kingdom of Great Britain and Northern Ireland v. Council of the European Union and European Parliament*, Action brought on 1 June 2012. OJ 2012, C 273/2.
14. See on the *Meroni* doctrine in the past few years, e.g. S. Griller & A. Orator, 'Everything under Control? The 'Way Forward' for European Agencies in the Footsteps of the *Meroni* Doctrine', *European Law Review* 35, no. 1 (2010): 3–35; M. Chamon, 'EU Agencies: Between *Meroni* and *Romano* or the Devil and the Deep Blue Sea', *Common Market Law Review* 48, no. 4 (2011): 1055–1075.
15. See Arts 290 & 291 TFEU. See *inter alia* H.C.H. Hofmann & A. Morini, 'Constitutional Aspects of the Pluralisation of the EU Executive through "Agencification"', *European Law Review* 37, no. 4 (2012): 419. More general on the introduction of the new hierarchy of norms, see J. Bast, 'New Categories of Acts after the Lisbon Reform: Dynamics of Parliamentarization in EU Law', *Common Market Law Review* 49 (2012): 885–928; P.P. Craig, 'Delegated Acts, Implementing Acts and the New Comitology Regulation', *European Law Review* 36, no. 5 (2011): 671–687.
16. The literature on European agencies is by now abundant. Recent publications include: M. Busuioc, *The Accountability of European Agencies. Legal Provisions and Ongoing Practices* (Delft: Eburon, 2010); E. Chiti, 'An Important Part of the EU's Institutional Machinery: Features, Problems and Perspectives of European Agencies', *Common Market Law Review* 46, no. 5 (2009): 1395–1442; E. Chiti, 'European Agencies' Rulemaking: Powers, Procedures and Assessment', *European Law Journal* 19, no. 1 (2013): 93–110; M. Busuioc, M. Groenleer & J. Trondal (eds.), *The Agency Phenomenon in the European Union. Emergence, Institutionalisation and Everyday Decision-making* (Manchester: Manchester University Press, 2012).

creation of *inter alia* the EEA[17] and the EMA.[18] In the aftermath of several scandals, for example, relating to food and maritime pollution at the end of the 1990s, European agencies were seen as an attractive solution for problems of lack of trust in, and credibility of, the EU and its regulation.[19] Up until that moment the EU institutions had not taken any particular vision or strategy on the creation and design of agencies thus leaving both functional and political interests to be determined at the micro-level of the founding regulations of agencies.[20]

In the 2000s however the European Commission took 'ownership' of the agen-cification process as part of a more general strategy in response to the need of an open government, accountability and new forms of partnerships between the different levels of European governance being in urgent need to (re)gain trust and credibility in the aftermath of various scandals.[21] It envisaged that agencies would play a role in the broader context of the exercise of the executive function and definition of the respon-sibilities of the institutions. It viewed agencies as being of great importance within the context of the guiding principles for administrative governance: less direct manage-ment, better control of delivery and greater cost-effectiveness,[22] making the delegation of a number of tasks and powers to agencies being non-majoritarian bodies into a new mode of governance.[23] The use of agencies was particularly promoted by the European Commission in its White Paper on European Governance, while recognizing that an overall framework should be created with provisions on the creation, operation,

---

17. Council Regulation (EEC) 1210/90 [1990] OJ L120/1, as amended by Council Regulation (EC) 933/1999 of 29 April 1999 on the establishment of the European Environment Agency and the European environment information and observation network [1999] OJ L117/1.
18. See the new Regulation (EC) 726/2004 of 31 March 2004 laying down Community procedures for the authorisation and supervision of medicinal products for human and veterinary use and establishing a European Medicines Agency [2004] OJ L136/1.
19. The importance of establishing agencies within the institutional setting of the EU was indeed underlined in 1999 by the Committee of Independent Experts, established after the Cresson affaire, that held that it was difficult to find in the Commission persons who had 'even the slightest sense of responsibility', and recommended delegation and decentralisation of day-to-day executive tasks to such bodies. See the Committee of Independent Experts in its First Report on 'Allegations Regarding Fraud, Mismanagement and Nepotism in the European Commission' of 15 March 1999, para. 9.4.25, available at: < http://www.europarl.europa.eu/experts/report1 _en.htm > , accessed on 8 July 2013.
20. See D. Curtin & R. Dehousse, 'EU Agencies: Tipping the Balance?', in *The Agency Phenomenon in the European Union. Emergence, Institutionalisation and Everyday Decision-making*, eds. M. Busuioc, M. Groenleer & J. Trondal (Manchester: Manchester University Press, 2012), 194.
21. Such as the BSE crisis, see E. Vos, 'EU Food Safety Regulation in the Aftermath of the BSE Crisis', *Journal of Consumer Policy* (2000): 227–255.
22. See Commission (EC), 'Reforming the Commission – Part I and II (Action Plan – White Paper) COM(2000) 200 final, 1 March 2000; Commission (EC), 'Shaping the new Europe' (Communi-cation) COM(2000) 154 final, 21 March 2000; Commission (EC), 'European Governance – A White Paper (White Paper) COM(2001) 428 final, 27 July 2001, 24; Commission (EC), 'European Governance: Better Lawmaking' (Communication) COM(2002) 275 final, 5 June 2002 and Commission (EC), 'Building our Common Future – Policy challenges and Budgetary means of the Enlarged Union 2007–2013 (Communication) COM(2004) 101 final/2, 26 February 2004, Annex 1.
23. See Curtin & Dehousse, *supra* n. 20, at 195.

and supervision of these agencies, in accordance with the principles of good governance.[24]

In the early 2000s we thus witnessed a third wave of creation of no less than another twenty agencies with the EU's enthusiasm for agencies seemingly unending.[25] Over the last decade however the agencification wave has come to a halt in view of the Commission's quest for reflection on the role and position of agencies and its announcement to put a moratorium on the creation of new agencies.[26] This could nevertheless not stop the spread of agencies, on the explicit request of the European Council,[27] also to the financial sector after the outbreak of the economic and financial crisis.[28] It is therefore safe to conclude that today European agencies have become an integral part of the EU's institutional structure and that they have become 'an established part of the way the EU operates'.[29]

The fascination of the EU institutions for European agencies has been elicited by a number of advantages that resort to agencies offers.[30] Agencies have been hailed as being able to deal with complex technical and scientific issues by providing expertise, introduce more, and more flexible, administrative capacity and efficiency and facilitate, coordinate and strengthen cooperation between national authorities. They have been praised as a means to (re)gaining trust and credibility, to improving implementation, to carrying out supervision and to increasing networking and participation of more actors, such as stakeholders and citizens. Following the American model, agencies have been introduced with the idea that sectoral regulation often requires a degree of technical complexity that can and should not be dealt with by an organization headed by politicians.[31] The creation of European agencies have thus allowed the European Commission greater room to concentrate on its core tasks and policy priorities,[32] as more specific and technical administrative tasks were delegated to these agencies. The creation of agencies herewith responded to the need for more uniformity in the implementation of EU policies where the harmonization model appeared to be less attractive while upholding the EU's system of decentralized implementation.[33] Notably, the *raison d'être* of agencies in the EU practice has also been more mundane and can be depicted as the outcome of the interplay of strategic and political interests

---

24. COM(2001) 428 final.
25. See M. Egeberg, M. Martens & J. Trondal, 'Building Executive Power at the European Level: Some Preliminary Findings on the Role of EU Agencies', ARENA Working Paper No. 10, June 2009, 9.
26. COM(2008) 135.
27. European Council Conclusions of 18–19 June 2009, paras 19–20.
28. In those times, Art. 235 EEC.
29. Joint Statement and Common Approach of the European Parliament, the Council and the European Commission on Decentralized Agencies adopted on 19 July 2012; < http://europa.eu/agencies/documents/joint
_statement_and_common_approach_2012_en.pdf > , accessed on 8 July 2013. See Annex 2 to this book.
30. See for a recent discussion Busuioc, Groenleer & Trondal, *supra* n. 16 and Busuioc, *supra* n. 16.
31. G. Majone, 'The Rise of the Regulatory State in Europe', *West European Politics* 17, no. 3 (1994): 77–101.
32. Majone (1996), *supra* n. 7.
33. R. Dehousse, 'Regulation by Networks in the European Community: The Role of European Agencies', *Journal of European Public Policy* 4, no. 2 (1997): 246–261.

in a power game between the institutions and Member States.[34] Hereby Member States' desire to gain prestige for having an agency seated in their territory has indubitably played a role. Exemplary of the latter is the fight for the seat of the EFSA.[35]

The prolific creation of agencies and the increasing delegation of a number of tasks to these bodies have nevertheless also been viewed with a more critical eye, fearing for example that agencies would become uncontainable entities of power, raising the question how to 'tame the Sorcerer's Apprentice'[36] and expressing severe doubts about the legitimacy of such non-majoritarian bodies.[37] Agencies thus have been considered to be problematic in terms of 'capture',[38] the difficult disentanglement of expert findings from political strategies,[39] independence,[40] their place within the

---

34. See e.g., R. Dehousse, 'Delegation of Powers in the European Union: The Need for a Multi-principals Model', *West European Politics* 4 (2008): 789–805; M. Groenleer, *The Autonomy of European Union Agencies: A Comparative Study of Institutional Development* (Delft: Eburon, 2009).

35. The most vivid 'discussion' on the seats of agencies is the one on the seat of the European Food Safety Authority, reported by the Reuters New agency during the Laeken Summit of 16 December 2001, which I would like to recall here again. Faced with the other candidate for the seat, Helsinki, the Italian Prime Minister Silvio Berlusconi argued that a European Food Safety Agency should be given to Parma in Italy on account of its famous cured ham. According to the Reuters news agency, the closing exchange of the 2001 Laeken Summit, as reported by diplomats who had access to verbatim notes, went like this:

    Italian PM Silvio Berlusconi: 'Parma is synonymous with good cuisine. The Finns don't even know what prosciutto is. I cannot accept this.'
    Austrian Chancellor Wolfgang Schuessel: 'I am not satisfied. We got nothing.'
    Swedish PM Goran Persson: 'This is no easy task. We had the problem during the Swedish presidency at Gothenburg. But it's strange that the IT [Information technology] agency should go to Spain.'
    Belgian PM Guy Verhofstadt (Chair): 'The gastronomic attraction of a region is no argument for the allocation of an EU agency.'
    French President Jacques Chirac: 'How would it be if Sweden got an agency for training models, since you have such pretty women?'
    Berlusconi: 'I already accepted the (European arrest) warrant. My final word is (shouts) No!'
    Schroeder: 'I love Parma, but you'll never get it if you argue like that.'
    Chirac: 'Lille is also a candidate. It lies in the heart of the (EU) political landscape.'
    Schuessel: 'The (EU) observatory on racism (in Vienna) has only 19 civil servants. Others have thousands.'
    Verhofstadt: 'That's it.' (Closes summit).
    See BBC News, 16 December 2001, < http://news.bbc.co.uk/1/hi/world/europe/ 1714264.stm > , accessed on 8 July 2013.

36. See S. Griller & S. Orator, 'Empowering European Agencies – or How to Tame the Sorcerer's Apprentice', *NewGov policy brief* no. 22, 2008, < http://www.eu-newgov.org/database/PUBLIC/ Policy_Briefs/NEWGOV_Policy_Brief_no22.pdf > , accessed on 8 July 2013.

37. See M. Everson, 'Independent Agencies: Hierarchy Beaters?', *European law Journal* 1, no. 2 (1995): 180–204; M. Busuioc, 'Accountability, Control and Independence: The Case of European Agencies', *European Law Journal* 15, no. 5 (2009): 599–615.

38. See R. Baldwin & C. McCrudden, *Regulation and Public Law* (London: Weidenfeld and Nicolson, 1987), 9–10.

39. M. Shapiro, 'The Problems of Independent Agencies in the United States and the European Union', *Journal of European Public Policy* 4, no. 2 (1997): 276–291.

40. See Everson, *supra* n. 37.

institutional balance of powers, their lack of constitutional basis and constitutional guarantees[41] as well as their transparency and accountability.[42]

Over the years the EU institutions have attempted to address such concerns. The European Commission in particular has hereby actively promoted the creation of a regulatory framework of what the Commission has called, regulatory agencies – nowadays indicated as decentralized agencies – and herewith to develop a clear overall vision on the role and place of agencies in the EU.[43] These initiatives have resulted recently in the adoption of a Joint Statement and Common Approach on decentralized agencies of the three institutions mentioned above. The content and implication of this approach will be discussed in the following sections.

§2.03 DEFINITION AND TAXONOMY

European agencies vary considerably as regards their tasks, powers and size. The following agencies currently exist:

- Agency for the Cooperation of Energy Regulators (ACER).[44]
- Body of European Regulators for Electronic Communications (BEREC).[45]
- Community Plant Variety Office (CPVO).[46]
- Education, Audiovisual and Culture Executive Agency (EACEA).[47]
- European Agency for Safety and Health at Work (EU-OSHA).[48]
- European Agency for the Management of Operational Cooperation at the External Borders (FRONTEX).[49]
- European Agency for the operational management of large-scale IT systems in the area of freedom, security and justice (IT Agency).[50]
- European Asylum Support Office (EASO).[51]
- European Aviation Safety Agency (EASA).[52]
- European Banking Authority (EBA).[53]
- European Centre for Disease Prevention and Control (ECDC).[54]

---

41. See K. Lenaerts, Regulating the Regulatory Process: "Delegation of Powers" in the European Community', *European Law Review* 18, no. 1 (1993): 42.
42. See Busuioc, *supra* n. 16; Groenleer, *supra* n. 34.
43. See Commission Communication on the operating framework for the European regulatory agencies, COM(2002) 718 and Commission Communication on a 'Draft Interinstitutional Agreement on the operating framework for the European regulatory agencies' COM(2005) 59 final.
44. Reg. 713/2009/EC (OJ 2009, L211/1).
45. Reg. 1211/2009 (OJ 2009, L337/1).
46. Reg. 2100/94 (OJ 1994, L227/1).
47. Dec. 2005/56/EC (OJ 2005, L24/35), replaced by Dec. 2009/336/EC (OJ 2009, L101/26).
48. Reg. 2062/94 (OJ 1994, L216/1).
49. Reg. 2007/2004 (OJ 2004, L349/1).
50. Reg. 1077/2011 (OJ 2011, L286/1).
51. Reg. 439/2010 (OJ 2010, L132/11).
52. Reg. 1592/2002 (OJ 2002, L240/1), replaced by Reg. 216/2008 (OJ 2008, L79/1).
53. Reg. 1093/2010 (OJ 2010, L331/12).
54. Reg. 851/04 (OJ 2004, L41/1).

- European Centre for the Development of Vocational Training (CEDEFOP).[55]
- European Chemicals Agency (ECHA).[56]
- European Defence Agency (EDA).[57]
- European Environment Agency (EEA).[58]
- European Fisheries Control Agency (EFCA).[59]
- European Food Safety Authority (EFSA).[60]
- European Foundation for the Improvement of Living and Working Conditions (EUROFOUND).[61]
- European GNSS Agency (GSA).[62]
- European Institute for Gender Equality (EIGE).[63]
- European Maritime Safety Agency (EMSA).[64]
- European Medicines Agency (EMA).[65]
- European Monitoring Centre for Drugs and Drug Addiction (EMCDDA).[66]
- European Network and Information Security Agency (ENISA).[67]
- European Insurance and Occupational Pensions Authority (EIOPA).[68]
- European Police College (CEPOL).[69]
- European Police Office (EUROPOL).[70]
- European Research Council Executive Agency (ERCEA).[71]
- European Railway Agency (ERA).[72]
- European Securities and Markets Authority (ESMA).[73]
- European Training Foundation (ETF).[74]
- European Union Agency for Fundamental Rights (FRA).[75]
- The European Union's Judicial Cooperation Unit (EUROJUST).[76]
- European Union Satellite Centre (EUSC).[77]
- European Union Institute for Security Studies (EUISS).[78]

---

55. Reg. 337/75 (OJ 1975, L039/1).
56. Reg. 1907/2006 (OJ 2006, L396/1).
57. Council Joint Action 2004/551/CFSP (OJ 2004, L245/17).
58. Reg. 1210/90 (OJ 1990, L139/1).
59. Reg. 768/2005/EC (OJ 2005, L128/1).
60. Reg. 178/2002/EC (OJ 2002, L031/1).
61. Reg. 1365/75 (OJ 1975, L139/1).
62. Reg. 1321/2004 (OJ 2004, L246/1), replaced by Reg. 912/2010 (OJ 2010, L276/11).
63. Reg. 1922/2006 (OJ 2006, L403/9).
64. Reg. 1406/2002 (OJ 2002, L208/1).
65. Reg. 726/2004 (OJ 2004, L136/1).
66. Reg. 302/93 (OJ 1993, L036/1).
67. Reg. 460/2004 (OJ 2004, L77/1).
68. Reg. 1094/2010 (OJ 2010, L331/48).
69. Council Decision 2005/681/JHA (OJ 2005, L256/63).
70. Council Dec. 2009/371/JHA (OJ 2009, L21/37).
71. Dec. 2008/37/EC (OJ 2008, L9/15).
72. Reg. 881/2004 (OJ 2004, L220/3).
73. Reg. 1095/2010 (OJ 2010, L331/84).
74. Reg. 1360/90 (OJ 1990, L131/1).
75. Reg. 168/2007 (OJ 2007, L53/1).
76. Council Decision 2002/187/JHA (OJ 2002, L63/1).
77. Council Joint Action 2001/555/CFSP (OJ 2001, L200/25).
78. Council Joint Action 2001/554/CFSP (OJ 2001, L200/1).

- Executive Agency for Competitiveness and Innovation (EACI).[79]
- Executive Agency for Health and Consumers (EAHC).[80]
- Office for Harmonization in the Internal Market (Trade Marks and Designs) (OHIM).[81]
- Research Executive Agency (REA).[82]
- Translation Centre for the Bodies of the European Union (CdT).[83]
- Trans-European Transport Network Executive Agency (TEN-TEA).[84]

The Translation Centre for the Bodies of the European Union (CdT) is different than the other agencies as it is to serve the other agencies with translation services and can therefore be seen as a support for the European agencies. The study of this agency therefore falls outside of the scope of this Chapter.

The agencies that will be discussed in this Chapter (and this edited volume) are indicated currently by the EU institutions as 'decentralized agencies' and can broadly be defined as bodies governed by European public law that are institutionally separate from the EU institutions and have their own legal personality. They are created by secondary legislation by the Council and/or European Parliament, they have clearly specified tasks and have a certain degree of administrative and financial autonomy. Accordingly, other independent bodies of the EU that are created by the Treaty itself, such as the European Investment Bank, fall outside the scope of this Chapter.[85]

The European Commission used to divide the agencies into regulatory agencies, operating in specific policy areas and executive agencies, carrying out specific EU programmes.[86] The use of the word 'regulatory' was however severely criticized by academics and the European Parliament for being inconsistent and rather deceiving as regards the nature of the agencies.[87] Faced with this critique and following the removal of the pillar structure by the Lisbon Treaty, the EU has recently modified its classification and rebaptised the category of 'regulatory' agencies into 'decentralized agencies'

---

79. Dec. 2004/20/EC (IEEA) (OJ 2004, L5/85), amended by Dec. 2007/372/EC (OJ 2007, L140/52).
80. Dec. 2004/858/EC (OJ 2004, L369/73).
81. Reg. 40/94 (OJ 1994, L011/1).
82. Dec. 2008/46/EC (OJ 2008, L11/9).
83. Reg. 2965/94 (OJ 1994, L3149).
84. Dec. 2007/60/EC (OJ 2007, L32/88).
85. Before the European Central Bank gained the official status of an EU institution (as introduced by the Lisbon Treaty), it was discussed in literature whether the European Central Bank should not be considered an as independent agency, see e.g., 'Executive Agencies within the EC: The European Central Bank – A Model?', editorial comment to *Common Market Law Review* 33 (1996): 623–631.
86. See e.g., COM(2002) 718 and COM(2005) 59 final.
87. See J.J. Rijpma, 'Hybrid Agencification in the Area of Freedom, Security and Justice and its Inherent Tensions: The Case of Frontex', in *The Agency Phenomenon in the European Union: Emergence, Institutionalisation and Everyday Decision-making*, eds. M. Busuioc, M. Groenleer & J. Trondal (Manchester: Manchester University Press, 2012), 85; Busuioc, *supra* n. 16; Curtin, *supra* n. 4, at 160–161; E. Vos, 'Independence, Accountability and Transparency of European Regulatory Agencies', in *Regulation through Agencies: A New Paradigm of European Governance*, eds. D. Geradin, R. Munoz & N. Petit (Cheltenham UK/Northampton MA, USA: Edward Elgar, 2005), 120–137. The term decentralized was explicitly proposed by the European Parliament in its 2009 Resolution on financial management and control of agencies, 23/04/2009, P6 TA (2009)074, para. 6.

in addition 'Euratom agencies' and 'executive agencies'.[88] While the use of the term 'decentralized agencies' is to be preferred over 'regulatory agencies' as it indicates more clearly the level at which the agencies are operating in the executive, as well as the geographical spread of agencies over the EU, it is key for a better understanding of the agency phenomenon and analysis to have several classifications of agencies instead of a single one.[89] The academic literature has come up with several classifications of agencies, varying from functional to instrumental typologies.[90] We argue that, depending on the purpose of analysis,[91] it is useful to distinguish agencies according to: (a) their functions, (b) their sheer size, (c) their legal basis, (d) the nature of their powers and the instruments that they can adopt, and (e) the way in which they can exercise their powers autonomously. Taken together agencies can roughly be classified according to a functional: (a) numerical (b) and legal taxonomy (c-e). For the purpose of our research the legal taxonomy is particular relevant.

[A]   Functional Taxonomy

From a functional perspective, agencies can be classified according to the five main tasks conferred upon agencies: (1) expertise, (2) information and cooperation, (3) provision of services (registration and certification), (4) supervision, inspection, and enforcement, and (5) execution of EU programmes. The provision of expertise and the delivery of scientific opinions are typical of agencies such as the EFSA and the EMA. The gathering of information and the creation of information networks is typical for agencies such as the EEA and the EMDDC, while the provision of a specific service, namely the registration of trade marks, is the main task of the OHIM and the CPVC. Supervision is the key mandate of the three new supervisory authorities in the financial sector the EBA ESMA and the EIOPA. The execution of specific EU programmes is the mandate of for example the EAHC and the EACEA. All agencies may serve both the EU institutions and the Member States (see section §2.08). While the first four types of agencies have in common that they are set up by the Council and the European Parliament for an indefinite period of time and are governed by a management board usually composed of Member States representatives (see below), the executive agencies are different from the other four types of agencies in that they are set up by the European Commission and are entrusted with purely managerial tasks and hence assist the Commission in implementing the EU's financial support programmes. They are set up for a fixed period and are strictly supervised by the Commission. These agencies also fall outside the scope of further analysis of this Chapter.[92]

It is noteworthy that increasingly a plurality of functions is conferred upon agencies, which makes it difficult to distinguish clearly the above-mentioned types. Examples of this mixed, or 'plural-functional' type, are the ECHA and the EASA that are

---

88. See < http://europa.eu/about-eu/agencies/index_en.htm > , accessed on 8 July 2013.
89. See also Griller & Orator, *supra* n. 14, at 10.
90. For an overview see Busuioc, *supra* n. 16, at 25–26 and Griller & Orator, *supra* n. 14, at 10.
91. See on the need for various classifications, Griller & Orator, *supra* n. 14.
92. Council Regulation (EC) No. 58/2003 (OJ L11, 16 January 2003).

tasked with the delivery of both expertise and services (issuance of environmental certificates, registration of chemicals), with inspection tasks also being conferred upon EASA.

[B]   Numerical Taxonomy

From a numerical perspective, agencies are different and vary in size (in staff and consequently in budget) enormously. The smallest agency is EIGE that employs approximately thirty persons, with an annual budget of approximately EUR 7 million.[93] The biggest agency is the OHIM employing 730 persons, having an annual budget of around EUR 418 million, entirely self-financed.[94]

[C]   Legal Taxonomy

From a legal perspective we can distinguish agencies in various manners, taking account of three aspects, legal basis, nature of powers, and instruments and autonomy in decision-making. The latter two are relevant for the analysis of delegation of powers to agencies. As regards their legal basis, we can distinguish agencies that have been created by a Commission act, a Council joint action, a Council act or a European Parliament and Council act. Agencies created by the Commission are meant to be purely to assist the Commission in the implementation of EU programmes and are called executive agencies. The three agencies that operate in the field of foreign security and defence policy, EDA, EUISS, and EUSC, are all established by a Council joint action. These agencies have a different organizational structure than the other agencies with, for example, in the case of EDA the defence ministers participating in the agency's administrative board. These agencies are therefore excluded from our analysis.

The former third pillar agencies, Europol, EUROJUST and CEPOL have been set up by the Council. This also holds true for the older agencies, set up in the 1990s and that did not undergo a revision or recast in the 2000s, as the strict view of foremost the Council's legal service was that the sole appropriate legal basis for the adoption of agencies was the former general clause Article 308 EC, the current flexibility clause of Article 352 TFEU. Hence agencies such as the Community Variety Plant Office and the European Agency for Safety and Health at Work, both created in 1994 and not having undergone a major revision, are based on a Council act by virtue of former 308 EC. The current more relaxed view holding that agencies should be created on the basis of the enabling policy legal basis, upheld by the Court,[95] as well as the changes brought by the Lisbon Treaty, will result in revisions in the founding acts of these agencies to be

---

93. See annual report 2011, < http://eige.europa.eu/sites/default/files/EIGE-Annual-Report-2011-web.pdf > , accessed on 8 July 2013.
94. See institutional budget for 2013, < http://oami.europa.eu/ows/rw/resource/documents/OHIM/institutional/budget/cb_12_s42_6-3_all_lang.pdf > , accessed on 8 July 2013.
95. Joined Cases C-154/04 and C-155/04, *Alliance for Natural Health and Others*, ECR 2005 I-06451.

adopted by both the European Parliament and the Council.[96] An example hereof is Frontex whose founding regulation still is a Council Regulation that has however been amended by a European Parliament and Council Regulation based on Articles 74 and 77(2) TFEU.[97] The same applies to the proposed amendment of the Europol founding decision that is now based on Articles 88 and 87(2b) TFEU.[98]

According to the nature of their powers and the instruments they have at their disposal, agencies can be divided into agencies with and without decision-making powers to adopt binding legal instruments. Only a few agencies have been allotted formal and binding decision-making powers, although it is noteworthy that increasingly binding decision-making powers are being conferred upon agencies. Such powers are, following the *Meroni* doctrine,[99] strictly circumscribed executive powers, mainly relating to the registration of trademarks and certain chemicals, and the issuance of certificates. These agencies adopt final and binding decisions on, for example, the registration of trademarks and chemicals, that individual actors can challenge before the General Court of the EU. At present, OHIM, CPVO, EASA, ECHA, EMA, ESMA, EBA, and EIOPA have powers to adopt binding decisions. ESMA's intervention powers that allow ESMA to prohibit or impose conditions on the entry by natural or legal persons into short sales or similar transactions, or to require such persons to notify or publicize such positions were challenged in 2012 before the Court by the UK for infringing the *Meroni* requirements.[100]

All other agencies adopt a variety of informal documents, such as recommendations, opinions, standards, guidelines, guidance documents, scientific reports, a code of conduct, an annual report, a work plan, and a strategic plan. In addition, they are also active at the global level, concluding informal agreements and memoranda of understanding with national or international organizations with a similar mandate.[101] Although most agencies have powers of an advisory nature, it may be clear that the scientific opinions given for example, by EMA or EFSA carry significant weight in Commission decision making.[102] EASA is very close to adopting quasi-binding rules, as it is empowered to adopt technical guidelines in relation to certification specifications while it prepares technical rules from which the Commission cannot deviate without

---

96. See Art. 85 TEU as regards Eurojust, Arts 87 and 88 TEU as regards Cepol and Europol.
97. As lastly amended by Regulation (EU) No. 1168/2011 of the European Parliament and of the Council OJ 2011, L304/1, based on in particular Art. 74 and Art. 77(2) points (b) and (d) TFEU.
98. COM(2013) 173 final. Proposal for a Regulation of the European Parliament and of the Council on the European Union Agency for Law Enforcement Cooperation and Training (Europol) and repealing Decisions 2009/371/JHA and 2005/681/JHA.
99. See section §2.07.
100. Case C-270/12, *UK v. Council and European Parliament*, brought before the Court on 1 June 2012. We will come back to this case below in section §2.07.
101. See A. Ott, E. Vos and F. Coman-Kund, in this volume.
102. See P. Craig, *EU Administrative Law* (Oxford: Oxford University Press, 2006), 155; M.B.A. Van Asselt & E. Vos, 'Wrestling with Uncertain Risks: EU Regulation of GMOs and the Uncertainty Paradox', *Journal of Risk Research* 11, no. 1–2 (2008): 281–300.

EASA's prior consent.[103] Moreover case law of the Court indicates that other acts of agencies may intend to produce legal effects vis-à-vis third parties, which consequently may be reviewed by the Court,[104] as is now also formally recognized by Article 263 TFEU.

As regards the autonomy to adopt specific acts, agencies may be divided into agencies that need prior approval for the conclusion of an act, agencies that need prior consultation with the Commission or agencies that can autonomously adopt acts. This typology has been revealed to be particular relevant for the assessment of whether in the exercise of their external relation tasks agencies have been delegated decision-making powers and whether this upsets the institutional balance of powers.[105]

§2.04 HYBRID NATURE

Apart from EUROFOUND and CEDEFOP that were created in 1975, agencification started to take place in the early 1990s, with the delegation of tasks of coordination and information gathering as well as the provision of expertise to agencies such as the EEA and EMA especially set up for that purpose by the Council. While agencies were still considered to be replacements of comitology structures in the 1990s, agencies in their teens and twenties demonstrate that they are not a replacement of comitology but rather of previously existing scientific committees, other advisory committees composed of (national) experts or joint committees such as the Joint Aviation Authorities in the case of EASA[106] and the Committee for Proprietary Medicinal Products in case of EMA.

Almost two decades of experience with European agencies has made clear that European agencies are, unlike their powerful and regulatory American counterparts, modelled on the basis of networks, with national counterparts and/or stakeholders. It is this strong interplay with their national counterparts that typifies European agencies. They have been designed to operate as a kind of *'primus inter pares'* with the national authorities, instead of being hierarchically placed above the national authorities, although in practice the agencies have a strong say and impact in the networks. EFSA has for example, been conceptualized as the apex of an interdependent network with various national authorities and other actors in a 'multi-level procedural labyrinth'.[107] It is also true that the role and position of the European agencies vis-à-vis their national

---

103. Art. 17(2b) of Regulation (EC) 216/2008 of the European Parliament and of the Council on common rules in the field of civil aviation and establishing a European Aviation Safety Agency, and repealing Council Directive 91/670/EEC, Regulation (EC) 1592/2002 and Directive 2004/36/EC, OJ 2008, L79/1.
104. Case T-411/06, *Sogelma v. EAR* [2008] ECR II-2771, paras 42 and 43.
105. See Ott, Vos and Coman-Kund in this volume.
106. See A. Schout, 'Changing the EU's Institutional Landscape? The Added Value of an Agency', in *The Agency Phenomenon in the European Union: Emergence, Institutionalisation and Everyday Decision-making*, eds. M. Busuioc, M. Groenleer & J. Trondal (Manchester: Manchester University Press, 2012), 71.
107. See P. Dąbrowska, 'EU Governance of GMOs: Political Struggles and Experimentalist Solutions?', in *Experimentalist Governance in the European Union: Towards a New Architecture*, eds. C.F. Sabel & J. Zeitlin (Oxford: Oxford University Press, 2010), 177–215.

counterparts partly depends on the topics dealt with so that the role EFSA plays as regards genetically modified organisms has been defined as a 'super-agency'.[108] Newer agencies with explicit goals to improve market integration, such as BEREC and ACER, moreover explicitly build on existing networks, in particular the networks of regulators and include them in their institutional structure or even conglomerate them to the formal agency as is the case with BEREC.[109] These network structures of agencies are all in line with and part of the composite or shared administration of the EU; agencies are 'betwixt and between'.[110] More recently we observe a new trend of agencies institutionalizing networks of national regulators with even legally complex constructions of an agency attached to a network, as the case of BEREC demonstrates.[111]

Most agencies dispose of some kind of hybridity, both institutionally, in their relation with and (in)dependence of the institutions and the Member States and substantively, in their multiple tasks.[112] This makes European agencies 'interesting hybrids'.[113] The hybridity of agencies is expressed in their organizational structure where representatives of both the institutions and Member States sit in their steering bodies (see section §2.05). The hybrid character of agencies, 'betwixt and between' EU institutions and Member States is even more apparent when taking account of the fact that agencies not only assist the EU institutions but also the Member States, for example, in the exercise of concluding cooperation arrangements at the global level. EASA for example, acts as 'the authorized representation of EU Member States' when concluding working arrangements with various third countries, as Australia and Brazil or international organizations, such as the Interstate Aviation Committee.[114] This thus adds another dimension to the 'double-hattedness' of agencies and the composite character of the EU executive,[115] so that we can speak of the 'triple-hatted' nature of agencies.

---

108. See E. Vos & F. Wendler, 'Food Safety Regulation at the EU Level', in *Food Safety Regulation in Europe. A Comparative Institutional Analysis*, eds. E. Vos & F. Wendler (Antwerp-Oxford: Intersentia, 2006), 65–138.
109. See M. Zinzani in this volume.
110. See Curtin, *supra* n. 4, at 174.
111. See Zinzani in this volume and M. Zinzani, *Market Integration through 'Network Governance'. The Role of European Agencies and Networks of Regulators* (Antwerp: Intersentia, 2012). See also D. Coen & M. Thatcher, 'Network Governance and Multi-level Delegation: European Networks of Regulatory Agencies', *Journal of Public Policy* 28, no. 1 (2008): 49–71 and D. Levi-Faur, 'Regulatory Networks and Regulatory Agencification: Towards a Single European Regulatory Space', *Journal of European Public Policy* 18, no. 6 (2011), 810–829.
112. See in relation to Frontex, Rijpma, *supra* n. 87, at 90.
113. See M. Everson, 'Agencies: The 'Dark Hour' of the Executive?, in *Legal Challenges in EU Administrative Law. Towards an Integrated Administration*, eds. H.C.H. Hofmann & A. Türk (Cheltenham: Edward Elgar, 2009), 131.
114. See working arrangement on the airworthiness between EASA and the Interstate Aviation Committee, < http://easa.europa.eu/rulemaking/docs/international/russia/intl_appro_IAC_EASA.pdf >, accessed on 8 July 2013. A similar wording is used in arrangements with Australia, Brazil, Japan, Singapore and Taipei. See for more examples Ott, Vos and Coman Kund in n. 81 of the Chapter in this volume.
115. See M. Egeberg & J. Trondal, 'EU-level Agencies: New Executive Centre Formation or Vehicles for National Control?', *Journal of European Public Policy* 18, no. 6 (2011): 883–884.

§2.05 SUI GENERIS EU AGENCY DESIGN

[A] Different but Similar Organizational Structure

Although the European agencies that we discuss in this Chapter are very different in tasks and size, they have a similar organizational structure.[116] They generally all consist of a management board (also called *inter alia*, governing or administrative board, college and in case of the three supervisory financial authorities, supervisory boards), scientific or advisory committees, an executive director, a secretariat and various networks. Management boards are the steering bodies of agencies and have the tasks to adopt the agencies' work programme and rules of procedure, and play a central role in the adoption of their budgets and the appointment and dismissal of their directors. Executive directors are the legal representatives of the agencies and are responsible for the day-to-day management of the agency including all staff matters. Scientific or technical committees are the beating hearts of agencies. They prepare the scientific opinions that are adopted as agencies' opinions, without intervention of other organs such as the management board or the executive director. They are often composed of experts for whom membership of these agency committees is an additional function to their existing jobs and who will come and meet in the committees, for example, once a month. Several additional bodies may exist, ranging from executive boards and budget committees to boards of appeal for agencies that have binding decision-making powers. It is noteworthy that the organs of some agencies have also been opened up to representatives of third countries – candidate, neighbouring, and associate countries – be it under specific conditions.[117]

[B] Less Is More?

The management boards of most agencies are composed of representatives of the Member States (one per country), representatives of the Commission (one to two) and for some agencies (one or two) representatives appointed by the European Parliament and/or representatives of stakeholder associations. This has resulted in large managements boards of up to forty members with an extreme account of eighty-four members

---

116. As said the executive agencies have a very different structure; they have a steering committee composed of five members appointed by the Commission and an executive director, who is appointed by the Commission as well.
117. See e.g., < http://ec.europa.eu/enlargement/pdf/financial_assistance/ipa/2011/pf_14_ipa_2011_participation_in_eu_agencies.pdf > , accessed on 8 July 2013; Commission Communication to the Council, Participation of candidate countries in Community programmes, agencies and committees, COM(99) 710 final. Accordingly, for EEA for example, bilateral agreements were negotiated with all 13 candidate countries to become member of the EEA, OJ 2001, L213. For participation of the neighbouring countries see Commission Communication on the general approach to enable ENP partner countries to participate in Community agencies and Community programmes COM(2006) 724 final. See for the Western Balkans: Communication from the Commission to the Council and Parliament – Preparing for the participation of the Western Balkan countries in Community programmes and agencies, COM(2003) 748 final.

in the case of EU-OSHA. The excellent study of Madalina Busuioc on the operation of management boards reveals that occasionally management board meetings of, for example, Europol may take up to 110–120 persons as Member State delegations are composed of three to four persons.[118] Meetings of large-sized management boards have therefore allowed for very little time for interventions and in-depth discussion on specific topics.[119]

Recognizing that the sheer size of management boards could impede any in-depth discussion, various founding regulations of agencies establish, in addition to large-sized management boards, smaller executive boards that prepare decisions, programmes and activities to be adopted by the management board, monitor implementation of management boards' decisions, as well as assist and advise the director. This seems a proper solution that accommodates both needs of large size and efficiency. This solution has now been taken over by the Common Approach on agencies.

[C]   Member States on the Boards

The question as to whether Member States should be represented on the boards was for many years a stern point of controversy between the institutions. On this matter the Council favoured a large(r)-sized board with all Member States being represented and the Commission a small board. It was one of the main reasons, together with the instrument (viz. interinstitutional agreement) to be used,[120] that prevented an agreement being reached on a common framework on agencies between the Council and the Commission. The Commission's view closely followed the Agency Working Group that prepared the 2001 Governance White Paper that viewed that the small size of management boards was:

> not solely to improve efficiency, but also to make representation more Community-minded'... 'the principle of at least one seat per Member State is not sustainable and this will lead the limited number of Member States to adopt positions from a Community perspective instead of acting as simple defenders of their national interests. This principle is confirmed by the experiences of the European Central Bank.[121]

Hence, the diverging opinions on the composition of the management boards between the Commission and the Council seem to find their roots in different views on the EU executive and the operation of agencies in it, as well who bears responsibility for acts of the management boards (see section §2.05[F]) in addition to an issue of size and efficiency. Hereby the Council has firmly held that in areas where Member States retain large responsibilities, all Member States must be on the boards of agencies.

---

118. Busuioc, *supra* n. 16, at 60.
119. *Idem*, at 74.
120. See Comte, *supra* n. 8.
121. Report drafted by the working group "establishing a framework for decision-making regulatory agencies" (group 3a) in preparation of the White Paper on Governance Work area 3 Improving the exercise of executive responsibilities (June 2001). SEC(2001) 340, p. 9.

Ever since it took on agencification as a new strand of governance in the 2000s, the Commission has indeed attempted to try to remove or at least reduce the number of seats for Member States in agencies' boards. The Commission thus repeated in its 2002 communication on an operating framework for agencies, that the experiences with large-sized management boards were 'not necessarily of value where it is a question of preserving the unity and integrity of the executive function at European level, essentially because they fail to take sufficient account of the Community dimension'.[122] This and the need for agencies to function effectively, led the Commission to plead for smaller administrative boards that would 'reflect the executive at Community level, while taking account of the expertise of the Member State executives'.[123] It also proposed to include representatives of interested parties, which would ensure that their views could be taken into account, but added that this should not give rise to any conflicts of interest or undermine proper management of the agency. This, in the Commission's view, would ensure greater transparency and might enhance public confidence.

The Commission was hereby particularly inspired by the EFSA model with a management board composed of one Commission representative plus fourteen members appointed by the Council in consultation with the European Parliament from a list drawn up by the Commission. Four of the latter members have a background in organizations representing consumers and other interests in the food chain. The Commission thus envisaged a fifteen-member administrative board, strongly emphasizing its independence, including six representatives appointed by the Commission and six by the Council – representing the national executives – and three, with no voting rights, representing the interested parties. The Commission viewed that the Parliament should not have any nominees on the boards as this would conflict with the Parliament's controlling function.

However, the Commission's calls and proposals for smaller management boards were unsuccessful. Member States' acceptance of the particular composition of EFSA's management board has remained quite extraordinary (with only a few other examples of small boards[124]) and should be understood against the backdrop of the crisis of confidence in EU regulation, its scientific advice, and the food industry in general following the BSE crisis,[125] calling for dramatically enhancing credibility and removing any inch of influence whatsoever. Hereby one has to realize that the price to be paid for the removal of the Member States from EFSA's Board was the creation of another organ

---

122. COM(2002) 718 final, pp. 8–9.
123. *Idem*, at p. 9.
124. Namely the Administrative Board of ACER with nine members, and the three newere supervisory authorities in the financial sector. Of the nine members of the management Board of ACER two are appointed by the Commission, two appointed by the European Parliament and five appointed by the Council (Art. 12, Reg. 713/2009/EC, OJ 2009, L211/1) who like with EFSA have to act in the public interest and the Management Board of EIGE with 19 members of which 18 appointed by the Council and one by the Commission (Art. 10 EIGE Foundation). The latter represent Member States but on a rotating basis. Both agencies have another organ in which all Member States (competent authorities) are represented.
125. See E. Vos, 'Reforming the European Commission: What Role to Play for EU Agencies?', *Common Market Law Review* (2000): 1113–1134.

in EFSA composed of the representatives of the national competent authorities (Advisory Forum). While the Commission has been easily convinced to accept European Parliament nominees still as members on the boards, it was not ready for many years to give in on the rule of one-seat per Member State, and at the same time fought to have a greater number of Commission representatives on the Boards. At last, after a four-year interinstitutional dialogue and a scandal around the conflicts of interests of a EFSA's board member,[126] the Commission was ready to accept the large-sized management boards with all Member States represented, two Commission representatives and, where appropriate, one member designated by the European Parliament and a fairly limited number of stakeholders' representatives.[127] The institutions hereby agreed to introduce a two-level governance structure 'when this promises more efficiency', and to create a small executive board in addition to the management board.[128] This seems to be a sound solution to the operational impracticalities currently linked to the large-sized management boards.[129] We continue to insist though that having a nominee appointed by the European Parliament seems to conflict with the oversight function the European Parliament has over the EU executive.[130]

[D]   Conceptual Underpinning for Having Member States on the Boards

The inclusion of Member State representatives may seem truly contradictory with the traditional concept and rationale of having agencies as non-majoritarian bodies operating as a fourth branch of government. The traditional arguments for resorting to regulatory agencies relate to the need of expertise in highly complex and technical matters, combined with a rule-making or adjudicative function that would be inappropriate for a government department to carry out. In this way, as has been forcefully argued by Giandomenico Majone, agencies' separateness from government is useful to relieve public administration from partisan politics, while agencies provide greater policy continuity than political executives because they are one step removed from election returns,[131] thus following the apolitical pursuit of economic autonomy and development.[132] Hereby, a tandem of technical regulatory efficacy and political independence, improved by means of institutional-legal accountability have acted as the legitimizing power of independent agencies within the regulatory state.[133] In this manner agencies are non-majoritarian bodies that are insulated from the political process. Seen in this perspective, introducing national representatives on agency boards and the political elements that the resort to agencies would precisely prevent

---

126. See e.g., < http://www.euractiv.com/euro-finance/eu-agencies-marred-conflict-inte-news-5125 87 >, accessed on 8 July 2013.
127. See the Common Approach (Annex 2 to this book), p. 5.
128. *Idem.*
129. See Busuioc, *supra* n. 37.
130. See for the Parliament's position on this, the Chapter by F. Jacobs in this volume.
131. Majone, *supra* n. 7.
132. M. Everson, 'Good Governance and European Agencies: The Balance', in *Which Regulatory Authorities in the EU?*, ed. D. Geradin (Cheltenham, Edward Elgar, 2005), 156.
133. M. Everson, 'A Comment on Chiti on Agencies', p. 1, < http://www.sv.uio.no/arena/english/ research/projects/cidel/old/Workshop_Firenze/commChiti.pdf >, accessed on 8 July 2013.

would go against the precise rationales of agencies and reduce the efficiency and effectiveness of agencies.[134] It is however important to realize that the non-majoritarian model of independent technocratic agencies clearly fails to take into account the value laden nature of especially health and safety and environmental regulation and that it is illusionary to think that the managerial and scientific tasks conferred upon agencies in these fields are merely technical and do not embrace political issues. The need for a 'political administration' and the demand to 'reintroduce politics into the apolitical sphere of economic regulation' has indeed been recognized in the literature.[135] In this way, EFSA's management board was considered as a blueprint for future agency design as it could act as a forum to weigh public interest and set parameters for social, political or economic action.[136] In practice the role model of EFSA's management board perished sadly when in 2010 in addition to EFSA staff members, quite ironically EFSA's board too, portrayed as an icon of independence, got involved in a scandal of conflicts of interests. Its Chair Diána Bánáti had remained secretly involved in the management of the International Life Sciences Institute Europe (ILSI), while being Chair of EFSA's board.[137]

We argue that is not only practically valid to have Member States on agency boards but also conceptually sound. The decision to have all Member States represented in the agencies' management boards is surely wise from a practical point of view. For does a 'Union-minded' implementation of EU legislation, to speak with the agency working group's language, not largely depend on the Member States? More fundamentally though, we view that having all Member States represented at agency boards is in line with the conceptual understanding of the EU executive as an integrated administration and is an expression of the composite[138] or shared character of the EU executive.[139] Member State involvement in the agencies' management boards should be considered as an expression of a 'Member State-oriented' institutional balance of powers principle, having due regard for the powers of both the Commission and the Member States.[140] Taking into account the origins of the division of powers between the institution reflecting the Member States' concern that the integrity of their own powers be maintained, this understanding of the institutional balance is based on the original ideas of distribution of powers have among the various institutions and generally recognizes that without Member States acceptance, it is impossible for the EU to develop or carry out regulatory policies. Therefore, the entire complexity of the EU structure may only be understood if the institutional balance of powers is widely

---

134. Everson, *supra* n. 132, at 156.
135. *Idem.*
136. Everson, *supra* n. 132, at 157.
137. See 'EU agencies stained by "conflicts of interest", wrongdoing', < http://www.euractiv.com/ euro-finance/eu-agencies-marred-conflict-inte-news-512587 >, accessed on 8 July 2013.
138. See L. Besselink, *A Composite European Constitution* (Groningen: Europa Law Publishers, 2008); G. Della Cananea, *L'Unione europea. Un ordinamento composito* (Bari: Laterza, 2003).
139. See Curtin, *supra* n. 4; H.C.H. Hofmann & A. Türk (eds.), *Legal Challenges in EU Administrative Law. Towards an Integrated Administration* (Cheltenham: Edward Elgar, 2009).
140. See for an elaboration of this concept, E. Vos, *Institutional Frameworks of Community Health and Safety Regulation, Committees, Agencies and Private Bodies* (Oxford: Hart Publishing, 1999), Chapter 2.5.

defined, encompassing not only the balance between the individual EU institutions but also the balance between the EU and the Member States. This underpins the management board design. At the same time, having Member States on the management boards should be considered to be in line with the philosophy underlying the subsidiarity principle, giving members the possibility to discern whether powers are exercised correctly at the EU level.[141] Surely this reasoning should be applied to the composition of only the management boards as the steering organs of the agencies and does not see to the composition of the scientific committees or other organs that need to deliver the 'objective', 'best possible', 'independent' scientific opinions.

Hence, with this choice made in the Common Approach to agencies to have Member States on the boards of agencies, the EU has eventually confirmed its departure from the regulatory agencies model as developed in the USA and has formally approved a sui generis EU agency design and the hybrid identity of EU agencies as part of the composite EU executive. Whether this model can be upheld in all policy areas will be discussed below in section §2.06[B].

[E]   Toothless Tigers?

Above we depicted the important role assigned to management boards as steering bodies of agencies by the founding regulations. In today's practice though, management boards do not seem to constitute a dominant component in the daily life of EU agencies.[142] This might be explained by the difficulties that management boards encounter in practice, in terms of their size and membership. The size together with a concurrent problem of lack of time for in-depth discussions, have led to poor efficiency and effectiveness of management boards in the agencies' experience.[143] Earlier, we expressed the opinion that large-sized management boards composed of representatives of all Member States together with representative of the Commission and, where appropriate, stakeholders is nevertheless theoretically sound and practically necessary. Meetings of such boards should be restricted to meetings of three to four times per year. Executive boards will be able to study and prepare the relevant dossiers to be discussed during these meetings in more depth which will benefit the discussions during the management board meetings.

As regards membership, a plethora of issues have been indicated to be problematic in practice; the lack of preparation for the meetings by the board members, a disinterest in the agency affairs by board members, the frequent change of members, a shortage of expertise as well as an emphasis on the national interests. Hence according to some agency directors, management boards are hardly operational, are not inspiring partners and do not help to steer the agencies. Moreover the frequent change in membership does not add to the institutional memory of agencies.[144] Surely this begs

---

141. *Idem.*
142. Egeberg & Trondal, *supra* n. 115, at 875.
143. M. Busuioc, 'European Agencies and their Boards: Promises and Pitfalls of Accountability beyond Design', *Journal of European Public Policy* 19, no. 5 (2012): 719–736.
144. See Busuioc, *supra* n. 16 , at 68–86.

for change. The lack of knowledge and interest of many national representatives of how agencies are working appears to be particularly worrying.[145] It is therefore key that board members, including national representatives, are equipped with the knowledge, expertise and interests needed to fulfil the tasks that are conferred upon them. An example hereof are the ECHA and EASA founding regulations which explicitly require the management board to ensure that there will be relevant expertise amongst the members in the field of general, financial and legal matters[146] and managerial capabilities.[147] Hereby we would like to argue that representiveness and expertise do not exclude each other. The need for managerial, administrative and budgetary skills of board members is now also recognized in the Common Approach.[148]

'Double-hattedness' of the members, coming from national authorities or ministries, has been reported in case of OHIM to lead to 'raging battles' of competition between national and European agency interests.[149] While this seems to be an atypical case, where serious doubts arise whether individual members are ill-suited for board membership, it must be accepted that the tension, competition and conflicts between national and European interests is inherent to the composite character of the EU executive. Importantly, having Member States on the board and reinforcing their role under the conditions just sketched is not likely to affect the Commission's powerful position regarding agencies. Here we must bear in mind the role of management boards as steering bodies that decide on work programmes, budgets and polities on transparency and conflicts of interests and hence do not have a say in the scientific content of opinions of agencies such as EMA. Moreover efficiency rationales for having agencies will not be undermined as the agency opinions are generally taken by organs other than the boards. Against this background, such a revised system of large-sized Member States boards together with smaller executive boards can only improve the quality of the boards' decision making and herewith the accountability and legitimacy of agencies.

[F]   Towards a 'Ministerial' Responsibility?

The most interesting and exciting provision of the Common Approach is without doubt the alert or warning system in paragraph 59. It deserves citation in full:

> An alert/warning system will be activated by the Commission if it has serious reasons for concern that an agency's Management Board is about to take decisions which may not comply with the mandate of the agency, may violate EU law or be in manifest contradiction with EU policy objectives. In these cases, the Commission will raise formally the question in the Management Board and request it to refrain from adopting the relevant decision. Should the Management Board set aside the request, the Commission will formally inform the European Parliament and the Council, with a view to allow the three institutions to react quickly. The

---

145. *Idem*, at 81.
146. Art. 79 of Reg. 1907/2006, OJ 2006, L396/1.
147. Art. 34 of Reg. 216/08/EC, OJ 2008, L79/1.
148. Common Approach, para. 10, see Annex 2 to this book.
149. See Busuioc, *supra* n. 16, at 83.

Commission may request the Management Board to refrain from implementing the contentious decision while the representatives of the three institutions are still discussing the issue.[150]

Although this provision is not explained anywhere, its origin lies undoubtedly in the quarrels between the Commission, the Council and the European Parliament about the question as to who bears political responsibility for acts of management boards. A central case in point was the affair over the alleged shelving of a report on anti-Semitism by the management board of the between the former European Monitoring Centre on Racism and Xenophobia (now Fundamental Rights Agency), that stirred a lot of political unrest taken up by the international press.[151] According to one of the authors of the report, Professor Bergmann, the Management Board had deliberately shelved the 112-page report because it concluded that Muslims and pro-Palestinian groups were behind much of the recent anti-Semitic violence in the EU.[152] This affair not only caused serious damage to the Centre's reputation, it also entangled the European Commission, which too was charged of fuelling anti-Semitism. Although the then President of the Commission Romano Prodi underlined the autonomy of the Centre and that the Commission was not responsible for the management board's decision to withhold the report, it served as a significant 'wake up call'[153] for individual Commissioners that they could be held accountable for agencies' actions. This has led the Commission to be much more alert as regards agencies' activities and from that moment onwards agency directors liaised directly with the Commissioners themselves rather than Commission directors-general.[154]

In the subsequent discussions on the regulatory framework for agencies the Commission thoroughly reflected on its political responsibilities in relation to agencies. It is therefore in this light that the alert or warning system must be seen. What does this system mean? Is this a kind of 'embryonic' 'ministerial' responsibility for agencies' acts in relation to EU Commissioners? A close reading of the text tells us that there is an obligation of the Commission ('will be activated') to raise the alarm if it has 'serious reasons for concern' that the relevant management board will adopt a decision that: (i) may not comply with the mandate of the agency, (ii) may violate EU law, or (iii) be in manifest contradiction with EU policy objectives. In that case, the procedure is as follows. The Commission will formally raise its concern in the management board and request it not to adopt the envisaged decision. If the management board does not honour the Commission's request, the Commission will formally inform and discuss the matter with the European Parliament and the Council. The Commission may then request the management board to refrain from implementing the contentious decision while the representatives of the three institutions are still discussing the issue. The alert system thus gives the Commission powers to bring the matter to the attention of the

---

150. Common Approach, see Annex 2 to this book.
151. See Groenleer, *supra* n. 34, at 259.
152. Racism report for EU ends in name calling, see < http://www.smh.com.au/articles/2003/11/27/1069825921685.html >, accessed on 8 July 2013.
153. See Groenleer, *supra* n. 34, at 130.
154. See Groenleer, *supra* n. 34, at 130. See for a detailed account of this affair, 258–260.

Council and the Parliament if it does not agree with an act that the management board envisages to adopt.

Even of more interest is the reverse situation in which the Commission does not raise the alarm. Does this mean that the Commission agrees with and assumes responsibility for that act so that if later on an act of a management board appears to be problematic, the Commission rightfully needs to answer for it? The text as such seems to give munitions for such argumentation. In view of the anti-Semitism affair for which the Commission was also attributed responsibility, the non-binding nature of the Common Approach as underlined by the three institutions does not seem to be of much help to the Commission, in any case not how its responsibility is viewed by other actors.

§2.06   AGENCIES BETWEEN INDEPENDENCE, CONTROL, AND CONFLICTING INTERESTS

The latter discussion brings us to the issue of independence of agencies accompanied by the need to control agencies and to let them account for their actions. It is apparent that the mushrooming of agencies within the European landscape necessitated that the EU institutions design mechanisms for keeping agencies under control and making them accountable. Ideally agencies should be subject to an effective system of supervision and control,[155] whereby the regulatory mandates may constantly be reviewed.[156] European agencies have been expressly designed as being dependent on various institutions, mainly the European Commission and to act as, or in, networks relying heavily on their national counterparts. As depicted above, European agencies have thus been designed in quite a different way than American agencies.[157] In this Chapter, two issues will be discussed: the design of control and accountability mechanisms and the issue of independence in view of the recent problems of conflicts of interests.

[A]   Manifold Control and Accountability Mechanisms

The first point relates to the design of mechanisms that encourage and respect agencies' autonomy but at the same time allow for keeping them under control and holding them accountable for what they do. This is a difficult but not impossible task as the practice demonstrates. First it is important to distinguish between control and accountability, with the term control to be understood broadly including accountability.[158] Control in this context denotes a situation where a principle has power over the delegate and covers a wide range of instruments employed by the principal to direct,

---

155. See White Paper on European Governance, COM(2001) 428 final, 24.
156. See Everson, *supra* n. 132.
157. See D. Geradin, 'The Development of European Regulatory Agencies: Lessons from the American Experience', in *Regulation through Agencies: A New Paradigm for EC Governance*, eds. D. Geradin, N. Petit & R. Munoz (Cheltenham, Edward Elgar, 2005), 215–245.
158. See Vos, *supra* n. 87.

steer and influence behaviour and decision making of the agent or delegate.[159] Accountability refers to the control ex post, to ascertain whether the agent or delegate has carried out its tasks correctly.

Accordingly we can distinguish between three types of control alongside a temporal dimension: ex ante, ongoing and ex post control, the latter being accountability. The design of European agencies includes an intriguing mix of control and accountability. In this way ex ante control is determined by the legal boundaries set in the founding regulations of agencies, such as the scope of action, powers, finances and the determination and position of the agencies' principals as well as the general principles that apply to or are declared applicable to agencies. Most prominently involved in the ex ante control are therefore the European Parliament and the Council as legislators. Ongoing control refers to the direct control by the principals in order to steer or influence the actions of the agencies. In this way, the autonomy of agencies is reduced and made more dependent of the controlling principals.[160] Examples hereof are the European Parliament's initiatives to link up a Member of European Parliament to a European agency to be able to follow this agency better,[161] the position of Member States as representatives in the management board or as competent authorities in other advisory organs of the agencies and more powerful, the above discussed alert or warning mechanism given to the Commission for actions of agencies' management boards. This kind of control sees therefore in particular to agencies' relations with the institutions and the Member States. It is most evident in the exercise of their external relations where some agencies are obliged to ask approval to the Council or Commission prior to the conclusion of international cooperation acts (for example, Europol and EASA) or consult with the Commission (for example, Frontex).[162] In how far the Council and the Commission make really use of these powers in practice is still a matter for research.

Ex post control equals accountability that carries out a retrospective process of information, discussion, and evaluation of agencies' actions. It expressly precludes direct intervention and herewith ongoing control. We observe five types of accountability: managerial accountability whereby in particular the supervisory roles that management boards play is key; political accountability that refers to the role of the European Parliament and the Council, administrative accountability, whereby the European ombudsman plays an important role in supervising general rules on transparency and access to documents;[163] financial accountability which concerns the role of the Commission's financial controller, the Council and the European Parliament as budgetary authorities, the latter of which is also responsible for the annual budgetary

---

159. Busuioc, *supra* n. 16, at 35 with reference to P.G. Rubecksen, K. Verhoest & M. Mac Carthaigh, 'Autonomy and Regulation of States Agencies: Reinforcement, Indifference or Compensation?', *Public Organization Review* 8, no. 2 (2008): 155–174.
160. Busuioc, *supra* n. 16, at 35–37.
161. See Jacobs in this volume.
162. See Ott, Vos and Coman Kund in this volume.
163. Special report from the European Ombudsman to the European Parliament following the own initiative inquiry into public access to documents, OJ 1998 C44/9. The Lisbon Treaty has formalised this type of control, now laid down in Art. 288 TFEU.

discharge (see below) and the Court of Auditors, and judicial accountability, that regards the possibility at last foreseen in Article 263 TFEU to challenge agency acts that have legal effect vis-à-vis third parties before the General Court.

Finally, it is important to observe that the EU does not have a concept such as a fully-fledged ministerial responsibility with EU Commissioners being responsible for European agencies (although now perhaps it has an embryonic version of it as set forth above).[164] In the absence of such a 'vertical' ministerial responsibility and faced with multiple principals, it is interesting to see that in the EU too, there is a growing interest in arrangements of what has also been called a 'horizontal responsibility' or 'public accountability',[165] paying much attention to responding to the clients of an entity or network.[166] All agencies have, for example, just as the Commission, adopted a code of conduct. In this context we should also consider arrangements relating to the partici- pation of interested parties and the public in general that are forcefully promoted by the European institutions.

Overall we can conclude that many arrangements to control and hold agencies accountable have been put in place. Shortcomings relate to the unfolding of account- ability mechanisms in practice as well as the tensions between the Parliament, the Commission, the Council, and Member States and the manifold control and account- ability mechanisms, referred to in literature as the problem of 'accountability over- load'.[167]

[B]   Independence and Conflicts of Interests

[1]   *European Parliament's Worries about Agencies' Independence*

The second point we address concerns the question of how we should deal with agency board, committee, and staff members as well as external experts who have a conflict of interest and thus how to guarantee an agency's independence. This situation has become particularly pertinent following the European Parliament's refusal to give some agencies, among which EFSA and EMA the budget discharge they had asked for two consecutive years, 2009 and 2010, precisely because of problems of independence of their experts and staff. The European Parliament for example, refused to give the EMA the discharge of the 2009 budget as it had 'grave' concerns about EMA's independence and considered that there is 'no proper guarantee of the independence of experts hired to carry out scientific evaluations of human medicines and some experts

---

164. See V. Mehde, 'Responsibility and Accountability in the European Commission', *Common Market Law Review* 40, no. 2 (2003): 423–442.
165. See also, D. Curtin, 'Delegation to EU Non-Majoritarian Agencies and Emerging Practices of Public Accountability', in *Regulation through Agencies: A New Paradigm for EC Governance*, eds. D. Geradin, N. Petit & R. Munoz (Cheltenham: Edward Elgar, 2005). See in general, Curtin, *supra* n. 4; M. Bovens, D. Curtin & P. 't Hart (eds.), *The Real World of EU Accountability. What Deficit?* (Oxford: Oxford University Press, 2010).
166. In The Netherlands, for example, several independent authorities adopted in 2002 a so-called 'charter on public responsibility'. See < http://www.publiekverantwoorden.nl/data/files/alg/ id21/HPV_concrete%20arrangement.pdf > .
167. Busuioc, *supra* n. 16, at 230.

had conflicting interests'. As a penalty, the Parliament decided to postpone the granting of the discharge of EMA's 2009 budget.[168] For the 2010 budget, the Parliament decided to postpone approval of the budgets of the EEA, EFSA, and EMA again for reasons relating to the lack of independence of staff and experts.[169] Crucial here was the problem of the 'revolving door' where board, committee or staff members resign their position to go to industry, and the Parliament expressed its serious concern about 'the failure of [EMA] and its Management Board to effectively address the matter of conflict of interests'.[170] Examples hereof are the case of the Chair of EFSA's Board who was involved in the management of a life science research institute, and after resignation took on again a management position at this institute and the case of EMA's executive director Thomas Lönngren who took up an advisory role within the private pharmaceutical sector just weeks after leaving his position with the agency.[171]

[2]   Independence as a Legal and Relative Concept

These problems highlight only one dimension of independence namely the independence from the market participants. We must therefore first try to understand what is meant by agencies' independence in general. Madalina Busuioc and Martijn Groenleer[172] prefer to speak of agencies' autonomy rather than their independence. This is important as it allows for a subtle assessment of the agencies' position vis-à-vis other parties and their accountability and it important to assess delegation of powers and financial means. In order to grasp the problem of the conflicts of interest however we cannot avoid addressing the legal significance of agencies' independence and to speak in terms of independence as it is the language used in the founding regulations, case law of the Court of Justice as well as in the recently proposed Law of EU Administrative Procedure.[173]

---

168. See 'EU Police College and Medicines Agency management not good enough, says Budgetary Control Committee' European Parliament News (Brussels 11 April 2011) < http://www.euro parl.europa.eu/nl/pressroom/content/20110411IPR17414/html/EU-Police-College-and-Medi cines-Agency-management-not-good-enough > , accessed on 8 July 2013. See also < http:// www.europarl.europa.eu/nl/pressroom/content/20110411IPR17414/html/EU-Police-College-and-Medicines-Agency-management-not-good-enough > , accessed on 8 July 2013. For a discussion < http://www.europarl.europa.eu/sides/getDoc.do?type=IM-PRESS&reference=201205 08IPR44653&format=XML&language=EN > , accessed on 8 July 2013.
169. For EFSA it moreover found that the average costs of the EFSA's 15-strong management board (EUR 92,630, or EUR 6,175 per member) were excessive and called for 'drastic cuts'.
170. See < http://www.europarl.europa.eu/sides/getDoc.do?type=IM-PRESS&reference=20120508 IPR44653&format=XML&language=EN > , accessed on 8 July 2013. In 2013 the European Parliament expressed still some concern for these agencies and proposed to postpone again the budgetary discharge for 2011, for the EEA, see the Parliament's report and proposal for a resolution of 25 March 2013, A70018/2013.
171. See REPORT on discharge in respect of the implementation of the budget of the European Medicines Agency for the financial year 2010 (C7-0281/2011 – 2011/2220(DEC)) Committee on Budgetary Control. A7-0107/2012.
172. See Chapter 8 in this volume.
173. European Parliament resolution of 15 January 2013 with recommendations to the Commission on a Law of Administrative Procedure of the European Union (2012/2024(INI)) P7_TA-PROV(2013)0004.

Generally the concept of independence refers to independence from executive and legislative powers, that is independence from politics and independence from market participants. It is clearly the latter dimension of independence that has been particularly troublesome with regard to EFSA and EMA and led the European Parliament to flex its muscles in postponing the budget discharge of EMA and EFSA. Article 298 TFEU stipulates that in the carrying out of their missions, the institutions, bodies, offices, and agencies of the Union shall have the support of an open, efficient, and independent European administration. Independence has indeed been viewed by the Commission in its White Paper on Administrative Reform of 2000 as one of the key principles of a European public administration.[174] This principle was further defined in the Code of Good Administrative Behaviour. This Code was adopted by the Commission in 2000, in order to ensure that the right to good administration, as laid down in the Charter of Fundamental Rights and now laid down in Article 298 TFEU, would be respected.[175] The Code thus stipulates that the staff of the Commission 'shall act independently within the framework of the policy fixed by the Commission and their conduct shall never be guided by personal or national interest or political pressure'.[176] The Code of Conduct of the European Parliament adds here that officials may not act by family interest and that they may not take part in a decision in which they, or any close member of their family, have a financial interest.[177] Independence is moreover recently proposed by the European Parliament to be included in what it has called the principle of impartiality, forming part of a Law of the EU Administrative Procedure stipulating that:

> the Union's administration shall be impartial and independent. It shall abstain from any arbitrary action adversely affecting persons, and from any preferential treatment on any grounds. The Union's administration shall always act in the Union's interest and for the public good. No action shall be guided by any personal (including financial), family or national interest or by political pressure. The Union's administration shall guarantee a fair balance between different types of citizens' interests (business, consumers and other).[178]

Independence may generally be considered to be free of both political and industry interests.[179] In the EU context this also refers to national interests. Independence often appears in secondary legislation and it is not easy to define what precisely it is. In the Court's case law on independence of supervisory authorities, the Court refers to its case law on the independence of judiciary bodies, inherent in the task of adjudication. Here the Court has held that independence has two aspects: external independence that concerns the protection against external intervention or pressure liable to jeopardize

---

174. COM(2000) 200 final.
175. On 1 November 2000, the code came into force. See, < http://europa.eu.int/comm/secre tariat_general/code/_docs/code_en.pdf > , accessed on 8 July 2013.
176. This is presented as a guideline for good behaviour in the code.
177. Art. 8 of the Code of Conduct of the European Parliament.
178. European Parliament resolution of 15 January 2013 with recommendations to the Commission on a Law of Administrative Procedure of the European Union (2012/2024(INI)), P7_TA-PROV(2013)0004.
179. D. Geradin & N. Petit, 'The Development of Agencies at EU and National Levels: Conceptual Analysis and Proposals for Reform", Jean Monnet Working Paper 01/04, NYU, 50.

the independent judgment of the relevant body involved and internal independence linked to impartiality that seeks to ensure a level playing field for the parties to the proceedings and their respective interests in relation to the subject-matter of those proceedings.[180] At the same time it is also clear that, as Advocate General Mazák held in Case C-518/07, independence is a relative term since it is necessary to specify in relation to whom or what and at what level such independence must exist.[181]

[3]   Independence and European Agencies

As regards external independence it is important to observe that the technical and scientific issues that various agencies deal with are in themselves not so neutral and objective as some may believe or argue. Collaborative research in the field of EU risk regulation revealed for example that risk assessment, a task conferred upon EFSA, is as such not a neutral exercise but rather a political act.[182] Clearly this should also be taken into account when reflecting on the need and criteria of independence. This discussion underlines the need for further research on this issue.

As regards internal independence, the high relevance of agencies' independence from industrial interests as regards staffing and membership, that is currently hotly debated, is generally agreed upon. European agencies should be independent of the market parties so as to avoid capture. Herewith particular reference is made to the membership of the technical and scientific organs of agencies that are to adopt the opinions of agencies on technical or scientific matters where in practice well-reputed scientists will always be likely to be or have been involved in industry or national affairs. The Commission observed in its 2002 Communication on the Operating Framework that the independence of the technical and/or scientific assessments of agencies is:

> in fact, their real *raison d'être*. The main advantage of using the agencies is that their decisions are based on purely technical evaluations of very high quality and are not influenced by political or contingent considerations.[183]

Independence from the national legislative, political and executive branches of government is however a more complex and controversial matter.[184] In this context we look closely at the role of national representatives as well as Commission representatives in agencies. Earlier we argued that agencies' management boards are rightly composed of Member States' representatives provided that their role is a steering one and that they do not adopt substantive binding decisions towards third parties. The

---

180. See e.g., Case C-506/04, *Wilson* [2006] ECR I-8613, paras 49–51. See more recently Case C-517/09 referring to that case in paras 38–40.
181. Opinion AG Mazák in Case C-518/07, para. 16.
182. See M.B.A. van Asselt, T. Fox, E. Versluis & E. Vos, 'Regulating Innovation, Trade and Uncertain Risks', in *Balancing between Trade and Risk, Integrating Legal and Social Science Perspectives*, eds. M.B.A. van Asselt, E. Versluis & E. Vos (London-New York: Earthscan/ Routledge, 2013), 247–275.
183. COM(2002) 718, p. 5.
184. See also A.T. Ottow & S.A.C.M. Lavrijssen, 'Independent Supervisory Authorities: A Fragile Concept', *Legal Issues of Economic Integration* 39, no. 4 (2012): 419–446.

new supervisory agencies in the financial sector and to some extent also BEREC and ACER take a somewhat unique position in the agency setting. Their founding regulations carefully avoid talking in terms of representatives of Member States or competent authorities. Instead, they put strong focus on the independence of members of their Boards of Supervisors, Management Boards, Chairperson and Executive Directors.[185] Article 46 of the founding regulations of these three agencies thus stipulates in general terms that also:

> The members of the Management Board shall act independently and objectively in the sole interest of the Union as a whole and shall neither seek nor take instructions from the Union institutions or bodies, from any government of a Member State or from any other public or private body.
> Neither Member States, the Union institutions or bodies, nor any other public or private body shall seek to influence the members of the Management Board in the performance of their tasks.

Similar wording is used for the members of the Boards of Supervisors, Chairperson, and Executive Directors. The strong focus on independence must be understood in the light of the supervisory tasks of these agencies, and the particular position of their counterparts in the national settings that are independent from other government structures. Yet, at the same time reality forces it to be admitted that in practice no independent (national) supervisory authority is completely independent of the political arena. In particular, the 'double-hattedness' of the members of these organs serving two masters indicates that independence is in practice a very fragile concept and underlines the relativeness of the concept of independence.[186] The shaping of a general legal concept of independence[187] with various criteria to safeguard independence of various categories of agencies seems therefore essential. The above-mentioned proposal of the European Parliament to have a general principle on impartiality and independence could be a first step in this direction. The adoption of clear rules and policies on how to deal with conflicts of interest for specific categories of agencies therefore seems key.[188] This has been recognized by the 2012 Common Approach and the Commission's roadmap implementing the Common Approach that focus on the independence of the scientific organs and experts of agencies.

---

185. See Arts 42 (Board of Supervisors), 46 (Management Board), 49 (chairperson) and 52 (director) of the funding regulations of the supervisory authorities (Regulation 1093/2010, *supra* n. 53, Regulation 1094/2010, *supra* n. 68, Regulation 1095/2010, *supra* n. 73).
186. See Ottow & Lavrijssen, *supra* n. 184.
187. See on the lack of a general legal concept of independence, C. Hanretty, P. Larouche & A. Reindle, *Independence, Accountability and Perceived Quality of Regulators*, a CERRE study, Brussels, 2012, see < http://www.cerre.eu/sites/default/files/report_container.pdf >, accessed on 8 July 2013. They would like to see uniformly applicable criteria.
188. Paragraph 20 of the Common Approach and para. 34 of the Commission's road map (see Annex 2 to this book). The need for a common framework is also suggested by the European Court of Auditors, Management of conflicts of interests of selected EU agencies, Special report No. 15, 2012.

§2.07   DELEGATION OF POWERS AND *MERONI*

Delegation of powers to European agencies, i.e., transfer of powers to agencies, which the latter exercises under its responsibility, has been discussed at length in the legal literature. The recent challenge by the UK brought before the CJEU arguing that specific powers delegated to the ESMA would breach the *Meroni* doctrine has resurrected this debate. The 'anti-delegation' or *Meroni* doctrine has been adhered to by the EU institutions in relation to agencies since the 1960s. This doctrine, better phrased as limited delegation doctrine,[189] only allowed for transferring very limited, defined powers to existing agencies. In so doing, arguably, the institutions followed the case law of the Court of Justice, in particular its *Meroni* case law of the late 1950s. In the *Meroni* cases,[190] the Court rejected the transfer of sovereign powers to subordinate authorities outside the EU institutions and ruled that only 'clearly defined executive powers' could be delegated, the exercise of which was to remain at all times subject to Commission supervision. Although the *Meroni* judgments related to the ECSC, their applicability to the EU Treaty has been generally accepted[191] and was confirmed by the CJEU in its case law in the 2000s. The *Meroni* case law would suggest that the following conditions apply to the admissibility of transferring sovereign powers to subordinate authorities outside the EU institutions:

- the delegating authority cannot delegate broader powers than it enjoys itself;
- only strictly executive powers may be delegated;
- discretionary powers may not be delegated;
- the exercise of delegated powers cannot be exempted from the conditions to which they would have been subject had they been directly exercised by the delegating authority, in particular the obligation to state reasons for decisions taken, and judicial control of decisions;
- the powers delegated remain subject to conditions determined by the delegating authority and subject to its continuing supervision.

Ultimately, these conditions would come down to requiring that the balance of powers will not be distorted. In *Meroni*, the Court considered that this balance would be distorted if discretionary powers were delegated to bodies other than those established by the Treaty. The underlying concern about the distinction between 'clearly defined executive powers' and 'discretionary powers' and the concern about the prohibition to delegate the latter to bodies other than the institutions seems to lie in the Court's understanding of democratic legitimacy, in which it must be possible to eventually

---

189. As rightly pointed out by G. Della Cananea at the workshop *The place of European agencies in the EU institutional structure*, University of Tor Vergata, Rome, 9 May 2013.
190. Cases 9/56 and 10/56 *Meroni v. High Authority* [1957–1958] ECR 133.
191. See e.g., Lenaerts, *supra* n. 41, at 41.

trace the powers of any rule-making body to the authority of a democratically-elected parliament.[192]

It is perhaps not surprising that we may observe that over the years agencies have obtained powers by the founding regulations that may well exceed the strictly circumscribed executive powers that the Court described in *Meroni*. As examples we may point to the impressive soft law powers conferred upon EASA and the far-reaching enforcement and intervention powers conferred upon the three supervisory authorities.[193] In practice we therefore observe the paradoxical situation in which the EU institutions, in particular the Commission, stress the possibility to delegate to agencies merely narrowly circumscribed powers whilst adopting in the legislative reality a much more indulgent attitude.[194] Earlier we argued that with the underlying rationale of the *Meroni* judgment of the Court, i.e., respect for the institutional balance of powers, a more lenient interpretation of delegation of powers to agencies could be achieved as long as the delegation of powers (from the EU legislature to EU agencies)[195] is accompanied by a reinforcement or rebalancing of the existing powers of the institutions provided that constitutional guarantees for decision making are safeguarded. This arguably will also depend on the understanding of the Commission's role in the EU executive post-Lisbon. Whether the Court will be ready to relax the strict interpretation of the *Meroni* doctrine will soon be seen when it needs to judge upon the powers that require ESMA, in exceptional circumstances, to prohibit or impose conditions on the entry by natural or legal persons into short sales or similar transactions, or to require such persons to notify or publicize such positions.[196] The Court will hereby need to

---

192. See C. Joerges, H. Schepel & E. Vos, 'The Law's Problems with the Involvement of Non-governmental Actors in Europe's Legislative Processes: The Case of Standardisation', EUI Working Paper, Law 99/9 (Florence 1999).

193. See A. Ottow, in this volume. See for a discussion of rulemaking powers of agencies, Chiti, *supra* n. 16, at 93–110.

194. This might be due to the tension between various DGs in the Commission whereby the policy DGs increasingly acknowledges the need to confer more powers on agencies in view of the growing complexity of the EU's tasks, and the Commission's Legal Service anxiously attempts to stick to the *Meroni* doctrine. G. Majone, 'Delegation of Regulatory Powers in a Mixed Polity', *European Law Journal* 3, no. 3 (2002): 329.

195. Delegation of powers may generally be defined as the transfer of powers from one organ or institution to another, which the latter exercises under its responsibility. In order to determine whether 'true' delegation has taken place three factors seem decisive: *i)* the nature of powers delegated (wide discretionary or narrowly circumscribed executive); *ii)* the amount of control that the delegating authority can exercise over the delegate and *iii)* the actual exercise of the powers (by delegate or delegating authority). The meaning of delegation in practice will therefore largely be determined by the degree to which real powers have been transferred. See also Ott, Vos and Coman-Kund in this volume. Although it is true that often the powers that are exercised by agencies were carried out at the national level and not by the EU, legally speaking these powers are first by means of the principle of conferral or attributed powers conferred upon the EU and it is the EU legislature that subsequently delegates such powers to agencies. This is also the case where European agencies become delegates of Member States as the founding regulation of an agency will clarify whether Member States may use European agencies to implement EU law. See for an example of the latter in the case of EASA, note 80 of Ott, Vos and Coman-Kund in this volume. See also below (section §2.08).

196. Art. 28 of Regulation (EU) 236/2012 of the European Parliament and of the Council of 14 March 2012 on short-selling and certain aspects of credit default swaps, OJ 2012, L86/1.

assess, in addition to the nature of powers, the amount of control that the Institutions can exercise over the agency and the actual exercise of the powers.[197]

§2.08 CONSTITUTIONAL RECOGNITION AND NEGLECT

'O agencies, where art thou?' This question is everything but a Shakespearean sonnet or comedy film but was the harsh reality until Lisbon, as agencies were far removed from the text of the Treaties. The Lisbon Treaty repaired this deficiency to some extent and made agencies prominently visible in various Treaty provisions. For example, agency acts now formally fall under the jurisdiction of the Court.[198] The Court may review the legality of agency acts 'intended to produce legal effects vis-à-vis third parties' and their failure to act, while it may also interpret agency acts in preliminary rulings.[199] Agencies are furthermore put on par with the institutions in a variety of provisions on internal security,[200] financial measures and independence of the European Central Bank,[201] complaints on instances of maladministration submitted to the Ombudsman,[202] audits,[203] fraud,[204] and citizenship.[205] Importantly, agencies, in the same breath as the institutions, are submitted to the principle of transparency (including access to documents),[206] the requirement of personal data protection[207] and the respect for the constitutional right of citizens to write questions and have answers in their own language.[208] They too are required to hold an open, efficient and independent administration.[209] The constitutionalization of the operation and decision-making procedures of agencies strengthens agencies as part of the EU executive and makes clear that they too are submitted to the constitutional values of

---

197. T. Hartley, *The Foundations of European Union Law* (Oxford: Oxford University Press, 2010), 127.
198. The lack of passive legitimation of agency acts before the Court in the EC Treaty, has however never prevented the Court from accepting jurisdiction, hence formally '*contra legem*' and unconstitutionally, for challenges against acts of the European Trade Mark Office. Thus, although not formally competent under the EC Treaty, in 1995, the former Court of First Instance expressly accepted jurisdiction to judge decisions of the OHIM and even amended its Rules of Procedure to this end. This practice was sustained by the Council who in view of the anticipated workload, especially stemming from litigation relating to these decisions, allowed the CFI to render judgment by single judge, see Council Decision 1999/291/EC, ECSC, Euratom, OJ 1999, L114/52.
199. Art. 263 TFEU moreover permits that the founding regulation of agencies lay down specific conditions and arrangements concerning actions brought by natural or legal persons against acts of these bodies, offices or agencies intended to produce legal effects in relation to them. The relevant Articles are: failure to act: Art. 265 TFEU, preliminary rulings: Art. 267 TFEU and plea of illegality: Art. 277 TFEU.
200. Art. 71 TFEU.
201. Arts 123(1), 124, 127(4), 130, 282(3) TFEU.
202. Art. 228(1) TFEU.
203. Art. 287(1) and (3) TFEU.
204. Art. 352(1) and (4) TFEU.
205. Art. 9 TEU.
206. Art. 15(1) and (3) TFEU.
207. Art. 16(2) TFEU.
208. Art. 24 TFEU.
209. Art. 298 TFEU.

transparency, openness, and participation. In view of the criticism on agencies' transparency,[210] *inter alia* in relation to the conflicts of interest *problématique*, this recognition is very important. Yet, it is also true that this constitutionalization will not solve the incoherencies that exist in practice where founding regulations stipulate transparency and participation in agency activities and decision making only in a very general way. Here shortcomings continue to exist as regards the role of participation, consultation and transparency in relation to binding and non-binding agency decisions[211] requiring a more general approach on these issues, for example, by means of an EU administrative act.[212]

Strikingly, any sign of agencies is lacking in the Treaty Article where they probably would fit best: the adoption of non-legislative acts, in particular Article 291 TFEU. The lack of reference to agencies in Article 290 TFEU is comprehensible as this is in line with the prevailing view that the *Meroni* doctrine only allows delegation of strictly circumscribed executive powers to agencies, while Article 290 TFEU refers to non-legislative acts of general application to supplement or amend certain non-essential elements of the legislative act. However, it may be wondered whether the administrative activities of agencies at the international plane should not be recognized too, for example, in Article 220 TFEU.[213]

The disregard of agencies in Article 291 TFEU is quite extraordinary in view of the composite character of the EU executive and the more remarkable, now that agencies do appear in the Treaties elsewhere. This constitutional neglect, we argue, may very well be due to the Commission's unitary view on the EU executive, set forth above. In order to understand this we need to go back to the chronicles of the negotiations prior to the Nice Treaty, where the introduction of a separate legal basis allowing for the creation of agencies was debated in various proposals. A last outcome in the negotiations was to have a new Treaty article, Article 256a of the former EC Treaty, which stipulated that:

> [w]here this appears necessary in order to carry out any of the activities provided for in Article 3, the Council, acting in accordance with the procedure laid down in Article 251, shall establish an agency having legal personality and confer on it powers to implement the rules which the Council lays down, without prejudice to Article 202. The rules governing languages applying to each of the agencies established on the basis of this Article shall be covered by Article 290.[214]

---

210. See *inter alia*, Court of Auditors 2012, *supra* n. 188.
211. Chiti, *supra* n. 16, at 104–108.
212. See D. Curtin, H. Hofmann & J. Mendes, 'Constitutionalising EU Executive Rule-making Procedures: A Research Agenda', *European Law Journal* (2013): 1–21.
213. See for an in-depth analysis Ott, Vos and Coman-Kund in this volume.
214. Conference of the Representatives of the Governments of the Member States, Brussels, 14 September 2000, CONFER 4770/00, at point 40, see < http://register.consilium.europa.eu/ pdf/en/00/st04/st04770-ad01.en00.pdf > , accessed on 8 July 2013. In an earlier proposal of 3 July 2000, it was proposed to add a new para. 3 to former Art. 7 of the EC Treaty which stipulated that: '[w]here this appears necessary in order to carry out any of the activities provided for in Art. 3, the Council, acting in accordance with the procedure laid down in Art. 251, shall establish an agency having legal personality and determine the rules applicable thereto.' See Conference of the Representatives of the Governments of the Member States,

The explicit reference to the conferral of powers on agencies to implement the rules that the Council would lay down however appeared difficult to swallow for the Commission and during a plenary session of the European Parliament in October 2000, the former president of the European Commission Romano Prodi swept the proposals as regards the agencies' legal basis aside. He argued that the insertion of a legal basis for the creation of agencies would risk creating conflicting centres of power, and that instead these agencies would need to operate under the authority of the Commission which is answerable to the Parliament for their actions.[215] This fear for competition with agencies and the focus on the Commission as the sole executive is also found in the Commission's 2001 the White paper on European Governance. This led academics to criticize the Commission for presenting itself as 'as the lone hero of European policy-making and implementation',[216] and which was argued to express a profound 'lack of understanding of the preconditions of successful multi-level governance in Europe'[217] and to deny the need for transnational partnership between the authorities of the various levels of governance. Although in the same White Paper, the Commission did acknowledge the merits of resorting to agencies, it blatantly focused on the Community method and the institutional triangle of the Council, Parliament and the Commission. This led it to suggest that the impact of comitology on its decision-making be diminished and to eliminate comitology for the adoption of delegated acts with a direct ex post[218] control mechanism on the exercise of the Commission's powers. It is precisely this thinking that has been codified in Articles 290 and 291 TFEU.

The disregard of agencies in Article 291 TFEU may constitute a conundrum for at least two reasons. First, most evidently, it confirms that the categorization of norms as introduced by the Lisbon Treaty is incomplete. For example, binding legal acts on the registration or refusal of a European Trade Mark adopted by the OHIM are clearly an act of executive nature and comparable with Commission decisions on the approval or refusal of an EU-wide approval of a novel food. However, while the latter decisions are implementing decisions in the sense of Article 291 based on comitology, OHIM's acts however do clearly not fall under this category, while OHIM as such is not recognized by Article 288 TFEU as an actor that can adopt acts 'to exercise the Union's competences'. This highlights the uncomfortable and even unconstitutional position of agencies as actors operating in the shadow of hierarchy that can adopt binding executive acts that would ultimately be at odds with the principle of conferral.

Brussels, 14 June 2000, CONFER 4750/00, at p. 89, see < http://register.consilium.europa.eu/pdf/en/00/st04/st04750.en00.pdf > , accessed on 8 July 2013.

215. Speech by R. Prodi before the European Parliament, 3 October 2002, SPEECH/00/352, see < http://europa.eu/rapid/press-release_SPEECH-00-352_en.htm?locale=EN > , accessed on 8 July 2013.

216. F.W. Scharpf, 'European Governance: Common Concerns vs. The Challenges of Diversity', New York Jean Monnet Working Paper 6/01, 2001, 8.

217. *Ibid.*

218. That is after the adoption and before the entry into force of the Commission act.

Second, importantly, it fails to acknowledge the composite character of the EU executive, where EU agencies occupy an increasingly important role, which is problematic in terms of accountability. Hereby it is noteworthy that European agencies operate not only as EU delegates but also as delegates of Member States in the implementation of EU law. The latter refers to the situation in which the founding regulations of agencies explicitly allow or mandate agencies to assist Member States in the implementation of EU law,[219] especially at the global level, as explained above.[220] Instructed to carry out certain tasks to implement the EU's framework on civil aviation safety by Regulation 216/2008, Member States may thus ask EASA to carry out various tasks on their behalf, in particular as regards the functions and tasks ascribed to Member States by applicable international conventions, in particular the Chicago Convention.[221] EU agencies herewith thus also become 'Member States' agencies. Although, in view of the Court's liberal attitude towards the 'borrowing' of EU institutions by Member States when implementing an international agreement outside the EU legal framework,[222] the 'borrowing' of European agencies by Member States to implement EU law, as permitted by EU law, seems as such not to be problematic. The absence of a constitutional status of agencies in Article 291 TFEU seems however to contribute to the blurring of responsibilities and to add to the complexity of EU decision making.

§2.09 CONCLUDING REMARKS

Almost four decades of experience with European agencies have made clear that European agencies are modelled on the basis of networks, with national counterparts and/or stakeholders. It is this strong interplay with their national counterparts that typifies European agencies. They have been designed to operate as a kind of *'primus inter pares'* with the national authorities, instead of being hierarchically placed above the national authorities, although in practice the agencies have a strong say and impact in the networks. These network structures of agencies are all in line with and part of the composite or shared administration of the EU; agencies have become crucial amalgams between EU institutions and Member States.

The hybridity of agencies is expressed in their institutional structure as well as in their multiple tasks. The Common Approach formally confirmed the hybrid and sui generis character of agencies with Member States on the management boards herewith departing formally with the regulatory agency model as developed at the national (for example, US) level. While having representatives of Member States on management

---

219. See for example also M. Chamon, 'The Influence of "Regulatory Agencies" on Pluralisms in European Administrative Law', *Review of European Administrative Law* 5, no. 2 (2012): 61–91, at 76–80.
220. See section §2.04.
221. See *inter alia*, Art. 17(e) of Regulation 216/2008, *supra* n. 52. See Ott, Vos and Coman Kund, in this volume.
222. See B. De Witte & T. Beukers, 'Case C-370/12, *Thomas Pringle v. Government of Ireland, Ireland, The Attorney General*, Judgment of the Court of Justice (Full Court) of 27 November 2012', *Common Market Law Review* 50, no. 3 (2013): 805–848.

boards is not only pragmatically wise but also conceptually sound, it is at the same time at odds with the principle of independence that the founding regulations impose on agencies and their organs, especially with the newer supervisory authorities. Extremely sensitive hereby is agency independence of political and national influence. This holds particularly true for the new supervisory agencies. While admittedly the new supervisory agencies are perhaps agencies unlike others, the 'double-' or even 'triple-hatted' nature of all agencies indicates that independence is in practice a very fragile and relative concept. Perhaps the most demanding challenge that the EU faces today is therefore how to guarantee agencies' independence while acknowledging at the same time that they are part of the composite executive power at EU level. It will require the shaping of a general legal concept of independence to safeguard independence of agencies from industry, political and national interest, taking account of however and accommodating the diversity of agency designs and tasks. Transparency on potential conflicts of interests is hereby an absolute minimum.

Over the years the European institutions have been confronted with both the need to confer more powers upon the agencies and the *Meroni* doctrine allowing only for the delegation of narrowly circumscribed powers to agencies. Practical considerations seem to have won notwithstanding much *Meroni* rhetoric used by the institutions and we thus observe that agencies have increasingly become powerful. We believe that the underlying rationale of *Meroni*, i.e., respect for the institutional balance of powers, would allow for a more lenient interpretation of delegation of powers to agencies as long as the delegation of powers (from the EU legislature to EU agencies) is accompanied by a reinforcement or re-balancing of the existing powers of the institutions provided that constitutional guarantees for decision making are safeguarded. Hereby it is important to observe that already many arrangements to control and hold agencies accountable have been put in place. Shortcomings today relate to the unfolding of accountability instruments in practice as well as to the manifold control and accountability mechanisms. The Common Approach has called for a streamlining of these controls.

The constitutionalization of the operation and decision-making procedures of agencies by the Lisbon Treaty strengthens agencies as part of the EU executive and makes clear that they too are submitted to the constitutional values of for example, transparency, openness, and participation. The constitutionalization of agencies will nevertheless not solve the incoherencies that exist in practice where founding regulations stipulate transparency and participation in agency activities and decision making only in very general way. Here deficiencies continue to exist as regards the role of participation, consultation, and transparency in relation to binding and non-binding agency decisions requiring a more general approach on these issues.

The absence of a constitutional status of agencies in Article 291 TFEU however seems to contribute to the blurring of responsibilities and to add to the complexity of EU decision making. It shows the uncomfortable and even unconstitutional position of agencies as actors operating in the shadow of hierarchy that can adopt binding executive acts that would ultimately be at odds with the principle of conferral. At the same time, it fails to recognize the composite character of the EU executive, where EU agencies occupy an increasingly important role, which is also problematic in terms of accountability.

European agencies are so torn between independence and dependence, EU and Member States, narrowly circumscribed and discretionary powers, constitutional recognition and disregard. This requires not only a further reflection on the role of agencies in the EU executive but also on the shared and composite character of the EU executive more generally.

CHAPTER 3

European Agencies: Barely Legal?

Michelle Everson

§3.01 INSTITUTIONAL BALANCE: BETWEEN CONSTITUTIONALITY AND THE RULE OF LAW

A recent contribution to the agency debate raises a tantalizing question: are twenty-first Century EU agencies legal, and if not, does this really matter?[1] The primary issue for lawyers in this case is one of the *'Meroni* doctrine', and its application to a new generation of European agencies, including important new agencies within the European System for Financial Supervision (ESFS),[2] who now exercise enhanced decisional discretion, and who may take decisions that are binding upon individuals.[3] The case of *Meroni*,[4] decided by the then European Court of Justice (ECJ), as far back as 1958, has long been held to preclude the direct and binding exercise of European competences by institutions not named by the European Treaties. By the same token, the current UK Government, has raised a direct objection to the operation of the new European Market and Securities Authority (ESMA) before the now Court of Justice of the European Union (CJEU), and, in particular, against Article 28 of the ESMA founding regulation,[5] which affords the Authority emergency powers to intervene, in order to prohibit financial services or products which might give rise to systemic risk within the European

---

1. D. Curtin & R. Dehousse, 'European Agencies: Tipping the Balance', in *The Agency Phenomenon in the European Union*, eds. M. Busuioc, M.Groenleer & J. Trondal (Manchester: Manchester University Press, 2013), 193–205.
2. Regulation (EU) No. 1092/2010 (ESRB Regulation); Regulation No. 1096/2010 (ECB Regulation); Regulation (EU) No. 1095/2010 (European Securities and Markets Authority); Regulation (EU) No. 1093/2010 (European Banking Authority); Regulation (EU) No. 1094/2010 (European Insurance and Occupational Pensions Authority).
3. M. Chamon, 'EU Agencies between *Meroni* and *Romano* or the Devil and the Deep Blue Sea', *Common Market Law Review* 48 (2011): 1055–1075.
4. Case 9/56, *Meroni & Co, Industrie Matallurgische S.P.A. v. High Authority* [1957–1958] ECR 133.
5. See, *supra* n. 2.

financial services market. The UK Government is relying both on *Meroni*, as well as the more recent case of *Romano*,[6] in foundation of its claim that the ESMA founding regulation is in conflict with principles of non-delegation within the EU.[7]

From the non-lawyerly, but highly realistic political-regulatory viewpoint, it is very hard to imagine that the CJEU will find against the emergency powers afforded ESMA. At a time of continuing economic crisis, as well as a (an almost) pan-European self-commitment to Banking Union and/or augmented formal institutional control over the private creation of money (aka creation of 'unsecured debt'),[8] judicial intrusion into a carefully crafted European system designed to control systemic risk, would surely represent a victory of law over common sense; or a foolish judicial disregard for the vital need to ensure continuing financial stability within Europe. Yet, the historic ECJ has provided us with a strong precedent in this regard: the case of Chernobyl,[9] whereby not even the immediate threat of radioactive contamination of foodstuffs within Europe was held to relieve the Council of its legislative duty to consult Parliament under the principle of the 'institutional balance'. Functionality, or a speedily effective response to an emergency situation, was not, in the Court's opinion, a sufficient justification for the negation of the principle of 'institutional balance' derived by the ECJ from the then Treaty's enumeration of the apportioned competences of individual European institutions (derived from Article 7 of the TEC).

The particular emphasis laid upon the principle of institutional balance in the case of Chernobyl, however, provides an immediate key to the very particular, and far broader, legal-constitutional tension which now bedevils the question of the legality of European agencies. As Jean-Paul Jacqué has famously noted, the notion of institutional balance – or the 'balance of powers' – as alluded to by the ECJ in justification of their *Meroni* Judgment, is a judicial construct, evolved within the context of the European Economic Communities in compensation for the absence within the European legal space of a principle of the separation of powers.[10] At core then, the ban on delegation of discretionary powers to institutions not named by the Treaty that was imposed by the Court, served, in the context of the time, to prevent 'the abuse of power', and more particularly, in *Meroni*, any potential abuse of power that might arise within the context of a delegation of powers from the High Commission under the then still-extant ECSC Treaty to a body constituted within private law.[11]

So far so apparently simple: nevertheless, simple recitation of Montesquieu's historically renowned reportage upon the nascent British Constitution – his observation that an abuse of sovereign power was then militated against by a division of power

---

6. Case 98/80, *Guiseppe Romano v. Institut national d'assurance maladie-invalidité* [1981] ECR 1259.
7. C-270/12, *United Kingdom v. Council and Parliament* (OJ 2012, C273/2).
8. See, for concepts of sound money, M. Everson, 'The Fault of (European) Law in (Social and Political) Economic Crisis', *Law & Critique* 24, no. 2 (2013): 107–129.
9. Case 70/88, *European Parliament v. Council of the European Communities* [1990] ECR I-2041.
10. J.-P. Jacqué, 'The Principle of Institutional Balance', *Common Market Law Review* 41, no. 2 (2004): 384–391.
11. See, for the distinction between *Meroni* and *Romano*, Chamon, *supra* n. 3.

between executive, legislative and judicial arms of government – masks great complexities within constitutional and legal history. These are complexities that are also only heightened within the current context of the evolution of European governance structures. Above all, and perhaps most presciently so in EU institutional terms, protection against the abuse of power may be understood in two ways: first, in purely formal legal terms, as an issue of personal protection; a matter which resides for the law in the existence of an identifiable and pursuable right for redress against an equally apparent abuse of formally-endowed authority (generally an ultra vires one). Yet, this is far from the end of the story. Instead, protection against abuse may also be understood in far broader political-constitutional terms. That is, as a matter of the establishment of an 'ideal' dispensation of powers between the various organs of state which are constituted within a distinct polity. Within the former understanding, legal certainty or the rule of law is paramount. Abuse of power is militated against by clear and formal enumeration of competences and by the provision of rights to individuals to demand judicial review where personal rights have been infringed upon. Within the latter scheme, by contrast, political realities and constitutional theory are predominant, with, for historical and contemporary example, James Madison's vision of the pluralistic dispersal of federal power continuing to vie for the 'power-controlling' soul of the US Constitution with James Hamilton's right-based concept of devolution of powers to individual Americans – a battle that determines the spread of competences amongst the institutions named by the US Constitution. In other words, the notion of the separation of powers is never an absolute one, subject instead to political, historical, and philosophical contingencies, which are generally fought to their conclusion within the space of the constitutional jurisdiction.

As has been suggested,[12] the evolving jurisprudence of the European Court – at least, to the degree that the remarks of its Advocate Generals allow us to surmise – around concepts of the balance of powers, or the institutional balance, reveals that, at different times, legal reasoning on the legitimate exercise of European competences has been variously informed by concerns about the rule of law, on the one hand, and by a broader vision of the constitutional dispensation of powers within Europe, on the other. Thus, for example, the case of *Romano*, decided within a later EC context of delegation of powers to a public rather than private authority, is also argued to differ from the earlier case of *Meroni*. That is, in its concern with the rule of law, the lack of an enumerated power of delegation from the Council and the absence of appropriate individual legal protection under the then Article 173 (TEC), governing judicial review. *Meroni*, by contrast is assumed to be a far closer reflection of the broader constitutional perception of the principle of institutional balance – one proposed by Jacqué – as being a means to contain and sustain the inherent tension within the EC/EU between its supranational and national characteristics; and more particularly so, to the degree that a related principle of non-delegation of powers may act to prevent any disguized transfer of national powers to supranational organs.

---

12. See, Chamon, *supra* n. 3.

However, to this one author (Chamon), there is similarly – in a final analysis – no difference in the distinction between *Meroni* and *Romano*, at least as regards the manner in which the cases might apply to the enhanced powers afforded all three of the new agencies established within the ESFS (including, the European Banking Authority (EBA) and the European Insurance and Occupational Pensions Authority (EIOPA)). On the one hand, the mention of European agencies within the new provisions of Article 263 TFEU, is not felt to be sufficient to ensure individual legal protection; at least as far as regards which acts undertaken by agencies may be deemed to 'have the force of law'.[13] Doubts still remain about the reach of judicial review within the EU, in particular, as regards acts of general application and 'pre-legal' implementing measures undertaken by the agencies (for example, establishment of joint supervisory standards). On the other hand, however, the very particular decision-making procedures established for European financial agencies, whereby the Commission's powers to reject regulatory standards suggested by the agencies are severely curtailed, may similarly be suggested to infringe upon the current manifestation of the non-delegation principle established within Article 290 (and 291) of the TFEU. The Commission has itself lodged objections on this basis to the creation of new financial services agencies:

> [A]s regards the process for the adoption of regulatory standards, the Commission emphasises the unique character of the financial services sector, following from the Lamfalussy structure and explicitly recognized in Declaration 39 to the TFEU. However, the Commission has serious doubts whether the restrictions on its role when adopting delegated acts and implementing measures are in line with Articles 290 and 291.[14]

As we shall see below, the primary concern of the Commission in this case is one that it could, as a consequence, be held to be liable for decisions taken in its name, over which it may nonetheless exercise very little practical control. By the same token, however, the de facto discretionary decision-making competences afforded new agencies within the ESFS – bodies established by simple regulations and not by the Treaty – in an area of day-to-day financial supervision (control of financial products), that was traditionally reserved to the Member States and which is now so central to the stability of the EU as a whole, cannot but raise concerns about disguised and uncontrollable mutations in the balance established between the institutional power centres of the EU. More specifically, concern must also arise within a differentiated EU, wherein there remains great potential for conflict between individual Member States, which have or have not committed themselves to enhanced European control of systemic risk within European Banking Union.

Seen in this light, the sanguine attitude of various authors, and more particularly, Deirdre Curtin and Renaud Dehousse,[15] to what might be termed the 'barely legal' nature of new European agencies might appear surprising. For Curtin and Dehousse, however, as exemplified by their curt dismissal of the 'theoretically perfect democratic

---

13. Chamon, *supra* n. 3, at 1070–1072.
14. Exemplary, the Commission statement on the establishment of ESMA, Interinstitutional File: 2009/0144(COD), Brussels, 10 November 2010 (12.11).
15. See, Curtin & Dehousse, *supra* n. 1.

legitimacy of the German parliament' propounded by the German Constitutional Court in its judgment on the Lisbon Treaty,[16] the core problem is not one of the exact legalities and perfect philosophical polities established at national level. We should not be too concerned that agencies appear increasingly to contravene the notion of institutional balance encapsulated within the *Meroni* doctrine. Much less should we be concerned about the rule of law in relation to agency decision-making. After all, the CJEU has always sought to establish appropriate rights of review whatever the deficiencies of the treaties.[17] Instead, we should simply concede that European agencies are, betimes ad hoc, but always necessary, responses to the administrative lacunae of a uniquely emerging and complex polity, maintaining intricate relations with supranational and national administrations, as well as political organs. Similarly, agencies perform a vast variety of vital functions, interacting between governance levels and responding to demands for coordination at national, supranational, and international level. We could no longer govern the EU without agencies.

Realism would appear to be uppermost: agencies are a fact of functional life within the EU whose operation should not be constrained by outmoded and inappropriate schemes of constituted national government. Yet, this is not to say that the attitude taken is wholly without its own normative or aspirational basis. Above all, Curtin and Dehousse are concerned that urgent measures must now be undertaken to design and manage 'appropriate accountability regimes' for European agencies.[18] At one level, a simple reflection of the editorial fact that the duo finds themselves commenting, in a concluding chapter, upon a volume dominated by political scientists, the emphasis which they lay upon a notion of accountability, rather than legality, is nonetheless also a measure of a feature specific to the principle of institutional balance within the EU. Far from being a monolith, the principle of institutional balance has, perforce, changed over the time of the development of the European Treaties. Seen in this light, the case of *Chernobyl* is doubly central to the evolutionary story of institutional balance within the EU. On the one hand, the case does reconfirm the degree of respect which must be maintained by each of the European institutions for powers and competences afforded the other institutions of the Union. On the other hand, however, continuity with regard to a principle of conferral of powers, is equally matched by a judicial and treaty-driven dynamism, whereby the Court has progressively strengthened the rights of the European Parliament with regard to its own competences, in moves which reflect the demand for additional democratic legitimation within the EU, and which have also, in their turn, been subsequently confirmed by treaty revision.[19] Alternatively, as the Community has mutated into the Union, the measure of 'constitutionality' within the Union has been both the adaptation of its governing principles, including the institutional balance, to the emerging shape of the European polity, as well as, the deployment of those principles to form the polity.

---

16. Curtin & Dehousse, *supra* n. 1, at 201.
17. Curtin & Dehousse, *supra* n. 1, at 200, with reference to the case of *Sogelma*, case T-411/06 [2008] ECR II-02771.
18. Curtin & Dehousse, *supra* n. 1, at 204.
19. See, for full details of this process, M. Everson & J. Eisner, *The Making of the European Constitution* (London: Routledge-Cavendish, 2007), Chapter 5.

To this exact degree, then, the emphasis placed by Curtin and Dehousse upon accountability, rather than formal respect for strictly delineated institutional competences, might be suggested to be a simple, but 'constitutionalist' reflection of the development of the vision of emergent governance within the EU within the terms of the second meaning of institutional balance, reflecting the effort to establish an ideal dispensation of powers amongst its institutions. Above all, and vitally so, although the principle of institutional balance as one of an institutional limitation of powers retains its place within the TEU – albeit in a far less eye-catching position (Article 13(1)) – it is absent from the TFEU, which now talks simply, in Article 7, of a principle of 'the conferral of powers', and, more importantly, may also be argued to have been partially alienated, in its spirit at least, by the new terms in which the delegation of powers is regulated in Articles 290 and 291 TFEU. Although the Lisbon Treaty has dispensed with much of the reformist lawyerly zeal of the draft constitutional treaty, Article 290 TFEU may yet give some measure of comfort to those who had hoped for comprehensive overhaul of the Community's Byzantine scheme of legislation and implementation. Above all, although the cumbersome historical distinction made between legislative instruments lives on in Article 288 TFEU (ex 249 TEC), the new Article 290 may be argued to have at last established a nascent 'hierarchy of norms' within the Union, placing explicit Treaty limits, as well as operational conditions (to be determined by the Council and by the European Parliament), upon the exercise of delegated powers and implementing competences by the European Commission. Thus, for example, a delegation of powers to the Commission 'to adopt non-legislative acts of general application' may now only occur where so stipulated within an originating legislative act, and only to the degree that such a delegated power 'supplement[s]' or 'amend[s] certain non-essential elements of that legislative act' (Article 290(1)). Equally, Article 290(2a) TFEU imposes a duty upon Parliament and Council 'explicitly' to detail the conditions upon which a power is exercised (for example, by means of a sunset clause detailing the temporal limits of the delegation); and further stipulates that 'delegated acts' may only 'come into force' where the Parliament and Council have raised no objections within a predetermined time limit (Article 290(2)(b)).

Accordingly, as noted, although at the formal legal level, the new Article 290 may and does raise concerns that acts of delegation to new European agencies are indeed barely legal, at least to the degree that they may be argued to entail 'essential' legislative elements, and to disenfranchise the Commission. It also raises a possibility that, post-Lisbon, the EU is moving beyond its own understanding of an institutional balance of powers to embrace the protection against an abuse of powers that can be afforded by a more conventional commitment to the separation of powers. Within this presumption, the position of Parliament is paramount. In that it now plays a major role in both condoning, and, vitally, revoking (outdated/misused) delegated powers, the primary concern around delegation within the EU might similarly be argued to have shifted. We are perhaps, in part at least, no longer concerned that acts of delegation may shift powers between institutions and, therefore, between national and supranational levels. Instead, we are now more determined to ensure that a European, rather than a national, public – via the representative medium of its democratically-elected MEPs – may exercise a greater degree of control over the evolving European executive, which similarly includes – most strikingly, within the concept of the 'networked agency'[20] – portions of national administrations.

Within this presumption of an increasing maturity within the European polity, the emphasis laid upon accountability appears to be far less complacent. Accountability, as well as its own partner mechanism of transparency, is just as surely one of the primary mechanisms whereby a popular (public) sovereignty might be assured within an ideal polity: the accountability of an executive to Parliament, and a Parliament to its voters, is a core means by which abuse of powers can be guarded against. Certainly, within our current European constellation we might be experiencing a tension between the rule of law (formal legal certainty) and constitutionality (new principles to regulate the inchoate but emerging EU polity). Nonetheless, the effort to guard against abuse of powers may be argued to continue, all potential illegality notwithstanding.

Is this then the end of the story? Are we simply experiencing a mutation in the institutional balance to an understanding of the European polity, within which European agencies will and can play a valued role? Is this a wholly normal cycle of constitutional development, comparable with periods of strain around, for example, the US concept of a separation of powers, wherein formal law has yet to match the developmental ideal of the dispensation of powers? This is certainly possible, and, might also be argued to be a feature of the development of the Union as a whole. However, Curtin and Dehousse also very briefly hint at a further – and very deep, political and pragmatic – problem. Disquiet is growing about the development of a European executive and more, particularly, is crystallizing around a question of its efficacy and efficiency. Similarly, such disquiet is growing at a period of intense crisis within which the normal motto of European institutional transformation and transformation – 'we will find a solution (eventually)' – has been brutally exposed, as the Euro crisis has revealed intractable inconsistencies in the national-supranational balance. Whatever, its final outcome, the Euro crisis has demonstrated that European projects can and may fail. The 'blind optimism' which has accompanied European integration,[21] has faltered. Under these circumstances, then, a disjunction between the current rule of law and a postulated future and desired constitutionality, undoubtedly presents great dangers of its own, a potential lack of transparency within which inefficiencies and poor governance may arise; an undermining of the prime formative output legitimacy of the EU, or, its ability to furnish good results.

---

20. Many European agencies find their primary role in the co-ordination of national regulatory activities; a unction also afforded new agencies within the ESFS. See, for networked agencies, G. Majone, 'Europe's Democratic Deficit: The Question of Standards', *European Law Journal* 4, no. 1 (1997): 5–28.
21. G. Majone, *The EU in Comparative Context: Regional Integration and Political Transaction Costs* (Cambridge: Cambridge University Press, forthcoming 2013).

§3.02   FROM 'INDEPENDENT' EXPERTISE TO A POLITICAL ADMINISTRATION?

[A]   Autonomy and Accountability in the Commission's Agency Model

A current Commission preference for European governance by means of European agencies or semi-autonomous expert bodies – most forcefully stated in its 2001 White Paper on European Governance – in large part derives from the historical failings in its own comitology structures that were exposed by the BSE crisis. The Commission's initial response to a lack of administrative capacity within its own structures was to turn to 'expertise' to aid in the daily business of administering the internal market. This expertise was likewise first concentrated within committee structures, or the system of comitology. BSE still functions as a potent warning to proponents of expert-led (technocratic) governance, especially with regard to the problem of what to do when technical expertise can no longer provide technical answers and of how to respond when diffuse hazard cannot be concretized as risk 'because the science has run out'. In the 1990s, however, the failure of scientific and administrative expertise at national and supranational level – both of quantification of the risks of human evolution of variant Creutzfeldt-Jakob disease and of adequate post-market control of the spread of 'mad cow' products – was primarily viewed within an institutional paradigm that stressed the subsequent need to act in order to improve and to ensure the quality and delivery of scientific and technical expertise. Above all, lack of transparency within the various ad hoc scientific committees established by the Commission to assess risks both exacerbated a lack of scientific independence at EU level[22] and foreclosed potential for independent epistemic review of scientific findings. In addition to highlighting the functional obscurantism of the comitology model, the BSE saga also revealed the need for permanently funded EU scientific expertise in order to facilitate long-term research upon the basis of which hazards could be transformed into quantifiable and therefore 'manageable' risks, as well as a demand for permanent oversight of implementation of EU standards at Member State level.[23]

Transparency and permanence are the hallmarks of the operations of expertise within regulatory agencies.[24] As a consequence, a radical expansion in the use of this vehicle followed the BSE scandal. This development has not been without its opponents, in particular Parliament, which has long standing concerns about the growth of the European executive.[25] Neither has it been viewed without ambivalence within the

---

22. Most 'European' experts involved were connected with the UK Government; see, for details, E. Vos, 'EU Food Safety Regulation in the Aftermath of the BSE Crisis', *Journal of Consumer Policy* 23 (2000): 227–255.
23. See, Vos, *supra* n. 22.
24. See, D. Demortain, *Scientists and the Regulation Of Risk: Standardising Control* (London: Edward Elgar, 2010).
25. Never a comitology fan or concerned that its competences might be surreptitiously siphoned off to the Commission in the fog of committee proceedings, Parliament is similarly wary that its competences may be ceded to powerful agency heads; see D. Geradin & N. Petit, 'The Development of Agencies at EU and National Levels', NYU, School of Law, Jean Monnet Working Paper Series (2004, 01/04).

Commission itself, especially in view of the danger that Commission powers might be themselves be alienated by the growth of new EU institutions.[26] Nevertheless, the functional demand for new governance vehicles within the EU remains strong; and perhaps especially so following miscarriage of the idealistic quest to create a self-consciously political European moment within the failed Constitutional Treaty. Equally, however, increasing EU recourse to the agency vehicle has also been facilitated by a prevailing consensus on the best mode of economic governance for modern markets.

In other words, although the existence of autonomous regulatory agencies, which operate at arms-length from conventional government has long been justified by the argument that areas requiring complex technical oversight are best governed by 'experts',[27] it has recently also been further facilitated by alterations in the manner in which the relationship between exercise of political power and market operation is viewed. More particularly, the argument traditionally used in order to justify the operation of independent central banks – one that a polity should guard against the danger that its own government will manipulate exchange rates for short-term political gain – finds a far more general application within the consensus that market operation should as far as is possible take place within its own autonomous sphere. 'Efficiency' is the leading criterion within a modern regulatory paradigm that seeks to refashion regulation in order to separate out the pursuit of general redistributive goals from sectoral regulatory aims. Assuming a higher normative commitment to autonomous market operation, efficiency-based regulatory models argue that the statist tendency to a political economy of 'corporatism' – distorting conflation of micro-economic market regulation with redistributive macro-economic policies – can be combatted by means of establishment of governing regulatory expertise within bodies that act independently from government.

Vitally, however, efficiency-based regulatory models have also gained in normative legitimacy as postulation of a concept of pareto-efficiency itself mediates against concerns that executive power should never be endowed with too broad a mandate. In other words, discretionary powers may be delegated to independent agencies where they have no redistributive consequences – which will always require majoritarian political oversight – and the subject-matter of regulation is value neutral in terms of welfare losses within the general populace.[28] Accordingly, and to the degree that pursuit of economic efficiency has become a self-limiting principle within the polity, the independence of regulatory agencies is transformed from constitutional spectre to positive constitutional good; one which must be positively protected from potential perversion within political process.

---

26. M. Everson & E. Vos (eds.), *Uncertain Risks Regulated* (London: Routledge, 2009).
27. F. Vibert, 'Better Regulation and the Role of EU Agencies', in *Better Regulation*, ed. S. Weatherhill (Oxford: Hart Publishing, 2007), 387–404.
28. G. Majone, 'Independence v Accountability: European Non-majoritarian Institutions and Democratic Government in Europe', EUI Working Papers (SPS) 1993/09 (1994).

In this analysis, an 'independent fourth-branch of government' is no stranger to our traditional 'separation of powers inspired', transmission-belt model of administration, whereby the legislature directs the executive. Instead, it is argued to be wholly integral to it, being no more than its most modern manifestation. The long-term will of the polity for efficient regulation is ensured rather than endangered by the shielding of regulatory expertise from political contingency. At the same time, however, the modernized transmission construct demands that an independent administration of expertise must also be subject to control, in order to ensure that it is capable of fulfilling its regulatory functions and performs them well (efficacy). The agency must consequently be made accountable to traditional institutions, as well as to the general public, in a manner that does not endanger its own autonomy, and is so, in this 'ideal vision', by means of a plural scheme of oversight – drawn from US experience – which ensures that 'no-one controls the agency, yet the agency is under control.'[29]

In large part based upon a Madisonian, or pluralist reading of the principle of a separation of powers within the US Constitution,[30] this US agency model would appear to have dominated Commission thinking on European agencies up until very recently. Certainly, the Commission retains its ambivalence towards agencies. Nevertheless, the agency vehicle provides it with a vital increase in its functional capacities, making it an institutionally powerful if sometimes reluctant proponent of an EU-specific model of agency operation. At the same time, however, when combined with a continuing respect for the *Meroni* doctrine – reserving final decisional powers for the Commission – a pluralist, US-inspired model of autonomous and accountable agencies, is attractive to the Commission on three counts:

- institutionalized agencies provide it with consistent and sustainable expertise;
- autonomous agencies accord with an internal market model of autonomous economic operations; and
- a pluralistic scheme of accountability lessens the danger that other EU institutions, or the Member States, will encroach upon Commission competences by means of their dominance of the new agencies.

Long-term Commission support for an agency model of autonomy and accountability can be gleaned from its various policy documents on governance in the EU, and, in particular, communications between itself and other EU institutions on the future of EU agencies. More specifically, the 2002 White Paper on Governance, the draft Inter-Institutional Agreement on Agencies and the 'Way Forward for Agencies', or Communication initially withdrawing the draft Inter-Institutional Agreement on Agencies.[31] Commission preferences for a justificatory model for agencies may be summarized as follows:

---

29. T. Moe, 'Political Institutions: the Neglected Side of the Story', *Journal of Law, Economics and Organization* 6, no. 2 (1990): 213–253; M. Everson, 'Independent Agencies: Hierarchy Beaters?', *European Law Journal* 1, no. 2 (1995): 180–204.
30. See, Everson, *supra* n. 29.
31. See, *supra* n. 9.

(1) *Agency creation and transmission*: Although full independence cannot be accepted within EU structures, agencies are still legitimated with reference to the (economic) principle of utility. They should only be established where the 'added' value of Community regulation can be demonstrated through cost-benefit analysis. Similarly, the balance of powers plays its own rhetorically justificatory role: agencies have a particular role to play in areas where the (executive) powers of the Member States must be pooled to avoid over-concentration of powers at Union level; a notion which finds its counterpart in the establishment of 'networked' supranational-national agency operation. Likewise, transmission-belt administration is assured by general restriction of the agency role to 'preparatory' decision-making in areas of 'technical expertise', where agencies can be supplied with 'a clear executive mandate'.

(2) *An agency structure of autonomy and accountability:* Plural theories of agency control, find their application in the stipulation that agencies must be placed within 'clear lines of accountability'. A degree of operational independence from the Commission is nonetheless established by virtue of their threefold division into a Director, administrative boards (executive boards) and scientific committees. The Director should typically be appointed subject to parliamentary approval. Administrative boards will be made up of representatives of the Commission, Council and, where necessary, Member States, as well as non-voting stakeholders. The members of the scientific committees of agencies are to be appointed in open public competition on the sole basis of their expertise. Independence is also assured by demands that Member State agencies operative within the EU national network, will be 'autonomous' of their own governments.

(3) *Ex ante and ex post accountability:* The (modern) transmission principle of administration is further secured by proposed imposition of a high degree of transparency upon agencies and the requirement that their proposed activities will always be laid down in an openly accessible annual work programme, which may likewise be subject to subsequent scrutiny in the light of the annual activity report. Agencies are also required to be subject to a further scheme of ex post financial, political, administrative, and judicial control, whereby significant oversight is furnished by the powers of the Court of Auditors, Council, and European Parliament to approve agency budgets, and by review of individual decisions before the CJEU (Article 263 TFEU).

(4) *Scientific transparency and public accountability:* The Commission also seeks to facilitate review of agency operation by broader epistemic communities. Transparent agencies should play a part in 'the validation of the scientific-technical basis for formal regulation' and will be 'held publicly accountable for this role'. Agencies are also ascribed an important function in relation to the integration of stakeholder views within public regulation, which occurs within the agency itself. Their role to 'analyse and stimulate public debate at both European and international level' attempts to reproduce the wider institutional legitimation, which arises as press and public follow the work of, for example, the policies of high-profile US agencies.

[B]   A Politicized Administration?

With the final publication of the Common Approach on European Agencies, or Inter-Institutional Agreement between Council, Parliament, and the Commission, concluded in July 2012,[32] a long period of negotiation between conflicting institutional positions on European agencies has come to an end. With the Common Approach and Commission Roadmap for its achievement,[33] the hope, at Union level, is accordingly one that, although a degree of diversity in the structures of European will remain a feature of this form of Union governance for the foreseeable future, a common set of operation principles for EU agencies will overcome any remaining concerns about their operation, facilitating their expansion.

The Commission has summarized the prime operating principles of the common agreement in its roadmap as 'more balanced governance, improved efficiency and accountability and greater coherence'. In greater detail, such principles will be served in the following manner:

- Governance: 'The implementation of the Common Approach will aim to clarify that management boards are expected to play a supervisory role to counter-balance the powers of the directors [of agencies].' In pursuit of this aim, the membership of supervisory/management boards will be streamlined, in order to mitigate a current tendency whereby they act as consultative assemblies, rather than active supervisors, although Parliamentary representatives will take their place on such boards 'where necessary'. Similarly, an 'alert-warning system' will be established whereby the Commission will be formally entrusted with the responsibility to warn the European Parliament and Council in case:

    it has serious reasons for concern that an agency's Management Board is about to take decisions which may not comply with the mandate of the agency, may violate EU law or be in manifest contradiction with EU policy objectives.

- Efficiency, accountability and transparency of agencies will be strengthened in relation to better coordination of joint agency resources, the establishment of better commonly respected standards governing day-to-day agency activities and a greater degree of openness with regard to the more unexpected functions which agencies have developed, for example, within the international sphere.
- 'Greater coherence in the way agencies function', or a greater degree of comparability between them will be provided by the harmonization of the voting rules in management boards, as well as through more informal practices, such as standard provisions for headquarter agreements on the basis of existing best practices.

---

32. 'Joint Statement of the European Parliament, the Council of the EU and the European Commission on decentralized agencies', available at < http://europa.eu/agencies/documents/joint_statement_and_common_approach_2012_en.pdf >, accessed on 15 July 2013.
33. See *supra* n. 32.

At first glance a very similar set of principles to those expounded within the White Paper, Inter-Institutional Agreement on Agencies and Way Forward, the Commission's Roadmap nonetheless hints at the very particular concerns of Council and Parliament, which are now to be found in the Common Approach and which may be argued to have vitally modified the Commission's agency scheme of autonomy and accountability. Above all, the Common Approach confirms a *fait accompli* already established by the temporal limitation imposed upon delegations of power to the Commission by Article 290 TFEU. All new agencies – mirroring the template adopted for the ESFS agencies – will be established with a 'sunset clause'. At one level a further means to ensure the efficiency and efficacy of agencies,[34] sunset clauses may, at the same time, act as a means to heighten 'political' control of agencies. In other words, a sword of Damocles hangs over agencies: 'fail to take note of political concerns around your operations, and you may find your mandate rescinded'. This soft means of the exercise of political power – an acceptable face of mandate control – similarly has the potential to harden within supervisory boards, on which Parliament might in the future also be represented, and which have now been consciously designed to counterbalance the powers of autonomous agency directors.

Within this particular constellation, therefore, a long-standing model of autonomy and accountability may find its nemesis in the increasing convergence between the EU agency model and the older template of tiered committee operation within which the technical expertise of scientific committees was always balanced by presentation of political views by Member State and Council representatives within regulatory committees.[35] Famously, the political-technical balance established in the case of comitology has been argued to have fostered a form of deliberative administration in which the political and the technocratic have come together to find the best regulatory solutions. But, will this also be the case for agencies? Is the agency model a suitable candidate for politicization? Perhaps not: the Commission's insistence on an 'alert-warning system' in relation to the operation of supervisory similarly hints at further tensions within the supposedly settled EU agency model. These potential tensions will be discussed below with specific reference to the potential inefficiency and lack of accountability which may have already arisen within the three agencies established within the ESFS.

---

34. As suggested by G. Majone & M. Everson, 'Institutional Reform: Independent Agencies, Oversight, Co-ordination and Procedural Control', in *Governance in the European Union*, eds. O. de Schutter, N. Lebesis & J. Patterson (Luxembourg, 2001), 129.
35. Ch. Joerges & J. Neyer, 'From Intergovernmental Bargaining to Deliberative Political Processes: The Constitutionalisation of Comitology', *European Law Journal* 3 (1997): 273–299.

§3.03   AGENCIES IN ACTION WITHIN THE ESFS: A TALE OF UNACCOUNTABLE INEFFICIENCY?

The ESFS was established by a series of EU regulations in 2010.[36] It comprises:

(1) The European Systemic Risk Board (ESRB), chaired by the President of the ECB and including governors of National Central Banks (NCBs), a Commission representative and the Chairs of the three ESAs. The role of the ESRB is to provide 'macro-prudential' supervision, or to identify and combat 'systemic risks', or hazardous financial activities, which threaten the functioning of the ESFS.

(2) Three ESAs who administer a complex series of common financial regulations for Banks, Insurers, and Financial Markets by means of establishment of the Binding Technical Standards (BTS) and jointly-established practices which inform micro-prudential supervision of financial institutions at national level. ESAs are also charged with identification of systemic risks within the ESFS and their notification to the ESRB. A Joint ESA Committee co-ordinates micro-supervision across the three sectors and strengthens macro-supervisory information flow.

(3) National Supervisory Authorities (NSAs), formally responsible for micro-prudential supervision at Member State level.

The ESFS is not the first endeavour to coordinate financial supervision at supranational level. Instead, it builds upon the regulatory principles, national regulatory networks, as well as European standard-setting committees for the financial services, established in the wake of the report of the 'Lamfalussy Committee' of Wise Men on the Regulation of European Securities Markets in early 2001.[37] However, lying between the Commission's establishment of its own comitology system and a far broader Union commitment to the ESFS, we find the collapse of Lehmann Brothers in late 2008 a significant change in the rhetorical justification for institutional reform at EU level, a host of new financial regulations, and a significant widening and deepening of supranational regulatory structures founded in independent expertise.

The Lamfalussy group was primarily concerned with the establishment of a globally competitive European market for financial services. At this stage, unwieldy EU regulation and discrepancies in national implementation were seen as regulatory failings, not because they accentuated obscurity within financial markets, but rather

---

36. Regulation (EU) No. 1092/2010 (ESRB Regulation); Regulation No. 1096/2010 (ECB Regulation); Regulation (EU) No. 1095/2010 (European Securities and Markets Authority); Regulation (EU) No. 1093/2010 (European Banking Authority); Regulation (EU) No. 1094/2010 (European Insurance and Occupational Pensions Authority).
37. Known as the European Financial Services Action Plan, and comprising, in particular, Commission Decisions, 2001/527/EC and 2001/528/EC (EU Securities Committee and Committee of European Securities Regulators); Commission Decision 2004/10/EC (Committee of European Banking Supervisors; Commission Decision 2004/9/EC (Committee of European Insurance and Occupational Pensions Supervisors).

since they led to differential treatment of financial instruments, both 'violating the prerequisite of the neutrality of financial supervision' in the EU market, and retarding adaption of European financial services 'to the pace of global financial market change'.[38] By rhetorical contrast, the 'high-level' de Larosière group on EU financial supervision convened in response to financial melt-down appeared to have returned to a more traditional concept of market failure, concluding that the system of European financial regulation must be strengthened and expanded: first, to improve an 'inadequate mix' of regulatory and supervisory skills, which had seen too little information gathered and shared 'on the global magnitude of global leveraging', and had likewise exhibited a catastrophic failure to 'fully understand or evaluate the size of the risks'; and second, to create a coordinated early-warning system to identify macro-systemic risks of a contagion of correlated horizontal shocks.[39]

In addition to imposition of straightened capital requirements on financial institutions, the regulatory and supervisory structure was significantly enhanced with the establishment of the ESFS and the creation of new, semi-autonomous authorities – or EU agencies – for the regulation and supervision of securities, banking, and insurance. This final development is particularly significant. Facing crisis, the European Parliament 'enthusiastically' welcomed the ESFS, discarding its long standing opposition to further consolidation of EU technocratic governance, in particular by means of supranational 'agencification'.[40]

Up until financial crisis, the supranational regulatory interest in financial services sought only to create a 'level competitive playing field' between EU and US regulatory structures and restricted itself to legislative harmonization of national prudential regulation.[41] First, it established the creditworthiness of individual financial institutions (1980s) to allow for creation of 'one-seat authorisations' for Europe-wide market actors (1990s). And second, it engaged in cooperative standard setting. Implementation of EU legislation and material supervision of the character of financial products was a matter for national authorities alone. The period since crisis, however, has seen a deluge of EU financial services regulation.[42] Major initiatives have focused on implementation of the risk-based Basel III international regulatory framework for banks, including its unexpected application to the insurance sector; in particular, the strengthening of each of its three pillars encompassing quantitative requirements (regulatory and economic solvency), qualitative requirements (risk management and supervisory oversight, including 'stress tests'), as well as market discipline (disclosure

---

38. See < http://ec.europa.eu/internal_market/securities/docs/lamfalussy/wisemen/final-report-wise-men_en.pdf >, accessed on 15 July 2013.
39. See < http://ec.europa.eu/internal_market/finances/docs/de_larosiere_report_en.pdf >, accessed on 15 July 2013.
40. Parliament had rejected a proposed Institutional Agreement on a common operating framework for EU agencies (COM(2005) 59 final) creating a factual moratorium on their establishment by demanding that the Commission undertake further review of the operations of such bodies already operating at EU level; see 'European Agencies – the Way Forward', COM(2008) 159 final.
41. P.O. Mülbert & A. Wilhelm, 'Reforms of EU Banking and Securities Regulation after the Financial Crisis', *Banking & Finance Law Review* 26 (2011): 187.
42. See, Mülbert & Wilhelm, *supra* n. 41.

and transparency). The regulatory initiatives have thus demanded a significant widening and deepening, both of EU legislation (Capital Requirement and Solvency Directives[43]), and vitally, of supranational standard-setting and supervisory oversight.[44]

Charged with overseeing this significantly enhanced regulatory framework, are the ESAs, which are also amongst the most powerful autonomous institutions ever established at EU level by virtue of their dual character as rule-making and supervisory authorities. Broadly similar to one another, the agencies are charged with 'improving the functioning of the internal market', 'ensuring the integrity, efficiency, and orderly functioning' of markets, combating 'regulatory arbitrage', 'consumer protection' and strengthening of 'international supervisory coordination' (Article 1 founding Regulations). They are also afforded one major domain of rule-making powers,[45] the power to make BTS. These standards comprise Technical Regulatory Standards for harmonization of the provisions of EU regulation and implementing Technical Standards to be applied at national level. Formally exercised by the Commission under competences delegated to the Commission by Parliament and Council under Articles 290 and 291 TFEU, BTS are nonetheless subject to a 'regulatory with scrutiny procedure',[46] which determines that, if opposed to the BTS proposed by an ESA, the Commission has the power only to delay its full adoption as a regulation or decision, subject to Parliamentary and Council scrutiny.[47]

The supervisory functions of the agencies are wide-ranging, relating primarily to the cooperative establishment of joint (risk-based) methodologies for national supervisory authorities through peer review and the issuing of recommendations and guidelines (Article 16 founding Regulations). Nevertheless, 'soft' supervision of national supervisory authorities crucially hardens in particular situations, including 'breach of Union Law', when the relevant agency can make recommendations to national supervisors and private actors and pursue (Commission) enforcement proceedings; 'emergency situations', or threats to systemic coherence where the relevant agency acts under the guidance of the ECB within the ESRB, addressing decisions to competent national authorities and, where necessary, individual financial institutions; and 'consumer protection', or action in the case of threats posed to the consumer by financial innovation, where the relevant agency may temporarily prohibit detrimental

---

43. Capital Requirements Directive (CRD III), 2010/76/EU (OJ L329/3 of 12 October 2010) for Banks, and the Solvency Directive for Insurers (Solvency II), 2009/138/EC (OJ L335/1 of 17 December 2009).
44. In addition, the EU has introduced important measures in securities markets. See, the Securities Regulation on Credit Rating Agencies (Regulation (EC) No. 1060/2009), the Directive on Alternative Investment Funds (Directive 2011/61/EU, OJ L174/1, of 1 July 2011), as well as proposed regulation on over-the-counter derivatives and short-selling: COM(2010) 484/5 and COM(2011) 482.
45. Art. 10 and Art. 15 founding Regulations. Similarly, the ESAs may contribute to the making of rules within the relevant 'College of Supervisors'. Colleges of Supervisors exist at supranational and international level and are responsible for global standard-setting.
46. Reproducing the traditional procedures of the Comitology Decision (1999/468/EC), laying down the procedures for decision-making within Comitology.
47. As a result, ESAs may be argued to exercise a 'hard power', backed by law, rather than a 'soft power', dependent upon their abilities to influence and convince the commission.

activities or products by means of powers conferred within the general regulatory framework of the EFSF, or under Article 18 emergency powers (Articles 17, 18, and 9 founding Regulations).

[A] Autonomy and Efficiency

With regard to the vital question of whether the ESFS is both a legitimate and effective response to crisis, primary doubts arise by virtue of potential for inefficiency and political interference within the ESAs. If the purpose of the ESFS is to promote the permissive consensus underlying expert-led market regulation, the partially autonomous status of ESAs could prove to be the worst of all possible worlds.[48] To the degree that the *Meroni* doctrine still applies, determining that Chairs of each agency – enjoined in the exercise of their powers 'neither [to] seek or [to] take instruction from the Union institutions' (Article 49 founding Regulations) – may find themselves in disruptive conflict with the Commission who is held accountable for ESA operations. Certainly, Commission-agency conflict is not new and is one which has largely been negotiated without fundamental upheaval within EU institutional relations. Nonetheless, additional strain arises as the sphere of delegated powers is also subject to Article 290 TFEU transmission strictures, encompassing both a permanent threat of recall of powers by Parliament and Council, and a 'sunset clause', in any case limiting delegation of the competence (exercised by ESAs) to the Commission to issue BTS for a period of four years (Article 11 founding Regulations). Although sunset clauses have proved to be a powerful tool within the US, ensuring that independent agencies are narrowly focused upon their mandates, their impact may prove to be counter-productive within this unusual constellation, whereby semi-autonomous institutions exercise the mandated competences of the Commission, which is, at the same time, which made vulnerable to Council or Parliament censure. Further, where BTS are issued by agencies under the regulatory with scrutiny procedure, potential for inter-institutional conflict heightens: both placing regulatory efficiency in doubt as renewed political influence may give rise to interventionism, and casting the Commission as perpetually rancorous looser in an institutional game of competence accrual.

Efficiency concerns have also been raised about the expansion of ESA activities to supervision and implementation at national level. In part, concern echoes objections to the general widening in the supranational regulatory competence, which it is argued has seen 'stealthy' neo-functionalist efforts to effect political integration by means of intensified EU market regulation, frustrate efficiency-oriented regulatory programmes at both national and European level.[49] Nevertheless, prevalence of regulatory arbitrage

---

48. N. Moloney, 'The European Securities and Markets Authority and Institutional Design for the EU Financial Market – A Tale of Two Competences: Part 1: Rule-making', *European Business Organization Law Review* 12, no. 1 (2011a): 41–86, as well as N. Moloney, 'The European Securities and Markets Authority and Institutional Design for the EU Financial Market – A Tale of Two Competences: Part 2: Rules in Action', *European Business Organization Law Review* 12, no. 2 (2011b): 177–225.
49. G. Majone, *Dilemmas of European Integration: The Ambiguities & Pitfalls of Integration by Stealth* (Oxford: Oxford University Press, 2005).

and contagion within the less intrusive Lamfalussy system weighed in favour of a hardening of the supranational supervisory competence,[50] and now gives rise to worries about potential for NSA- ESA conflict within hierarchical EU financial supervision.[51] Possible discord arises by virtue of the fact that regulatory standard-setting cannot easily be divorced from supervisory implementation. Instead, the relationship between standards and their on-going application is a necessarily complex one, not simply because understandings about regulatory aims may differ at each supervisory level, but rather because their successful achievement is necessarily context dependent.[52] Several factors militate in favour of local flexibility, or 'heterarchy', in implementation of BTS. First, ESAs are relatively inexperienced and are currently understaffed. Second, regulatory goals will also necessarily require adaptation in view of varied national institutional supervisory structures. Above all, however, complex Basel III regulatory methodologies not only require an intense degree of local knowledge in order to overcome informational asymmetries, but also demand regulatory-implementing flexibility to allow for experimentation with regard to rapid financial innovation, as well as for immediate response to systemic shock. Equally, experimentalist localism may act as a 'safety-valve' within the system, easing contagion potential through a supervisory plurality that guards against the danger that undue centralization will itself facilitate systemic shock.[53]

[B]   Accountability and Transparency

An interesting peculiarity of ESA structure, which may mediate inefficiency effects, is the self-contained nature of expertise assembled within the authorities. Possibly as a consequence of heightened influence afforded to the Parliament and Council, the desire for political voice within the agencies is dampened: ESA establishment has not experienced the unseemly scramble for parliamentary representation within the agency more generally witnessed within the Union.[54] Instead, expertise headlines the agency in the character of the Board of Supervisors, which is made up of the heads of each NSA, as well as non-voting representatives from the Commission and ESRB (Article 40 founding Regulations), and is subject to a concept of 'technocratic excellence'. The Chairperson of the insurance ESA, for example, is to be appointed 'on the basis of merit, skills, knowledge of financial institutions and markets and of experience relevant to financial supervision and regulation' (Article 48(2) EIOPA Regulation). National interest is also purged with regard to the establishment of duties of ESA independence (Article 42 founding Regulations). Political arbitrage is combated by

---

50. P. Snowden & S. Lovegrove, 'The New European Supervisory Structure', *Compliance Officer Bulletin* 83 (2011): 1.
51. J. Black, 'Restructuring Global and EU Financial Regulation: Capacities, Coordination and Learning', LSE Law, Society and Economy Working Papers 18/2010, London School of Economics and Political Science.
52. See, Moloney (2011b), *supra* n. 48.
53. See, Black, *supra* n. 51 and Moloney (2011b), *supra* n. 48.
54. For details of the efforts of the EP to gain parliamentary representation within the management board of the European Food Standards Agency, see Vos, *supra* n. 22.

simple majority voting in both Supervisory and Management Boards: The sole decisional criteria are technocratic in nature, shorn of political interest and thus – under theories of expert deliberation – facilitative of the objectivity and epistemic cooperation that might ensure ESFS efficiency.

Given the technocratic coherence of the ESAs, the primary legitimating mechanism for their operation is the establishment of an effective scheme of plural accountability, which ensures that each agency is both competent, and acts only within its technical mandate. In this case, all the common control mechanisms apply: ex ante control of multi-annual work programmes and budgets by multiple EU institutions, including the Court of Auditors (Article 62 founding Regulations); on-going control of agency activities by means of parliamentary committee hearings, as well as inter-agency oversight within the joint committee of the ESA (Article 54 founding Regulations); and, ex post multi-institutional control both of budgets and annual reports. In addition, agency decisions addressed to individual actors may be reviewed by an independent Board of Appeal and by the CJEU (Article 61 founding Regulations). Accordingly, and despite doubts about the budgetary adequacy of the agencies,[55] it appears fair to state that, in structure at least, 'no one controls the ESAs, yet the ESAs are under control'.

Final doubts about the accountability of agencies within the EU must nonetheless remain, particularly with regard to their transparency and public responsiveness. These worries have accompanied EU agency operation from its outset.[56] However, the concern that EU agencies are unable to generate their own public communities of review is necessarily heightened in the case of ESAs. In contrast to the US, EU institutional literature is strangely devoid of the theme of 'agency capture'.[57] Instead – in line with efficiency-based consensus – industry actors are regarded as 'stakeholders' within the regulatory process, representatives of autonomous market process whose views must be taken seriously in the establishment of sensitive oversight schemes. The same philosophy has been applied to ESAs who are mandated to establish 'stakeholder' groups (Article 37 founding Regulations) – comprising market actors, as well as consumers and academics – and to consult them prior to issuing BTSs. However, within the financial services sector, it was exactly this close relationship between regulator and regulated that contributed to financial collapse. Above all, the joint application of risk-based models of economic solvency fostered particularly intense relations between regulators and regulated within which the fatal complacency arose that tolerated and even welcomed unsustainable business models as wealth-creating vehicles of innovation, which were also of benefit to (disadvantaged) consumers. Agency capture potential was instead replaced with the far more subtle, but no less catastrophic danger posed by creation of a dominant 'rationality', a shared mode of thinking – or 'cognitive failure' – which could not recognize, let alone tolerate dissent. Accordingly, in establishing its own epistemic community of review, the ESFS as a

---

55. Moloney (2011b), *supra* n. 48.
56. See, Everson, *supra* n. 29.
57. Exemplary, see, M. Shapiro, *Who Guards the Guardians? Judicial Control of Administration* (Athens: University of Georgia Press, 1988).

whole is surely charged with identifying voices, not of partnership, but of dissent – 'mavericks'– and of identifying challenges to its own philosophies and methodologies.[58] In this regard, a vital question remains: Where might these malcontents come from?

Within the US, a vital element of legitimate agency operation is the broader public that attaches to particular and identifiable institutions, such as the Environmental Protection Agency. In three decades of operation, and despite the use of modern transparency methods (websites), no such agency public has arisen within the EU. In part, the problem is one of a lack of a European press; the absence of a European public sphere of communication and a tendency to 'renationalise' European decision-making within a fragmented nationally-focused media. The problem is also institutional: No general public right to challenge the actions of European Agencies has been established. The reformulated Article 263 TFEU considerably widens the parties who might request CJEU review of ESA implementing acts. Equally, efforts are now underway to establish a European Procedures Act.[59] Nonetheless, the publicity and 'post-legislative' control generated by class action claims is still absent from the EU system. The problem, however, is also specific to financial services. Confidentiality matters: In the case of emergency action to combat systemic risk, in particular, there are powerful reasons that weigh against wide-scale provision of public information.

§3.04   A COMPLEX EUROPEAN EXECUTIVE WITH A TROUBLED FUTURE?

Although established prior to the conclusion of the Common Approach on European agencies, the agencies now operating within the ESFS are a good exemplar for the difficulties that will continue to plague the vehicle of agency governance at EU level. Certainly, post-financial crisis, a very good case may be made for enhanced regulatory and supervisory powers at EU level, which are concentrated within the permanent and expert structures of agency operation. Yet, at the formal level of legal certainty and the notion of the rule of law, EFSF ESAs undoubtedly challenge our accepted vision of the balance of powers. The direct rule-making and supervisory competences of the agencies that are exercised at national level – especially to the degree that the European Commission has little control over them – may be construed as a breach of the *Meroni* doctrine. Equally however, to the degree that the *Meroni* doctrine can be dismissed as an unwarrantedly formal and outmoded expression of a constitutional principle of the balance of powers within the Union that seeks instead, and by contrast, to establish an 'ideal' dispensation of competences between the established and newer institutions of the Union and the Member States – one which also seeks to enhance the functionality and accountability of EU governance – grave problems remain.

---

58. See, Black, *supra* n. 51.
59. European Parliament resolution of 15 January 2013 with recommendations to the Commission on a Law of Administrative Procedure of the European Union (2012/2024(INI)) P7_TA-PROV(2013)0004.

Above all, where the Common Approach takes forward the theme established in Articles 290 and 291 of the TFEU – one of an increasing politicization of the model of executive governance extant within the EU – tensions just as surely arise between the 'accountability' and the 'efficiency' of the agency model within Europe. Certainly, sunset clauses and various political limitations on the exercise of delegated competence within the EU, as well as increased political representation within European executive structures (of the European Parliament), may reflect a necessary trend towards the establishment of a separation rather than balance of powers model within the EU. At this one level, then, the European Parliament may be argued to be a vital representative of the EU citizen within the European executive; a new form of accountability within the EU, which might compensate for weaknesses in current schemes of agency accountability. Nevertheless, the institutional tensions which such a construct may create between Commission, Parliament, as well as the Council, may further undermine the efficient operations of EU agencies, especially with regard to their increased powers exercised at national level.

Agencies undoubtedly have a future within the EU. Importantly, as EU competences increase with regard to post-crisis regulation, agencies will become evermore complex, active at national, as well as supranational and international level. Functionality may well demand that the formal constellation of the balance of powers as we currently recognize it, must be dispensed with in regard to agency operation. Nevertheless, as efforts continue to identify the ideal dispensation of powers within the emergent EU, urgent attention must be paid to the efficacy of this vital vehicle of EU governance.

PART III   European Agencies: New, Old
Roles and New Generations

CHAPTER 4

EU Agencies as a Solution to Pan-European Implementation Problems

Michael Kaeding & Esther Versluis

§4.01 INTRODUCTION

EU rules do not entail any guarantee for timely and correct implementation. In twenty years the European Single Market has not been completed; in fact non-compliance with EU law represents a serious and alarming threat to the EU project as a whole. A recent Commission scoreboard illustrates that seventy-four Single Market directives had not yet produced their full effects due to lack of national implementation measures in one or more Member States.[1] In addition, Member States grant themselves too often an extra six to nine months after the deadline has expired to adopt the implementing legislation.[2] Next to delayed transposition,[3] European directives are too often implemented incorrectly,[4] which leaves us with a highly fragmented European 'regulatory

1. European Commission, Internal Market Scoreboard (2010) < http://ec.europa.eu/internal_market/score/docs/score22_en.pdf > , p. 13.
2. M. Kaeding, 'Lost in Translation or Full Steam Ahead? The Transposition of EU Transport Directives across EU Member States', *European Union Politics* 9, no. 1 (2008): 115–144.
3. E. Mastenbroek, 'Surviving the Deadline. The Transposition of EU Directives in the Netherlands', *European Union Politics* 4, no. 4 (2003): 371–395; M. Kaeding, 'Determinants of Transposition Delay in the European Union', *Journal of Public Policy* 26, no. 3 (2006): 229–253; D. Toshkov, 'Embracing European Law: Compliance with EU Directives in Central and Eastern Europe', *European Union Politics* 9, no. 3 (2008): 379–342; B. Luetgert & T. Dannwolf, 'Mixing Methods: A Nested Analysis of EU Member State Transposition Patterns', *European Union Politics* 10, no. 3 (2009): 307–334; B. Steunenberg & M. Kaeding, 'When Time goes bye... The Transposition of Maritime Directives across EU Member States', *European Journal of Political Research* 48 (2009): 432–454; M. Haverland, B. Steunenberg & F. van Waarden, 'Sectors at Different Speeds: Analyzing Transposition Deficits in the European Union', *Journal of Common Market Studies* 48, no. 5 (2010): 1–27.
4. G. Falkner, O. Treib, M. Hartlapp & S. Leiber, *Complying with Europe. EU Harmonisation and Soft Law in the Member States* (Cambridge: Cambridge University Press, 2005); E. Versluis, 'Even

patchwork', deterring citizens and businesses from exercising their rights.[5] If we are to compete successfully in an increasingly aggressive global market, while many other economies continue to get stronger, all parts of the EU must make an effort.[6] What can EU agencies contribute to put the Single Market 'back on track'? How can EU agencies contribute to improving domestic implementation records?

The first reference to potential involvement of European agencies in stimulating domestic implementation was made in the European Commission's White Paper on European Governance of 2001. It was explicated here that '[t]he creation of further autonomous regulatory agencies in clearly defined areas will improve the way rules are applied and enforced across the Union'.[7] In other words, EU agencies are to contribute to the efficient and flexible implementation of EU legislation and policies, particularly in areas requiring decisions based on technical or scientific considerations, while at the same time encourage the harmonization of regulatory practices in the Member States. This is rooted in the belief that agencies – through (independent) expertise and apolitical, high quality evaluations – will produce better results.[8]

Where are we roughly a decade later? There is currently a lot of talk about EU agencies – not only because of the recently concluded reflection period that was initiated, or perhaps better 'revived', by the Commission in 2008 with its Communication 'European Agencies – The Way Forward'.[9] The latest Joint Statement, adopted in July 2012, states that agencies perform a wide range of important tasks, of which their contribution to the implementation of important Union policies is the first to be mentioned. When carefully analysing this Joint Statement, however, it becomes clear that no word is said about what agencies actually do to improve implementation, nor does it indicate any kind of vision on how EU agencies should play a role in this stage of the policy process that was initially considered a core task of the Member States.

Rules, Uneven Practices: Opening the 'Black Box' of EU Law in Action', *West European Politics* 30, no. 1 (2007): 50–67; T. Börzel, T. Hofmann, D. Panke & C. Sprungk, 'Obstinate and Inefficient: Why Member States Do Not Comply With European Law', *Comparative Political Studies* 43, no. 11 (2010): 1363–1390.

5. Implementation is defined as 'the process by which national law is modified in accordance with Community law' (P. Eijlander & W. Voermans, *Wetgevingsleers* (Den Haag: Boom Juridische uitgevers, 2000) 257. Member States involved in making EU legislation must implement Community legislation that induces policy change including the legal transposition, application and enforcement process (S. Prechal, *Directives in European Community Law. A study of directives and their Enforcement in National Courts* (Oxford: Oxford University Press, 1995) 5–6.

6. M. Kaeding, *Towards an Effective European Single Market* (Wiesbaden: Springer, 2012) argues that the answer is not to give up on rules, but rather to develop and implement good quality rules. Presenting both timely and relevant forms of European policy instruments in the field of financial services, public administration, transport, working conditions and social protection, he shows which kind of policy instruments work and under what circumstances help to overcome many of the impediments to using alterative policy instruments at the European level.

7. European Commission (2001): < http://eur-lex.europa.eu/LexUriServ/site/en/com/2001/com 2001_0428en01.pdf >, p. 24.

8. F. Gilardi, 'Policy Credibility and Delegation to Independent Regulatory Agencies: A Comparative Empirical Analysis', *Journal of European Public Policy* 9, no. 6 (2002): 873–893; G. Majone, 'Delegation of Regulatory Powers in a Mixed Polity', *European Law Journal* 8, no. 3 (2002): 262–275.

9. European Commission (2008): < http://eur-lex.europa.eu/LexUriServ/LexUriServ.do?uri=COM: 2008:0135:FIN:EN:PDF >, p. 135.

Also, most of the academic debate concerns questions of accountability,[10] autonomy,[11] and legitimacy[12] – next to current heated institutional battles surrounding financial errors, ethics tests, green facades, and Caribbean trips.

All in all, a public and scholarly debate surrounding the added value of EU agencies, when it comes to domestic implementation of EU rules, is still in its infancy.[13] This leads us to the overarching question to be addressed in this chapter: Is the creation of EU-level agencies, centralizing (or at least coordinating) certain implementation tasks, a solution to deal with the pan-European implementation problem?

In this chapter we first provide further insight into what EU agencies actually offer to improve implementation of European legislation at the Member State level. Section §4.02 provides an overview of the nine EU agencies that currently have specific implementation tasks, and outlines what they entail. Hereafter, we turn to the academic literature. After outlining the theoretical expectations, why agencies are expected to provide a cure for domestic implementation problems, we turn to available empirical insights highlighting the main lessons to be learned from the field's first case studies. The concluding section will reflect further on these lessons to draw from EU agencies' involvement in domestic implementation of EU rules.

§4.02   IMPLEMENTATION TASKS OF EU AGENCIES

Today there are more than forty agencies. In addition, some EU agencies' mandates have been – or are in the process of being – considerably widened. In total, these entities employ almost 8,000 members of (most temporary) staff and their combined annual EU administrative budget (or subsidy) is around EUR 1 billion (excluding the Joint Undertaking for ITER, Fusion for Energy).

Various scholars have categorized EU agencies in different ways. Flinders[14] distinguished two categories of executive and regulatory agencies, Geradin and Petit[15]

---

10. M. Bovens 'Analysing and Assessing Accountability. A Conceptual Framework', *European Law Journal* 13 (2007): 447–468; M. Busuioc, 'Accountability, Control and Independence. The Case of European Agencies', *European Law Journal* 15 (2009): 599–615; M. Busuioc, *The Accountability of European Agencies: Legal Provisions and Ongoing Practices* (Delft: Eburon, 2010).
11. M. Groenleer, *The Autonomy of European Union Agencies. A Comparative Study of Institutional Development* (Delft: Eburon, 2009).
12. M. Shapiro, 'The Problems of Independent Agencies in the United States and the European Union', *Journal of European Public Policy* 4, no. 2 (1997): 276–291; C. Lord, 'The European Parliament and the Legitimation of Agencification', *Journal of European Public Policy* 18, no. 6 (2011): 909–925.
13. M. Groenleer, M. Kaeding and E. Versluis, 'Regulatory Governance through Agencies of the European Union? The Role of the European Agencies for Maritime and Aviation Safety in the Implementation of European Transport Legislation', *Journal of European Public Policy* 17, no. 8 (2010): 1212–1230; C. Gulbrandsen, 'EU and the Implementation of International Law: A Case of 'Sea-level Bureaucrats'', *Journal of European Public Policy* 18, no. 7 (2011): 1034–1051; E. Versluis and E. Tarr, 'Improving Compliance with European Union Law via Agencies: The Case of the European Railway Agency', *Journal of Common Market Studies* (forthcoming).
14. M. Flinders, 'Distributed Public Governance in the European Union', *Journal of European Public Policy* 11, no. 3 (2004), 520–544.
15. D. Geradin & N. Petit, 'The Development of Agencies at EU and National Levels: Conceptual Analysis and Proposals for Reform', *Jean Monnet Working Paper*, 01/04, 2004.

identified a third category of decision-making agencies and Vos[16] referred to four distinct types with information, management and two categories of regulatory agencies. The Commission now speaks of decentralized agencies, Euratom agencies and executive agencies. What has been less prominent in such classifications is the 'implementation' role that EU agencies have started to take up more and more. When we analyse agency competences, we see that nine EU agencies with (semi-)regulatory functions are invested with a variety of tasks related to ensuring that rules are implemented and enforced effectively and uniformly (see Table 4.1). While in principle all agencies can be expected to contribute to implementation in general terms – for example, reports issued by the Fundamental Rights Agency are expected to have some influence on domestic-level implementation across Member States – here we only resort to those agencies with explicit implementation tasks. This group consists of: ACER (Agency for the Cooperation of Energy Regulators), EASA (European Aviation Safety Agency), EBA (European Banking Authority), ECHA (European Chemicals Agency), EFCA (European Fisheries Control Agency), EIOPA (European Insurance and Occupational Pensions Authority), EMSA (European Maritime Safety Agency), ERA (European Railway Agency) and ESMA (European Securities and Markets Authority).

Table 4.1   Specific Implementation Tasks of EU Regulatory Agencies at the Member State Level

Name of EU Agency	Creation Budget Staff*	Specific Implementation Tasks at the Member State Level
ACER (Agency for the Cooperation of Energy Regulators) Ljubljana, Slovenia	2009 5,000 40	ACER's purpose is to assist the national regulatory authorities in exercising their regulatory work at community level and, where necessary, coordinate their action. This includes monitoring the implementation of relevant Union legislation and policies as well as the functioning of the internal market for energy.
EASA (European Aviation Safety Agency) Cologne, Germany	2002 34,399 574	EASA's objective is to establish and maintain a high uniform level of civil aviation safety in Europe. To this end, the agency is tasked with developing certification specifications and guidance material for the application and the

16. E. Vos, 'Agencies and the European Union', in *Agencies in European and Comparative Perspective*, eds. L. Verhey & T. Zwart (Antwerp: Intersentia, 2003), 113–148.

Name of EU Agency	Creation Budget Staff*	Specific Implementation Tasks at the Member State Level
		implementation of Regulation (EC) 216/2008. In addition, the agency monitors the application of EU legislation in the field of civil aviation safety by carrying out standardization inspections of the competent authorities in the Member States.
EBA (European Banking Authority) London, UK	2010 5,073 46	EBA's aim is to ensure that regulations concerning the financial sector are implemented properly to preserve financial stability, to ensure confidence in the financial system and to protect consumers of financial services. To these ends, EBA's tasks are *inter alia* to ensure consistency in the application of relevant EU law which includes mediating and settling disagreements between national authorities and peer review analyses of the competent authorities.
ECHA (European Chemicals Agency) Helsinki, Finland	2006 DG 503	ECHA's objective is to ensure consistent implementation of the REACH Regulation (registration, evaluation, authorization, and restriction of chemical substances) and CLP Regulation (classification, labelling and packaging of chemical substances). Its so-called enforcement forum coordinates a network of national enforcement authorities, promotes best practice and coordinates harmonized enforcement projects and joint inspections.
EFCA (European Fisheries Control-Agency) Vigo, Spain	2005 12,849 53	EFCA's main task is to ensure the Member States' uniform compliance with the rules of the Common Fisheries Policy. In order to achieve this aim, the Agency coordinates Member States' activities of control and inspection in the fisheries sector

Name of EU Agency	Creation Budget Staff*	Specific Implementation Tasks at the Member State Level
EIOPA (European Insurance and Occupational Pensions Authority) Frankfurt, Germany	2010 4,267 46	EIOPA's mission is to promote a sound regulatory framework and consistent supervisory practices in the financial sector in order to protect the rights of policyholders, pension scheme members and beneficiaries and contribute to the public confidence in the European Union's insurance and occupational pensions sectors. To these ends, EIOPA's tasks are *inter alia* to ensure consistency in the application of relevant EU law which includes mediating and settling disagreements between national authorities and peer review analyses of the competent authorities.
EMSA (European Maritime Safety Agency) Lisbon, Portugal	2002 54,936 208	EMSA's objective is to ensure a high level of maritime safety and security and prevent pollution caused by ships. To this end, EMSA assists the Commission in monitoring the implementation of relevant EU legislation relating, for example, to classification of societies, certification of marine equipment, the training of seafarers and ship security.
ERA (European Railway Agency) Valenciennes, France	2004 25,304 144	ERA's objective is to contribute, on technical matters, to the implementation of Union legislation aimed at improving the competitive position of the railway systems by enhancing interoperability and at developing a common approach to safety on the European railway system. Thereby, the agency shall contribute to the creation of a European railway area without frontiers and guarantee a high level of safety.
ESMA (European Securities and Markets Authority) Paris, France	2010 6,785 58	ESMA's aim is to ensure that regulations concerning the financial sector are implemented properly to preserve financial stability, to ensure confidence in the financial system and to protect consumers of financial services.

* As authorized under the 2011 union budget.

As clearly expressed in Articles 4 and 291(1) TFEU, it is the Member States which have to fulfil European commitments and 'to adopt all measures of national law necessary to implement legally binding Union acts'. While traditionally a clearly defined task of the Member States, we gradually see increasing involvement of EU agencies in the implementation of European legislation. Looking at the nine 'enforcement'- agencies, it becomes clear that the transport sector sets the scene: EASA and EMSA (both set up in 2002) were the first agencies to obtain implementation powers. Particularly EMSA derives its existence from devastating implementation failures. In response to the 1999 oil tanker Erika accident, which sank off the coast of France causing one of the greatest environmental disasters in the world, EMSA was created with the explicit expectation that the new body would lead to better implementation of EU maritime safety rules. This is not to say that these agencies formed the first attempt at organizing European involvement in domestic implementation. Already in the late 1980s, early 1990s, the Commission and particularly the European Parliament pushed for a rather powerful EEA with extensive decision-making and enforcement powers, but notorious 'environmental laggards' blocked this idea in the Council of Ministers.[17]

Since the early 2000s, EASA and EMSA have rapidly been followed by seven other agencies, particularly related to DG MOVE and DG MARKT. In fact, the overall creation of EU agencies has been a rather recent trend. While the first agencies were all established under the consultation procedure to allow maximum intergovernmental control, in parallel, a strict interpretation of the *Meroni* judgment by the Commission led to hardly any delegation of powers to (semi-)independent agencies as this would entail a loss of powers.[18] In the area of competition, for example, the Commission has actively resisted the establishment of a European Cartel Office.[19] Dehousse even goes as far as stating that the Commission only accepts the creation of an agency 'if convinced that an extension of its own powers is not likely to be approved by the Council.'[20] It thus appears that agencies are only 'allowed' when there is agreement between both Member States and the Commission.[21] Often it seems to require a crisis of some sort – see the transport agencies and the far-reaching powers of the agencies lately established in the financial sector – or a broad willingness across Member States for harmonization in particular areas (chemicals), as well as a willingness of the Commission to 'hand over' responsibilities and to be 'able to deliver' (food safety).

Not all nine agencies have the same set of enforcement competences – some agencies have more direct and stronger implementation tasks than others. Overall, the following direct and indirect implementation tasks can be identified.

---

17. R.D. Kelemen, 'The Politics of 'Eurocratic' Structure and the New European Agencies', *West European Politics* 25, no. 4 (2002): 93–118, at 101.
18. Vos, *supra* n. 16; X.A. Yataganas, 'Delegation of Regulatory Authority in the European Union. The Relevance of the American Model of Independent Agencies', *Jean Monnet Working Paper*, 3/01, 2001.
19. G. Majone, 'The New European Agencies: Regulation by Information', *Journal of European Public Policy* 4, no. 2 (1997): 252–275, at 263.
20. R. Dehousse, 'Delegation of Powers in the European Union: The Need for a Multi-Principals Model', *West European Politics* 31, no. 4 (2008): 789–805, at 796.
21. The co-decision procedure (now ordinary legislative procedure) has been applied since the creation of the European Food Safety Authority in 2002. The European Parliament has therefore also become a partner which has to be taken into the equation.

Table 4.2   EU Agency Activities Affecting Domestic Implementation

Category	Specific Activity	Empowered Agency
Activities to impact decision making	(Drafting) decisions	All agencies
	Certification	EASA
Capacity-building activities	Training	EASA, EFCA, EMSA
	Providing technical assistance	EMSA
	Providing equipment	EFCA
Activities to explain the rules on paper	Guidelines, recommendations, opinions, reports	All agencies
Activities to disseminate information in practice	Consultation, workshops, conferences, network meetings	All agencies
Activities to enforce action in Member States indirectly	Issuing implementation standards	EASA, EBA, ECHA, EFCA, EIOPA, ESMA
	Monitoring	All agencies
	Peer reviewing	EBA, ERA (pilot)
	Cross-auditing	ERA (pilot)
	State or on-site visits	EASA, EMSA, ERA, ESMA
	Investigations	ACER, EASA, EMSA
	Inspections	EASA, EFCA, EMSA, ESMA
	Issuing warnings or inquiries	EIOPA, ESMA
Activities to enforce action in Member States directly	Bindingly settling disputes between Member States	ESMA
	Prohibiting activities or products	EIOPA, ESMA
	Issuing sanctions	EASA

Comparing this set of 'enforcement'-agencies, we see striking similarities but also crucial differences. Overall, all agencies somehow have an impact on decision making. While some have more impact than others, all agencies issue draft non-legislative proposals for the Commission, to be decided upon via delegated or implementing acts.[22] Only EASA can bindingly issue certificates for aircrafts, engines, and parts. Only a handful of agencies also have the possibility to impact Member States' implementation capacity directly. Some agencies, the ones with inspection power, provide training to national inspectors, but only the fisheries agency has the budget available to provide equipment when needed. All agencies have tools to explain the rules on paper, or to disseminate information in practice.

Differences come with agencies taking a direct or indirect coercive stand at Member State level. Agencies have an indirect coercive force when performing activities that provide the Commission with the relevant and necessary input to start

---

22. A. Hardacre & M. Kaeding, *Delegated and Implementing Acts – The New Comitology* (Maastricht: EIPA, 2011).

infringement procedures. Direct coercive force refers to those agencies which single-handedly impact Member States' implementation records, without necessarily interference of the Commission.

All nine 'enforcement'-agencies monitor Member State activities and report to the Commission respectively. This provides the Commission with potential ammunition to start infringement procedures. The transport and fisheries agencies can conduct inspections at the Member State level ('inspecting the national inspectors'), and two of the financial sector agencies can issue warnings or inquiries. This last category really provides a grey zone between indirect and direct coercive force, as these activities could be seen as the first step of the infringement procedure. There is, however, no direct coercive power as the agencies are, in the end, dependent on the Commission for officially starting the procedure. Only three of the nine agencies have the possibility to enforce action at the Member State level directly. Two of the most recently established financial sector agencies have the possibility to bindingly settle disputes between Member States and/or to actually prohibit certain activities or products. The aviation safety agency is the only agency with the competence to issue fines directly for detected infringements.

§4.03 EU AGENCIES AS A CURE FOR EU IMPLEMENTATION PROBLEMS?

[A] From Theoretical Expectations ...

The expectation that agencies can stimulate domestic implementation is not new. Haas argued already in 1992 that transnational networks of knowledge-based professionals, or epistemic communities, can play a crucial role in closing the 'implementation gap' in a more informal and decentralized way. In particular, Majone[23] addressed the importance of agencies in facilitating 'the development of behavioural standards and working practices that create shared expectations'. Dehouses,[24] in the same year argued that agencies could ensure that 'the actors in charge of implementation of Community policies behave in a similar manner'. He particularly expected agencies to have an impact via the pan-European networks by which they can promote 'horizontal cross-fertilization among national administrations'.[25] Kelemen[26] later reiterated this point by stressing that agencies particularly play a crucial role in providing a platform to diffuse regulatory practices via the coordination of networks of national authorities. Overall, this body of literature thus particularly stresses the potential added value of agencies in stimulating the creation of, and allowing the diffusion of, common behavioural standards or regulatory practices via their ability to create and coordinate European networks.

---

23. Majone, *supra* n. 19, at 272.
24. R. Dehousse, 'Regulation by Networks in the European Community: The Role of European Agencies', *Journal of European Public Policy* 2, no. 2 (1997): 246–261, at 254.
25. Dehousse, *supra* n. 24, at 255.
26. R.D. Kelemen, 'The Politics of 'Eurocratic' Structure and the New European Agencies', *West European Politics* 25, no. 4 (2002): 93–118.

[B]   ... To the Latest Empirical Insights

Most empirical insights derived from case studies on EU agencies and their role in domestic implementation[27] support most theoretical expectations. A strong focus on agencies' potential added value in bringing together national experts in transnational networks and their ability to stimulate learning is apparent. Table 4.2 displays that agencies have an extensive repertoire of instruments aimed at explaining rules or norms and/or disseminating information to their disposal.

First and foremost, their added value lies in stimulating learning. By stimulating learning agencies add to the harmonization and convergence of national practices, thus contributing to a uniform implementation of EU legislation. The organization of inspections by EMSA and EASA, where a team of specialists from various Member States inspects the national authority of one Member State, makes it possible to do just that. In addition, they represent learning platforms for European and national stakeholders. By organizing workshops and training through networks of national authorities, EMSA and EASA have started to contribute to the diffusion of implementation practices across Europe via the diffusion of knowledge, values, and ideas. They can 'add most value when they refrain from using a hierarchical and centralized approach, and when they spur informal learning among national regulatory authorities'.[28] And EU agencies stimulate learning outside the EU. Gulbranden's study[29] shows how Norwegian inspectors indicate a positive impact of participation in EMSA's training on their own inspection behaviour.

Furthermore, informality plays a strong role in triggering cross-fertilization. In the context of ERA an agency official stated that:

> We don't start with any agenda and that's quite powerful. There is no law behind it. By being the place where all actors meet we have acted as a catalyst for all the actors to work together and to exercise their own responsibilities.[30]

This informality is also underlined by the findings of Gulbrandsen in analysing the impact of training conducted by EMSA on Norwegian inspectors, where a respondent

---

27. For example, Groenleer et al. *supra* n. 13; M. Egeberg & J. Trondal, 'EU Level Agencies: New Executive Centre Formation or Vehicles for National Control?', *Journal of European Public Policy* 18, no. 6 (2011): 868–887; Gulbrandsen, *supra* n. 13; M. Maggetti & F. Gilardi, 'The Policy-making Structure of European Regulatory Networks and the Domestic Adoption of Standards', *Journal of European Public Policy* 18, no. 6 (2011): 830–847; E. Versluis, 'Catalysts of Compliance? The Role of European Union Agencies in the Implementation of EU Legislation in Poland and Bulgaria', in *The Agency Phenomenon in the European Union. Emergence, Institutionalisation and every Decision-making*, eds. M. Busuioc, M. Groenleer & J. Trondal (Manchester: Manchester University Press, 2012), 172–190; M. Egeberg, M. Martens & J. Trondal, 'Building Executive Power at the European Level: On the Role of European Union Agencies', in *The Agency Phenomenon in the European Union. Emergence, Institutionalisation and every Decision-making*, eds. M. Busuioc, M. Groenleer & J. Trondal (Manchester: Manchester University Press, 2012), 19–41; Versluis &Tarr, *supra* n. 13.
28. Groenleer et al. *supra* n. 13, at 1226.
29. Gulbranden, *supra* n. 13.
30. Versluis & Tarr, *supra* n. 13.

indicated that 'what was useful were those things we inspectors from different countries discussed after the course, in the evenings. That was incredibly useful.'[31]

The impact of knowledge dissemination or learning is another important aspect, but sometimes overrated. Learning is no magic bullet. Those who do not want to learn will not be reached by dissemination of information. The ERA case shows that Member States most open to learning are the smaller and newer Member States with relatively little experience and expertise in a policy field.[32] This observation is in line with the findings of Maggetti and Gilardi[33] who argue that – in the context of the Committee of European Securities Regulators – newcomers to the European network have a stronger relationship. They also identified that countries with larger financial industries take a more central position in the network. A lack of learning – or more specifically a lack of using guidelines issued by EU agencies – is not always a matter of unwillingness. Sometimes countries might want to use guidelines but are simply unable to:

> If I tell an Italian judge, I remove these measures because ERA says so, they will not take this into account. There is a problem with the legal status of the advice. It's only an interpretation, it's not written in the law. ERA's guidelines should become binding, otherwise I cannot work with them.[34]

As regards direct capacity-building activities such as providing technical assistance or equipment, empirical evidence on how these activities are taken up and how they are perceived at the Member State level is almost non-existent – mainly due to the fact that these powers have only recently been granted to some EU agencies. We do know, however, that the Central and Eastern European Member States, in particular, would very much welcome it if EU agencies were to take up this capacity-building role more strongly.[35] Furthermore, EU agencies can play a more indirect facilitating role by providing ammunition for national agencies to use against their own national government. The EASA case illustrates this nicely:

> We have actually benefited from the recommendations of EASA on imposing a safeguard clause for Bulgaria. The problems as they stand are technical, not political. For example, on the grounds of EASA's reports, we have asked the government for more resources.[36]

One final observation seems to be appropriate here. Not all Member States appreciate the EU agencies in the same manner, and thus it is very likely that their responses – i.e., their domestic implementation behaviour – will not be influenced the same by EU agency activities. In the context of ERA and EASA, for example, powerful and resourceful Member States seem to oppose a strong agency with hierarchical means while less powerful and resourceful Member States wish for a strong agency.[37] The EU consists of twenty-eight different Member States, and EU agencies are not uniform

---

31. Gulbranden, *supra* n. 13, at 1045.
32. Versluis & Tarr, *supra* n. 13.
33. Maggetti & Gilardi, *supra* n. 27.
34. Versluis & Tarr, *supra* n. 13.
35. Versluis & Tarr, *supra* n. 13.
36. Versluis, *supra* n. 27; see also Versluis & Tarr, *supra* n. 13.
37. Versluis, *supra* n. 27 and Versluis & Tarr, *supra* n. 13.

actors acting the same under all circumstances. Nor are the Member States very similar in their responses to, or perception of, agency behaviour.[38] What will work in the Polish aviation sector, will not necessarily have the same success – or can even be counter-productive – in the British agricultural sector or in the Greek financial market sector.

To conclude there is evidence for an incremental evolution of agency involvement in domestic implementation. In line with Egeberg and Trondal,[39] empirical evidence shows that international administrations expand their tasks at their own initiative and thus EU agencies become more involved in domestic implementation than formally prescribed. Gradually, more and more implementation powers are being transferred to the agency level, which corresponds to the evolutionary character of the institutionalization and strengthening of agencies and networks, rather than comprehensive revolution typifying the ongoing transformations of the European regulatory space.[40] Evidently, this does not come automatically. Martens,[41] for example, offers an insightful analysis of the Commission's and Member States' reluctance in transferring far-reaching implementation tasks (i.e., inspection tasks) to the European Environment Agency.

§4.04   CONCLUDING DISCUSSION

What does the empirical reality about EU agency involvement in implementation tell us? Why should EU agencies be involved in tasks which represent the core of national competences? Why do we find, nevertheless, evidence for an incremental transferral of implementation power away from the national to the European level?

Once accepted as nodes in transnational networks of 'inspection' professionals, EU agencies can play an important role in closing the 'implementation gap' and thereby facilitate the functioning of the Single Market. Next to the Commission, the EU agencies' key interlocutors are primarily national agencies.[42] Consequently, agencies' networks with national regulatory authorities will prove to be crucial tools for ensuring the implementation of EU law. Networks represent 'an effort to harmonize the fragmented institutional landscape.'[43] But Member States will have to commit themselves in terms of number and quality of the staff assigned by them. They should assign sufficient and adequate staff in the framework of their cooperation with the agency. This is how national agencies will become 'networked'[44] when successfully implementing EU legislation.

---

38. Egeberg & Trondal, *supra* n. 27, at 882.
39. M. Egeberg & J. Trondal, 'EU Level Agencies: New Executive Centre Formation or Vehicles for National Control?', *Journal of European Public Policy* 18, no. 6 (2011): 868–887.
40. M. Thatcher & D. Coen, 'Reshaping European Regulatory Space: An Evolutionary Analysis', *West European Politics* 31, no. 4 (2008): 806–836.
41. M. Martens, 'Voice or Loyalty? The Evolution of the European Environment Agency (EEA)', *Journal of Common Market Studies* 48, no. 4 (2010): 881–901.
42. Egeberg & Trondal, *supra* n. 39, at 883.
43. D. Levi-Faur, 'Regulatory Networks and Regulatory Agencification: Towards a Single European Regulatory Space', *Journal of European Public Policy* 18, no. 6 (2011): 810–829, at 811.
44. Egeberg & Trondal, *supra* n. 27.

EFCA, for example, already relies on an information network consisting of the Commission and relevant authorities of the Member States in order to exchange relevant information available regarding joint control and inspection activities within Union and international waters. Next to the Commission, EASA also relies on the national aviation authorities exchanging any information available to them in the context of the application of the founding regulation and EASA's implementing rules. AGNA, the Advisors Group of National Authorities, for example, assists EASA in its rulemaking tasks, a tool which also exists for the representatives of the agency's stakeholders. ECHA relies on a Forum for Exchange of Information on Enforcement which is tasked with coordinating a network of Member States authorities responsible for the enforcement of the agency's founding regulation. ERA's networks of national safety authorities and national investigation bodies facilitate the cooperation between these national authorities and allow active exchanges of experience for the purpose of harmonizing national authorities' decision-making criteria across the Union. The meetings are convened on a regular basis with high participation of the Member States representatives. Both networks have proven to be helpful in identifying early stages possible problems with implementation of the EU legislation in the railway field.

However, domestic implementation problems differ per policy and Member State. Compliance problems occur following one or a combination of the following factors:[45] (a) non-compliance out of opposition or unwillingness; (b) out of unclear rules or a lack of expertise; and/or (c) due to administrative capacity problems.

When analysing the EU agency activities affecting domestic implementation (see Table 4.2), and comparing this with the first empirical insights (see section §4.03), we find that EU agencies seem to play a prominent role in combating compliance problems of the second category (unclear rules or lack of expertise). At the moment, EU agencies, first and foremost, seem to concentrate on disseminating information and explaining the rules. Under these circumstances, however, EU agency activities appear limited and narrowed down to only one aspect of non-compliance with a reduced impact on domestic implementation. Few agencies have the possibility to influence Member States' (administrative) capacity to comply directly, despite the fact that these problems often represent major compliance obstacles.

Does this observation lead us to the conclusion that EU agencies should categorically receive more competences to impact on domestic implementation directly? The example of ERA shows that not all actors necessarily see the added value of EU agencies being granted more enforcement powers. Following the current discussion whether or not ERA's tasks should be expanded, ERA staff is not entirely in favour of this either:

> The Member States are afraid of the Commission because the Commission can do nasty things to them and they all know they are not complying. Because we come from the sector and we meet the people all day every day at the working parties, thus people tell us things they don't tell the Commission.[46]

---

45. For example, O. Treib, 'Implementing and Complying with EU Governance Outputs', *Living Rev. Euro. Gov.* 3, no. 5. URL (cited on 2 December 2012): < http://www.livingreviews.org/lreg-2008-5 > .
46. Versluis & Tarr, *supra* n. 13.

In sum, ERA staff is afraid of losing the comfortable position they now have with all parties based on trust, and thus sharing relevant information with the agency. National authorities know that the agency can always refer cases to the Commission which is then able to start an infringement procedure. As a Polish respondent stated in relation to EASA:[47]

> In comparison to the JAA system,[48] EASA is far more efficient in ensuring implementation and in forcing states to live up to their commitments. The domestic aviation authorities are far more afraid of EASA than of JAA.

In sum, while the current dissemination and information tasks potentially do not solve all domestic implementation problems – in particular problems related to capacity or unwillingness – we have to be careful in concluding that more competences will provide the magic bullet. More competences might disturb the balance of power between the EU agency, their network of national agencies and the Commission. More empirical insight into how the new powerful agencies in the financial sector fare in stimulating domestic implementation is crucial in this respect.

---

47. Versluis, *supra* n. 27, at 182.
48. The system of Joint Aviation Authorities in use before the EU set up EASA.

CHAPTER 5

European Agencies on the Global Scene: EU and International Law Perspectives

*Andrea Ott, Ellen Vos & Florin Coman-Kund**

§5.01 INTRODUCTION

In the almost forty years of experience with European agencies,[1] it has become apparent that for a good operation and functioning of these agencies to fulfil their mandate, they need to interact with related third countries' authorities and international organizations. Interestingly, already the founding regulations of the first established agencies, the European Centre for the Development of Vocational Training (CEDEFOP) and the European Foundation for the Improvement of Living and Working Conditions (EUROFOUND), instructed the agencies to 'cooperate as closely as possible with specialized institutes, foundations and bodies in the Member States or at international level'.[2] When looking at the current global practice of agencies, we observe a variety of actions closely linked with the mandate and powers that agencies received by their founding regulations. Collaboration varies from a mere cooperation in training matters, the organization of common events such as workshops, conferences

---

* The authors would like to thank Bruno De Witte for his comments on an earlier version. The usual disclaimer applies.
1. The first Community agencies, now EU agencies, were the European Centre for the Development of Vocational Training (Cedefop) and the European Foundation for the Improvement of Living and Working Conditions (EUROFUND), both established in 1975.
2. Art. 3(2) of Regulation (EEC) 1365/75 of the Council of 26 May 1975 on the creation of a European Foundation for the improvement of living and working conditions [1975] OJ L139/1 (Eurofound's founding act). A similar provision is found in Art. 3(2) of Regulation (EEC) 337/75 of the Council of 10 February 1975 establishing a European Centre for the Development of Vocational Training [1975] OJ L39/1(Cedefop's founding act), that reads '2. In carrying out its tasks, the centre shall establish appropriate contacts, particularly with specialized bodies, whether public or private, national or international, with public authorities and educational institutions and with workers "and employers" organisations.'

and research and capacity building activities, to more substantial cooperation in the form of the development of common procedures, the exchange of (confidential) information and personal data (European Police Office, hereinafter EUROPOL), cooperation in joint operations (European Agency for the Management of Operational Cooperation at the External Borders of the Member States of the EU, referred to as Frontex), and mutual acceptance of the findings of the partner competent authority (for example, European Aviation Safety Agency, hereinafter EASA) in the context of certification of aviation products and organization approval. The European Centre for Drugs and Drug Addiction (EMCDDA) has, for example, signed a Memorandum of Understanding with the United Nations Office on Drugs and Crime (UNODC) and, on specific assignments, this agency works together with the Joint United Nations Programme on HIV/AIDS UNAIDS and the World Health Organization (WHO).[3] EASA has an impressive record of cooperation with air safety and civil aviation authorities around the globe.[4] Another example is the European Food Safety Authority (EFSA) which cooperates with food agencies from Japan and the US and is active within the *Codex Alimentarius* Commission.[5]

Hence we observe that together with the EU's ambitions to acquire a more significant and articulated status at the global level, European agencies present an increasingly prominent international dimension.[6] This international dimension of agencies is threefold.[7] First, agencies have themselves acquired a larger breath than being 'pure EU' bodies, as third countries may participate in agencies' internal structures. This form of external participation is created to allow EU candidate countries, the European Economic Area (EEA) and the European Neighbourhood Policy (ENP) countries, to familiarize themselves with the EU and its programmes.[8] Second, they increasingly give support to the EU institutions in global fora; an example of which is the support given by EFSA to the European Commission in the context of the *Codex Alimentarius* Commission.[9] Third, they increasingly cooperate with third

---

3. See *Ramboll, Eureval, and Matrix's Insights. Evaluation of the EU Decentralised Agencies Conclusions at System Level*, Final Report, Vol. III 'Agency level findings', December 2009. Evaluation for the European Commission ABAC Contracts No. 30-CE-0230814/00 Specific contract No. 003, at 111, available online at: < http://www.europarl.europa.eu/meetdocs/2009_2014/documents/libe/dv/evaluation_eu_agencies_vol_iii_/evaluation_eu_agencies_vol_iii_en.pdf > , p. 111. This will be referred hereafter as the 'Ramboll report.'
4. See website of EASA at < http://easa.europa.eu/rulemaking/international-cooperation-working-arrangements.php > , accessed on 1 February 2013.
5. See website of EFSA, < http://www.efsa.europa.eu/en/networks/international.htm > , accessed on 1 February 2013. In relation to the Codex Alimentarius, see M.D. Masson-Matthee, *The Codex Alimentarius Commission and Its Standards* (The Hague: T.M.C. Asser Press, 2007), 127–128.
6. See generally: A Ott, 'EU Regulatory Agencies in EU External Relations: Trapped in a Legal Minefield Between European and International Law', *European Foreign Affairs Review* 13, no. 4 (2008): 515.
7. F. Coman-Kund, 'Assessing the Role of EU Agencies in the Enlargement Process: The Case of the European Aviation Safety Agency', *Croatian Yearbook of European Law and Policy* 8 (2012): 338.
8. Commission Communication to the Council, Participation of candidate countries in Community programmes, agencies and committees, COM(99) 710 final. See further: Ott, *supra* n. 6, at 528–539; and Coman-Kund, *supra* n. 7, at 338.
9. See E. Vos, 'Responding to Catastrophe: Towards a New Architecture for EU Food Safety Regulation?', in *Experimentalist Governance in the EU,* eds. C.F. Sabel & J. Zeitlin (Oxford: Oxford University Press, 2010), 151–176. In relation to the European Medicines Agency (EMA),

states' authorities, international programmes and organizations. Here agencies at times conclude various forms of arrangements such as memoranda of understanding and working arrangements as independent actors. Most often, this global aspect has been explicitly recognized in the founding regulations of the agencies that mention the need for agencies to cooperate with third countries and international organizations (see Annex on the typology of EU agencies in view of their external relations powers below).

While the two first aspects of the international dimension of European agencies are certainly of great interest, they do not cause pressing legal problems. The third aspect, however, is more problematic. The issue of European agencies as global actors at the international plane therefore forms the focus of our analysis. Notably, this aspect has been largely neglected in the debate on European agencies both by the literature[10] and the EU institutions.[11] The global dimension of agencies was indeed not put on the agenda of the institutions in their attempt to rethink and reconceptualize agencies.[12] The recently adopted Common Approach on agencies however finally recognizes the importance of the agencies' international relations and calls for a clear strategy to be adopted to make sure that the agencies remain within their mandate and within the existing institutional framework.[13] Herewith the institutions acknowledge at last that the active involvement of agencies in the areas of the *acquis communautaire* beyond the EU's borders and their cooperation with third countries and/or international organizations may currently be problematic in relation to, for example, the legal nature of the acts that agencies adopt, both from an EU and international law perspective and the EU's institutional balance of powers post-Lisbon.

This Chapter will therefore attempt to clarify what it precisely is, in legal terms, that European agencies do on the global plane. To this end it will address two vital

---

see, for instance, E. Vos, 'Making Informal International Law Accountable: Lessons from the EU', in *Informal International Lawmaking*, eds. J. Pauwelyn, R.A. Wessel & J. Wouters (Oxford: Oxford University Press, 2012), 368, and M. Groenleer, 'Linking up Levels of Governance: Agencies of the European Union and their Interaction with International Organisations', in *The Influence of International Institutions on the European Union*, eds. O. Costa & K-E Joergensen (Basingstoke: Palgrave Macmillan, 2012), 135.

10. See however Ott, *supra* n. 6, at 515; and specifically on EASA and Frontex: Coman-Kund, *supra* n. 7, at 358 and M. Fink, 'Frontex Working Arrangements: Legitimacy and Human Rights Concerns Regarding "Technical Relationships"', *Merkourious* (2012): 20, < http://www.merko urios.org/index.php/mj/article/viewFile/URN%3ANBN%3ANL%3AUI%3A10-1-112855/54 >, accessed on 1 February 2013.

11. The Ramboll Report also describes some activities on international cooperation in Vol. III 'Agency level findings', *supra* n. 3.

12. See Commission (EC), 'European Agencies – The way forward' (Communication) COM(2008) 135 final. See, however, Commission (EC), 'Draft Interinstitutional Agreement on the operating framework for the European regulatory agencies' COM(2005) 59 final, which touches upon the participation of third countries in the EU agencies (at p. 20), as well as on the international activities of these bodies (at pp. 20–21). It should be noted, however, that the draft interinstitutional agreement proposed by the Commission was not supported by the Council and has been withdrawn consequently by the Commission via COM(2008) 135.

13. Common Approach annexed to the Joint Statement of the European Parliament, the Council of the EU and the European Commission on Decentralized Agencies of 19 July 2012, pct. 25 – available on the official website of the European Commission, < http://ec.europa.eu/ commission_2010-2014/sefcovic/headlines/news/2012/07/2012_07_17_joint_agreement_age ncies_en.htm >, accessed on 1 February 2013.

issues: the legal nature of the acts that agencies adopt in the global setting from both a European and international law perspective and the question as to whether agencies' global activities upset the EU's internal institutional balance of powers.[14] How should, for example, agreements and working arrangements, that some agencies are empowered to conclude, be defined both under EU and international law? Does the fact that these agencies are legally mandated to cooperate with third countries mean that the agreements concluded by agencies are legally binding for the whole EU? Adding to this problem is that the conclusion of agreements and working arrangements by the European Commission is already legally questionable.[15] This contribution aims to provide for general answers through an analysis of the precise mandate and powers as well as the practices of various agencies. This is not an easy task as the mandate, powers and/or instruments given to agencies vary enormously while, from an international law perspective, the question of international legal personality and treaty-making powers of agencies is ambiguous.[16]

This Chapter will aim to find a way through the great variety of external relations' activities of agencies. To this end it will give a typology of the agencies in view of their external relations powers (section §5.03). This typology will serve both to define the legal nature of acts agencies are empowered to adopt and/or have accordingly adopted in practice, and to examine whether the EU's institutional balance of powers has been upset. It will thus carefully analyse the powers conferred upon various agencies (section §5.04) and draw some general conclusions (section §5.05). To understand how the external actions of European agencies can be qualified and how their status in the global scene can be determined, it is nevertheless essential first to take a step back and determine how international agreements are defined and how treaty-making in the EU is organized (section §5.02).

§5.02   AGENCIES' ACTIONS IN LIGHT OF INTERNATIONAL AND EU LAW

[A]   Defining an International Agreement

According to the third rapporteur on the law of treaties for the UN International Law Commission Gerald G. Fitzmaurice:

---

14. Thus, it is beyond the scope of this contribution to give a comprehensive evaluation of the international activities of the EU agencies, as this would require an in-depth analysis of the differences and commonalities in the legal mandates and tasks of EU agencies, in the wording between the specific provisions, as well as the practice of agencies in adopting specific acts, working arrangements and/or agreements.
15. See already Case C-327/1991, *France v. Commission* [1994] ECR I-3641, Opinion of AG Tesauro delivered on 16 December 1993, the case note on this judgment by J. Kingston 'External Relations of the European Community. External Capacity versus Internal Competence', *International & Comparative Law Quarterly* 44 (1995), 659–670 and Ott, *supra* n. 6, at 523–525.
16. See G. Schusterschitz, 'European Agencies as Subjects of International Law', *International Organisations Law Review* (2004): 163–188; Ott, *supra* n. 6, at 526.

a treaty is an international agreement in a single formal instrument (whatever its name, title or designation) made between entities both or all of which are subjects of international law possessed of an international legal personality and treaty-making capacity, and intended to create rights and obligations, or to establish relationships, governed by international law.[17]

According to international treaty law practice, it is not decisive how the treaty is named[18] and whether the treaty is formally signed but whether the parties have the intention to create obligations under international law.[19] Furthermore it makes no difference whether the treaty is concluded on behalf of states or is concluded on behalf of governments, ministries or state agencies as these actions will bind the state.[20] The 1969 Vienna Convention on the Law of Treaties between States (VCLT) and 1986 Vienna Conventions on the law of Treaties between States and International organizations are silent on the question which state branches can conclude international agreements. Article 7 of both Conventions only presents the assumption that the state is represented by the head of state, head of government and ministers of foreign affairs. It furthermore depends then on the constitutional practice of the respective state. A party can be a state, a state agency or an intergovernmental organization;[21] however, this excludes public bodies which have a legal personality separate from the state.[22] International organizations or any other subject of international law can conclude international agreements based on their mandate of their founding treaty.[23] For the purpose of this Chapter the term international agreement will be used to indicate treaty, agreement or arrangement.

[B] Inter-agency Agreements

For a good understanding of the role of agencies in EU external relations, we need to highlight another aspect of international treaty-making, namely that states and international organizations can also engage in executive or administrative agreements. Such agreements are characterized as binding international agreements between the

---

17. G.G. Fitzmaurice, 'Third Report on the Law of Treaties', *Yearbook of the International Law Commission* II (1958): 24. The definition under Art. 2 of the 1969 Vienna Convention on the Law of Treaties (1155 U.N.T.S. 331, 8 I.L.M. 679) of an international agreement is straightforward: an international agreement is concluded between states in a written format; see further A. Aust, *Modern Treaty Law*, 2nd edn. (Cambridge: Cambridge University Press, 2007), 16–23.
18. Names such as treaty, agreement or arrangement, code or statute have been used in state practice, see D.P. Myers, 'The Names and Scope of Treaties', *American Journal of International Law* 51 (1957): 575 and J. Klabbers, *The Concept of Treaty in International Law* (The Hague: Kluwer Law International, 1996), 42–44.
19. Aust, *supra* n. 17, at 20.
20. Aust, *supra* n. 17, at 58 and Klabbers, *supra* n. 18, at 103.
21. See for the US practice: Circular 175 Procedure of the US State Department, 1 U.S.C. §181.2, < http://ecfr.gpoacc ess.gov/cgi/t/text/text-idx?c=ecfr&tpl=/ecfrbrowse/Title22/22cfr181_main_02.tpl >, accessed on 1 February 2013.
22. Aust, *supra* n. 17, at 58.
23. This is also confirmed in the 1986 Vienna Convention on the Law of Treaties between States and International Organisations or between International Organisations which however has not entered into force yet. See further Aust, *supra* n. 17, at 400.

executive branch which do not require ratification by parliament. In a comparative law approach, comparing national constitutional law provisions and practice, this has been structured by the literature into treaties concluded in the name of the state, treaties concluded in the name of the government and treaties concluded in the name of a government department and a ministry.[24] For example, Switzerland, United Kingdom and USA recognize so-called agency-to-agency agreements as international agreements.[25] Such executive or agency-to-agency agreements regulate detailed technical cooperation and do not necessarily include political obligations which require ratification through parliaments.[26] Generally these inter-agency agreements are concluded between a state agency or local government and an agency of a foreign state or an international organization but also can be concluded between international organizations.[27]

The US State Department has clarified explicitly that agency-level agreements are international agreements if they satisfy the necessary criteria such as identity of parties, significance of the arrangement and its form.[28] In practice, ministries, but also independent agencies, can be engaged in these activities depending on the constitutional framework. Federal agencies in the United States are also able to conduct international activities and can conclude international agreements, although this requires prior consultation with the US Secretary of State.[29] In Germany the involvement of agencies in the conclusion of executive agreements also has a long tradition and is explicitly mentioned in Article 59(2) of the German Constitution (*Grundgesetz*). For example, the German Federal Aviation Office was empowered to represent the German Ministry of Transport to conclude an agreement on the implementation of aspects of the International Civil Aviation Code with the Danish Ministry of Transport, which was also represented by an agency, the Danish Centre for Aviation.[30]

---

24. D. Hollis, 'A Comparative Approach to Treaty Law and Practice', in *National Treaty Law and Practice. The American Society of International Law,* eds. D. Hollis, M.R. Blakeslee & L.B. Ederington (Leiden: Martinus Nijhoff, 2005), 1.
25. Hollis, *supra* n. 24, at 17.
26. See F.A. Mann, 'Zur Auslegung von Verwaltungsabkommen durch den Bundesgerichtshof', *Zeitschrift für Ausländisches öffentliches Recht und Völkerrecht* 35(1975): 723 and Klabbers, *supra* n. 18, at 97.
27. See J. Erne, 'Primary and Secondary Law-making in the Renewed EU', *Trames* 14, no. 3 (2010): 265.
28. See Art. 181.2 b of the Circular 175 Procedure of the US State Department, *supra* n. 21 ('the fact that an agreement is concluded by and on behalf of a particular agency of the US government, rather than the US government, does not mean that the agreement is not an international agreement') and see discussion by J. Pauwelyn, R. Wessel & J. Wouters, 'Informal International Lawmaking: An Assessment and Template to Keep it Both Effective and Accountable', in *Informal International Lawmaking,* eds. J. Pauwelyn, R.A. Wessel & J. Wouters. (Oxford: Oxford University Press, 2012), 500.
29. D.J. Kuchenbecker, 'Agency-level Executive Agreements. A New Era in U.S. Treaty Practice', *Columbia Journal of Transnational La*w 18, no. 1 (1979–1980): 20.
30. Agreement between the Federal Ministry of Transport, Building and Urban development of the Federal Republic of Germany and the Ministry of Transport of the Kingdom of Denmark on the implementation of Art. 83*bis* of the Convention on International Civil Aviation, represented by the Federal Aviation Office and the Danish Transport Authority, Centre for Aviation, available at < http://www.lba.de/SharedDocs/Downloads/B/B1_Genehmigungen/83bis/ICAO-Daenemark_de_engl.pdf?__blob=publicationFile >, accessed on 3 February 2013) (< http://www.lba.de/DE/Betrieb/Genehmigungen/83bis/ICAO_Daenemark.html?nn=20280 >).

In Estonia, such inter-agency agreements are also considered as international agreements and are concluded on behalf of a state authority in the area of its competences.[31] The Republic of Kosovo has agreed on a law on international agreements in which ministries and state agencies may conclude, within their competence, agreements or memoranda with institutions of other states and international organizations only if such agreements do not contain legally binding obligations on the government.[32] In France, government agencies are able to conclude *arrangements administratifs*, which are defined as government agency agreements, to implement existing treaties or to deal with matters within the scope of the agency's jurisdiction. However, such agreements only bind the agency on the national level but not the French government internationally.[33] Also in Japan government agencies generally have no independent authority to negotiate and conclude international agreements.[34]

The European Commission has argued in light of this – though inconsistent – state practice that it would be able to conclude internationally binding administrative agreements. This view however has been rebutted (and without further discussion) in the ruling *France v. Commission* by the Court that stated that international agreements are concluded solely by the Council.[35]

To summarize, an international treaty can be concluded by a state agent on behalf of the state or international organization with another international party if the conditions are met that this agent can represent the state/international organization according to the constitution and the interpretation of the respective text gives rise to the intention that both parties want to be bound. Moreover, if an entity within a state or international organizations has separate international legal personality, this entity can conclude international agreements in its own right. Hence, in order to establish whether an act is an international agreement, it is important to identify who is able to conclude such agreements on behalf of the EU and whether at the executive level, for example the Commission or even EU agencies, could be considered to be able to conclude binding international agreements.

---

31. As example an agreement between ministries is mentioned, see Erne, *supra* n. 27, at 265.
32. Art. 12, Republic of Kosovo, Law No. 04/L-052 on international agreements, < http://www. mfa-ks.net/repository/docs/Ligji_per_marreveshjet_nderkombetare_(anglisht).pdf > , accessed on 3 February 2013.
33. Hollis, *supra* n. 24, at 18. However, see for Bulgaria the Law for the International Agreements of the Republic of Bulgaria, November 2001 where a minister or head of an administrative body can be mandated to conclude such an international agreement, see Art. 9(2), < http://ciela. sliven.net/laws/Law_for_the_international_agreements_of_the_republic_of_Bulgaria.htm > , accessed on 3 February 2013.
34. Hollis, *supra* n. 24, at 21.
35. CJEU, Case C-327/91, *French Republic v. Commission* [1994] ECR I-3641.

[C]   International Agreements According to EU Law

[1]   Do Multiple International Legal Personalities Exist in the EU?

International agreements thus require the ability to act on the international plane which is determined by international legal personality. International organizations can acquire international legal personality according to their founding treaties and in the case of the EU this is now codified by Article 47 TEU.[36] In this way, it is beyond doubt that the different institutions (Commission, Council, or European Parliament) of the Union do not have separate international legal personality.

International law literature is however undecided whether multiple international legal personalities of international organizations can at all be considered as also having individual organs of an international organization endowed with such legal personality.[37] Practice in EU law, however, shows a careful tendency to recognize the European Central Bank and the European Investment Bank as having a separate international legal personality, with reference to their independence, practice and powers under their founding acts.[38] In a further consecutive step, literature sources have argued for an international legal personality of EU agencies by referring to the general provisions in all founding regulations that agencies have legal personality.[39] These provisions however refer to the agencies' internal legal personality. Yet international legal personality of agencies cannot per se be excluded but could only be established by a case-by-case analysis of agencies' external relations mandate, and their practice and powers to act externally, as we will see below (sections §5.04 and §5.05).

[2]   Institutional Balance in EU External Relations

International legal personality is therefore closely linked to the ability to conclude international agreements.[40] It needs to be determined, within such an international organization, which competent organ is able to conclude international agreements on behalf of the organization. This is usually the supreme organ but this does not preclude other organs from acting when powers have been delegated to them.[41] According to the wording of Article 218 TFEU, the power to conclude international agreements for the Union is conferred upon the Council. This entails that the Commission cannot conclude binding international agreements with third countries, as the CJEU has held in its case

---

36. H. Schermers & N. Blokker, *International Institutional Law: Unity within Diversity* 5th rev. edn. (Leiden: Martinus Nijhoff Publishers, 2011), 991.
37. Schermers & Blokker refer in this regard to the European Investment Bank, *supra* n. 36, at 994.
38. Especially on the European Central Bank: see C. Zilioli & M. Selmayr, 'Recent developments in the Law of the ECB', *Yearbook of European Law* (2006): 1, with extensive references to literature in n. 362 at p. 78.
39. R. van Ooik, 'The Growing Importance of Agencies in the EU: Shifting Governance and Institutional Balance', in *Good Governance and the European Union*, eds. D. Curtin & R. Wessel (Antwerp: Intersentia, 2005), 132.
40. Aust, *supra* n. 17, at 16.
41. Schermers & Blokker, *supra* n. 36, at 1136–1137, see also Art. 7 of the 1986 Vienna Convention, *supra* n. 23.

law. Thus, as the Court held in the above mentioned case *France v. Commission*, the Commission's attempts to conclude administrative agreements of a binding nature[42] with the US government on the application of competition rules were a violation of the distribution of powers in external relations. In this case the CJEU was confronted with a dilemma that such an agreement could be interpreted as an internationally binding agreement according to international customary law but would violate the balance of powers established in Article 218 TFEU. The Court however ruled that Article 218 TFEU assigns the Council with the power to make international agreements while the Commission is empowered to prepare this treaty-making in negotiations under the guidance of the Council.[43]

With this rather strict interpretation of the institutional balance in treaty-making, the Court failed in this case to engage in the discussion on administrative agreements raised by Advocate General Tesauro in his opinion. The latter had argued that certain arrangements by specific administrative entities, with a view to establishing forms of cooperation with the authorities of other states, would be not be governed by international law. However, he further concluded that a comparison could not be made to the executive power to conclude administrative arrangements by Member States' governments since an independent and general executive function carried out by the Commission could not be identified.[44] The Court however did not go along with this argument. As a result the Commission has been clearly denied a mandate to conclude executive agreements in light of Article 218 TFEU. Yet, where it is clear throughout the negotiations that the intention of the parties is not to enter into a legally binding commitment, the Court has held in its second ruling in *France v. Commission* that Article 218 does not preclude the adoption of 'guidelines' by the European Commission together with an international partner.[45] Furthermore, it has not been clarified by the Court whether the extensive practice of the Commission to engage in contractual relations with international organizations is infringing Article 218 TFEU.

The Commission has over the years developed an extensive practice to organize the EU's relations with international organizations[46] through such examples as exchange of letters,[47] a financial administrative framework

---

42. In his Opinion, AG Tesauro gives a good description as defining them as 'agreements in a simplified form, without parliamentary action, and normally concern technical and administrative matters, whose implementation does not entail legislative amendments or which supplement or define pre-existing agreements concluded in accordance with the usual procedures' (para. 32), Case C-327/91, *France v. Commission* [1994] ECR I-3641.
43. Case C-327/91, *France v. Commission* [1994] ECR I-3641, paras 24–37. In a subsequent case, the Court did accept that the Commission can agree on non-binding guidelines, considering that such actions would not violate Treaty provisions – see Case C-233/02, *France v. Commission* [2004] ECR I-2759.
44. Case C-327/91, *France v. Commission* [1994] *ECR* I-3641, Opinion of AG Tesauro, delivered on 16 December 1993, para. 22 and para. 32.
45. In the guidelines on regulatory cooperation and transparency agreed between the US and the Commission it is expressively worded that it 'intends to apply on a voluntary basis', Case 233/02, *France v. Commission*, [2004] ECR I-2759, para. 2.
46. See generally R. Frid, *The Relations between the EC and International Organisations: Legal Theory and Practice* (The Hague: Kluwer Law International, 1995), 127–129.
47. For example, Arrangement in the form of an exchange of letters between the European Economic Community and the International Council for the Exploration of the Sea, OJ L149/14-16 of

agreement,[48] a framework agreement,[49] an administration agreement,[50] and a contribution agreement.[51] Looking at the content of some of the agreements concluded by the
Commission with international organizations, they are intended to be considered legally
binding. Taking the Financial and Administrative Framework Agreement with the
United Nations[52] as an example, it states that the EU is represented by the Commission
and establishes rules in its text about the entry into force and the termination of the
Agreement. In its content it regulates the details of cooperation such as reporting and
other related matters. Other agreements with international organizations have similar
provisions.[53]

As regards the question as to whether the Commission is able to represent the
Union and such a text constitutes an international agreement the literature is divided.

---

10 June 1987 (where the Commission represented the Community); Exchange of letters between
the World Health Organisation and the Commission of the European Communities concerning
the consolidation and intensification of cooperation, OJ 2001 C1/04 of 4 January 2001.

48. For example, Financial Administrative Framework Agreement between the European Community, represented by the Commission of the European Communities and the United Nations
(2003) information available at < http://ec.europa.eu/europeaid/work/procedures/
implementation/practical_guide/previous_versions/2003/fafa_en.htm (visited on 3 February
2013). The agreement itself is available at < http://ec.europa.eu/echo/files/partners/
humanitarian_aid/fafa/agreement_en.pdf > , accessed on 3 February 2013.

49. For example, Framework Agreement between the European Commission (the 'Commission')
and the World Organisation for Animal Health ('OIE') of 2010 available at < http://
ec.europa.eu/europeaid/work/procedures/financing/international_organisations/
other_international_organ
isations/documents/framework_agreement_oie_signed.pdf > , accessed on 3 February 2013;
Framework Agreement between the Commission of the European Communities (the 'Commission') and the International Monetary Fund ('IMF') of 2009 < http://ec.europa.eu/europeaid/
work/procedures/financing/international_organisations/other_international_organisations/
documents/fa_ec_imf_signed_12_january_2009.pdf > , accessed on 3 February 2013.

50. See, for instance, Art. 3 of the Trust Funds and Cofinancing Framework Agreement between The
European Community represented by the Commission of the European Communities and
the International Bank for Reconstruction and Development, The International Development
Association and the International Finance Corporation (2009) – available at < http://ec.europa.
eu/europeaid/work/procedures/financing/international_organisations/other_documents_rela
ting_world_bank/documents/signed_contract_20_march_2009bis_en.pdf > , accessed on 3
February 2013.

51. See Guide on relations with international organisations, Member States, beneficiary countries
and other donors: Delegated cooperation and co-financing (2011) – available at < http://
ec.europa.eu/europeaid/work/procedures/financing/international_organisations/documents/
guide_on_relations_with_ios+na+bc_en.doc > , accessed on 3 February 2013. See also General
conditions on contribution agreements with international organisations – available at < http://
ec.europa.eu/europeaid/work/procedures/financing/international_organisations/documents/
c2_contribution_agr_gc_en.pdf > , accessed on 3 February 2013.

52. Financial Administrative Framework Agreement between the European Community, represented by the Commission of the European Communities and the United Nations (2003), *supra*
n. 48.

53. Framework partnership agreements [FPAs] and contribution agreements are concluded routinely by the Commission on behalf of the EU with international organizations in the area of
humanitarian aid – see more info on the following links: < http://ec.europa.eu/echo/partners/
humanitarian_aid/fpa_en.htm > and < http://ec.europa.eu/echo/partners/humanitarian_aid/
fpa_int_en.htm > ; see for an example of a FPA concluded with IOM in 2011 – < http://ec.
europa.eu/europeaid/work/procedures/financing/international_organisations/other_internati
onal_organisations/documents/framework_agreement_iom.pdf > , accessed on 3 February
2013.

In principle, two opposing views can be observed. The first view relying on the argument of the cooperation of administrations[54] argues that the Commission is able to conclude binding international agreements with international organizations according to Article 220 TFEU under the condition that such agreements do not touch upon the realm of political and legal commitment under Article 218 TFEU and only cover technical and management tasks in relations with international organizations.[55] These agreements, being based on Article 220 TFEU, will consequently also bind the Union.[56] According to Article 220 TFEU the Commission (now post-Lisbon together with the High Representative for the Foreign Affairs and Security Policy) shall maintain the relations with international organizations. However, if such agreements would touch upon the political content with clear-cut obligations, this would nevertheless violate Article 218 TFEU and the assigned powers of the Council, as it stipulates clearly that the 'Council shall authorize the opening of negotiations, adopt negotiating directives, authorize the signing of agreements and conclude them' and thus infringe the institutional balance of powers as laid down in Article 13(2) TFEU.

Whether such international agreements are invalid under international law is a different question. The agreements concluded by the Commission will have to be considered in light of Article 46 of the 1969 VCLT.[57] This Article stipulates that violations of internal rules can only be invoked by a contracting party in order to invalidate its consent to be bound by a treaty in cases that the violation of the internal rule results in manifest infringement and the violation concerned an internal rule of fundamental importance. Article 218 TFEU could be considered to be such an internal rule but the CJEU also acknowledged in its ruling C-327/91 that in practice it will be difficult to prove that such a norm (internal rule) is of fundamental importance. That the internal rule is of fundamental importance would need to be objectively evident to any state conducting itself in the matter in accordance with normal practice and good faith.[58]

The second view maintains that any binding international agreement is a violation of the powers of the Council in EU external relations and such Commission arrangements will not qualify as international agreements and therefore only include a political commitment and are informal arrangements between the Commission and the international organization.[59]

When we look at the above mentioned example of the Commission's Framework agreement with the United Nations, it is clear that the latter interpretation of denying

---

54. B. Dutzler, 'Representation of the EU and the Member States in Internatonal Organisations', in *External Economic Relations and Foreign Policy in the European Union*, eds. S. Griller & B. Weidel (Vienna: Springer Publisher, 2002). 159.
55. See Frid, *supra* n. 46, at 127; Dutzler, *supra* n. 54, at 159; K. Schmalenbach, 'Article 220 TFEU, para. 8', in *EUV/AEUV Commentary*, eds. Ch. Calliess & M. Ruffert, 4th edn. (Munich: Beck Publisher, 2011).
56. Ott, *supra* n. 6 with further literature reference in n. 61.
57. This provision is also binding on the EU as customary international law. See generally Schmalenbach, *supra* n. 55, para. 8.
58. A. Watts, *The International Law Commission 1949-1998* (Oxford: Oxford University Press, 1999), 898.
59. I. MacLeod, I.D. Hendry & S. Hyett, *The External Relations of the European Communities* (Oxford: Clarendon Press, 1996), 167.

international binding status for these Commission agreements concluded under Article 220 TFEU is contradicted by the very content of this Framework Agreement which indicates with its wording a clear intention by both parties to be bound. Consequently it is correct to argue that certain but limited treaty-making powers rest inherently with the Commission in Article 220 TFEU.[60] Furthermore, it is too restrictive and formal to deny the Commission the use of international agreements in the management of relations with international organizations and they may be permitted as long these agreements respect the limits set by Article 220 TFEU and Article 218 TFEU.

The above indicates that respect for the institutional balance of powers in the field of external relations entails that treaty-making powers rest with the Council, as laid down in Article 218 TFEU. Hence the Council is responsible for binding international agreements to which the European Parliament needs to give its consent since Lisbon. The Commission has no power to conclude international agreements with third countries; however, it can be argued that managerial tasks in coordination with international organizations can be regulated by international agreements according to Article 220 TFEU. In the framework of a cooperation of administrations the Commission can also engage in international agreements which will also bind the Union only with international organizations (and not with third states). In addition, the Commission is always able to conclude non-binding arrangements with third parties as long as it becomes clear in the text of such an arrangement that it cannot be considered legally binding.

§5.03   EU AGENCIES: DELEGATION AND TYPOLOGY IN VIEW OF THEIR INTERNATIONAL POWERS

[A]   Delegation

As we set forth in the introduction, the precise reference to international collaboration as well as the nature of and the instruments used vary significantly among the agencies. In view of this great diversity, it is important to clarify what forms of powers have been conferred upon agencies to act at the global level. For our discussion of agencies' global activities, it is therefore decisive to establish whether agencies as part of an executive power[61] manoeuvre in a situation comparable to the Commission or the Council and whether such tasks have been and/or can be delegated to them by the legislator with the observance of the institutional balance enshrined in Article 218 and Article 220 TFEU.

European agencies have the task to assist the Commission and the Council in the implementation of Union policies.[62] They generally have been delegated, in line with

---

60. See Dutzler, *supra* n. 54 and Schmalenbach, *supra* n. 55.
61. D. Curtin, *Executive Power of the European Union* (Oxford: Oxford University Press, 2009), 52.
62. See generally S. Griller & A. Orator, 'Meroni Revisited: Empowering European Agencies between Efficiency and Legitimacy', *NewGov* (2007) 04/D40, < http://www.eu-newgov.org/database/DELIV/D04D40_WP_Meroni_Revisited.pdf > , accessed on 4 February 2013; E. Chiti, 'An Important Part of the EU's Institutional Machinery: Features, Problems and Perspectives of

the (in)famous *Meroni* case law of the late 1950s,[63] clearly defined limited executive powers[64] which are subject to judicial review, so as to respect the institutional balance of powers.[65] From this we can argue that in principle treaty-making is a form of 'external legislation making' and that European agencies cannot be put in the position to conclude binding international agreements or working arrangements without a clear tie to the primary actors in EU external relations law: the Council and Parliament (in relation to international agreements under Article 218 TFEU) and the Commission (in relation to working agreements with international organizations under Article 220 TFEU).

For our analysis, it is therefore important to define the relationship that agencies have with the EU institutions in the exercise of their global activities and whether and what powers have been delegated to them. To this end it is important to define what delegation is. Delegation of powers may generally be defined as the transfer of powers from one organ or institution to another, which the latter exercises under its responsibility. This definition may not be entirely satisfactory as the formal position does not always correspond with the practice: a formal delegation of powers has been made without transfer of responsibility while formally no real authority has been delegated and real powers are exercised by the other organs.[66] In order to determine whether 'true' delegation has taken place three factors seem decisive: (i) the nature of powers delegated (wide discretionary or narrowly circumscribed executive powers); (ii) the amount of control that the delegating authority can exercise over the delegate and (iii) the actual exercise of the powers (by delegate or delegating authority).[67] In the *Meroni* cases, the Court indeed distinguished between a 'true' delegation of the powers conferred upon the delegating authority and a situation where the authority grants the powers to a delegate, the performance of which remains subject to oversight by the

---

European Agencies', *Common Market Law Review* 46 (2009): 1395, M. Chamon, 'EU Agencies between Meroni and Romano or the Devil and the Deep Blue Sea', *Common Market Law Review* 48 (2011): 1055, and Chapter 1 to this volume.

63. Case 9/56, *Meroni & Co, Industrie Metallurgiche SpA v. High Authority of the European Coal and Steel Community* [1958] ECR 133 and Case 10/56, *Meroni & Co, Industrie Metallurgiche SpA v. High Authority of the European Coal and Steel Community* [1958] ECR 157; cases where the Court has referred to Meroni in later case law include: Case C-255/04, *Commission v. France*, ECR [2006] I-5251; Case C-240/03 P, *Comunità montana della Valnerina v. Commission*, ECR [2006] I-731; Case C-301/02 P, *Carmine Salvatore Tralli v. European Central Bank*, ECR [2005] I-4071, Case 98/80, *Giuseppe Romano v. Institut national d'assurance maladie-invalidité*, ECR 1981 Page 01241, see generally: Chamon, *supra* n. 62, at 1055–1075; K. Lenaerts 'Regulating the Regulatory Process: "Delegation of Powers" in the European Community', *European Law Review* 18, no. 1 (1993): 23; E. Vos, 'Reforming the European Commission: What Role to Play for EU Agencies?', *Common Market Law Review* 37 (2000): 1113; G. Majone, 'Delegation of Regulatory Powers in a Mixed Polity', *European Law Journal* 8, no. 3 (2002): 326; E. Vos, 'Agencies and the European Union', in *Agencies in European and Comparative Perspective*, eds. L. Verhey & T. Zwart (Antwerp: Intersentia, 2003).

64. See very recently, Case C-270/12, *United Kingdom of Great Britain and Northern Ireland v. Council of the European Union*, European Parliament on the powers conferred upon ESMA. App 11844/12 on 1 June 2012 (pending).

65. Curtin, *supra* n. 61, at 145.

66. T. Hartley, *The Foundations of European Union Law*, 7th edn. (Oxford: Oxford University Press, 2010), 127.

67. Hartley, *supra* n. 66.

authority which assumes full responsibility for the decisions of the delegate.[68] According to the Court, in the latter situation no 'true' delegation takes place. Whether or not delegation has taken place to agencies, which may upset the institutional balance of powers, thus depends on these three factors. At the same time it is helpful to remind that the question of delegation is a matter of degree and does not necessarily have a yes or no answer. The meaning of delegation in practice will therefore largely be determined by the degree to which real powers have been transferred.[69]

[B]   Disciplining the Reality: Typology

The above makes clear that it is vital to establish the nature of powers delegated and the degree of supervision by the EU authorities. Hereby it is key to determine whether powers (and which ones) have been delegated to the agencies. To this end it is important to establish whether some kind of control is exercised by the Council or the Commission. We may observe that various agencies' founding regulations do require some form of control. For the purpose of our analysis, we can divide the agencies into agencies that have obtained explicit powers, and hence a mandate to act internationally, and agencies that have not obtained explicit powers in this regard and where the founding regulation is completely silent on this point. With respect to the latter it remains unclear whether and/or how these agencies may act at all. Such agencies, i.e., Body of European Regulators for Electronic Communications (BEREC), Community Plan Variety Office (CPVO), European GNSS Agency (GSA), and European Agency for the operational management of large-scale IT systems in the area of freedom, security and justice (IT Agency),[70] therefore remain outside of the scope of our analysis. According to the formal powers they have obtained, subjected to various degrees of supervision in a broad sense,[71] we can therefore classify agencies roughly into three types (see for a detailed overview the Annex on the typology of EU agencies in view of their external relations powers):

(1) agencies that, for the conclusion of an act of international cooperation, need to ask prior approval by either the Council or the Commission (category 1);

(2) agencies that must ask for the opinion of the Commission prior to concluding an act of international cooperation (category 2); and

(3) agencies whose founding acts do not provide expressly for supervision by the Commission or the Council (category 3).

The requirement of prior approval for agency global action is important for our analysis so as to determine whether the EU is bound by an act of an agency as well as who is

---

68. See Case 9/56, *Meroni*, *supra* n. 63, at 147–149 and Case 10/56, *Meroni*, *supra* n. 63, at 169–171.
69. Hartley, *supra* n. 66, at 127.
70. Regulation (EU) No. 1077/2011 of the European Parliament and of the Council of 25 October 2011 establishing a European Agency for the operational management of large-scale IT systems in the area of freedom, security and justice [2011] OJ L286/1.
71. See on the various ways EU agencies may be classified, Vos in this volume.

responsible for the act. The prior approval or consultation by the EU institutions will be decisive to establish whether powers have (lawfully or non-lawfully) been delegated to the agencies and whether the institutional balance has been upset.

Hence, powers and/or obligations have been conferred upon category 1 agencies to cooperate with third countries and/or international organizations but these agencies may conclude an instrument of cooperation only after approval of the Commission or the Council. 'Category 1 agencies' thus refers to four agencies, viz.: EASA, CEPOL, Europol, and EUROJUST. 'Category 2 agencies' may or must consult with the Commission. This is the case with EMCDDA, FRA, ETF, and Frontex. For this category the Commission is associated with external actions of the concerned agencies but cannot prevent the final conclusion of arrangements. Powers and/or obligations have been conferred upon category 3 agencies instead to cooperate with third countries and/or international organizations without further specification of supervision. The vast majority of agencies fall into this category.

Category 1 agencies have thus to be distinguished from categories 2 and 3 agencies as, for the latter, the Commission and the Council can prevent the final decision-making process and therefore have to be considered responsible for creating binding obligations on behalf of the Union, should these obligations be considered binding. We will see in sections §5.04 and §5.05 what this will mean for the legal nature of the acts of the latter agencies and the institutional balance.

§5.04 EU AGENCIES' EXTERNAL ACTIONS: EXAMPLES OF PROVISIONS AND PRACTICE

Our analysis reveals that it is important to look at the precise provisions stipulated in the founding regulations and the practice of the agencies on the international plane. Only in this way can we determine the precise nature of the agencies' acts and whether the global dimension of agencies interfere with the institutional balance. Our categorization of the agencies thus helps to identify the powers of agencies and whether they may carry them out autonomously or where there is some kind of control by the EU institutions.

For the purpose of our analysis, we will need to look at concrete provisions in the legal foundations of agencies as well as the practice of the conclusion of working arrangements or cooperation agreements. To this end, we will give a few examples of the three categories of agencies that have different powers and instruments and vary in their constraints on the use of these instruments.

[A] Category 1: Prior Approval by the Commission or Council

As the Annex on the typology of EU agencies in view of their external relations powers shows, there are only four agencies that need to ask for prior approval for their global action. Since the 2008 amendment of its founding regulation, EASA is required to ask for prior approval from the Commission for the conclusion of international working arrangements, while CEPOL, Europol, and EUROJUST need to ask for prior approval from the Council before they conclude agreements with third countries or international organizations. For the purpose of our analysis we will analyse EASA and Europol.

[1]   EASA

EASA's international cooperation in the form of working arrangements requires prior Commission approval.[72] EASA is assigned with tasks which fall into the categories of rulemaking, certification and standardization. In the field of rulemaking, EASA assists the Commission in drafting legislation, it can adopt soft law in form of non-binding documents (for example, on airworthiness) and assist third countries in setting up common aviation safety standards as regards certification.[73] EASA derives its international mandate from Article 27 of its founding regulation according to which:

> the agency may cooperate with aeronautical authorities with third countries and the international organisations competent in matters covered by this Regulation in the framework of working arrangements concluded with those bodies, in accordance with the relevant provisions of the Treaty.

Though EASA was established already in 2002,[74] it is noteworthy that only the amended 2008 founding regulation has added that such cooperation requires the prior approval of the Commission.[75] EASA has been very active in its international relations and has concluded numerous working arrangements with other aeronautical authorities in third states, both in Europe such as Iceland, Norway, Switzerland, and Serbia and elsewhere such as, Australia, Brazil, China, Hong Kong, New Zealand, and Vietnam.[76] These working arrangements cover cooperation in the field of civil aviation in the form of the collection and exchange of information on the safety of aircraft using EU airports and airports of the relevant country, airworthiness and environmental type-certification of aeronautical products, parts and appliances, approval of aircraft

---

72. Art. 27 of Regulation (EC) 216/2008 of the European Parliament and of the Council of 20 February 2008 on common rules in the field of civil aviation and establishing a European Aviation Safety Agency, and repealing Council Directive 91/670/EEC, Regulation (EC) No. 1592/2002 and Directive 2004/36/EC [2008] OJ L79/1, as last amended by Regulation (EC) 1108/2009 of the European Parliament and the Council of 21 October 2009 amending Regulation (EC) No. 216/2008 in the field of aerodromes, air traffic management and air navigation services and repealing Directive 2006/23/EC [2009] OJ L309/51 (hereafter referred to as 'EASA founding regulation').
73. See especially Arts 19 and 20 of the Basic EASA Regulation. Art. 12 covers the acceptance of third-country certifications.
74. Regulation (EC) 1592/2002 of the European Parliament and of the Council of 15 July 2002 on common rules in the field of civil aviation and establishing a European Aviation Safety Agency [2002] OJ L240/1.
75. Art. 18 of Regulation (EC) 1592/2002 did not refer to the Commission's approval but only mentioned in very general words that working arrangements must be concluded to 'in accordance with the relevant provisions of the Treaty.'
76. See generally on this the information available on the official website of EASA in the section 'International Cooperation – Working Arrangements' < http://easa.europa.eu/rulemaking/international-cooperation-working-arrangements.php > , accessed on 4 February 2013. On the different types of working arrangements used by EASA in the context of EU enlargement: Coman-Kund, *supra* n. 7, 363–365.

design organizations and of production and maintenance organizations, coordination of joint (operational) measures and projects, standardization inspections and training.

Due to extensive practice, the international partners of EASA vary and the wording of its working arrangements is not alike.[77] Differences in the wording of the working arrangements would moreover require each and every of the 100 agreements to be studied in order to identify whether there is an intention to legally bind the EU, which falls beyond the scope of this contribution. Here we will give only a few outstanding examples. The international partners of EASA are all involved in the control and management of civil aviation but their international legal status differs. The cooperation with Russia is organized through the Interstate Aviation Committee (IAC) which was established by international agreements between twelve states of the former Soviet Union and is an international organization.[78] From this legal status it can be assumed that the IAC has treaty-making powers when it concludes a working arrangement with EASA. Moreover, it is noteworthy that in this working arrangement with the IAC the preamble mentions that EASA explicitly represents the Member States and not the EU.[79] EASA representing the Member States can be traced back to the EASA founding regulation setting common rules on aviation safety at the EU level and entrusting the implementation tasks to the Member States and the Commission together with EASA.[80] A similar or identical provision concerning the Member States'

---

77. According to the information available on the website of EASA, it transpires that up to date the agency has concluded more than 100 working arrangements of different types with international partners all over the world; it should be noted however that about half of these working arrangements have been concluded only with the Chinese competent authority, due to the specific circumstances of the international cooperation framework with China – < http:// easa.europa.eu/rulemaking/international-cooperation-working-arrangements.php > (accessed on 11 February 2013).

78. See the official website of ICAO < http://legacy.icao.int/icao/en/assembl/a36/wp/wp056_ en.pdf > (accessed on 4 February 2013).

79. See working arrangement on the airworthiness between EASA and the Interstate Aviation Committee, < http://easa.europa.eu/rulemaking/docs/international/russia/intl_appro_IAC_ EASA.pdf >, accessed on 4 February 2013.

80. Thus recital (13) of the preamble of Regulation 216/2008 already specifies that certification tasks are to be executed at national level, while EASA can also be empowered in certain cases to conduct certification tasks (such empowerment is operated via the founding regulation itself and its implementing rules). Art. 17(2)(c) stipulates explicitly the task of EASA to carry out on behalf of the Member States functions and tasks assigned to them by applicable international conventions, in particular the Chicago Convention. Following this line, Art. 20(1) specifies that EASA is to carry out (where applicable and as specified in the Chicago Convention) on behalf of the Member States the function and tasks of the state of design, manufacture or registry when related to design approval. Furthermore, Art. 23(1)(b) authorizes EASA to issue and renew authorizations proving the capability of third-country operators, unless a Member State carries out the functions and tasks of the state of operator. Last but not least, Art. 27(3) on EASA's international cooperation stipulates that the agency shall assist Member States to respect their international obligations (in particular those under the Chicago Convention). Since airworthiness certification requirements and tasks are covered by the Chicago Convention (to which only Member States are parties, not the EU) but, on the other hand, Member States transferred the competence to the EU to adopt common rules in the area of aviation safety, Regulation 216/2008 (and before that, Regulation 1592/2002) has foreseen the possibility for EASA to act on behalf of the Member States in relation with the outside world. Another interesting situation is that provided for in Art. 12 of Regulation 216/2008, according to which EASA may issue certificates on behalf of any Member State in application of an agreement concluded by one of the Member

authorization is also included in the preamble or the content of working arrangements concluded with Australia, Brazil, Japan, Vietnam, Singapore, and Taipei.[81] The intention to be legally bound is included in all of these arrangements and the wording in the preamble can be understood to mean that EASA concludes an agreement on behalf of the EU Member States. A particular feature of these working arrangements is that they cover certification-related matters and the wording of these arrangements (authorized representation of EU Member States) reflects the regulatory oversight tasks which still belong to Member States.

In other examples in the practice of EASA, the wording of the arrangements indicates whether they should be considered legally binding. The working arrangement between EASA and Armenia states at point 10.2 that, 'This working arrangement, of technical and practical nature, regulates the working relations between the Parties. It is not legally binding for the EU and the Republic and Armenia'.[82] It should also be noted that the working arrangements concluded with third countries in order to ensure the transition from the Joint Aviation Authority (JAA) system to the EASA system specify that they do not affect the legal responsibilities of the parties under relevant international agreements (for example, Albania; Azerbaijan; Georgia; Moldova; San Marino; Serbia; Turkey; Ukraine).[83] Without having analysed all of its over 100 working arrangements, we can argue that those EASA arrangements concluded with third countries on cooperation in civil aviation, that include a sentence indicating that this working arrangement does not affect or limit in any way the rights and obligations stemming from international agreements, in all likelihood will not be considered to be binding under international law and will be considered soft law under international law.

When applying the criteria whether an international agreement is at issue, the agreement with the IAC can be considered an international agreement. The text provides for the intention to be legally bound and the partner of EASA is able to conclude such an international agreement. However, what does it mean that the authorization to conclude such an agreement is derived not from EU but from the

---

States with a third country (such an example is the working arrangement concluded between EASA and the Civil Aviation Authority of Israel on the implementation of the Agreement between Israel and Italy concerning the airworthiness certification, approval or acceptance of imported civil aeronautical products and the acceptance of maintenance services entered into force on 2 May 1990, < http://easa.europa.eu/rulemaking/docs/international/israel/IP_Israel.pdf > (accessed on 4 February 2013).

81. For instance working arrangement between EASA and the Civil Aeronautics Administration in Taipei, < http://easa.europa.eu/rulemaking/docs/international/taipei/WA%20CAA%20Taipei.pdf > (accessed on 4 February 2013) and in the one with competent aviation authority from Saudi Arabia, < http://easa.europa.eu/rulemaking/docs/international/saudi-arabia/GACA-EASA-WA-signed%20Version18.03.08.pdf > (accessed on 4 February 2013).

82. Working arrangement between the European Aviation Safety Agency (EASA) and the General Department of Civil Aviation at the Government of Republic of Armenia < http://easa.europa.eu/rulemaking/docs/international/armenia/WA%20ARMENIA.pdf > (accessed on 4 February 2013).

83. See the official website of EASA in the section 'International Cooperation – Working Arrangements' < http://easa.europa.eu/rulemaking/international-cooperation-working-arrangements.php > , accessed on 4 February 2013.

Member States? The Commission's approval on its own would only lead to a binding international agreement in the case of cooperation with an international organization as in the case of the IAC. This mandate derives from Article 220 TFEU but is limited to technical agreements with international organizations and excludes cooperation with third countries. The Commission might also be active in external relations with third countries but with due respect to Article 218 TFEU only in the form of a non-binding action or through soft law. Under these conditions the institutional balance in EU external relations is observed. In case of EASA, this approval entails that there is no true delegation as the action remains subject to continuing oversight by the Commission due to mandatory approval. Consequently it could be argued that this form of authorization does not breach *Meroni*.[84] Thus if an international agreement between EASA and an international organization is concluded it could be considered authorized by Article 220 TFEU and the powers given to the Commission. In case such an agreement would be concluded with a third country, the agency and the Commission have to respect the limits of Article 220 TFEU. Legally binding cooperation with third countries would overstep the mandate inherent in Article 220 TFEU and need to be measured for its binding force under international law by Article 46 VCLT. However, the more likely interpretation is that the authorization of EASA in these cases, as in cases of the IAC and the third countries Taipei and Saudi-Arabia, derives directly from the Member States and their inherent treaty-making powers. EASA not only acts in this area on behalf of the Commission but also on behalf of Member States. When acting on behalf of the Member States, Articles 220 or 218 TFEU will become irrelevant. This analysis leads to a rather novel legal construction as it is different from international agreements concluded by the Member States with international partners in the form of an inter-agency agreement discussed under section §5.02[B]. In this case an EU agency concludes an international agreement on behalf of the Member States. The latter situation is quite peculiar as we see that Member States 'borrow' EASA for tasks relating to powers for which they are responsible.[85] Consequently this necessitates more empirical research on this matter.

[2]   Europol

Europol is a category 1 agency as it needs to ask for prior Council approval in its international activities. Europol was founded originally through a convention between the Member States[86] and was only on 1 January 2010 transformed into an EU agency.[87]

---

84. Case 9/56, *Meroni, supra* n. 63, 150–152 and Case 10/56, *Meroni, supra* n. 63, 173. As concerns the application of the Meroni scenario to EU agencies cf. Lenaerts, *supra* n. 63, at 40–49; E. Vos, *Institutional Frameworks of Community Health and Safety Regulation. Committees, Agencies and Private Bodies* (Oxford: Hart Publishing, 1999), 200–203; Vos, *supra* n. 63, at 129–133.
85. See also H.C.H. Hoffmann & A. Morini, 'Constitutional Aspects of the Pluralisation of the EU Executive through "Agencification"', *European Law Review* 37, no. 4 (2012), 419–443, at 431.
86. Convention based on Art. K.3 of the Treaty on European Union, on the establishment of a European Police Office (Europol Convention) OJ 1995 C316/2.
87. Council Decision 2009/371/JHA of 6 April 2009 establishing the European Police Office (Europol) [2009] OJ L121/37, hereafter referred as 'Europol's founding decision.'

Europol's mission is to support its Member States in preventing and combating all forms of serious international crime and terrorism. It facilitates the exchange of criminal intelligence between police, customs and security services. Article 23 of Europol's Founding decision regulates cooperative relations with third countries and international organizations, and foresees the conclusion of such agreements with these countries. Europol's change of legal status from an international organization to an EU agency is interesting not only from the perspective of international law but also from an EU law perspective. It was considered to have international legal personality in the areas assigned to it,[88] while being, at the same time, under the strict control of the Council, which was approving these cooperation agreements with third countries. The Commission always emphasized, however, the weaknesses of the democratic control of Europol and stressed that this issue could be addressed limiting Europol's 'own possibilities of concluding agreements with third states and such agreements should be in the future be negotiated on behalf of the EU.'[89] The Commission subsequently suggested under the heading 'relations with third bodies' that administrative arrange-ments with third bodies might be concluded.[90] The Council did not follow this suggestion and the 2009 new Council Decision kept the original wording of the Europol Convention and the final text still refers to agreements to be concluded by Europol.

In addition to the founding act, Council Decision 2009/934/JHA of November 2009 covers the implementing rules governing Europol's relations with partners, including the exchange of personal data and classified information.[91] Article 2 of Council Decision 2009/934/JHA stipulates that Europol should use the instruments of cooperation agreements and working arrangements in the relations with its partners. Article 4 of Council Decision 2009/934/JHA highlights the procedure of concluding cooperation agreements. These agreements are only concluded once the Council has decided, after consulting the European Parliament,[92] to determine a list of third states and international organizations with which Europol shall conclude agreements and after having received final approval of the Council.[93] The list of the international partners with whom Europol was directed to conclude agreements had been adopted in the form of a Council Decision.[94]

---

88. See for instance S. Peers, *EU Justice and Home Affairs Law*, 3rd edn. (Oxford: Oxford University Press, 2011), 932, and Ott, *supra* n. 6, at 516. See on this the Australian Federal Police with a legally incorrect but interesting formulation: 'Australia became a member of Europol in 2007 through the signing of an *International Treaty* which allows the Australian Federal Police, State and Territory Police, Customs and Border Protection and the Australian Crime Commission (collectively known as Competent Authorities) to exchange intelligence and interact with other Europol member countries', < http://www.afp.gov.au/policing/international-liaison/europol.aspx > (accessed on 5 February 2013).
89. Commission Staff Working Document, Brussels 20 December 2006, SEC (2006) 1682, p. 17.
90. *Supra* n. 89 and further: Ott, *supra* n. 6, at 531–532.
91. Council decision 2009/934/JHA of 30 November 2009 adopting the implementing rules govern-ing Europol's relations with partners, including the exchange of personal data and classified information OJ [2009] L325/6.
92. According to Art. 26(1)(a) of Europol's founding act.
93. According to Art. 23(2) of Europol's founding decision.
94. Council Decision 2009/935/JHA of 30 November 2009 determining the list of third States and organisations with which Europol shall conclude agreements [2009] OJ L352/12.

Europol has through its separate development under the Convention developed already quite far-reaching cooperation which can be divided into operational and strategic agreements with non-EU States such as Australia, Canada and the US and operational and strategic agreements with three international organizations (i.e., Interpol; the United National Office on Drugs and Crime, and World Customs Organization).[95] The nature of the cooperation agreements can vary, ranging from operational cooperation, including the exchange of personal data, to technical or strategic cooperation.[96] Looking at the content of these agreements, they have characteristics of international agreements, namely how they are worded, what they cover and how they are put into force. However, it must be noted that many of these agreements and arrangements have been concluded in the pre-agency phase. This is different with the Agreement on operational and strategic cooperation between Monaco and Europol which was concluded as the first agreement after Europol became an agency. From its wording and structure it does not differ from pre-agency agreements, a lot of factors such as the party involved (government of Monaco), the wording of the text, the provisions on entry into force and validity and termination indicate that this agreement is concluded as a binding agreement.[97] It can also be assumed that the legal status of Europol has not changed since the transformation into an agency. Due to the identical wording of its Founding Decision and the former convention, clearer indications would be needed to deny Europol the ability to conclude international agreements and Europol's limited international legal personality remains unchanged.

Importantly, the specific position of Europol in comparison to other agencies is also expressed in the requirement that external action needs to be approved by the Council, the EU institution, as we noted above, that is mandated to act for the EU on the international plane. In the case of Europol a strict supervision of treaty-making powers are organized by Council Decision 2009/935/JHA in which the Council determines with which third states and organizations Europol shall conclude agreements. Therefore, both primary EU law and the institutional balance are observed, as it is ultimately the Council that concludes the agreements or is strictly supervising Europol in its action so that no true delegation to this agency takes place.[98] This view is supported by the legal framework[99] and international cooperation practice of Europol, already before becoming an EU agency, where the approval of the Council is explicitly referred to both

---

95. See for details and for the texts of the agreements the official website of Europol, External co-operation section: < https://www.europol.europa.eu/content/page/external-cooperation-31 > (accessed on 5 February 2013).
96. See for details and for the texts of the agreements the official website of Europol, External cooperation section: < https://www.europol.europa.eu/content/page/external-cooperation-31 > (accessed on 5 February 2013).
97. Agreement on Operational and Strategic Co-operation between the Government of HSH The Sovereign Prince of Monaco and the European Police Office, done on 6 May 2011 available at: < https://www.europol.europa.eu/sites/default/files/principalityofmonaco.pdf > (accessed on 5 February 2013).
98. Curtin calls this a formal rubber-stamping exercise on behalf of the Council but does not lead to a complete shift of powers to an organ outside the Treaties, Curtin, *supra* n. 61, at 160.
99. See Art. 2 of Council Act of 3 November 1998 laying down rules concerning the receipt of information by Europol from third parties (1999/C 26/03) [1999] OJ C26/17 and Art. 2 of Council Act of 3 November 1998 laying down rules governing Europol's external relations with

in the relevant legal acts regulating Europol's international tasks and in the agreements concluded by Europol. A clear example of the practice of Europol after becoming an EU agency forms the agreement that Europol concluded with the principality of Monaco of 2010 where Europol, although signing the agreement in its own name, refers to the fact that the Council gave Europol 'the authorization to agree to the present agreement between the principality of Monaco and Europol'.[100]

Yet, in this case, the neglect of the role of the European Parliament is problematic under EU law as since Lisbon the role of the European Parliament in Article 218 TFEU has been reinforced with requiring the consent of the European Parliament for international agreements as a rule.[101] Clearly, the European Parliament does not play this role in the agreements concluded by Europol. Here, as with all other European agencies, the Parliament's involvement is restricted to an indirect control by being co-responsible for the budget of agencies. And according to Article 26 of the Europol Council Decision, the European Parliament will be consulted to determine the list of third states and organizations with which Europol shall conclude agreements. It could now be argued that this very limited participatory right of the European Parliament is comparable to the national constitutional system and executive or agency-to-agency agreements. In some EU Member States, as highlighted above, the practice is accepted that government agencies or other government entities conclude international agreements on technical matters which do not require ratification by Parliament. The same practice applies for the Commission agreements concluded on the basis of Article 220 TFEU with international organizations.

However, in the case of Europol it is doubtful whether these agreements are just technical agreements with reference to their content and aims, while it is moreover highly disputable whether such a practice of executive agreements is recognized in EU law. Article 218 TFEU does not foresee that executive agreements exist without the consent by the European Parliament. In Case C-327/91, *France v. Commission*, Advocate General Tesauro denied the practice of administrative agreements,[102] and the CJEU has not further explored this interpretation.[103] The only exception to the participatory rights of the European Parliament foreseen in Article 218(6) TFEU and where the European Parliament will only be informed in case the legal basis does not refer to the ordinary or special legislative procedure or the agreement relates to the CFSP. Hence, the current practice of Europol's international cooperation breaches Article 218 TFEU by disregarding the European Parliament's powers.

---

third States and non-European Union related bodies (1999/C 26/04) [1999] OJ C26/19 adopted under the 1995 Europol Convention.

100. See preamble to the Agreement on Operational and Strategic Co-operation between the Government of HSH The Sovereign Prince of Monaco and the European Police Office, *supra* n. 97.

101. Art. 218, para. 6(a)(v) TFEU (agreements covering fields to which either the ordinary legislative procedure applies or the special legislative procedure where consent by the European Parliament is required) in combination of Arts 88 and 84 TFEU in light of the ERTA doctrine.

102. Case C-327/91, *France v. Commission* [1994] ECR I-3641, Opinion of AG Tesauro, delivered on 16 December 1993, paras 33–34.

103. See Court's judgment in Case C-327/91, *France v. Commission* [1994] ECR I-3641.

The current legal framework of Europol is consequently investigated and the Commission will introduce a new draft Regulation in 2013 which will change the legal base in line with Article 88(2) TFEU, and which should also reflect the primary law demand for greater 'scrutiny of Europol's activities by the European Parliament, together with national Parliaments'.[104]

[B] Category 2: Prior Consultation with the Commission

Also category 2 agencies can be counted, namely EMCDDA, FRA, ETF and Frontex. Frontex is one of the category 2 agencies as, subsequent to the 2011 amendment to its founding regulation,[105] cooperation with third states by Frontex requires prior Commission consultation. Yet it should be underlined that as regards its international cooperation with international organizations, no specific provision is made with regard to Commission's involvement, which makes that Frontex also falls in category 3. Frontex is of interest as being an agency that deals with borders and it has a broad range of activities with third countries and international organizations.[106] Frontex was established by Council Regulation in 2004 and became operational in 2005[107] in order to improve 'the integrated management of Union's external borders.'[108] Just like other EU agencies, Frontex represents the institutional substitute of more informal cooperation mechanisms already in place in the management of external borders area.[109]

In order to manage external borders efficiently, international cooperation is a must. This is reflected in Frontex's founding act that stipulates the international dimension of the Agency in two separate articles. Article 13 provides the framework for

---

104. Art. 88(2) TFEU. Draft Regulation on the European Union Agency for Law Enforcement Cooperation and Training (Europol), COM(2013) 173 final. See further: Communication from the Commission to the European Parliament and the Council on the procedures for the scrutiny of Europol's activities by the European Parliament, together with the national Parliaments, COM(2010) 776 final and E. Disley, B. Irving, W. Hughes & B. Patruni, 'Evaluation of the implementation of the Europol Council Decision and of Europol's activities', *RAND Europe*, < https://www.europol.europa.eu/sites/default/files/publications/rand_evaluation_report. pdf > (accessed on 5 February 2013).
105. Council Regulation (EC) 2007/2004 of 26 October 2004 establishing a European Agency for the Management of Operational Cooperation at the External Borders of the Member States of the European Union [2004] OJ L349/1, as last amended by Regulation (EU) 1168/2011 of the European Parliament and of the Council of 25 October 2011 amending Council Regulation (EC) 2007/2004 establishing a European Agency for the Management of Operational Cooperation at the External Borders of the Member States of the European Union [2011] OJ L304/1, hereafter referred to as 'Frontex founding regulation.'
106. We will discuss the relevant legal provisions for FRONTEX's relations with international organizations under category 3 in the Annex on the Typology of EU Agencies.
107. 'Parliamentary oversight of security and intelligence agencies in the European Union' (Study), EP 2011, p. 52 – available at: < http://www.europarl.europa.eu/document/activities/cont/20 1109/20110927ATT27674/20110927ATT27674EN.pdf (accessed on 5 February 2013).
108. See Art. 1(1) of Council Regulation 2007/2004, *supra* n. 105.
109. See J.J. Rijpma, 'Hybrid Agencification in the Area of Freedom, Security and Justice and its Inherent Tensions: The Case of Frontex', in *The Agency Phenomenon in the European Union: Emergence, Institutionalisation and Everyday Decision-making*, eds. M. Busuioc, M. Groenleer & J. Trondal (Manchester: Manchester University Press, 2012), 87–88. See also S. Peers, 'The European Union's Area of freedom, security and justice architecture after the Lisbon Treaty', in *Parliamentary Oversight of Security and Intelligence Agencies in the European Union*, Study European Parliament, 2011, at 400.

cooperation with international organizations, while Article 14 regulates the interactions between Frontex and third countries and their competent authorities. In the 2004 founding act, Frontex's international cooperation provisions with international organizations and third countries organizations were drafted similarly. In both cases, international cooperation would be '...in accordance with the relevant provisions of the Treaty', and the 'working arrangement' was the preferred instrument to formalize such cooperation. There were also differences between the two categories of subjects. The working arrangements with international organizations also had to be concluded in compliance with the provisions on the competences of the relevant international organization. Conversely, in its relations with third countries, the Agency was also asked '...to facilitate the operational cooperation between the Member States and third countries in the framework of the EU external relations policy'.

Article 14(1) states explicitly that one of the aims of the cooperation entered into by Frontex with third countries is '...to promote European border management standards'. Next, the scope of the working arrangements concluded with competent third country authorities are clearly limited '...to the management of operational cooperation.'[110] Furthermore, Frontex is allowed to deploy liaison officers in third countries and to receive liaison officers from third countries.[111] Additionally, express provision is made for the Agency to launch and finance, within the scope of its mandate, technical assistance projects in third countries.[112] Next, the peculiar position of Frontex in the management of external border areas is illustrated by Article 14(7). This provision allows the Member States to include provisions on the competence of the Agency in bilateral agreements with third countries on operational cooperation at external borders. Last but not least, the 2011 amendment makes the conclusion of the working arrangements with third countries, as well as the decisions regarding the deployment/receiving of liaison officers, dependent on the prior opinion of the Commission and full information of the European Parliament.[113]

In practice, Frontex has established numerous working arrangements with third countries under different headings. According, to its website and activity reports,[114] by June 2012, Frontex had concluded working arrangements (or similar formalized cooperation instruments) with a number of competent authorities of third countries.[115]

---

110. Art. 14(2) of Frontex founding regulation, *supra* n. 105.
111. Art. 14(3)–(4) of Frontex founding regulation, *supra* n. 105.
112. Art. 14(5) of Frontex founding regulation, *supra* n. 105.
113. Art. 14(8) of Frontex founding regulation, *supra* n. 105.
114. It appears that a Memorandum of cooperation has been concluded by Frontex with the Swiss competent authority on 4 June 2007, but this is not mentioned on Frontex website. However, this memorandum is considered as redundant because Switzerland is now participating in the Schengen acquis – see J.J. Rijpma, *Building Borders: The Regulatory Framework for the Management of the External Borders of the European Union* (PhD thesis, Florence: European University Institute, 2009), 333.
115. Viz. the Russian Federation, Ukraine, Croatia, Moldova, Georgia, the Former Yugoslav Republic of Macedonia (FYROM), Serbia, Albania, Bosnia and Herzegovina, the United States, Montenegro, Belarus, Canada, Cape Verde, Nigeria, Armenia and Turkey. Furthermore, the Agency has also concluded working arrangements with the CIS Border Troop Commanders Council and the MARRI Regional Centre in the Western Balkans, but these entities are given apparently a slightly different status as the cooperation instruments are concluded under.

Similar to other agencies, the cooperation instruments concluded by Frontex bear various labels.[116] However, in spite of the diversity in the labels of instruments, it appears that all these instruments are seen by Frontex as 'working arrangements' under Articles 13–14 of the founding act.[117] Furthermore in terms of content, the working arrangements with the competent authorities of third countries explicitly set the framework for cooperation between Frontex and its partners. More specifically, these instruments provide for cooperation in operational activities, the launching of and participation in common projects, technical assistance (for example, trainings and research), exchange of information and best practices, deployment of liaison officers, etc.[118]

Of great relevance is that the working agreements or memoranda of cooperation concluded by Frontex routinely include a sentence stating that they do not constitute an international agreement and they do not fulfil international obligations of the EU.[119] Consequently, these international cooperation instruments concluded by Frontex with third countries are not legally binding under international law and will be considered guidelines or soft law which do not violate EU primary law.

Art. 13 of Frontex founding act. See the official website of Frontex, < http://www.Frontex.eur opa.eu/partners/third-countries > (accessed on 5 February 2013). See also Frontex's General Report 2009, < http://www.frontex.europa.eu/assets/About_Frontex/Governance _documents/Annual_report/2009/gen_rep_2009_en.pdf >, p. 9–10 (accessed on 5 February 2013); Frontex's General Report 2010, < http://www.frontex.europa.eu/assets/About_ Frontex/Governance_documents/Annual_report/2010/frontex_general_report_2010.pdf >, p. 10 (accessed on 5 February 2013); Frontex's General Report 2011, < http://www.fro ntex.europa.eu/assets/About_Frontex/Governance_documents/Annual_report/2011/General _Report_2011.pdf >, pp. 13–14 (accessed on 5 February 2013).

116. These range from 'working arrangement' (e.g., Ukrainian competent authority) to 'memoran-dum of cooperation' (e.g., Switzerland), 'memorandum of understanding' (e.g., Turkey), 'terms of reference' (e.g., Russian Federation) – see Frontex general activity reports 2009, 2010 and 2011, *supra* n. 115.

117. See for instance, Frontex press release on the working arrangement with UNODC where it is stated that that was the sixth international organization with which the Agency concluded a working arrangements (although in the case of IOM and ICPMD the instruments concluded are labelled differently) – < http://www.Frontex.europa.eu/news/Frontex-signs-working-arrange ment-with-unodc-4JlIBZ > (accessed on 5 February 2013). See also Frontex webpage on cooperation with third countries, where the list of third states with whom working arrange-ments have been concluded includes all the partners of Frontex regardless of the label used for each specific instrument – < http://www.Frontex.europa.eu/partners/third-countries > (ac-cessed on 5 February 2013).

118. See also *Parliamentary oversight of security and intelligence agencies in the European Union* (Study), *supra*, n. 107, p. 54.

119. See for instance, Terms of reference on the establishment of operational co-operation between European Agency for the Management of Operational Cooperation at the External Borders of the Member States of the European Union (Frontex) and the Border Guard Service of the Federal Security Service of the Russian Federation done on 14 September 2006, pct. 6; Working arrangement establishing operational cooperation between European Agency for the Manage-ment of Operational Cooperation at the External Borders of the Member States of the European Union (Frontex) and the National Security Council of the Republic of Armenia done on 22 February 2012, pct. 6; Working arrangement establishing operational cooperation between European Agency for the Management of Operational Cooperation at the External Borders of the Member States of the European Union (Frontex) and the Ministry of Internal Affairs of the Former Yugoslav Republic of Macedonia done on 19 January 2009, pct. 7.

[C]   Category 3: General Mandate for International Action

As the Annex on the typology of EU agencies in view of their external relations powers demonstrates, the vast majority of agencies have a general mandate to cooperate with third countries and/or international organizations without any specification of supervision in the sense of prior consultation or prior approval. Looking at the practice of some of these agencies we find that activities include foremost collaboration on technical and administrative aspects, exchanges of information (including specific confidentiality arrangements sometimes), trainings and workshops.

Agencies like EFSA and EMA have been very careful in designing their cooperation with their international partners. As far as we can oversee it, all acts of cooperation contain an explicit statement that the acts do not create legally binding obligations.[120] This practice has been formalized for the three European Supervisory Authorities, of which the founding regulations explicitly stipulate that administrative arrangements concluded by the agencies cannot create legal obligations for the EU and the Member States.[121] At the same time, these arrangements cannot prevent Member States and their competent authorities from concluding bilateral or multilateral arrangements with third countries.[122] Accordingly, EBA, ESMA and EIOPA are entitled to establish relations and to conclude formalized cooperation instruments called 'administrative arrangements' with international organizations and with the administrations of third countries but these arrangements cannot create legal obligations for the EU and the Member States. Consequently the international actions taken by the three supervisory

---

120. See for instance, the Memorandum of Cooperation between Food Safety Commission of Japan and European Food Safety Authority, signed on 4–7 December 2009, pct. 1(2) available on EFSA's website < http://www.efsa.europa.eu/en/networks/international.htm > (accessed on 5 February 2012). As regards EMA, see Cooperation between the Pharmaceutical Inspection Co-operation Scheme and the European Medicines Agency signed on 28 December 2010 available on EMA's website: < http://www.ema.europa.eu/docs/en_GB/document_library/Other/2011/02/WC500102054.pdf > (accessed on 5 February 2012) and the Exchange of Letters between the Food and Drug Administration (FDA) of the United States of America (US), on the one side, and the European Commission (in its pharmaceutical regulation capacity) and the European Agency for the Evaluation of Medicinal Products (EMEA) on 12 September 2003, available on EMA's website: < http://www.ema.europa.eu/ema/index.jsp?curl=pages/part ners_and_networks/document_listing/document_listing_000228.jsp&mid=WC0b01ac058003 176e > (accessed on 5 February 2012).
121. See the identically worded Art. 33 of Regulation (EU) 1093/2010 of the European Parliament and of the Council of 24 November 2010 establishing a European Supervisory Authority (European Banking Authority), amending Decision No. 716/2009/EC and repealing Commission Decision 2009/78/EC [2010] OJ L331/12 (EBA's founding regulation); Art. 33 of Regulation (EU) 1094/2010 of the European Parliament and of the Council of 24 November 2010 establishing a European Supervisory Authority (European Insurance and Occupational Pensions Authority), amending Decision No. 716/2009/EC and repealing Commission Decision 2009/79/EC (EIOPA's founding regulation) (OJ 2010 L331, p. 48); and Art. 33 of Regulation (EU) 1095/2010 of the European Parliament and of the Council of 24 November 2010 establishing a European Supervisory Authority (European Securities and Markets Authority), amending Decision 716/2009/EC and repealing Commission Decision 2009/77/EC of the European Parliament and of the Council of 24 November 2010 establishing a European Securities and Markets Authority (OJ 2010 L331, p. 84) (ESMA's founding regulation).
122. *Ibid.*

authorities with third country authorities cannot be considered as binding international law and consequently do not upset the EU's institutional balance.

As we pointed out above, Frontex has concluded working arrangements or similar formalized cooperation instruments with a variety of international organizations such as with United Nations Commissioner of Refugees (UNHCR),[123] Interpol,[124] International Organization for Migration (IOM),[125] International Center for Migration Policy Development (ICMPD),[126] Democratic Control of Armed Forces (DCAF) based in Switzerland,[127] and with UNODC.[128]

It is important to note that the working arrangements Frontex concludes with international organizations – in difference to the ones concluded with third countries discussed above – do not include such a clear statement about their international legal statement and it could be questioned whether some of them can be considered international agreements. This might be not relevant in so many cases as for example, the case of a working arrangement, the Geneva Centre for the DCAF demonstrates. The Centre is first of all established under private law and consequently not equipped with international law capacity. This criterion already excludes an international agreement. In the case of a working arrangement with Interpol, this is different. Interpol is an international organization but its legal status is still disputed as it has not been established by an international agreement between its members.[129] As regards its wording, this arrangement seems to be similar to an international agreement but Frontex's action is not legitimized by the Founding Regulation through an approval by the Commission, just like for actions of category 1 agencies. Instead the Commission is only consulted. Hence, this seems to be a binding action that is breaching EU primary law (Articles 218 and 220 TFEU) and the *Meroni* doctrine, as contrary to the Commission's role vis-à-vis EASA actions, the role of the Commission in these actions is not clarified.

§5.05 AGENCIES GLOBAL ACTIVITIES: OVERALL ANALYSIS

Our analysis of the global practice of the various agencies reveals that not all three categories of agencies will give rise to legal difficulties in the sense that they would or could create international binding agreements. Hereby our categorization of agencies' activities and powers in the global scene and the differentiation into EU and international law are key.

Our analysis of the international mandates of the agencies laid down in the founding regulations reveals that the legislator has over the years become much more

---

123. According to Frontex's General Report 2010, *supra* n. 115, p. 11.
124. According to Frontex's General Report 2009, *supra* n. 115, p. 11.
125. According to Frontex's General Report 2009, *supra* n. 115, p. 11.
126. See Frontex press release on 29 June 2009 – < http://www.Frontex.europa.eu/news/Frontex-s-cooperation-with-icmpd-enters-into-force-phjFME > (accessed on 5 February 2013).
127. According to Frontex's General Report 2011, *supra* n. 115, p. 14.
128. See Frontex press release on 23 April 2012 – < http://www.Frontex.europa.eu/news/Frontex-signs-working-arrangement-with-unodc-4JliBZ > (accessed on 5 February 2013).
129. Schermers & Blokker, *supra* n. 36, at 40.

aware that a careful drafting of the external relations' tasks of agencies is required to prevent misunderstandings and/or legal uncertainties. This is also recognized by the Joint statement of the European Parliament, the Council of the EU and the European Commission on decentralized agencies added to the Common Approach to agencies as adopted in June 2012.[130] According to this document the agencies' international relations should be streamlined and the strategy worked out with the partner DGs in the Commission should ensure that agencies are not seen as representing the EU position to an outside audience or as committing the EU to international obligations.

The provisions in relation to the new supervisory authorities in the financial sector, discussed above, clearly indicate that they want to prevent the impression that international agreements are drafted by agencies. For category 1 agencies CEPOL, EUROJUST, and Europol, the founding regulations have no difficulty in referring to 'agreements'. This could be explained by the fact that this category of agency anyway requires prior approval by the Council and therefore falls under the supervision of the classical organ engaged in EU external relations. Furthermore, in the case of Europol, we are confronted with a former international organization with an independent international legal status to conclude international agreements.

Importantly, the analysis of all provisions on EU agencies international cooperation reveals that most provisions reflect the general legal constraint that these actions based on secondary law are not allowed to infringe primary law.[131] As argued above (section §5.04), such actions cannot violate the institutional balance and especially not the institutional balance established in EU external relations.

[A]   EU Law Perspective

From an EU law perspective, agencies' global action need to be in conformity with the principle of institutional balance of powers and the limits set by the Court in its *Meroni* and *Romano* case law and the Treaty norms of Articles 218 and 220 TFEU. The examples of category 2 and 3 agencies show that these actions will not be approved by the Commission or Council but also do not create binding international agreements as this is stated clearly in various working arrangements concluded by Frontex in relation to third countries.

More problematic are the agencies discussed in categories 1 and 3. For category 1, we have argued that this chain of approval could imply that Commission and Council have mandated agencies EASA and Europol to act in the international field. In category 3, Frontex cooperation arrangements with international organizations do not include any statement on their legal status. They could be considered exceptionally as international agreements but then have no mandated chain of approval by the

---

130. Common Approach annexed to the Joint Statement of the European Parliament, the Council of the EU and the European Commission on Decentralized Agencies of 19 July 2012, *supra* n. 13, pct. 25. See Annex 2 to this book.
131. This is formulated in some of the rules in the founding regulations that international cooperation needs to comply with relevant Treaty norms.

Commission. Frontex would act on its own and Frontex has no independent international legal personality. Nevertheless, the analysis under international law would depend on the interpretation of Article 46 VCLT.

In category 1, Europol acts, having come from a different background. It is a more privileged agency looking at its development history and its approval deriving from the Council. The Council maintains full responsibility so that we can argue that no true delegation to this agency has taken place.[132] However, when Europol is able to conclude international agreements on behalf of the Union, without restrictions, then this also needs to be controlled further by the Parliament as otherwise it can argued to be a circumvention of the institutional balance enshrined in Article 218 TFEU.

[B]   International Law Perspective

In the case of EASA, we have explained that, exceptionally, a few arrangements could be considered international agreements. This is the case for the agreement concluded with the IAC whereas binding arrangements with third countries would at the same time violate EU law principles if it is not argued that these arrangements are mandated directly by Member States. In the case of Frontex, this agency can conclude an international agreement with international organizations under the condition that their international partner is able to act on the international plan and the wording of such an arrangement gives rise to the interpretation that it is intended to be legally binding. The consequences of this discrepancy between the EU law status and international law need to be determined by principles of interpretation developed under the VCLT. Violations of internal rules can only be invoked against a contracting party in cases of manifest infringement and in the case of an internal rule of fundamental importance. However, whether breaches of Article 218 TFEU are of fundamental importance in the sense of Article 46 VCLT is doubtful due to strict criteria established by this Article.

§5.06   CONCLUSIONS

Our analysis shows that external actions of EU agencies can have different implications depending on the wording in the founding regulations, their institutional background and the practice developing with third countries and international organizations. Legal uncertainty exists for the external action of these agencies as they differ in mandate, international partners and instruments of action. Our analysis of some of the provisions and practice shows that the majority of EU agencies does not and cannot conclude international agreements and will make this clear to their international counterparts.

It has been stressed that in practice these activities of agencies are not perceived as problematic.[133] However, this could be explained by a simplified assumption that we are not dealing with international agreements at all, which is contradicted already by

---

132. See Case 9/56, *Meroni, supra* n. 63, 147–149 and Case 10/56, *Meroni, supra* n. 63, 169–171. See section §5.03[A] of this contribution.
133. Coman-Kund, *supra* n. 7, at 367.

Europol's status under EU law and its scope of activities. Also in the case of EASA as global actor difficulties persist. The agency's activities give the impression that this agency wants to conclude binding commitments with third countries administrative bodies and international organizations but they can only do so if these arrangements are recognized as international agreements.

The 2012 Common Approach on decentralized agencies recognizes the importance and complexity in these fields and emphasizes a streamlining of agencies' international relations. However, we argue that a general streamlining of agencies in this respect is counterproductive in view of the different tasks and ways of control of agencies laid down in their founding regulations. Therefore, agencies' international activities should be examined on the basis of the typology developed in this contribution in combination with the nature of tasks conferred upon the agencies. Depending on the nature of acts that agencies conclude, the rights of European Parliament need to be strengthened as required by Article 218 TFEU. This is clearly the case in relation to agreements concluded by Europol. As for the majority of the Frontex and EASA working arrangements we concluded that no international agreement is produced but that we are confronted with soft law which is not binding on the parties from the perspective of international law. The past practice in some Member States such as France of creating their own category of administrative agreements of binding nature has been denied for the EU by literature[134] and Advocate General Tesauro in the case *France v. Commission* until now.[135] According to the evolution in EU and international law, the majority of non-binding arrangements concluded by agencies with third countries and international bodies escape judicial scrutiny for the lack of intent to produce legal effect, while the European Parliament would not be able to monitor them nor a legal review would be possible. For the few agreements which can be considered international legally binding, their effect in EU law depends on which institution approves the action. While in case of prior Council approval, this is relatively straightforward and results in no further problem under the condition that the rights of the European Parliament are observed, the approval by the Commission requires a closer in-depth look as exemplified in the example of EASA.

It seems that traditional concepts of international law, constitutional law and administrative law need to be re-adapted for the demands of a fast developing reality of new emerging global actors. This is addressed in the new debate about global administrative law which discusses practices of public bodies or international organizations which act internationally outside international law but will produce normative effects in the international sphere.[136] However, this new branch of research is currently primarily busy categorizing such new developments[137] and cannot provide concrete

---

134. P. Eeckhout, *EU External Relations Law*, 2nd edn. (Oxford: Oxford University Press 2011), 206–207.
135. Opinion of AG Tesauro, *supra* n. 15.
136. B. Kingsbury & L. Casini, 'Global Administrative Law of International Organisations Law', *International Organisations Review* 6 (2009): 324.
137. B. Kingsbury, N. Krisch & R.B. Stewart, 'The Emergence of Global Administrative Law', *New York University Public Law and Legal Theory Working Papers*, 2005, Paper 17, < http://lsr. nellco.org/nyu_plltwp/17 > (accessed on 5 February 2013); S. Cassese, 'Administrative Law

answers yet. Hereby global administrative law does not necessarily result in a common approach, but it suggests that experiences in national administrative law need to be taken into account. This current discussion relates to international administrative law concepts of the nineteenth century in which an idea of transnational governance already appears with distinctive administrative law principles.[138] Until this can be achieved, EU agencies' ever-growing activities in global governance will continue to challenge the existing understanding of institutional balance, international legal actors and treaty-making instruments. They require more attention and legal scrutiny with a necessary flexibility in an ever-changing international environment.

Without the State? The Challenge of Global Regulation', *New York University Journal of International Law and Politics* 37 (2005): 663; B. Kingsbury & L. Casini, 'Global Administrative Law Dimensions of International Organisations Law', *New York University Public law and Legal Theory Working Papers*, 2010; E. Chiti & R. Wessel, 'The Emergence of International Agencies in the Global Administrative Space: Autonomous Actors or State Servants?', in *International Organizations and the Idea of Autonomy: Institutional Independence in the International Legal Order*, eds. R. Collin & R.D. White (Oxon: Routledge, 2011), 142–159.
138. See on this M. Ruffert & C. Walter, *Institutionalisiertes Völkerrecht* (Munich: Beck Publisher, 2009), 219 and Kingsbury & Casini, *supra* n. 136, at 327.

ANNEX

TYPOLOGY OF EU AGENCIES IN VIEW OF THEIR EXTERNAL RELATIONS POWERS
(BASED ON THE CRITERION OF CONTROL/SUPERVISION OVER THEIR LEGAL
INSTRUMENTS FOR INTERNATIONAL COOPERATION ACCORDING TO THE
PROVISIONS OF THEIR FOUNDING ACTS)*

Agency	Category 1 Prior approval by the Council or by the Commission	Category 2 Prior Commission consultation	Category 3 No express provision for Commission or Council supervision / controls
Agency for the Cooperation of Energy Regulators (ACER)	-	-	Article 19 of Regulation (EU) 1227/2011
European Centre for the Development of Vocational Training (Cedefop)	-	-	Article 3(2) of Regulation (EEC) 337/1975
European Police College (CEPOL)	Council approval for cooperation agreements – Article 8(3) of Decision 2005/681/JHA	-	-
European Aviation Safety Agency (EASA)	Commission approval for working arrangements – Article 27 of Regulation (EC) 216/2008	-	-
European Asylum Support Office (EASO)	-	-	Articles 49–50 and 52 of Regulation (EU) 439/2010
European Banking Authority (EBA)	-	-	Article 33 of Regulation (EU) 1093/2010

Agency	Category 1 Prior approval by the Council or by the Commission	Category 2 Prior Commission consultation	Category 3 No express provision for Commission or Council supervision / controls
European Centre for Disease Prevention and Control (ECDC)	-	-	Articles 9 and 11 (2) of Regulation (EC) 851/2004
European Chemicals Agency (ECHA)	-	-	Articles 77 and 120 of Regulation (EC) 1907/2006
European Environment Agency (EEA)	-	-	Articles 2 and 15 of Regulation (EC) 401/2009
European Fisheries Control Agency (EFCA)	-	-	Article 4 of Council Regulation (EC) 768/2005
European Food Safety Authority (EFSA)	-	-	Articles 23 and 33 of Regulation (EC) 178/2002
European Institute for Gender Equality (EIGE)	-	-	Articles 4(5) and 8 of Regulation (EC) 1922/2006
European Insurance and Occupational Pensions Authority (EIOPA)	-	-	Article 33 of Regulation (EU) 1094/2010
European Medicines Agency (EMA)	-	-	Articles 28c(1), 28d, 52, 57(1), 58 of Regulation (EC) 726/2004

Agency	Category 1 Prior approval by the Council or by the Commission	Category 2 Prior Commission consultation	Category 3 No express provision for Commission or Council supervision / controls
European Monitoring Centre for Drugs and Drug Addiction (EMCDDA)	-	Prior Commission opinion for working arrangements – Article 20 of Regulation (EC) 1920/2006	
European Maritime Safety Agency (EMSA)	-	-	Article 2 of Regulation (EC) 1406/2002
European Network and Information Security Agency (ENISA)	-	-	Article 3 of Regulation (EC) 460/2004
European Railway Agency (ERA)	-	-	Article 1 of Regulation (EC) 881/2004
European Securities and Markets Authority (ESMA)	-	-	Article 33 of Regulation (EU) 1095/2010
European Training Foundation (ETF)	-	Prior Commission opinion for co-operation agreements (containing working arrangements) – Article 3(6) of Regulation (EC) 1339/2008	-
European Agency for Safety and Health at Work (EU-OSHA)	-	-	Article 3(1) of Regulation (EC) 2062/1994

Agency	Category 1 Prior approval by the Council or by the Commission	Category 2 Prior Commission consultation	Category 3 No express provision for Commission or Council supervision / controls
European Foundation for the Improvement of Living and Working Conditions (EUROFOUND)	-	-	Article 3(2) of Regulation (EEC) 1365/1975
The European Union's Judicial Cooperation Unit (EUROJUST)	Council approval for agreements – Article 26a of Decision 2002/187/JHA		
European Police Office (EUROPOL)	Council approval for agreements – Article 23 of Decision 2009/371/JHA		
European Union Agency for Fundamental Rights (FRA)		Prior Commission opinion for administrative arrangements – Article 8(3) of Regulation (EC) 168/2007	
European Agency for the Management of Operational Cooperation at the External Borders (FRONTEX)		Prior Commission opinion for working arrangements with third countries– Article 14 of Regulation (EC) 2007/2004	Working arrangements with international organisations – Article 13 of Regulation (EC) 2007/2004
Office for Harmonisation in the Internal Market (Trade Marks and Designs) (OHIM)	-	-	Title XIII 'International Registration of Marks' of Regulation (EC) 207/2009

* Please note that the following EU agencies have been deliberately excluded from this typology: Body of European Regulators for Electronic Communications (BEREC); Community Plant Variety Office (CPVO); European GNSS Agency (GSA); and the European Agency for the operational management of large-scale IT systems in the area of freedom, security and justice (IT Agency) as their founding acts do not contain explicit provisions on the external powers/tasks of these bodies.

CHAPTER 6

The New European Supervisory Architecture of the Financial Markets

Annetje Ottow

§6.01 INTRODUCTION

The financial supervisory landscape changed dramatically on 1 January 2011, when the European networks of national regulatory authorities were converted into independent, European supervisors. This transformation was a first step towards more Europeanization of the supervision on financial markets. Although the national supervisory authorities have retained primary responsibility for supervising financial institutions in line with the home country model, these new European authorities are given independent powers to intervene at a national level.

And a new move towards greater Europeanization and centralization is clearly underway. Recently, it has been decided for the banking sector to establish a Single Supervisory Mechanism (SSM), where the supervisory tasks of the national supervisors will be taken over by the European Central Bank (ECB) in relation to significant banks.[1] The primary responsibility for supervising a significant part of the banking activities in the Euro zone will be in the hands of the ECB. This new system is setting aside – as far as the Euro zone is concerned – the old home country control model and causes a significant shift in the case of supervisory tasks from a national to a European level. Although the national banking authorities remain actively involved in the day-to-day practice, a real transfer of powers from the national to the European level

---

1. Memo European Commission, Brussels, 10 September 2012, MEMO 12/12/656. This proposal has been revised in the Proposal for a Council regulation conferring specific tasks on the European central Bank concerning policies relating to the prudential supervision of credit institutions – Presidence compromise, 3 December 2012, 2012/0242 (CNS), EF 287 ECOFIN 1011 (not officially published). This contribution is based on this new compromise. However, many details are yet unknown and (substantial) changes might be introduced in a later stage.

will take place. These developments make the European supervisory landscape highly complex, with an entwining of European and national authorities. It can be expected that this Europeanization process will also occur in other financial areas in the near future.

This chapter examines this new supervisory structure for the financial sectors and the way in which powers are divided between European and national authorities.

§6.02   EUROPEANIZATION: THE NEW TREND

Over the past two decades, the Member States have seen many different market regulators being set up under the influence of European law. Market liberalization has resulted in regulatory authorities being created for the purposes of monitoring the liberalization process and promoting competition. These authorities play a key role in implementing and enforcing European rules. As the parties responsible for overseeing the national markets, they have to ensure that the decisions they take result in European legislation being applied correctly. Indeed national implementation practices are to a large degree 'coloured' by the specific features of the various national systems and the implementation practices of the national regulators. It is not only the powers assigned to the national regulators, but also the applicable rules on decision making, the powers of enforcement and the supervisory practices that have a critical influence on the way in which national regulators perform the tasks entrusted to them. Although there are similarities between national practices, there are also major differences and these lead to disparities in the way the applicable European rules are implemented. In the absence of minimum or maximum harmonization standards,[2] this can result in a downward spiral, with disparities distorting competition within the internal market. From this perspective, this reliance on correct national implementation can be seen as a major shortcoming in the European legislative system.[3]

Although the work of these national regulatory authorities is based on the principle of Member States' institutional and procedural autonomy, European law has a major impact on their activities and the way in which they operate.[4] This 'Europeanization' is multi-faceted and does not always manifest in the same way in the various sectors.[5] In addition to the influence of European law at the national level, various European networks of national regulators have also been set up over the years and are

---

2. On the harmonization of financial regulation, see, for example, G. Hertig, 'Regulatory Competition for EU Financial Services', *Journal of International Economic Law* (2000): 349–375.
3. R. Baldwin & M. Cave, *Understanding Regulation* (Oxford: Oxford University Press, 1999), 159; R. Baldwin et al., *Understanding regulation. Theory, Strategy and Practice* (Oxford: Oxford University Press, 2012), 388–408 and J.H. Jans et al., *Europeanisation of Public Law* (Groningen: Europa Law Publishing, 2007), 200–201.
4. For a discussion of the European influence on the legality principle via European Court of Justice (ECJ) case law and various European sector directives, see S. Lavrijssen & A.T. Ottow, 'The Legality of Independent Regulatory Authorities', in eds. L.F.M. Besselink, F. Pennings & S. Prechal, *The Eclipse of Legality Principle in the European Union* (The Hague: Kluwer Law International, 2010), 73–96.
5. A.T. Ottow, 'The Europeanisation of Supervision of Competitive Markets', *European Public Law*, no. 1 (2012): 191–221.

playing a role in the further harmonization, implementation, and enforcement of European law. A recent development has been the transformation of these networks into ESAs alongside the national regulatory authorities and to which are being assigned centralized, European powers. These developments make the European regulatory landscape highly complex, with an entwining of national and European authorities.

This chapter focuses on this process of recently accomplished Europeanization in the financial markets. In section §6.03 the original home state control mechanism of the financial directives will be set out. This system formed the basis of the financial supervision regime but is currently dismantled for the banking sector. In section §6.04 the old networks of the national regulatory authorities and the Lamfalussy process will be explained, as these structures also formed the building blocks for the setting-up of the new ESAs. These new authorities will be sketched out in section §6.05. With the proposed introduction of the SSM for the banking sector in 2013, the ECB will play a central role for the supervision of banks in the Euro zone. A new supervisory division of the ECB, separated from its monetary functions, will be established.[6] This new SSM will also be explained in section §6.05. The powers of these new institutions will be dealt with in section §6.06 and the institutional structure in section §6.07. Special attention is given to the *Meroni* issues in section §6.08 and the enforcement powers in section §6.09.

§6.03 THE ORIGINAL STARTING POINT: NATIONAL SUPERVISION ('HOME STATE CONTROL MODEL')

Until recently, European supervision was based wholly on the system of home state control. Financial directives, including the Banking Directive,[7] operated on the basis of a system whereby a bank licensed by a European Member State was permitted to establish a branch in another Member State without having to apply for a new licence. The licence issued by the home state operated as a 'European passport';[8] the host Member State was not permitted to require national authorization for a branch of a credit institution that had already been granted a licence in another Member State.[9] For supervision, the opportunities in the host Member State were also limited, as the

---

6. Communication from the Commission to the European Parliament and the Council. A roadmap towards a Banking Union. Brussels, 12 September 2012, COM(2012) 510 final; Proposal for a Council regulation conferring specific tasks on the European Central Bank concerning policies relating to the prudential supervision of credit institutions, Brussels, 12 September 2012, COM(2012) 511 final; Proposal for a regulation of the European Parliament and of the Council amending Regulation (EU) No. 1093/2010 establishing a European Supervisory Authority (European Banking Authority) as regards its interaction with Council Regulation (EU) No. .../... conferring special tasks on the European Central Bank concerning policies relating to the prudential supervision of credit institutions, Brussels 12 September 2012, COM(2012) 512 final.
7. Directive 2006/48/EC of the European Parliament and of the Council of 14 June 2006 relating to the taking up and pursuit of the business of credit institutions (recast), OJ EU 2006, L177, pp. 1–200 (the 'recast Banking Directive').
8. De *bevoegdheden van de Nederlandsche Bank inzake Icesave* (The authority of the Dutch Central Bank in the case of Icesave). Research by A.J.C. de Moor-Van Vugt & C.E. du Perron for the Ministry of Finance, 11 June 2009, 13 (report on the Icesave Affair).
9. Art. 16 recast Banking Directive.

national regulator in the host country was only entitled to supervise the branch's liquidity,[10] while the competent regulatory authority in the home state was responsible for prudent supervision of the credit institution as a whole.[11] This system contributed greatly to the liberalization and internationalization of national financial markets. The European financial directives impose requirements on national supervision and set rules for harmonization.

This system stood or fell with the quality of the national supervisory system and was based on the assumption of mutual confidence between the regulators. National regulatory authorities were highly reliant on each other as they based themselves on each other's supervision and needed to be able to rely on the other party's quality and reliability. It is this aspect that formed a weak link in the chain of European supervision. As the credit crisis demonstrated, mutual confidence was not automatically present and could result in an enforcement deficit, with too little supervision to ensure correct application of European rules.[12] Various reports, including the well-known *De Larosière* report,[13] compiled in response to the financial crisis, highlighted that the system of home state control, which relied solely on national supervision, was no longer 'fit for purpose' in an increasingly internationalized market. The supervisory structures proved unable to evolve in line with market dynamics, and greater coordination and a more extensive cross-border approach were needed,[14] as illustrated by the 'Icesave affair'.[15] The Icesave Report examines the extent of the powers that were available to the Dutch Central Bank ('DNB') in respect of the Icelandic bank Icesave's (online) banking activities in the Netherlands. Icesave's head office was in Iceland and the bank's activities in the Netherlands were performed through a branch. The reporters concluded that the system of the European passport and the Banking Directive[16] meant that the regulatory body in the host state (in this case, DNB) had only limited powers. As soon as the host state regulator deems measures to be necessary that extend beyond supervision of the branch's liquidity, it requires the cooperation of the regulatory body in the home state (in this case, the Icelandic regulator FME).[17] The report's conclusions included the view that the European system needed to be

---

10. Art. 41 recast Banking Directive.
11. Art. 40 recast Banking Directive.
12. For a discussion of the European enforcement deficit, see, for example, A.T. Ottow, *Supervising Telecommunications. The Influence of European and Dutch Administrative Procedural Law (Telecommunicatietoezicht, de invloed van het Europese en Nederlandse bestuurs(proces)recht)* (The Hague: SDU, 2006), 171–173.
13. *De Larosière report* (high-level group on financial supervision in the EU, chaired by Jacques de Larosière), Brussels, 25 February 2009, and *The Turner Review: A Regulatory Response to the Global Banking Crisis*, Financial Services Authority, London, March 2009.
14. Communication from the Commission, *European Financial Supervision*, Brussels, 27 May 2009, COM(2009) 252 final, p. 2. Cf. *De Larosière report*, 41 ('led to an erosion of mutual confidence among supervisors') and 72 ('distrust between supervisors').
15. *De bevoegdheden van de Nederlandsche Bank inzake Icesave* (The authority of the Dutch Central Bank in the case of Icesave). Research by A.J.C. de Moor-Van Vugt & C.E. du Perron for the Ministry of Finance, 11 June 2009. See also the report (in Dutch) of the De Wit Parliamentary Commission on the Icesave affair, *Parliamentary Papers II*, 2009–2010, 31 980, no. 4.
16. Arts 29–37 recast Banking Directive (Directive 2006/48/EC).
17. Report on the Icesave affair, 31.

amended so as to allow regulatory authorities in the host state greater powers to intervene.[18]

§6.04 OLD NETWORKS OF NATIONAL REGULATORY AUTHORITIES AND THE LAMFALUSSY PROCESS

As explained above, cooperation between the national regulatory authorities played a vital role in determining the success of the system in the home state control model. Over the years this cooperation was channelled via European networks of national regulatory authorities. In the case of the financial sectors, this involved the following networks:

- CESR (Committee of European Securities Regulators).
- CEBS (Committee of European Banking Supervisors).
- CEIOPS (Committee of European Insurance and Occupational Pensions Supervisors).

These networks played a vital role in the European harmonization process and constituted an important building block in the process of integrating the financial markets.[19] All these networks are (or were) structured along similar lines, albeit one more informally than the other. Although the various networks have differing objectives, their key aim is to facilitate the exchange of information between national regulators. Essentially the tasks of the various networks can be divided into three categories: expertise, coordination, and peer review.

The networks were the result of the wish to achieve greater cooperation within the EU, in line with the obligation under Article 10 of the EC Treaty (now, after amendment, Article 4.3 of Treaty on EU) to work together loyally to facilitate the achievement of the agreed Treaty objectives. Rather than seeking to establish a comprehensive alternative for European supervision, the purpose of these networks was to achieve closer alignment of national regulatory authorities and practices. The way in which these networks worked together was complex, informal, and not always transparent,[20] with national interests playing a role and the application of European directives not always proceeding smoothly.[21] Nevertheless, the harmonizing effect – whether formal or informal – that these networks have had on national application practices should not be underestimated.[22] National regulators looked to each other in

---

18. Report on the Icesave affair, 69.
19. For the various tasks of these networks, see Ottow, *supra* n. 4.
20. S. Lavrijssen & L. Hancher, 'Europese regulators in de netwerksectoren: Revolutie of evolutie?', *SEW* no. 11 (2007): 447–463.
21. See, for example, the critical comments by the CESR in its 2004 report: CESR, Preliminary Progress Report 'Which supervisory tools for the securities markets? An analytical paper by CESR', October 2004, Ref. No. 04-333f, 18.
22. N. Moloney, 'EU Financial Market Regulation after the Global Financial Crisis: "More Europe" or More Risks?', *Common Market Law Review* 47 (2010): 1364, which refers to various CESR examples in which the network informally influenced harmonisation: 'some progress was, however, being made in drilling beneath the rules.'

the event of new developments or to see how rules are being applied and followed the guidelines and recommendations issued within the network. These networks played an important role in the 'Lamfalussy process',[23] a decision-making process for financial regulation at four different levels that was introduced in 2001.[24] The Lamfalussy process set out to create a mechanism for, on the one hand, achieving convergence of supervisory practices in the European financial sector and, on the other hand, for ensuring that Community legislation on financial services was able to respond quickly and flexibly to developments in the financial markets.

Under this process financial regulation is passed at four levels.[25] Level one of the Lamfalussy process comprises a framework directive issued under the normal legislative procedures provided for in Article 294 TFEU.[26] This framework directive sets out core principles, without going into any further detail. At level two the technical details are elaborated and the Commission proposes implementing measures. These proposals are submitted to the European Parliament and the Council of Ministers ('the Council') for approval. The Council is represented by comitology committees, comprising civil servants from the ministries of finance of the Member States. These committees have both a regulatory and an advisory role and represent three areas of the financial sector: pensions, banks and insurance. At level three, the 'level 3 committees' – the three European networks of financial supervisory authorities referred to above – advise the Commission on the feasibility of measures proposed at level two. At level four the Commission enforces the timely and correct transposition of EU legislation into national law and may take action against a Member State if transposition is not compliant with European law.

While binding directives and regulations were issued at levels one and two, the committees at level three issued guidelines, recommendations and standards for applying European rules. These are non-binding ('soft law')[27] and had only indirect effect – via the national application practice. The level three committees had no powers to introduce binding measures or issue binding decisions. In other words, compliance with these regulations was reliant on the powers of the national regulatory authorities.

Certain fault lines in the system were becoming evident even before the financial crisis broke out.[28] There was too much variation in the ways that European regulations were being implemented in practice at the national level and the system proved to be

---

23. Final report of the Committee of Wise Men on the Regulation of European Securities Markets, 15 February 2001.
24. D. Alford, 'The Lamfalussy Process and EU Bank Regulation: Another Step on the Road to Pan-European Regulation?', *Annual Review of Banking and Financial Law* (2006): 397.
25. Communication from the Commission, *Review of the Lamfalussy process – Strengthening supervisory convergence*, Brussels, 20 November 2007, COM(2007) 727final, p. 2.
26. In this legislative procedure the European Parliament and the Council jointly decide on a proposal from the Commission.
27. A.P.W. Duijkersloot, 'The Principle of Legality and the "Soft Law" Regulation and Supervision of Financial Markets', in eds. L.F.M. Besselink, F. Pennings & S. Prechal, *The Eclipse of the Legality Principle in the European Union* (The Hague: Kluwer Law International, 2010), 171–186.
28. European Commission, *Review of the Lamfalussy process – Strengthening supervisory convergence*, COM (2007) 727 final.

too inflexible to respond effectively to developments in the markets.[29] The fact that the networks lacked powers to issue binding decisions was also seen as an increasingly pressing problem.[30]

§6.05 NEW FINANCIAL AUTHORITIES

[A] EBA, ESMA, and EIOPA

In response to the *De Larosière* report, the Commission took the steps needed to amend European financial supervision. In its Communication of 27 May 2009, the Commission announced proposals to introduce major changes to European financial supervision.[31] The Commission believed there is a need for regulators at the European level, given that there are still too many inconsistencies in national implementing practices and that further coordination is necessary. These ultimately resulted in three regulations to establish three new European authorities.[32] The new supervisory framework, the European System of Financial Supervision (ESFS), comprises the following:

(i) European Systemic Risk Board (ESRB), which is responsible for identifying and assessing potential threats to financial stability arising from macro-economic developments and from developments within the financial system as a whole ('macro-prudential supervision');

(ii) European System of Financial Supervisors (ESFS), comprising a network of national financial supervisors working with new European Supervisory Authorities (ESAs) to safeguard financial soundness at the level of individual

---

29. E. Ferran, *Understanding the New Institutional Architecture of EU Financial Market Supervision*, in *Financial Regulation and Supervision. A Post-Crisis Analysis,* eds. E. Wijmeersch (Oxford: Oxford University Press, 2012), 122–125, where she highlights the fact that the networks could not impose binding standards as one of the key weaknesses of the Lamfalussy level-3 architecture.
30. Ferran, *supra* n. 29, at 120–122.
31. Communication from the Commission, *European Financial Supervision*, Brussels, 27 May 2009, COM(2009) 252. For a discussion of these proposals, see R.J. de Doelder & I.M. Jansen, 'Een nieuw Europees Toezichtraamwerk', *Tijdschrift voor Financieel Recht* 12 (2010): 17–23 and C.M. Grundmann-van de Krol, 'Een nieuw 1/2, Europees toezichtkader', *Ondernemingsrecht* 15 (2010): 618–624.
32. Regulation (EU) No. 1093/2010 of the European Parliament and of the Council of 24 November 2010 establishing a European Supervisory Authority (European Banking Authority), amending Decision No. 716/2009/EC and repealing Commission Decision 2009/78/EC (OJ EU, L331/12, the 'EBA Regulation'); Regulation (EU) No. 1095/2010 of the European Parliament and of the Council of 24 November 2010 establishing a European Supervisory Authority (European Securities and Markets Authority), amending Decision No. 716/2009/EC and repealing Commission Decision 2009/77/EC (OJ EU, L331/84, the 'ESMA Regulation') and Regulation (EU) No. 1094/2010 of the European Parliament and of the Council of 24 November 2010 establishing a European Supervisory Authority (European Insurance and Occupational Pensions Authority), amending Decision No. 716/2009/EC and repealing Commission Decision 2009/79/EC (OJ EU, L331/48). The structure of all three regulations is the same. In principle, this paper refers solely to the EBA Regulation, unless stated otherwise.

financial institutions and to protect consumers of financial services ('micro-prudential supervision').[33]

The three new ESAs are: European Banking Authority (EBA), European Insurance and Occupational Pensions Authority (EIOPA) and European Securities and Markets Authority (ESMA). The structures of these three authorities are essentially the same. Rather than establishing a centralized, integrated European authority, the European legislator has opted to maintain supervision by the national regulatory authorities at a national level for the different sectors, but to have this supervision more emphatically guided by the ESAs for the various sectors.

An outline of the responsibilities in the old and new European supervisory financial landscapes is set out below:

Table 6.1   Responsibilities in the New and Old European Financial Landscapes

	European Financial Supervisors	
Macro supervision	Before 2011	Since 2011
	–	ESRB
Micro supervision	Before 2011	Since 2011
Banks	CEBS	EBA
Securities	CESR	ESMA
Insurance / Pensions	CEIOPS	EIOPA

[B]   A New Additional European Authority: ECB as European Prudential Supervisor

In the last two years of the financial and monetary crisis, it became more and more evident that a further restructuring at the European level of the banking sector was necessary. The European Commission recently presented proposals to design a single banking supervision mechanism in the euro area, further strengthening its response to the crisis. More steps for an integrated bank crisis management and European control were unavoidable.[34] Due to the financial crisis, governments invested trillions of Euros to rescue their national banks, as a result of which the national financial situation of many Member States became very fragile. To break the link between the Member States and their banks, the European Stability Mechanism (ESM) is proposed to recapitalize banks directly at the European level, breaking the vicious circle between

---

33. Communication from the Commission, *European Financial Supervision*, Brussels, 27 May 2009, COM(2009) 252, p. 3.
34. Report by the presidents for the European Council, the Commission, the Euro group and the ECB of 26 June 2012, < www.consilium.europa.eu/uedocs/cms_data/docs/pressdata/en/ec/1313 59.pdf > .

banks and Member States.[35] For that purpose, a single European supervisory system for banks is required, which enables a 'fully rigorous and independent supervision'[36] for the banking sector. Direct and central supervisory control will be given to the ECB for significant banks in the Euro zone. The national supervisory authorities will remain responsible for the less significant banks, unless the ECB takes over the supervisory tasks in specific cases. As a consequence, the home state control mechanism will no longer exist for the banking sector with respect to significant banks in the Euro zone (and for those countries joining the ESM): the NRAs no longer have any formal control over the banking institutions established in their country. This is a fundamental change of the supervisory system in the Member States. A complicated cooperation system between the national supervisory authorities and the ECB is introduced, which still needs to be worked out in more detail in a later stage.

§6.06 POWERS OF THE EUROPEAN FINANCIAL SUPERVISORS

[A] European Systemic Risk Board

The primary task of the ESRB is to oversee macro-prudential supervision within Europe, with the ECB playing a key role in this process. The Board has not been assigned any binding powers but instead is only able to issue warnings and recommendations. The role that this new body gains will depend very much on its influence in the day-to-day practice Whether it will genuinely have an influence in emergencies will depend on the body's informal authority, given that it has no formally binding powers.

[B] European Supervisory Authorities

The three new ESAs have been assigned important tasks and powers in order to help achieve greater convergence between national application practices and to allow rapid intervention in the event of conflicts between national supervisory authorities[37] and in emergencies. The ESAs are authorized to:

---

35. Memo European Commission, Brussels, 10 September 2012, MEMO 12/12/656. This proposal has been revised in the Proposal for a Council regulation conferring specific tasks on the European central Bank concerning policies relating to the prudential supervision of credit institutions – Presidence compromise, 3 December 2012, 2012/0242 (CNS), EF 287 ECOFIN 1011. This contribution is based on this new compromise. However, many details are yet unknown and (substantial) changes might be introduced in a later stage.
36. *Idem*, p. 2.
37. In the Proposal for a regulation of the European Parliament and of the Council amending Regulation (EU) No. 1093/2010 establishing a European Supervisory Authority (European Banking Authority) as regards its interaction with Council Regulation (EU) No. ...../... conferring special tasks on the European Central Bank concerning policies relating to the prudential supervision of credit institutions the powers of the ECB are extended to the ECB: Arts 4, 18(1) and 35(1) to (3): see section §6.07 of this chapter.

   (i) Devise and propose technical standards (a 'single technical rule book'), which are put to the Commission for endorsement;[38]

  (ii) Issue guidelines for interpretation and conduct peer reviews ('best practices') with which the national supervisory authorities will make every effort to comply in their decision making;[39]

 (iii) Facilitate and coordinate actions of national supervisory authorities in the event of emergencies;[40]

 (iv) Take binding decisions in the event of disagreements between national supervisory authorities;[41]

  (v) Support and guide the functioning of colleges of supervisors;[42]

 (vi) Build a common supervisory culture within the European Union;[43]

(vii) Give advice and deliver opinions to the Commission and the European Parliament, both in response to requests and otherwise;[44]

(viii) Give designations to national authorities in the event of failure to comply with European obligations and, if these designations are not followed, to issue specific instructions to the relevant financial institutions.[45]

Although the original idea had been to grant powers to these supervisory authorities to adopt binding technical standards, this was not included in the final text. These powers are now reserved for the Commission, which will adopt a single technical rule book at the instigation of the ESAs.[46] This binding single rulebook represents a significant step towards further harmonization of essential and binding standards and, therefore, of national implementing practices. This in turn should result in less divergence and will improve matters compared with the current situation. The regulations also include significant and binding procedures for resolving disputes between national supervisors and for decision making in emergencies in order to prevent situations such as Icesave. It is the Council, however, and not the ESAs that first has to determine whether an emergency exists.[47]

[C]   The New Role of the ECB

Under the proposed new Supervisory Mechanism for Banks (SSM), the ECB will be empowered to take over the supervisory activities of the NRAs of the significant banks

---

38. Arts 10 and 15 EBA Regulation.
39. Arts 8 and 16 EBA Regulation.
40. Art. 18 EBA Regulation.
41. Art. 19 EBA Regulation.
42. Art. 21 EBA Regulation.
43. Art. 29 EBA Regulation.
44. Arts 8, 32 and 34 EBA Regulation.
45. Art. 17 EBA Regulation.
46. Arts 10 (regulatory technical standards) and 15 (implementing technical standards) EBA Regulation provide a complex procedure for developing standards, whereby the Commission has the opportunity, within certain periods and after consultations, to endorse and also possibly amend standards proposed by the EBA.
47. Art. 18(2) EBA Regulation. Once it has been determined that an emergency exists, the ESA may then adopt the individual decisions required (Art. 18(3) EBA Regulation).

in the euro area as from 1 March 2014 (although it is not certain whether this deadline will be met). In the 'presidency compromise' of 3 December 2012, amending the proposals of the Commission of 12 September 2012, a reallocation of the division of the tasks between the ECB and the national supervisory authorities has taken place: the ECB will no longer be responsible for all credit institutions established in the euro zone and participating Member States, but the national authorities remain responsible for direct supervision over 'less significant' institutions[48] (based on size, economic importance and cross-border activities[49]) as well as for those for which no public financial assistance has been requested nor received directly or indirectly from the EFSF or the ESM.[50] The ECB will be granted key specific supervisory tasks which are indispensable to ensure the detection of risks threatening the viability of banks. It will be empowered to require banks to take the necessary remedial actions.

The ECB will, *inter alia*, be the competent authority for authorizing credit institutions (banks) falling within their powers, assessing qualifying holdings, ensuring compliance with the minimum capital requirements, ensuring the adequacy of internal capital in relation to the risk profile of a credit institution, conducting supervision on a consolidated basis and supervisory tasks in relation to financial conglomerates. The ECB will also ensure compliance with provisions on leverage and liquidity, apply capital buffers and carry out, in coordination with resolution authorities, early intervention measures when a bank is in breach of, or is about to breach, regulatory capital requirements. The ECB will be vested with the necessary investigatory and supervisory powers to perform its tasks. Active involvement of NRAs within the SSM is provided for to ensure the smooth and efficient preparation and implementation of supervisory decisions, as well as the necessary coordination and information flow regarding issues of both local and European reach, in order to ensure financial stability across the Union and its Member States.[51] Therefore, the NRAs carry out (assisting the ECB) the day-to-day assessment of a bank's situation and on-site verifications, implementing general guidance or regulations issued by the ECB.[52] In fact, they can be seen as the 'local branches' of the ECB. For the supervision by the NRAs over non-significant banks, the ECB can issue regulations, guidelines and general instructions giving guidance to the NRAs for their supervisory tasks.

All tasks not explicitly conferred upon the ECB will remain with national supervisors. For example, national supervisors will remain in charge of consumer protection and the enforcement of money laundering regulation, and of the supervision

---

48. Art. 5(6) of the 3 December proposal.
49. Art. 5(4)(a) of the 3 December proposal. A bank is considered 'less significant': (i) if the total value of its assets does not exceed 30 billion euro, or (ii) if the ratio of its total assets over the GDP of the participating home member state does not exceed 20% (unless the total value of its assets is below EUR 5 billion). This would mean that the ECB would supervise approximately 150 significant banks (from the 6,000 in total in the eurozone).
50. Art. 5(4)(b) of the 3 December proposal.
51. Communication from the Commission to the European Parliament and the Council. A Roadmap towards a Banking Union, p. 7.
52. Proposal for a Council regulation conferring specific tasks on the European Central Bank concerning policies relating to the prudential supervision of credit institutions, p. 5.

of third country credit institutions establishing branches or providing cross-border services within a Member State.[53]

Concluding, the new role of the ECB as a new prudential supervisor is a major step towards more centralization. For the banking sector, European supervision will be in place, with a shift from the NRAs towards the ECB. The ECB will have the most important supervisory and enforcement powers over the European significant banks.

§6.07   THE NEW INSTITUTIONAL STRUCTURE

The innovation is in the institutional structure, with the European networks (the 'level three committees') being converted into EFAs. Looking at the structure and powers of these new European vehicles, the European regulatory networks would seem to have been placed in a more solid structure. There is, however, no centralized European control in all areas, with the exception for the credit rating agencies (as discussed in section §6.08[B]) and for the banking sector (as discussed in sections §6.06[C], §6.07[C] and 6.08[C]). The influence of the NRAs is still significant. In other words, the EFAs cannot yet be seen as real 'Euroregulators', but it is an evolutionary process.[54] Although these new authorities are more than the so-called network plus entities,[55] their existence is still depending on the influence of the NRAs. It is very much the question whether these entities should actually be categorized as regulators, both in view of their governance structure and given their tasks and powers.

[A]   Influence of the NRAs in the ESAs

How 'European' are these new ESAs in reality? From a perspective of the structure and powers of these new European vehicles, it would seem that the old European networks have simply been repackaged into a more solid structure and there is no question of genuinely centralized European command. Power remains concentrated at the level of the national regulators as these bodies can substantially influence the ESA at a board level. For each European Financial Supervisor, the central body is the Board of Supervisors. This Board comprises the heads or chairs of the national regulators and is chaired by the ESA chairperson.[56]

Representatives of the European Commission, the ESRB, the ECB and the other two ESAs attend meetings as observers, but do not have voting rights. Although voting generally requires a simple majority (with each member having one vote), many important decisions require a qualified majority.[57] This applies, for example, in respect of acts relating to regulatory and implementing technical standards, guidelines and

---

53. Communication from the Commission to the European Parliament and the Council. A roadmap towards a Banking Union, p. 7.
54. Compare: H. Hofman, 'Mapping the European Administrative Space', *West European Politics* 31, no. 4 (2008): 662–676.
55. Lavrijssen & Hancher 2007, *supra* n. 20.
56. Arts 6 and 43 EBA Regulation.
57. A qualified majority in accordance with Art. 16(4) of the Treaty on European Union, together with the protocol (No. 36) on the transitional provisions attached to the Treaty on European

recommendations, for budgetary matters as well as in respect of requests by a Member State to reconsider a decision by the authority to temporarily prohibit or restrict certain financial activities.[58] This means that the national regulatory authorities have an important voice in and, therefore, influence on decisions taken by the ESAs. In addition to the Board of Supervisors, there is also a Management Board (comprising the chair of the ESA, representatives of the national regulatory authorities and the Commission),[59] an Executive Director[60] and a Board of Appeal.[61] In addition, a Joint Committee, within which the ESAs have to work together to resolve cross-sectoral issues and promote consistency within the various financial sectors, has been established.

Although these new European entities certainly enjoy a degree of independence, problems of independence existing at a national level have now, in essence, been transferred to the European level because of the substantial influence that the national bodies have on these new European authorities.[62] If this structure is compared with, for example, that of the European Data Protection Supervisor, referred to by the European Court in the *Commission v. Germany*[63] as a perfect example of complete independence, the question arises whether these structures will in practice prove sufficient to safeguard independence.[64]

[B]   Influence of the Commission

The Commission is clearly playing an important role in this process of Europeanization, also as the director of the new architecture that is being put in place. Furthermore, the Commission's influence on all these new structures is considerable: as well as attending meetings of the European networks as an observer, it is represented (as a voting or non-voting member) on the boards of the European regulatory authorities, while also being able to intervene in decisions and draft decisions and having a role in adopting technical standards. In this way to a certain degree it serves as a counterweight to the new European regulators, in part under the watchful eye of the Council and the European Parliament. For the Commission the Euroregulators act as an

---

Union and the Treaty on the Functioning of the European Union. Note that under the new Proposal for amending the EBA regulation, Arts 41, 42 and 44 will be amended, regarding the majority rules in certain matters.

58. See, for example, consideration 53 of the EBA Regulation.
59. Arts 6 and 47 EBA Regulation.
60. Arts 6 and 53 EBA Regulation.
61. Arts 6 and 60 EBA Regulation.
62. A differing view has been expressed by Chiti, who believes that these new authorities enjoy a certain degree of independence, specifically vis-à-vis producers, consumers and political institutions such as the Commission. He does not, however, address the influence of national governments on these bodies. See E. Chiti, 'An Important Part of EU's Institutional Machinery: Features, Problems and Perspectives of European Agencies', *Common Market Law Review* 46 (2009): 1429.
63. ECJ 9 March 2010, *Commission v. Germany*, case C-518/07, *Tijdschrift voor Toezicht*, No. 3-2010, pp. 78–86, annotated by A.T. Ottow. This case has been followed by the recent judgment of the ECJ 16 October 2012, *Commission v. Austria*, case C-614/10, not yet published.
64. See on the independence principle within the European context: S. Lavrijssen & A. Ottow, 'Independent Supervisory Authorities: A Fragile Concept', *Legal Issues of Economic Integration* 39, no. 4 (2012): 419–445.

important vehicle for obtaining greater control over national regulators, even though the influence that these national regulators have on the European bodies remains considerable. However, the issue of vesting powers in European bodies without the Commission being able to exercise any influence still remains a taboo subject.[65]

[C]   The Position of ECB: Embedding Its Independence

It is the first time that the ECB will be vested with supervisory tasks (prudential supervision). So far, the ECB was only responsible for carrying out monetary functions with a view to maintaining price stability in accordance with Article 127(1) TFEU.[66] The exercise of supervisory tasks has the goal to protect the safety and soundness of credit institutions and the stability of the financial system. In order to avoid conflicts of interests between the monetary and supervisory functions and to ensure that each function is exercised in accordance with the applicable objectives, the ECB should ensure they are carried out in full separation.[67]

How is this separation realized? This is a key question, with important consequences to ensure no conflict of interests. According to the proposed Council Regulation, a separate Supervisory Board responsible for decisions on supervisory matters should be set up. The Supervisory Board will have to submit draft decisions to the ECB Governing Council. These decisions will be deemed adopted, unless objected to by the Governing Council.[68] New provisions on due process have been introduced in the amended proposal of 3 December 2012.[69] An internal review is now added, where a panel of review can confirm, abrogate or amend the decision in question.[70] However, no additional accountability requirements have been included for the supervisory tasks of the ECB.[71] It remains to be seen how this separation of functions within the ECB will be actually implemented and guaranteed in practice. It is clear that potential conflicts between the two functions of the ECB are there. It seems unavoidable that the ECB will give preference to its monitory responsibilities in case of a conflict. Also the influence of the NRAs, as being represented in the Supervisory board, and the controlling powers of the EBA will have an impact on the decisions of the ECB.

---

65. Chiti, *supra* n. 59, at 1434. This is also evident from the Communication from the Commission to the European Parliament and the Council, 'European agencies – The way forward', Brussels, 11 March 2008, COM(2008) 135 final.
66. For the ECB its independence regarding its current monetary tasks is laid down in Art. 130 TFEU. See, ECJ, *Commission v. ECB*, case C-11/00, [2003] ECR I-7147. See further: Ch. Ziglioli & M. Selmayr, 'The Constitutional Status of the European Central Bank', *Common Market Law Review* 44 (2007): 355–399.
67. See consideration 35 of Proposal for a Council regulation conferring specific tasks on the European Central Bank concerning policies relating to the prudential supervision of credit institutions.
68. Art. 19(3) of the 3 December proposal.
69. Art. 17a of the 3 December proposal.
70. Art. 17b of the 3 December proposal.
71. E. Ferran & V. Babes, *The European Single Supervisory Mechanism*, Legal Research Papers Series, University of Cambridge, Faculty of law, Paper No. 10/2013, March 2013, pp. 12–16.

[D]   *Meroni* Issues

The *Meroni* doctrine[72] is an important element to be considered when establishing European regulatory authorities and assigning tasks and powers to such bodies. The issue at stake in *Meroni* involved the Commission delegating its discretionary powers to a body established under private law.[73] The conventional view on the ruling in this case is that the Commission is not entitled to delegate powers involving a discretionary element to European bodies, such as the newly established European regulators. As far as the Commission's proposals to establish these new bodies in the various sectors are concerned, it can generally be stated that these 'Euroregulators' have powers of a purely technical and advisory nature and no regulatory tasks, let alone powers involving any element of discretion. The Commission has clearly been mindful – in the light of the *Meroni* case – not to grant any regulatory powers to the EFAs. Instead, they can only propose draft rules (such as technical standards) to the Commission, which can then decide whether to endorse them.[74] Similarly, it is only the Council and not the ESAs, as had originally been intended, that is authorized to take a decision in an emergency. The right to take an individual decision in respect of an individual financial institution may prove contentious as this could constitute the exercising of discretionary powers, and that would conflict with the ruling in the *Meroni* case.

An important question is whether greater transparency and accountability of the European authorities can resolve the problems identified in the *Meroni* case.[75] The requirement for independence needs to be matched by a requirement for sufficient transparency; in other words, a need for accountability.[76] This is to ensure that the various bodies are subject to proper control.[77] Important new provisions to guarantee proper control are included in most of the arrangements, albeit not always to the same extent.[78] Take, for example, the ESAs. The new regulations contain substantial procedures on transparency and accountability, which were not available when the

---

72. C-5/56 *Meroni* [1958] ECR 133.
73. See, for example, H. van Meerten & A.T. Ottow, 'The Proposals for the European Supervisory Authorities (ESAs): The Right (Legal) Way Forward?', *Tijdschrift voor Financieel Recht* 1/2, no. 12 (2010): 11–15, including the references.
74. See Arts 10 to 15 Regulation 1093/2010. The Commission can amend draft rules only in certain specific circumstances. The European Parliament and the Council may object to the Commission's endorsement of these standards (Art. 13).
75. A useful discussion of *Meroni* from an accountability perspective can be found at < http://www.eu-newgov.org/database/DELIV/D04D40_WP_Meroni_Revisited.pdf >.
76. See, for example, D. Curtin, 'Delegation to EU Non-majoritarian Agencies and Emerging Practices of Public Accountability', in eds. D. Gerardin et al., *Regulation through Agencies in the EU. A New Paradigm of European Governance* (Cheltenham/Northampton: Edward Elgar, 2005), 88–119; E. Vos, 'Reforming the European Commission: What Role to Play for EU Agencies?', *Common Market Law Review* 37 (2000): 1113–1134.
77. See, for example, Art. 15, para. 5, and Art. 16, para. 8, Regulation 713/2009 (ACER) and Art. 5, para. 5, and Art. 13 Regulation 1211/2009 (BEREC).
78. Recent research into European agencies has shown that although in many cases little fault can be attributed to the mechanisms of accountability; mistakes are sometimes made in the actual control activities by those responsible for supervising the European institutions. See M. Busuioc, 'European Agencies: Pockets of Accountability', in eds. M. Bovens, D. Curtin & P. 't Hart, *The Real World of EU Accountability. What Deficit?* (Oxford: Oxford University Press, 2010) and M. Busuioc, *The Accountability of European Agencies: Legal Provisions and Ongoing Practices*

Court of Justice ruled on the *Meroni* case. In the EBA Regulation, for example, it is not only the involvement of the European Parliament in several procedures that is foreseen;[79] the Union budgetary procedure is also applicable, while consultation procedures with important stakeholders have been included[80] and new appeal and judicial review mechanisms[81] introduced. All in all, the establishment of these new bodies cannot be compared with the situation in the *Meroni* case as sufficient safeguards have been put in place to compensate for the substantial independence of these authorities.[82]

As a result of the additional decision steps to be made, the major objections existing in respect of the Lamfalussy process essentially continue to apply. There are still many stages involved in the decision-making process, and the new authorities cannot adopt and impose technical standards directly. Nevertheless, their influence (albeit informal) will be greater in practice, certainly under the pressure of various additional enforcement powers and it is in these new powers that the innovative impact of the new institutional structure will be felt.

§6.08   NEW ENFORCEMENT POWERS: A MAJOR SHIFT TOWARDS EUROPEANIZATION

From a perspective of enforcing European financial regulations there has been a significant shift towards Europeanization. Traditionally enforcement has been the autonomous responsibility of the Member States via national supervisory authorities. Although the European networks achieved quite some progress in the convergence of national supervisory practices,[83] considerable differences remained. One of the conclusions of the *De Larosière* report was that many national supervisory authorities had too few sanctioning powers to ensure compliance with European standards. In December 2010, the Commission published a Communication on reinforcing the sanctioning regimes in the financial services sector.[84] In its Communication the Commission recognized that a proper functioning supervisory system needs to have efficient and sufficiently convergent sanctioning regimes. The Commission carried out a review in order to examine sanctioning regimes across Member States. The review focused on the application of EU directives by Member States with regard to the banking, insurance and securities sector. Following this review, the Commission

---

(Delft: Eburon, 2010). See also M.L.P. Groenleer, *The Autonomy of European Union Agencies. A Comparative Study of Institutional Development* (Delft: Eburon, 2009).
79. Arts 34 and 50 Regulation 1093/2010, for example.
80. See, for example, Art. 10, para. 1, and Art. 37 Regulation 1093/2010, which introduces a new body (the Banking Stakeholders Group) that has to be consulted on important new technical standards and rules. See also Art. 1(5) of the proposal for the Regulation amending the EBA regulation, amending Art. 4 of the current EBA regulation.
81. Arts 60 and 61 Regulation 1093/2010: appeal procedure with a Board of Appeal and to the Court of Justice.
82. Lavrijssen & Ottow, *supra* n. 64, at 442–443.
83. Moloney, *supra* n. 22, at 1364 ('supervisory convergence').
84. Commission, 'Reinforcing sanctioning regimes in the financial services sector' (Communication) COM(2010) 716 final.

concluded that the sanctioning regimes in those sectors show considerable divergences across Member States.[85]

The Commission identifies in its Communication several divergences and weaknesses across Member States. Some NRAs do not have certain important types of sanctioning powers for certain violations at their disposal. Also, the levels of administrative fines vary widely across Member States and are too low in some Member States. In addition, some NRAs cannot address administrative sanctions to both natural and legal persons. NRAs do not take into account the same criteria in the application of sanctions. Divergence exists in the nature (administrative or criminal) of sanctions provided for in national legislation. Finally, the level of application of sanctions varies across Member States. Thus, the Commission comes to the conclusion that sanctioning regimes across Member States diverge considerably. These divergences may lead to a situation in which sanctions are not applied in an 'effective, proportionate, and dissuasive' manner.

In the new legislation, many steps have been taken to transfer enforcement powers from the NRAs to the European level: the ESAs and the ECB. This process is a major step in improving the harmonization and effectiveness of the enforcement of financial regulation. This transfer of enforcement powers will be discussed in the following sections.

[A]   The First Shift: Direct Interventions by the ESAs

The three new regulations establishing the ESAs represent a novum in European law, with the European authorities being given powers to intervene directly – bypassing the national supervisory authorities – and issue instructions to the relevant financial institution.[86] Grundmann-van de Krol refers to this power as the 'knight's move', as in a game of chess.[87] This is a three-step enforcement mechanism.[88] Where a breach of Union law is detected under Article 17(3) of the EBA Regulation, the EBA can address a recommendation to the competent national authority. If the competent national authority does not comply with the recommendation within the time limit, Under Article 17(4) of the EBA Regulation the Commission may issue a reasoned opinion requiring the competent authority to comply with Union law. If the competent authority does not comply with the formal opinion, under Article 17(6) the EBA may adopt an individual decision addressed to a financial institution.

When an ESA (for example, EBA) is requested to settle a disagreement between two or more national competent authorities under Article 19(2), the EBA may take up a mediation and if the competent authorities have failed to reach an agreement the EBA

---

85. Commission, 'Reinforcing sanctioning regimes in the financial services sector' (Communication) COM(2010) 716 final, p. 6.
86. See Art. 17 EBA Regulation. The ESA can issue such an individual instruction, providing it first gives the competent national authority the opportunity to comply with the European obligations. If the competent national authority continues to fail to comply, the ESA may issue a binding decision requiring the relevant financial institution to take the necessary measures.
87. Grundmann-van de Krol, *supra* n. 31, at 622.
88. Recitals 28 and 29, the EBA Regulation.

may take a binding decision under Article 19(3). If the concerned authorities fail to comply with this decision the EBA may adopt an individual decision addressed to a financial institution under Article 19(4). These supporting tools are important since the new binding powers are based on the failures of national supervision regimes. Although these new binding powers are heavily conditioned and are only intended to be used as a last resort measure, these new powers are significant.[89] Evidently the Union extends its competence where decentralized enforcement fails. The new EBA Regulation represents the EU taking over ex-post enforcement.[90]

Some authors argue that with the EBA's competences to bypass national authorities in law enforcement against an individual financial institution, the Union supervisory network is centralized to some degree.[91] Indeed, the significance of this development should not be underestimated, given that it effectively represents a direct transfer of powers relating to specific supervisory activities from a national to a European level. The new financial supervisory authorities can directly take a binding decision on a financial institution if a national supervisor continues to infringe directly applicable EU law by failing to take the required measures.[92] This represents an innovative and effective instrument for avoiding an enforcement deficit at a national level, alongside the opportunity available to the Commission under Article 258 TFEU to initiate infringement procedures. Appeals against individual decisions in such situations can be lodged with the Board of Appeal of the ESA,[93] while decisions by the Board of Appeal can be appealed at the European Court of Justice.[94]

This knight's move forms the first shift towards more European enforcement powers.

[B]   The Second Shift: Single Supervision by the ESMA on Credit Rating Agencies

There has also been a second shift towards power at a European level in that various financial directives, including the new European Regulation on credit rating agencies, further extend the enforcement powers of the EFAs.[95] On 1 July 2011 responsibility for

---

89. Recital 32, the EBA Regulation.
90. Moloney, *supra* n. 22, at 1335.
91. A. Lefterov, 'How Feasible is the Proposal for Establishing a New European System of Financial Supervisors?' *Legal Issues of Economic Integration* 38, no. 1 (2011): 39.
92. The provisions concerned have to be established on a case-by-case basis. According to Art. 17(1) EBA Regulation, the provisions in any event include regulatory and implementing technical standards established in accordance with Arts 10 and 15. In the event of directive provisions, terms will need – in line with ECJ case law – to be sufficiently precise and unconditional. See, for example, J. Prinssen, *Doorwerking van Europees recht. De verhouding tussen directe werking, conforme interpretatie en overheidsaansprakelijkheid* (The Hague: Kluwer, 2004), Chapter 2, and M.J.M. Verhoeven, *The Costanzo Obligation. The Obligations of National Administrative Authorities in the Case of Incompatibility between National Law and European Law* (Antwerp: Intersentia, 2011).
93. Art. 60 EBA Regulation.
94. Art. 61 EBA Regulation.
95. Regulation (EU) No. 513/2011 of the European Parliament and of the Council of 11 May 2011 amending Regulation (EC) No. 1060/2009 on credit rating agencies, OJ EU, L145, p. 30. See also

supervising credit rating agencies passed almost entirely from the national supervisory authorities (the AFM in the case of the Netherlands) to the ESMA. The latter has been given extensive powers, including the right to impose sanctions directly.

When the Board of Supervisors finds that a credit rating agency has, intentionally or negligently, committed an infringement related to conflicts of interest, organizational, or operational requirements, it must impose a fine.[96] The ESMA has no margin of discretion to choose what remedy fits best. When the Board of Supervisors has found an infringement that is listed in Annex III of the Regulation it must impose a fine in accordance with the limits as laid down in the Regulation. The minimum and maximum amount of the fine are fixed, the ESMA cannot exceed these limits. However, ESMA is following its own enforcement policy and introducing a more risk based approach. In practice, ESMA has shown so far to take a rather pragmatic approach and follows a risk based enforcement style and take a wide margin of discretion.[97] Only in exceptional cases it will impose sanctions. Just recently, the European Commission published further rules of procedure for the exercise of ESMA's powers to impose fines or periodic penalty payments. Such rules were adopted and clarified by means of a Delegated Regulation.[98] This regulation is inspired by the procedure rules used by the Commission in competition cases. Currently, one sanctioning procedure is pending, in which ESMA is following the procedures of the delegated regulation. This will be the first sanction decision of ESMA.

This new centralization does not mean, however, that NRAs have been made redundant. The NRAs remain responsible for the oversight of the users of credit ratings.[99] Moreover, the ESMA is dependent upon an appropriate cooperation agreement with the NRAs. NRAs should provide information,[100] assist the ESMA,[101] or carry out investigations and on-site inspections on its behalf.[102]

Regulation (EU) 513/2011 has two interesting aspects. First, it sets aside the responsibility of NRAs and gives an exclusive responsibility of registration and supervision of credit rating agencies to the ESMA. A similar centralization at the

---

European Commission, Non-paper of the Commission's services on the amendment to the proposal for a regulation amending regulation (EC) No. 1060/2009 on credit agencies, Brussels 28 October 2010. Explanatory notes on the proposal in the Letter from the Minister of Foreign Affairs, 30 August 2010, *Parliamentary Papers II*, 2009–2010, 22 112, No. 1051.

96. Art. 36a Regulation (EU) 513/2011 amending Regulation (EC) 1060/2009 on credit rating agencies [2011] OJ L145/30.

97. Credit rating agencies Annual report 2012. Application of the regulation (EC) No. 1060/2009 as amended according to Art. 21(5), www. ESMA.europa.eu.

98. Commission delegated regulation (EU) No. 946/2012, OJ L282, 16 October 2012, p. 23.

99. Recital 9 Regulation (EU) 513/2011 amending Regulation (EC) 1060/2009 on credit rating agencies [2011] OJ L145/30.

100. Art. 27 Regulation (EU) 513/2011 amending Regulation (EC) 1060/2009 on credit rating agencies [2011] OJ L145/30.

101. Art. 23c (4) and Art. 23d (5) Regulation (EU) 513/2011 amending Regulation (EC) 1060/2009 on credit rating agencies [2011] OJ L145/30.

102. Art. 23d(6) Regulation (EU) 513/2011 amending Regulation (EC) 1060/2009 on credit rating agencies [2011] OJ L145/30.

European level is also expected to occur in other areas.[103] This represents a significant challenge for ESAs, such as the ESMA, with the question being whether the ESAs have sufficient capacity to take on these supervisory tasks.[104] In practice they will remain largely reliant on the enforcement capacity of the national supervisory authorities. Cooperation between the ESMA and the various NRAs remains necessary.

[C]   The Third Shift: Direct Enforcement by the ECB

The third and last shift towards Europeanization of enforcement powers are the new supervisory powers of the ECB. Not only has the ECB the exclusive competence to decide on the authorizations of banks (and its withdrawal),[105] it has also the powers to impose administrative pecuniary sanctions of up to twice the amount of the profits gained or losses avoided because of the breach where those can be determined, or up to 10% of the total annual turnover of a legal person in the preceding business year in as far as there is an infringement of direct applicable EU law.[106] In addition, it has investigatory powers (requiring information and conducting on-site inspections).[107] The ECB will, however, need the assistance of the NRAs for the day-to-day assessment and the execution of the supervisory tasks over significant banks. A hybrid mixed administration system will come into existence, where the division of tasks and powers is blurred and not always transparent. New rules on procedures and judicial protection will need to be developed.

§6.09   CHALLENGES FOR THE FUTURE

The institutional landscape of financial supervision has changed dramatically by the establishment of the ESAs and the new supervisory tasks of the ECB. However, the level of influence strongly depends on the powers of the ESA. The powers of the ESA range from issuing recommendations and opinions to taking binding decisions and overstepping NRAs. The influence of ESAs on the application of Union law by NRAs should not be underestimated. Although the opinions and recommendations are not legally binding, high-quality recommendations and opinions cannot simply be ignored by the NRAs. If these recommendations are also based on the common practices and experiences of the NRAs, this might have a significant convergence effect of the

---

103. A similar centralization at a European level has occurred in two other areas: Regulation 648/2012 on OTC derivatives, central counterparties and trade repositories (EMIR) and Regulation 236/2012 on short selling and certain aspects of credit default swaps.
104. See, for example, the information on the ESMA website (www.esma.europa.eu): at the 2010 year-end, the organization had 47 staff members, while a total of 70 is expected by the end of 2011. Of this total, some 15 employees are shown as focussing on assessing the credit rating agencies operating in the EU.
105. Art. 13 Proposal for a Council regulation conferring specific tasks on the European Central Bank concerning policies relating to the prudential supervision of credit institutions.
106. Art. 15(1) Proposal for a Council regulation conferring specific tasks on the European Central Bank concerning policies relating to the prudential supervision of credit institutions.
107. Arts 9–12 Proposal for a Council regulation conferring specific tasks on the European Central Bank concerning policies relating to the prudential supervision of credit institutions.

enforcement practices. By using their powers adequately, the ESAs contribute to a more consistent application of Union law across Member States. The establishment of the ESAs will contribute to greater convergence across Member States.

Also the new instrument of the ESAs regarding the 'knight's move' will have a convergence effect; the threat of such an intervention will force the NRA to take the appropriate measures. In addition, the new, to be developed, practice of the ESMA regarding the credit rating agencies and of the ECB regarding banks will serve as an example for the European enforcement practice. It is to be hoped that the ESMA and the ECB will not only focus on sanctions/penalties, but will also take into account the other instruments available regarding enforcement.

In the longer term this trend towards greater centralization of enforcement may have far-reaching consequences for the NRAs as these authorities will have to transfer powers to the European supervisors, as is the case now for credit agencies and credit institutions (as from 2013). In the field of enforcement, which has traditionally been an autonomous responsibility of the Member States, power is now also shifting towards Europe. This is certainly the correct direction in the case of markets that are highly internationally focused, such as the credit ratings market and the banking sector, given that fragmented supervision of such markets, involving a diversity of enforcement practices, is simply not effective. In those cases, the NRAs will become no more than local branches of the European regulators (ESMA and ECB), as the central decision makers. At the same time, however, local (in other words, national) supervision will remain necessary in markets with limited or no cross-border activities[108] and in all cases the local knowledge of the national supervisory authorities will be needed if proper supervision is to be performed. Overlooking this new institutional structure, a complicated Supervisory Bermuda Triangle between the NRAs, ECB, and the EBA is created. It remains to be seen how the tasks will be divided and how the cooperation will actually take place. In any event the risk does exist that the division of powers is confusing and that complicated cooperation structures must be developed.

The structuring of financial supervision in Europe is a process of evolution. Although significant new steps have now been taken by the establishment of the ESAs and the SSM for the banking sector, it remains a long-term process. The establishment of ESAs and the transfer of tasks to the ECB can certainly be regarded as historic, but these authorities remain largely reliant on the Commission and the NRAs. In view of the continuing internationalization of these markets, this process of Europeanization will inevitably continue, with national supervisory authorities increasingly becoming the right hand of the European supervisors and losing more and more of their autonomy. The current system will prove insufficiently robust. And that means that achieving full integration of the national supervisory systems, via centralized European control, will be the challenge in the period ahead.

---

108. Cf. Ottow, *supra* n. 4.

CHAPTER 7

Towards a New Agency Model? The Example of Telecommunications[*]

Marco Zinzani

§7.01 INTRODUCTION

The telecommunications sector is an EU regulatory field in which the powers in relation to the definition of rules are shared among actors placed at different governance levels, none of which can operate independently from the others. The relationships between the national and the EU levels are governed by both formal and informal coordination rules, which naturally implies overlaps and strong interdependencies. Over the past two decades, the sector has been characterized by an institutional 'network trend': all the attempts to create a true EU regulatory agency have failed and networks have become (and continue to be) a key player of regulatory policy making.[1]

The first set of sectoral directives, back in the 1990s,[2] already foresaw the creation of bodies independent of the telecommunications organizations for the

---

[*] This chapter draws upon the author's research findings presented in M. Zinzani, *Market Integration through 'Network Governance'. The Role of European Agencies and Networks of Regulators* (Antwerp: Intersentia, 2012): Chapter 4: 'Networks of Regulators in the EU Telecom Field', 159–224.
1. E. Sutherland, 'A Single European Regulatory Authority', paper presented to the 17th Biennial Conference of the International Telecommunications Society, *The Changing Structure of the Telecommunications Industry and the New Role for Regulation*, Montreal, 24–27 June 2008; S. Simpson, 'Supranationalism and Its Limits in European Telecommunications Governance – The European Electronic Communications Markets Authority Initiative', *Information, Communication and Society* 12, no. 8 (2009); D. Levi-Faur, 'Regulatory Networks & Regulatory Agencification: Toward a Single European Regulatory Space', *Jerusalem Papers in Regulation & Governance* (2010): 13.
2. See Commission Directive 90/388 on competition in the markets for telecommunications service, Art. 7; Directive 88/301 on the competition in the markets in telecommunications terminal equipment; Directive 90/387 on the establishment of the internal market for telecommunications

administration of regulation at the national level. A concrete attempt to create a European agency to regulate the single European market in telecoms was made in 1994 with the so-called Bangemann report, calling for a transfer of regulatory responsibilities from the national to the European level.[3] At that time, few Member States had independent national regulatory authorities (NRAs). The idea of a single regulator appealed to market operators with cross-border activities, while it met the opposition of the national governments and the few existing national regulators, concerned about their prerogatives.[4] Again, in the 1999 Communications Review,[5] the Commission proposed to establish a pan-European regulator, the High Level Communications Group. It would have consisted of representatives of all relevant national regulatory bodies and the Commission and it would have brought the national regulators under the structures and the control of the Commission.[6] The Commission claimed that stronger EU-wide coordination was necessary since the NRAs were delegated more power under the new regulatory framework. National governments and regulators, however, strongly opposed the creation of such a body. The failed attempts to create an agency were thus followed by the establishment of a permanent Communications

---

services through the implementation of open network provisions; Directive 90/544 on the frequency bands for pan-European land-based public radio paging; Directive 91/263 on the approximation of the laws of the Member States concerning the telecommunications terminal equipment; Directive 91/287 on the frequency band for digital European cordless telecommunications; Directive 92/44 on the application of open network provision to leased lines; Directive 93/97 supplementing Directive 91/263 in respect of satellite earth station equipment; Directive 94/46 amending Directive 88/301 and Directive 90/388 in particular with regard to satellite communications; Directive 97/51 amending Directives 90/387 and 92/44 for the purpose of adaptation to a competitive environment in telecommunications; Directive 95/62 on the application of open network provisions to voice telephony; Comm. Directive 96/2 amending Directive 90/388 with regard to mobile and personal communications; Comm. Directive 96/19 amending Directive 90/388 with regard to the implementation of full competition in telecommunications market; Directive 97/13 on the common framework for general authorizations and individual licenses in the field of telecommunications services; Directive 97/33 on the interconnection in telecommunications with regard to ensuring universal service and interoperability through application of the principles of the open network provision; Directive 98/13 on telecommunications terminal equipment and satellite earth station equipment; Directive 98/61 amending Dir. 97/33 with respect to operator number portability and carrier pre-selection.

3. European Commission, *Europe and the Global Information Society: Recommendations to the European Council [Bangemann Report]* (Brussels, 1994). See D. Kelemen, 'The Politics of Eurocratic Structure and the New European Agencies', *West European Politics* 25, no. 4 (2002): 110. See also D. Coen & M. Thatcher, 'Network Governance and Multi-Level Delegation: European Networks of Regulatory Agencies', *Journal of Public Policy* 28, no. 1 (2008): 60.

4. M. Michalis, *Governing European Communications. From Unification to Coordination* (Plymouth, UK: Lexington Books, 2007), 157.

5. European Commission, *Communication from the Commission to the Council, the European Parliament, the Economic and Social Committee and the Committee of the Regions – Towards a New Framework for Electronic Communications Infrastructure and Associated Services – The 1999 Communications Review*, COM/99/0539 final.

6. M. Groenleer & M. Kars, 'Regulation and Governance of the European Telecommunications Sector: From Network to Agency?', paper presented at the ECPR Standing Group on Regulatory Governance, on the occasion of the conference *(Re)Regulation in the Wake of Neoliberalism. Consequences of Three Decades of Privatization and Market Liberalization*, 5–7 June 2008, Utrecht, available at < http://regulation.upf.edu/utrecht-08-papers/mgroenleer_kars.pdf > , 13.

Committee (COCOM), a comitology committee,[7] and by the setting up of networks of regulators: first, the Independent Regulators Group (IRG) and then the European Regulators Group (ERG). In 2007 the Commission promoted the establishment of a telecoms agency, the European Electronic Communications Market Authority (EE-CMA). This proposal also failed and eventually the Body of European Regulators for Electronic Communications (BEREC) and the Office were created, formally integrating into European law the powers and responsibilities of the existing ERG.

It is important to note that the institutional developments briefly mentioned above took place almost simultaneously with the inter-institutional dialogue on the work of EU agencies[8] which, after a few years of difficult negotiations, eventually resulted, in June 2012, in the Common Approach of the European Parliament, the Council of the EU and the European Commission on decentralized agencies (hereinafter, the 'Common Approach').[9] Considering that the latter is intended to lay down a framework as regards, *inter alia*, the role and position of the agencies in the EU institutional landscape and their structure, functioning and supervision,[10] its guidelines and general recommendations have to be considered when assessing a body such as the BEREC. Accordingly, where appropriate, this chapter will highlight certain features which appear to distinguish the BEREC from the 'model agency' of the Common Approach.

In general, this chapter shows how the institutional design of electronic communications regulation has progressively evolved in the EU, going from a loose network of regulators to a hybrid institutional model, through an enhanced network of regulators. The first forms of cooperation between national regulators are explored; then, the features of the structures created in 2009 with the Third telecoms reform package are analysed. The focus is on the following questions: what is the result of the institutional process of reform realized by the Third telecoms package? What is the BEREC? What are its features? How significant is the difference between the old networks of regulators and the BEREC? What problems does the BEREC pose from a legal perspective? What are the commonalities and the differences between the BEREC and the classic EU regulatory agencies? Does the BEREC represent a new agency model? Finally, do the guidelines of the Common Approach suit the BEREC?

---

7. The Cocom was established under the 2002 Framework Directive to assist the Commission in carrying out its executive powers under the regulatory framework governing telecoms in the EU. It was composed of senior officials from the Member State authorities responsible for telecoms and exercised its functions through 'advisory', 'regulatory' and 'regulatory with scrutiny' committees in accordance with general comitology procedures. It also provided a platform for the exchange of information on market developments and regulatory activities. Its members used to meet five times a year in Brussels.
8. See the letter from the President of the Commission dated 7 May 2008, ref. 10120/08.
9. See Annex II to the document 'Evaluation of European Union agencies', Council of the European Union, 18 June 2012, ref. 11450/12.
10. See the Joint Statement of the European Parliament, the Council of the EU and the European Commission on decentralized agencies, Annex I, ref. 11450/12. See Annex 2 to this book.

§7.02   THE COOPERATION AMONG EUROPEAN TELECOM
REGULATORS

National regulators play a central role in the institutional framework for the EU regulation of telecoms. A 'NRA' is defined by Article 2(g) of Directive 2002/21 (hereinafter, the 'Framework Directive')[11] as 'the body or bodies charged by a Member State with any of the regulatory tasks assigned in this Directive and the specific directives'. Elaborating on this definition, the Court of Justice has argued that it emphasizes 'the potentially pluralist nature' of NRAs.[12] It was left to the Member States to decide upon the form and powers of their NRAs; in any case, the Member States had to guarantee the independence of the NRA or authorities in order to ensure the impartiality of their decisions.[13]

Since their creation in the 1990s, the national regulators have felt the need to establish institutional cooperation mechanisms for their action to be effective. Some duties of cooperation were formally included in the Framework Directive. Article 7(3), for instance, required the NRAs to inform the Commission and all other authorities about their envisaged decisions. Once they had received the notification, the Commission and the other authorities had one month to make comments. The duty extended to decisions relating to the procedure for market definition, market analysis and the identification of operators with Significant Market Power (SMP)[14] and to decisions resolving disputes between firms which would affect intra-Community trade.[15] However, some practical problems constrained the efficiency of the notification mechanism of Article 7.[16]

NRAs were thus brought together in networks, in order for them to look beyond their borders and take a European perspective on their respective activities. Very soon, the networks began to conduct benchmark exercises, to form study groups and to issue policy documents and non-binding guidelines on a variety of regulatory issues.[17] As observed by Hancher and Larousse, the creation of EU regulatory networks marked a

---

11. Directive 2002/21/EC of the European Parliament and of the Council of 7 March 2002 on a common regulatory framework for electronic communications networks and services, *OJ* L108/33, 24 April 2002.
12. See Case C-82/07, *Comisión del Mercado de las Telecomunicaciones v. Administración del Estado*, [2008] ECR I-1265, para. 19.
13. See Recital 11 and Art. 3(3) of the Framework Directive. Obviously the independence requirement was particularly important considering that the Member States had considerable financial interests in the telecommunications markets through their shares in national monopolists (incumbents).
14. Arts 15 and 16 of the Framework Directive.
15. See Recital 38 of the Framework Directive.
16. See M. de Visser, *Network-Based Governance in EC Law. The Example of EC Competition Law & EC Communications Law* (Oxford: Hart Publishing, 2009), 207. De Visser notes, in particular, that few NRAs offer observations on each other's proposed decisions, mainly because of time and language constraints.
17. L. Hancher & P. Larouche, 'The Coming of Age of EU Regulation of Network Industries and Services of General Economic Interest', in *The Evolution of EU Law*, eds. G. De Burca & P. Craig (Oxford: Oxford University Press, 2010): 745.

significant step away from the starting point approach towards an 'integrative approach'.[18] Through the establishment of networks, the Commission and the regulatory networks started to work together in the framework of the same enforcement community. A not perfectly defined separation of roles applied, with the Commission taking care of the supervisory and policy making functions and the NRAs dealing with the application of the law. The first European institutional forum to be established for the cooperation of national regulators, paving the way for further cooperation, was the IRG.

[A]   The Predecessors of the BEREC: The IRG as a Loose Network of Regulators

The IRG was established in 1997 as a group of European NRAs. In a certain way, the establishment of the group was a reaction to the calls for a pan-European regulator; at the same time, it also represented a contribution by the more experienced NRAs to support the newer regulators.[19] Interestingly, despite the successive creation of strengthened networks of regulators, the IRG currently still exists. In particular, in 2010 the IRG decided to continue to run the Group in parallel to the European body of regulators (first the ERG, then the BEREC) for at least three years.

The main goal of the IRG is to provide a forum for discussion and the exchange of ideas and expertise between its members and with other experts regarding regulatory issues in the electronic communications sector. It also promotes the consistent application of the European regulatory framework for electronic communications networks and services in all the Member States, and the development and consolidation of the internal market for electronic communications networks and services in Europe. The IRG, in particular, commissions, prepares and publishes documents, reports, presentations, analyses, 'principles of implementation and best practices' (PIBs), which are examples of benchmarking, and other studies to inform the market regarding regulatory strategies and developments. It then monitors the application by its members of the latter, in order to promote transparency and to ensure the effectiveness of guidance and the continual development of best regulatory practices. Finally, it maintains a dialogue between its members and stakeholders, including market participants and consumers, and it cooperates with other regulatory networks internationally.[20]

The IRG is composed of a General assembly, a Board of Directors, a Contact Network and a small Brussels-based secretariat. It is established from the meetings of presidents of the various NRAs and is formed outside the Community/EU framework. The IRG is still registered as a not-for-profit organization under Belgian law (ASBL). The membership is open to any NRAs in the electronic communications sector which

---

18. *Ibid.*
19. Michalis, *supra* n. 4, at 157.
20. Art. 5, Independent Regulators' Group Statutes, available at < http://www.irg.eu/streaming/ IRG-Statutes_EN_090402FINAL.pdf?contentId=545921&field=ATTACHED_FILE > (accessed on 30 October 2012).

satisfies the conditions laid down in Article 7 of the Statutes of IRG.[21] At the present time, the IRG has thirty-six members which correspond to twenty-eight EU Member States, four EFTA members and four candidate countries to the EU.

The IRG is a flat organization which produces policy outcomes based on agreement and consensus reached through extensive communication between network members. It is also a forum where national regulators can meet without the presence of the Commission. It is a body that exists and operates outside the realm of EU law; even in the recent process of reform of the legal framework for communication networks and services, it has rejected all the Commission attempts to incorporate its coordination activities into the EU framework.[22] Its membership is identical to that of the ERG first and then the BEREC; yet, it has continued to exist alongside the ERG and the BEREC. It seems that regulators are keen on keeping the IRG as an institutional context which allows them to work through an alternative organization outside the control mechanisms to which European bodies are subject and against any possible intrusion by the national governments and/or the Commission, which might threaten the independence of the national regulators.

[B]   The Predecessors of the BEREC: The IRG as an Enhanced Network of Regulators

The ERG for electronic communications networks and services was created in 2002 to have in place a suitable mechanism to encourage cooperation and coordination between NRAs and the Commission.[23] Members of the Group were the Heads of the independent NRAs of each Member State, established to oversee the day-to-day interpretation and application of the provisions of the relevant Directives of the regulatory framework. The Commission was represented at an appropriate level at ERG meetings and provided the secretariat to the ERG. EFTA States and EU candidate countries also participated in the work of the ERG. Decision 2002/627/EC establishing the ERG was repealed as from 1 June 2010, when the ERG formally ceased to exist.[24]

---

21. The NRA must regulate its national electronic communications market and, in the case of EU members, be the NRA notified to the European Commission under the Framework Directive; be independent of its government and operators and be in a country which is an EU Member State, and EFTA state, an EU acceding country or a candidate for membership of the EU which has (or is working towards) a liberalized electronic communications market (according to EU standards).
22. B. Eberlein & E. Grande, 'Beyond Delegation: Transnational Regulatory Regimes and the EU Regulatory State', *Journal of European Public Policy* 12, no. 1 (2005): 102.
23. Commission Decision of 29 July 2002 establishing the European Regulators Group for Electronic Communications Networks and Services, 2002, L200/38 as amended by Commission Decision 2004/641/EC of 14 September 2004, 2004, *OJ* L293/30 and Commission Decision 2007/804/EC of 6 December 2007, *OJ* L323/43.
24. See Commission Decision of 21 May 2010 establishing the European Regulators Group for Electronic Communications Networks and Services (2010/299/EU).

The ERG was composed of a Plenary,[25] a Chair,[26] a Secretariat,[27] and a Contact Network.[28] The detailed work of the ERG was undertaken through expert working groups or project teams. The former were standing groups dealing with issues related to a similar theme.[29] The latter were ad hoc groups set up to deal with specific regulatory issues. The ERG occasionally also organized one-day seminars for the NRAs. The goal of these meetings was to consider and debate selected topics of relevance for the decision-making practices of the national authorities. The range of the ERG's powers included both advisory and coordination responsibilities. The ERG could also play a role in the context of cross-border dispute resolution. Finally, the ERG provided the forum through which joint transnational market analyses were undertaken by the Commission and the NRAs.[30] The ERG also produced PIBs and reports.

Looking at the features of multi-level policy networks, as identified by the political science literature,[31] it is rather clear that the ERG was a network in the 'technical' sense of the word. The ERG did not possess legal personality; the ERG, as a regulatory network, merely represented a paradigm of cooperation between the Commission and the regulatory networks, an institutional infrastructure with a strong network design through which the NRAs interacted in a variety of ways with each other and with the Commission for a consistent exercise of their functions. At the same time, the ERG was far from the supranational decision-making body that the Commission might have wished for: it was rather intergovernmental in nature, acting only through soft law instruments. The role of the ERG was to facilitate the cooperation between network members in the course of the decision-making processes and to allow the Commission and the NRAs to exchange information. Its output fell within the realm of soft law and, in many cases, lacked visibility. Nevertheless, the network had a role to

---

25. The Plenary meeting was attended by the Heads of the NRAs. There were normally four regular plenary meetings each year. The decisions of the Plenary were taken by consensus. The Commission was always present on the occasion of the Plenary meetings and reported on the workings of the Art. 7 procedure, meetings of the comitology committee and regulatory proposals.
26. The ERG Chair was elected for an annual term by his/her peers and s/he was also the IRG Chair.
27. The ERG Secretariat consisted of a number of staff (only three in 2003) based in Brussels and appointed by the European Commission. The Secretariat acted as a link between the European Commission and the ERG. In particular, it prepared ERG meetings, agendas and annual reports; it assisted the Chair in the preparation and implementation of the Work programme, and it identified the issues arising in the Commission which needed to be brought to the attention of the ERG.
28. The Contact Network was attended by senior representatives of the national regulators and was chaired by a representative of the ERG Chair. It usually met before the ERG plenary meetings: its main role was to facilitate the work of the ERG.
29. In 2006, the ERG working groups (WGs) were: the Significant Market Power WG; the Mobile Market WG; the Fixed Network WG; the Regulatory Accounting WG; the End Users WG. Source: IRG/ERG, 'A Guide to Who We Are and What We Do', *ERG (06) 03*, February 2006.
30. See Commission Guidelines on market analysis and the assessment of significant market power under the Community regulatory framework for electronic communications networks and services, 2002, *OJ* C165/6, 139. The market analysis may eventually lead to the imposition of remedies. Each NRA is then required to adopt a decision which implements the agreed remedy for the territory over which it exerts its powers.
31. See T.A. Borzel, 'Organizing Babylon – On the Different Conceptions of Policy Networks', *Public Administration* 76 (1998): 254 and Coen & Thatcher, *supra* n. 3, at 50.

play in framing policies to guide the national regulators in the administration of the relevant European rules. The Common position on remedies, agreed upon in April 2004, can be listed here as one of the most significant achievements of the ERG:[32] in a particularly sensitive field, where the European Commission had no veto powers, the document aimed at providing guidance and fostering a consistent application of remedies across the EU, while allowing for flexibility to accommodate the national preferences.

The functioning of the ERG promoted respect for commitments agreed upon by representatives of the national authorities, making it possible for the Commission to interact with a single counterpart and for the national authorities to be part of the broader EU administration. Moreover, given that, in principle, the output of the ERG was in line with the European interest, because of the position of the network itself, the Commission was likely to consider it attentively during the decision-making processes. It can thus be concluded that the ERG responded to a clear need both on the part of the national authorities and of the Commission.

The ERG's main contribution to the EU telecoms regulation was to pool together technical expertise, ensure the sharing of information and provide a framework for regulatory cooperation. However, the ERG was not entirely successful in bringing about regulatory convergence and consistency. Its capacity to foster harmonization was questionable from the beginning considering that it could not take legally binding decisions, but it could only assume a coordinating role. Its main failings were due to the decision-making procedures of the body, the lack of available administrative support, the loosely defined nature of its responsibilities and the tendency of the ERG itself to operate mainly as a body concerned with the protection of national interests rather than the development of a true European telecoms regulatory approach.[33] The ERG decided on a consensus basis, which is, at the end of the day, a very intergovernmental dynamic.[34] Eventually the common positions and opinions of the ERG had to accommodate a wide range of views. Even deciding on ERG rules of procedure required agreement among Member States and was dependent on the Commission: in fact, the rules were to be adopted by consensus or, in the absence of consensus, by a two-thirds' majority vote, subject to the approval of the Commission. The lack of administrative support was another obstacle for the ERG: with a small secretariat, the network did not have the resources, technical competence or authority to initiate actions effectively.

---

32. The document has been subsequently amended. See ERG, Revised ERG Common Position on the Approach Remedies in the ECNS Regulatory Framework, ERG (06) 33, May 2006.
33. See European Commission, Explanatory memorandum, 13 November 2007 (0249): '(...) all ERG common approaches are factually based on consensus, making such common approaches difficult and slow to achieve. They are indeed impossible to achieve where there are substantial differences of opinion or interest between different regulators. The loose cooperation that results has not allowed its documents to go beyond rather general statements in a number of important and controversial issues.'
34. Only in exceptional cases, where there was a real need for a common perspective but consensus proved unattainable, the ERG rules of procedure allowed for acts to be made by two-thirds majority. See Arts 4.1–4.3, 'Rules of Procedure for ERG', ERG (03)07, 2003.

§7.03 THE BEREC AND THE OFFICE

The creation of the BEREC and of the Office was long and laborious.[35] In its 2007 proposal for a review of the telecoms package, the European Commission suggested to establish a new European authority, the EECMA, to serve as its main advisor on all European regulatory affairs and to deliver more consistency of regulation throughout European telecoms markets.[36] The EECMA, which would have merged with the ERG and the European Network and Information Security Agency (ENISA),[37] would not have been able to issue binding decisions but it would have provided a framework for the cooperation between NRAs (like the ERG). Its main decision-making body would

---

35. It can be observed already that a long process of definition of institutional structures is hardly in line with the transient nature of regulation in a sector, such as telecoms, which is characterized by innovation and rapid technological progress. The last decades, for instance, have witnessed extremely rapid developments in each and every aspect of the telecommunications sector, including the introduction of new products, internet based services, the digitalization, the progressive convergence of broadcasting, information technology and telecommunications services, etc.

36. For Commissioner Viviane Reding, the EECMA had to 'operate unambiguously and transparently on the sound basis of Community law and would hence have the legitimacy and legal authority to participate fully in the process leading to Community law decisions which affect market players across Europe. Only such a regulatory body created by the European Parliament and the Council could operate in a transparent manner and be accountable to the democratically elected representatives of the people'. See V. Reding, Letter to Roberto Viola and Daniel Pataki, dated 6 December 2007, available at < ec.europa.eu >. In its proposal for EECMA, the Commission explicitly challenged the soft governance character of the ERG, which was delivering only 'loose coordination among regulators' ultimately resulting in 'lowest common denominator' regulatory solutions. Interestingly, in a letter by Fabio Colasanti, Director General of the Information Society and Media Directorate General of the European Commission, dated 30 January 2007 (available at < ec.europa.eu >), it was stressed that Commissioner Reding was open 'for considering an alternative road: to develop the ERG into a 'body with teeth (...) that could be in charge itself, instead of the Commission, of ensuring consistency of regulation in the internal market, including the (...) Art. 7 procedure'. Before proposing the establishment of the EECMA, the Commission shortly considered establishing a Single European Regulatory Authority with centralized decision making involving discretionary powers on trans-boundary as well as on national matters. See European Commission, 2007, Impact Assessment, SEC 2007 1472, 65. The Authority would have had strong implications for the institutional balance, transferring regulatory powers from national regulators to the centralized level. However, legal considerations (broadly referred to by the Commission as 'institutional concerns') rendered the option unfeasible. See L.C.P. Broos, M.A. Heldeweg & R.A. Wessel, 'European Organization of Telecom Regulators and the Impact on the Pace of Telecom Innovations: Is EU Modesty Hampering Innovation in Telecom? Think Global, Act Local...', paper presented at the *Second Annual Conference on Competition and Regulation in Network Industries*, Centre for European Policy Studies, Brussels, Belgium, 2009. Interestingly, the EECMA was a major novelty in the 2007 Commission's proposal, especially since the 2006 impact assessment had concluded that the time was not ripe for creating a pan-European telecoms regulator, as the costs would outweigh the benefits. See A. Renda, 'The Review of the EU Telecoms Framework: A Tale of the Anti-Commons', in *Monitoring EU Telecoms Policy 2009*, ed. M. Cave et al. (Madrid: NEREC, 2009), 12.

37. Regulation (EC) No. 460/2004 of the European Parliament and of the Council of 10 March 2004 establishing the European Network and Information Security Agency, [2004] *OJ* L77/1, as amended by Regulation (EC) No. 1007/2008 of the European Parliament and of the Council of 24 September 2008 amending Regulation (EC) No. 460/2004 establishing the European Network and Information Security Agency, as regards its duration, [2008] *OJ* L293/1. ENISA has its seat in Heraklion, Greece.

have been composed of the heads of the NRAs, which would have had the possibility to take decisions on the basis of simple majority voting, and an Executive Director.[38] It would have been an independent body established within the EU institutional framework, with a significant supranational dimension for the European telecommunications policy field. The arguments in favour of a new strong authority were, just to name a few, the internalization of cross-country externalities, the economies of scale in regulatory decisions, the potential help to the Commission in facing the increased burden from the proposed extended veto power on remedies[39] and the need to replace the ERG, that had proven to be weak and lacking accountability.

However, the necessity to establish the EECMA as an agency, as well as the strengthening of the Commission's powers, was questioned by both the European Parliament and the Council.[40] The arguments against included the observations that markets were not sufficiently integrated, that the governance of the authority, including the EECMA Administrative Board,[41] would not have guaranteed independence, that accountability was not ensured and that the simple majority voting might have created problems.[42] In addition, it was unclear what the balance of powers would have been between the Commission and the new authority. Moreover, there was no significant industry support for a single regulator. Eventually, the proposal was rejected by both the Council and the Parliament during the autumn of 2007.[43] In 2008, rather than

---

38. Commission's proposal for a Regulation of the European Parliament and the Council establishing the European Electronic Communications Market Authority, Art. 27(1).
39. The regulatory remedies are the legal consequences to be imposed following a market analysis carried out under the Framework Directive.
40. See J. Loades-Carter, 'EU Telecoms Proposals Get Mixed Reception', *Financial Times*, 29 June 2006. As reported by Klotz, in a first exchange of views on the telecoms package in the Industry Committee of the European Parliament, several MEPs raised concerns on the shifting of power to the Commission envisaged by the proposal. Moreover, they asked the Commission how it intended to guarantee the impartiality of the Agency and deal with possible conflicts of competencies between national regulators and the Agency. See R. Klotz, 'The Liberalization of the EU Telecommunications Markets', in *EC Competition and Telecommunications Law*, ed. C. Koenig et al., (Alphen aan den Rijn: Kluwer Law International, 2009), 100. A number of big Member States, including Germany, France and the UK, voiced their firm opposition in the Council. The UK government, in particular, argued that the existing NRA's network, the ERG, should have been allowed to continue its work to improve the exchange of best practices among national regulators. See S. Taylor, 'London Calling the Shots on Network Rules', *European Voice*, 6–12 December 2007.
41. The Board would have had half of its members appointed by the Council of Ministers and half by the European Commission, which would have thus had a strong influence on the functioning of the Authority.
42. See the example offered by A. Renda, 'The New Telecoms Package: Ripe for Reform, Again?', paper presented at the conference *What Comes Next in Electronic Communications? A Review of the New EU Framework*, Institut d'Études Juridiques Européennes, Liege, 2010, 30: assuming that neither a NRA nor the incumbent had wanted to undertake functional separation and that the Commission, backed by the EECMA, had rejected all other remedies, then the NRA would have been forced to choose separation under the new Art. 13a. This would have eventually led to the de facto imposition of functional separation in one country against the will of the regulator and of the regulated, thanks to a simple majority vote by the EECMA and with no real possibility of appeal.
43. It must be noted that national regulators and policy makers also strongly argued against the idea of losing power to a European authority. See Broos, Heldeweg & Wessel, *supra* n. 36. The European Parliament, already in first reading, expressed its doubts on the need to appoint a new

setting up the EECMA as a new regulatory 'super agency' in the field of telecoms, it was agreed to create a much leaner organization with the objective to become the main advisor, both for the European Commission and the national regulators, in the field of regulating the electronic communications market, enabling consistency in the application of EU rules and, at the same time, attracting support from the Member States.[44] Eventually, BEREC and the Office were established by Regulation 1211/2009,[45] after an agreement on the final elements of the reform package was reached on 24 November 2009.[46]

---

body with 134 staff and with only an advisory role, especially in a context where *ex ante* regulation was supposed to be phased out in favour of *ex post* antitrust scrutiny.

44. The new organization, originally referred to as BERT (Body of Regulators in Telecom) was supposed to be set up as an association of NRAs without independent legal personality, established as a private law body with a mandate until 2014, and hosting a conciliation procedure for cases in which the Commission expressed doubts on remedies proposed by the NRAs. The national regulators should have supported the goals of BERT to promote greater regulatory coordination and coherence. They should have taken utmost account of common positions issued by BERT when adopting their decisions for their own home markets. BERT would not have had a partially supranational Administrative Board. It would have received only a third of its budget from the EU, the rest coming from the national level through contributions by the NRAs. In the course of the legislative process leading to the adoption of the regulation establishing the new authority, the latter was given different names. In November 2008 the Commission replaced the originally proposed EECMA by proposing a 'Body of European Telecoms Regulators' ('The Body'). This would have had less tasks and powers than the EECMA, but still it was 'supposed to reinforce the cooperation between national regulatory authorities and to establish confidence by virtue of its independence'. The Commission also restated its role as an EU agency. In February 2009, the Council took the common position not to be convinced of the necessity of institutional change: 'the Commission, to a large extent supported by the Parliament, has proposed to change the (inter) institutional set-up and, consequently, the balance of power between the various actors, regulatory authorities, the EU institutions and other stakeholders. (...) Although the Council believes that an update of the regulatory framework for electronic communications would be beneficial for the sector, it is of the view that this could be achieved by improving the current arrangements rather than by setting up alternative mechanisms. (...) The Council has opted to give the ERG formal status in a Community regulation by laying down a more precise definition of its tasks, its functioning and its relations with the Community institutions. (...) the Council has opted for a different type of legal act from that proposed by the Commission'. Having said this, the Council eventually agreed to introduce a new entity instead of upgrading the ERG, but still suggested another name for the Body: 'Unlike the European Parliament, the Council considered that the name GERT (Group of European Regulators in Telecoms) would have been more appropriate for the new body than BERT (Body of the European Telecoms Regulators). It felt, however, that GERT should neither have had the characteristics of an agency nor legal personality'. In this context, it is worth noting that such a 'saga' on the name of the body, at present, would have been contrary to the Common Approach, pursuant to which a standard term should be used for future agencies: 'European Union agency for...'. See the Common Approach, section I, para. 1. Moreover, considering the BEREC's specific features, as further described below, it appears difficult that the current name of the body might be aligned to the recommended standard denomination.

45. Regulation (EC) No. 1211 of the European Parliament and of the Council of 25 November 2009 establishing the Body of European Regulators for Electronic Communications (BEREC) and the Office, *OJ* L337/1, 18 December 2009.

46. The BEREC Regulation came into effect 20 days after its publication in the Official Journal. With publication of the Regulation in the Official Journal on 18 December 2009, the BEREC therefore came into being on 7 January 2010. The inaugural meeting to establish the BEREC was held on 28 January 2010 in the setting of the Palais d'Egmont in Brussels. The transposition of the telecoms package was due by 26 May 2011.

The institutional design of the BEREC and of the Office is original. The outcome of the long discussions in the European Parliament and the Council is indeed a two-tier institutional structure. Two entities work side by side: on one hand, there is the BEREC; on the other hand, the Office. The BEREC is supported by the BEREC Office, established as a new, small agency with the task of providing professional and administrative support services to the BEREC. Overall, the BEREC replaces the ERG but falls short of the European super-regulator which the Commission had called for.

The recitals of the BEREC Regulation hint at the debate over a super-regulator which preceded the agreement on the EU reform package. Between the lines, the conflicting opinions during the process of negotiating of the Regulation are reflected in the justifications provided for the need for a stronger central regulatory function on one hand, and the need to do so in accordance with the principles of subsidiarity and proportionality on the other.[47] Similarly, while the Commission stresses that the ERG had made a positive contribution towards consistent regulatory practice by facilitating cooperation among NRAs and between NRAs and the Commission, it also adds that 'continued and intensified cooperation and coordination among NRAs will be required to develop further the internal market in electronic communication network and services'.[48] Notably, the BEREC was established by a Regulation of the European Parliament and of the Council and not by a Commission Decision, as was the case with the ERG. This clearly shows the intention to institutionalize the BEREC and confer upon it a high legal status. However, while the Office is a classical (small) European agency, the BEREC itself is not de jure an EU agency and does not have legal personality.[49] In the next section, we are going to have a closer look at the structure and functioning of the BEREC.

[A]   Analysis of the BEREC

[1]   Institutional Structure

The BEREC is comprised of a single organ, the Board of Regulators, consisting of the heads or nominated high-level representatives of the twenty-eight NRAs established in

---

47. See, for instance, Recital 3. While it recalls that 'the need for the EU regulatory framework to be consistently applied in all Member States is essential for the successful development of an internal market for electronic communications networks and services', it also stresses that 'the EU regulatory framework sets out objectives to be achieved and provides a framework for action by national regulatory authorities (NRAs), whilst granting them flexibility in certain areas to apply the rules in the light of national conditions'.
48. Recital 5, Regulation 1211/2009. See also N. Geach, 'The Regulatory Framework Directive 2002/21/EC', in *Electronic and Mobile Commerce Law: An Analysis of Trade, Finance, Media and Cybercrime in the Digital Age*, ed. C. Wild et al. (Hatfield: University of Hertfordshire Press, 2011), 403.
49. It is interesting to note that in the arrangements proposed by the Commission, the authority would have had legal personality. On the contrary, in the arrangements proposed by the EP and the Council the authority, like the ERG, would not have had legal personality. Eventually a compromise was found by adding a supporting office to the BEREC with legal personality. It was thus mainly in response to pressure from the Commission that the BEREC's secretariat was made an EU body.

each Member State with the primary responsibility for overseeing the day-to-day operation of the markets for electronic communications networks and services. BEREC members are expected to act independently of any government, of the Commission or of any other public or private entity.[50] The EU Commission, EFTA States, and EU candidate countries participate as observers to the Board of Regulators. The Board of Regulators is assisted by a working group (Contact Network) composed of senior representatives of all members, including the European Commission and the other observers, to prepare the decisions to be taken by the Board of Regulators.[51] External experts may also be invited to take part in the meetings of the Board.[52] The Board appoints a Chair and a Vice-Chair from among its members, and their term in office is one year.[53] The plenary meetings of the Board, according to Article 4(6) of Regulation 1211/2009, shall occur at least four times a year in ordinary session to which the Commission must be invited. The Commission, or at least a third of the Board's members may request the convening of additional meetings. These meetings are to take place in a different place each time.[54] In exceptional circumstances, decisions

---

50. Every year, the members of the Board of Regulators must make a declaration of commitment to fulfil their duties and a declaration of interests which could be prejudicial to their independence in writing. These include any financial interests exceeding EUR 50,000 and/or voting rights of 5% or more per company and any work/activities performed during the previous five years in public or private companies operating within the electronic communications sector. In addition, at each meeting, members shall declare any interest which could be considered to be prejudicial to their independence with respect to any point on the agenda. The declaration of such interests will eventually lead to their exclusion from any vote on the relevant point. See Art. 19, BEREC Rules of Procedure of the Board of Regulators, *BoR (10) 03* and Annex 2 to the Rules of Procedure.

51. Art. 1(3), Rules of Procedure of the Board of Regulators, *BoR (10) 03*. In general, the Contact Network ensures the coordination of proposals to be considered by the Board of Regulators. To this end, it shall aim to resolve outstanding differences of opinion between the members; ensure that papers proposed to be submitted for consideration by the Board of Regulators are duly and timely prepared and, with the assistance of the Administrative Manager, agree the draft agenda for each meeting of the Board of Regulators. It shall also act as 'a filter and facilitator between Expert Working Groups, on one hand, and the Board of Regulators, on the other hand, with the assistance of the Office'. Interestingly, the Contact Network also operates as an informal network whose members are the key contact points between national regulatory authorities for seeking and exchanging information on regulatory issues.' See Art. 12, BEREC Rules of Procedure.

52. Art. 1, Rules of Procedure of the Board of Regulators, *BoR (10) 03*.

53. Art. 2(1) of the Rules of Procedure of the Board of Regulators, *BoR (10) 03*, states that 'before serving her/his term as Chair for one year, the Chair shall first serve one year as Vice-Chair. She/he shall also serve as Vice-Chair for the year following her/his term as Chair'. The Regulation does not provide for the possibility of extension of the one year term served by the Chair and Vice-Chairs. The first Chair of the BEREC, for 2010, was John Doherty, chair of the Irish regulator, ComReg. The BEREC Chair for 2012 is Dr Georg Serentschy, CEO of the Austrian Regulatory Authority for Broadcasting and Telecommunications (RTR-GmbH). As the BEREC Chair for 2013 and Vice-Chair for 2012 the Board of Regulators appointed Dr Leonidas Kanellos, President of the Hellenic Telecommunications and Post Commission (EETT).

54. See Art. 4(3), Rules of Procedure of the Board of Regulators, *BoR (10) 03*: 'any member wishing to host a Board of Regulators meeting shall submit a proposal to the Office. In the event of more than one proposal being received for a particular meeting, the Member planned to chair BEREC for the concerned period shall have the final decision. In the event that no proposal for hosting a meeting is presented by a Member, the Board or Regulators may request the Office to make a proposal to organize the meeting at a suitable place.'

which cannot wait until a plenary meeting are made by the Board of Regulators via electronic procedures. The Board of Regulators met on five occasions in 2010 and on four occasions in 2011.

The Board of Regulators may also decide to create Expert Working Groups, open to all members and observers, to assist with the performance of the tasks and functions of the BEREC and request the Office to provide support.[55] The Expert working groups draw together senior experts from the BEREC Member authorities, and therefore are the main channel for the NRAs to express their commitment to the work of the BEREC. In 2010, Expert Working Groups met on fifty-six occasions over a total of sixty-four days, with some of the meetings being held over two days. In addition to the meetings, the Working Groups conducted their activities electronically via conference calls and email exchanges.[56]

The voting procedure of the BEREC represents a significant innovation with regard to the system previously adopted by the ERG. The Board of Regulators shall act by a two-thirds majority of all its members unless otherwise provided in Regulation 1211/2009, in the Framework Directive or in the specific Directives.[57] It can be observed that this innovation could, on paper, make the BEREC more efficient than the ERG. The decisions of the Board are published and must include an indication of any reservations by any member NRA if it so requests.

[2]   Powers

Like the ERG, the BEREC aims at ensuring the consistent application of the EU regulatory framework and a better functioning of the internal telecom market. According to the founding regulation:

> BEREC should continue the work of the ERG, developing cooperation among NRAs, and between NRAs and the Commission, so as to ensure the consistent

---

55. Art. 11, BEREC Rules of Procedure. In accordance with the BEREC work programme for 2010, in May 2010 the Board of Regulators created 11 expert working groups and designated the relative chairs for 2010. These groups are: the Benchmarking working group; the BEREC-RSPG cooperation working group; the Convergence and Economic Analysis working group; the Framework Implementation working group; the End-User working group; the International Roaming working group; the Net Neutrality working group; the Next Generation Networks working group; the Remedies monitoring working group; the Regulatory Accounting working group and the Termination rates working group. See Decision of the Board of Regulators on the establishment of BEREC Expert Working groups, *BoR (10) 23*.

56. BEREC – Body of European Regulators for Electronic Communications, 'Annual Report 2010' (2011), 20.

57. According to these pieces of legislation, decisions will be taken by a simple majority when giving opinions on the Commission's analysis of remedies notified by national regulators. As for the quorum necessary for meetings, it 'shall be achieved when at least two-thirds of all voting members are present or represented by proxy'. See Art. 8, BEREC Rules of Procedure. It is interesting to note that the weighting voting system which characterizes the voting rules for the Member States in the Council has not been imported into BEREC's decision-making process. This reinforces the idea that the members of the Board should act independently, in the European interest and not as representatives of specific national interests. Furthermore, in contrast to the ERG, the decisions adopted by the Board of Regulators do not require approval by the Commission. See Art. 5.4 of the ERG Decision.

application in all Member States of the EU regulatory framework for electronic communications networks and services, and thereby contributing to the development of the internal market.[58]

In this sense, the BEREC can be seen as 'the last stage' of the administrative integration process in the communications sector.[59]

Similar to the role of its predecessors, the functions to be undertaken by the BEREC are characteristic of soft governance. The roles and tasks of the BEREC are set out in Articles 2 and 3 of the founding Regulation. Article 2 states that the BEREC shall develop and disseminate among NRAs regulatory best practice, such as common approaches, methodologies or guidelines on the implementation of the EU regulatory framework. In general, it should have an advisory role for national telecoms regulators when decisions have cross-border implications. On request, it shall provide assistance to NRAs on regulatory issues.[60] It shall also deliver opinions on the draft decisions, recommendations, and guidelines of the Commission, referred to in Regulation 1211/2009, the Framework Directive and the specific Directives. Then, it shall issue reports and provide advice and deliver opinions to the European Parliament and the Council, upon a reasoned request or on its own initiative, on any matter regarding electronic communications within its competence.[61] These reports can ultimately be authoritative, and the BEREC seems to be aware of this possibility. In fact, it is not uncommon to find, in BEREC reports, normative sentences like:

> coordination through BEREC could be used (...) to promote rapid implementation of any viable approach across Europe and not only in 1 or 2 Member States.[62]

---

58. Regulation (EC) No. 1211/2009 of the European Parliament and Council of 25 November 2009, Recital 8.
59. M. Quaranta & A. Di Amato, 'Chapter 19. Italy', in *Media, Advertising, & Entertainment Law Throughout the World*, ed. A.B. Ulmer (New York: Thomson West, 2011).
60. The condition that the onus remains on national regulators to seek assistance may 'limit the extent to which this role will actually be performed in practice'. See F. Rizzuto, 'Reforming the "Constitutional Fundamentals" of the European Union Telecommunications Regulatory Framework', *Computer and Telecommunications Law Review* 16, no. 2 (2010).
61. According to the BEREC Work Programme 2010, *BoR (10) 15 rev 1*, May 2010, in 2010 the Body was expected to deliver, among others, the following: a report on the operation of the Roaming Regulation 717/2007/EC in Member States as requested by the Commission; a report on Next Generation Networks Access; a report on the Regulatory principles of Open Access; reports on the conformity of national regulatory practices with ERG Common Positions on wholesale broadband access, wholesale unbundled access and wholesale leased lines; a report on regulatory accounting; a report on business services market; a report on convergent services regulation; a report on the impact of bundled offers in retail and wholesale market analysis; a report on cross-border enforcement; a report on accessibility services for disabled end-users; a report on the remedy of Functional Separation as foreseen in Arts 13a and 13b of the Access Directive; a report on issues related to the ability of consumers to switch service providers. It must be highlighted that the BEREC will play an important role in providing advice on radio frequency harmonization, including making analyses and reporting, identifying means for the development of new services, maintaining a register of spectrum use across the EU and providing advice on the common procedures for granting authorizations.
62. See BEREC, BEREC Response to the European Commission 'Public Consultation on a Review of the Functioning of Regulation (EC) No. 544/2009 (the 'Roaming Regulation')', *BoR (11) 09*, February 2011, 9. The BEREC adds that 'it would be happy to elaborate this idea further if the Commission finds merit in it'.

Or

> the point of this analysis is only to show that it should be possible to set a Eurotariff cap for 2015 which 'approaches' domestic rates, without causing network operators to price below costs or retail providers to suffer a margin squeeze.[63]

Similar sentences confirm the view that the soft law instruments of BEREC could actually 'harden', becoming de facto binding requirements. Sometimes the language of the BEREC is milder. An example is, from the same document, the sentence:

> BEREC welcomes this opportunity to discuss a further possible regulatory approach, linked to regulated access. The suggestion is to explore the possibility of inserting into the Roaming Regulation a new provision: requiring [Mobile Network Operators] to provide access for the purposes of providing a retail roaming service on reasonable request and on reasonable terms.[64]

In other instances, the BEREC declares that the aim of its reports/opinions is that of providing guidance to the NRAs.[65] Obviously, only future practice can prove whether or not the 'normative' language by BEREC is actually destined to be transformed into legislation; because of the technicalities of the field, one might expect this to be the case.

Finally, on request, the BEREC shall assist the European Parliament, the Council, the Commission and the NRAs in relations, discussions and exchanges with third parties; and assist the Commission and NRAs in the dissemination of regulatory best practices to third parties. Article 3(1) of the Regulation contains a long list of the specific tasks which have to be performed by the BEREC, with regard, in particular, to the delivering of opinions, the provision of assistance to NRAs, the assistance to the Commission, the monitoring and reporting function on the electronic communications sector. In particular, the BEREC will play a role in reviewing remedies chosen by the NRAs, pursuant to Article 7 and 7a procedures.[66] Some of these tasks are not new; rather, they are areas in which the ERG would have had an opinion in any event. However, under the new framework, the Commission and the NRAs are required to take utmost account of BEREC opinions, recommendations, guidelines, advice or regulatory best practices. This means that BEREC documents are expected to have a greater impact. Nevertheless, the European courts have already established that the obligation to take utmost account of an opinion does not affect the discretion afforded to the final decision maker to take whatever decision it considers as the most

---

63. *Ibid.*
64. *Ibid.*, 19.
65. See, for instance, the draft report on relevant market definition for business services, *BoR (10) 46 Rev1*.
66. See Art. 7(2) Framework Directive. Under this provision, effective as of May 2011, BEREC keeps track of regulatory measures notified by the NRAs to the European Commission under Art. 7 Framework Directive, as well as the Commission's concerns as expressed in their comments letters. See the combined Polish cases PL/2011/1255-1256-1257-1258 and the Polish case PL/2011/1260 in BEREC Annual Report 2011, *BoR (12) 48*, 12.

appropriate. The final regulatory decision-making power remains therefore with the Commission or the NRAs respectively.[67]

The BEREC met for the first time on 28 January 2010, supported by the encomia of the sponsoring Commissioners.[68] The BEREC Work Programme 2010, which was a follow-up to the activities which the ERG had initiated, focused on three regulatory issues: harmonization, emerging challenges, and changes to the legal regulatory framework.[69] In particular, the BEREC undertook considerable activity in relation to the field of international roaming, convergence of the telecoms markets and net neutrality. During the third plenary meeting of the Body of European Regulators of Electronic Communications in Helsinki in May 2010, the Board of Regulators approved the BEREC opinion on the draft recommendation on regulated access to Next Genera-tion Access networks (NGA).[70] This was the first BEREC opinion formally requested by the European Commission under the new European regulatory framework. The Commission subsequently modified its recommendation on the matter in line with the amendments proposed by the BEREC and adopted it in September 2010. Over the course of its first year of activities alone, in 2010, the BEREC Board of Regulators published thirty-seven documents, including ten consultations, while the Management Committee published twelve documents.[71] These figures show a significant 'activism'

---

67. F. Rizzuto, 'The Harmonised Enforcement of European Union Telecommunications Law: The Case Law of the European Judicature on the Constitutional Fundamentals', *Computer and Telecommunications Law Review* Part 1: 37; Part 2: 67 (2009).
68. See N. Kroes, European Commissioner for Competition Policy, *The important role of the Body of European Regulators for Electronic Communications*, Inaugural meeting of the BEREC Palais d'Egmont, Brussels, 28 January 2010 Reference: SPEECH/10/15, available at < http://europa. eu/rapid/pressReleasesAction.do?reference=SPEECH/10/15&format=HTML&aged=0&language =EN&guiLanguage=en > (accessed on 30 October 2012): '(...) a strong and independent BEREC is the best chance for this success. Not only for BEREC, but also in reinforcing the efforts of national regulators who might sometimes feel their independence is under pressure back home. (...) the EU Legislator has established BEREC to ensure the "consistent application" of the telecoms Regulatory framework. This is quite different from "harmonisation." In Europe's diverse telecom markets, I do *not* believe in a one-size-fits-all approach will work. We are all aware that BEREC is not a European super-regulator. However, as a body of experienced national regulators, I think you are well placed to deliver this consistent application of the regulatory framework.' See also V. Reding, Member of the European Commission responsible for Information Society and Media, *A new beginning for EU telecoms regulation: EU telecoms regulator starts work*, First meeting of the Board of Regulators of BEREC and the Management Committee of the Office 28 January 2010, Egmont Palace Brussels, Reference: SPEECH/10/13, available at < http://europa.eu/rapid/pressReleasesAction.do?reference=SPEECH/10/13 > (accessed on 30 October 2012): '(...) The new European telecoms regulator BEREC will provide a force for consistent regulation across the EU. It will be an essential partner for the European Commission in strengthening the single market also in the telecoms sector. (...) We move from the loose form of cooperation "behind closed doors" that has existed in the past within the European Regulators Group, to a more transparent and efficient approach which moves the regulators from a simple advisory body of the Commission towards an institution of its own'.
69. BEREC – Body of European Regulators for Electronic Communications, 'Annual Report 2010', 4.
70. In the coming years, the main technological trends are expected to be guided by the passage from traditional ways to the Next Generation Network or IP-based networks to a growing use of wireless communications and deployment of fibre in the local access networks.
71. BEREC – Body of European Regulators for Electronic Communications, 'Annual Report 2010', 6.

of the BEREC, if compared to the previous experience of the ERG.[72] It must also be noted that the BEREC has produced several studies and issued opinions on its own initiative, mainly collecting and elaborating information provided by the NRAs.

[B]   Analysis of the Office

[1]   Institutional Structure

The Office is an EU body established in order to provide professional and administrative support to the BEREC. The Office has legal, administrative, and financial autonomy[73] and must enjoy the most extensive legal capacity under the national law of each Member State. It is funded by a subsidy from the EU budget and from voluntary contributions from the Member States or their NRAs for specific items of operational expenditure.[74] The Office is composed of a Management Committee and an Administrative manager, who is to be the head of the Office. The number of staff is limited to the number required to carry out its duties; it is estimated in particular that the number of employees will not exceed twenty-eight.[75] The Office formally came into existence in May 2010 with the announcement of its seat in Riga, Latvia[76] and it obtained full autonomy in September 2011. The official opening took place on 14 October 2011.[77]

The composition of the Management Committee, which is supposed to act as the 'Management Board', as per the Common Approach, is identical to that establishing the Board of Regulators and is subject to the same voting rules; the only difference is that the Commission representative has voting rights. This composition of the Management

---

72. See < http://www.erg.eu.int/documents/erg/index_en.htm > (accessed on 30 October 2012). In the course of its existence, the ERG adopted slightly more than 100 documents in total.
73. The revenues and resources of the Office consist of a subsidy from the European Union and contributions from the Member States or from their NRAs made on a 'voluntary basis'. See Art. 11, Regulation 1211/2009. The Board approves the voluntary financial contribution from Member States or NRAs before they are made. The approval must be unanimous if all Member States or NRAs are contributing or by simple majority if a number of Member States or NRAs have decided to make a contribution. Each Member State shall also make sure that NRAs have the adequate financial resources required to participate in the work of the Office.
74. The 2010 budget for the Office prepared by the Commission at the beginning of 2009 provided for an expenditure of EUR 3.67 million, covering a staff of 18 persons. In this context, it is important to recall that in order to guarantee the independence of the BEREC and the Office, the Member States must ensure that NRAs are properly financed. This is a provision which indirectly seeks to ensure that the participation and work of the NRAs in the BEREC is ensured. The planned budget for 2012 of the BEREC Office amounts to EUR 4.44 million.
75. The ceilings for the staff recruitment were fixed as follows: 18 agents in 2010, 22 in 2011 and 28 in 2012–2013. A high number of national experts (up to 10) is expected to be seconded to the Office.
76. The decision on the location of the Office was obviously a matter for the Council. The Board of Regulators expressed its clear preference for locating the secretariat/support function in Brussels as the best way to achieve the effective and efficient functioning of the BEREC. Among the factors for that choice, the Board listed the proximity to the EU institutions, facilitating BEREC's communication with the EU institutions; enabling it to carry out its role fully; the establishment and support to BEREC's Expert Working Groups and the transparency and interaction with stakeholders, which are mainly based in Brussels. The final decision on the location of the BEREC was taken in May 2010.
77. See BEREC Office, Management Committee, Annual Activity Report, 3 July 2012, MC (12) 16, 9.

Committee, which does not include either any member designated by the European Parliament or any stakeholders' representative, however, clearly falls short of the requirements set forth in the Common Approach.[78] Similar to the Board of Regulators, the Management Committee of the Office is also assisted by a working group (Contact Network), composed of senior representatives of all members to prepare the decisions to be taken by the Committee itself and a similar regime applies to observers.[79] The rules for the appointment and the term and the duties of the Chair and Vice-Chairs of the Management Committee are the same as those for the Chair and Vice-Chairs of the Board of Regulators of the BEREC.[80] Yet, the plurality of internal bodies appears to be far from the governance structure envisaged by the Common Approach if one considers, for instance, the necessity of the appointment of a single 'Director'.[81] It is noteworthy that the regular meetings of the Management Committee are held at the same date and venue as the meetings of the Board of Regulators.[82]

The Administrative Manager is appointed by the Management Committee for a three-year term with the possibility of extending it for another three years if justified.[83] He or she is responsible for the day-to-day management of the Office. The other staff of the Office is divided into three areas: administration and finance, executive support, and programme management. Staff members are to be appointed as officials of the EU.[84]

[2]   Powers

The Office provides professional and administrative support services to the Board of Regulators,[85] collects information from NRAs, and transmits information and regulatory best practices to them.[86] The Office also supports the Chair of the Board[87] and

---

78. Common Approach, section II, para. 10.
79. Art. 1(3), Rules of Procedure MC Office.
80. Art. 2, Rules of Procedure MC Office.
81. See Common Approach, section II, paras 14 et seq.
82. Art. 4, Rules of Procedure MC Office.
83. The first administrative manager of the Office, Ando Rehemaa, formally took up his position on 1 October 2010.
84. It will also be possible for the Office to have seconded national experts from the Member States on a temporary basis and for a maximum of three years.
85. This includes ICT, Legal, HR and other support. The BEREC Office also supports the BEREC in its tasks mentioned in Art. 2(b) and (e) of the BEREC Regulation.
86. See section 2.1, BEREC Office Work Programme 2011, *MC (10) 39* BEREC Office WP 2011_final: 'The foreseen tasks of BEREC-Office to support BEREC in this regard include: data collection from NRAs, including verification and presenting the results to the experts and the Board of Regulators; periodically ask NRAs about new regulatory decisions and conformity with BEREC Common Positions; analyse the remedies proposed by NRAs and Commission concerns expressed in comments letters; support in contacting external stakeholders/ external parties; conduct studies; support the Working Group in producing the yearly report on regulatory accounting; exchange of best practices and technical expertise.'
87. This includes press and communications support, managing relations with external stakeholders and logistical support to CN and plenary.

supports and manages the expert working groups that may be formed by the Board.[88] As explained above, the Board of Regulators and the Management Committee appear to have identical compositions, but different functions. In short, while the former is accorded the authority to adopt all advisory acts, the latter is charged with supporting the work of the former. In particular, the tasks of the Management Committee concern its relationship with the Administrative Manager, the staff, budget and financial issues and the functioning of the Office in general.

[3]   Overall Compliance of the BEREC and the Office with the Principles of Good Governance

The Regulation establishing the BEREC contains specific provisions dealing with the political control over the body. The Board of the BEREC is required to adopt an annual work programme before the end of the preceding year to which it relates; upon adoption, it has to be notified to the Council, the Commission, and the European Parliament.[89] An annual report must also be produced specifying in details the BEREC's activities and sent to the same bodies as well as to the European Economic and Social Committee and the Court of Auditors by 15 June each year.[90] On the basis of any issues within the annual report, the Chair of the Board may be summoned to address the European Parliament.

Article 1 of Regulation 1211/2009 requires the BEREC to carry out its tasks independently, impartially, and transparently. According to Articles 18 and 22, the BEREC and the Office are committed to carry out their activities with a high level of transparency, ensuring that the public and any interested parties are given objective, reliable and easily accessible information, in particular in relation to the results of their work. In addition, the management of documents held by the BEREC is governed by Regulation 1049/2001 EC.[91] The practical rules for the implementation of Regulation 1049/2001 regarding public access to the documents held by the BEREC have been adopted by the Board of Regulators of the BEREC in May 2010[92] and reflect the usual rules with regard to access to documents in the EU. The BEREC and the Office shall not disclose to third parties any processed or received information for which confidential treatment has been requested. This provision obviously protects business secrets. The publication or making available to the public or any stakeholder of any BEREC documents requires the prior approval of the Board of Regulators.[93] This, in any case,

---

88. This contains logistical and administrative support. For the organization and coordination of e.g., Art. 7 FD ad hoc Expert Teams, see Art. 6(2) item 5 BEREC Regulation.
89. Art. 5(4) Regulation No. 1211/2009.
90. Ibid.
91. Regulation (EC) No. 1049/2001 of the European Parliament and of the Council of 30 May 2001 regarding public access to European Parliament, Council and Commission documents, OJ L145, 31 May 2001, 43.
92. Decision by the Board of Regulators of the Body of European Regulators for Electronic Communications (BEREC) concerning the transparency and access to documents at the BEREC, BoR (10) 26.
93. See Art. 4(2) of Decision BoR (10) 26: 'The Board of Regulators, assisted by the Office, shall take decisions regarding confirmatory applications.'

cannot prejudice the right of access to BEREC documents under EU legislation.[94] All BEREC documents approved for publication by the Board of Regulators are published on a website which is run by the Office.[95] These documents include the brochures and other documents meant for the general public issued by the BEREC and any document adopted by the Board of Regulators for publication, as foreseen by the annual work programme of the BEREC; all press releases issued by the BEREC; the work programme of the BEREC; the BEREC annual report and the agendas and conclusions of the Board of Regulators and Contact Network meetings.[96]

Specific rules are laid down in order to avoid conflicts of interest. According to Article 21 of the BEREC Regulation, the Members of the Board of Regulators and of the Management Committee, the Administrative Manager and the staff of the Office shall make an annual declaration of commitments and a declaration of interests which might be considered to be prejudicial to their independence.[97] As a rule, therefore, any person facing a conflict of interest situation is under a duty to inform and discuss the best way of avoiding that the conflict of interest having an impact on the validity of the decisions. The declarations are published on the BEREC website and entered in a register held by the Office. According to the BEREC internal guidelines, cases that could lead to a conflict of interest include a situation:

> where a Member of the Board of Regulators and/or of the Management Committee, the Administrative Manager or the staff of the Office are in a position to make or make a decision, or are in a position to act or do act, motivated by other or additional considerations than the best interests of BEREC.[98]

The example appears to be vague, and in any case the document itself adds that 'it is recognized that it is often difficult to objectively assess whether a conflict of interest situation exists.'[99] Moreover, it is not clear what the consequences are when a conflict of interest is found and how far BEREC members, who declare to have a conflict of interest, are excluded from the decision-making process. The internal guidelines only provide that:

> the Administrative Manager, the Management Committee or the Board of Regulators will jointly evaluate whether a declared interest constitutes a conflict. As a

---

94. Art. 17, BEREC Rules of Procedure.
95. Art. 18, BEREC Rules of Procedure. The public register of BEREC documents has been operational since 1 August 2012 and is maintained only electronically.
96. Art. 8(1), Decision by the Board of Regulators of the Body of European Regulators for Electronic Communications (BEREC) concerning the transparency and access to documents at the BEREC, *BoR (10) 26*.
97. See the model for the annual declaration of interests of the members of the Management Committee (Annex 3 to *MC (10) 02*). In particular, the members of the Management Committee are required to declare, among others, any work/ activities during the previous five years in public or private companies operating within the electronic communications sector; any financial interest in companies relevant to the operating area of BEREC during the previous five years and exceeding EUR 50,000 and/or voting rights of 5% or more per company, work and activities, whether or not remunerated, for and/or on behalf of companies or organizations relevant to BEREC.
98. See *MC (11) 02* Declaration of interest_Rev_1.
99. *Ibid.*

result of such assessment, the matter will be brought to the attention of the Board of Regulators/Management Committee.[100]

Arguably, clearer rules on the consequences of the establishment a conflict of interest should have been laid down; yet, the current policy appears to be in line with the relevant guidelines provided for in the Common Approach.[101]

With regard to public consultation, the BEREC Regulation lays down the applicable general principles. In particular, Article 17 sets an obligation on the BEREC to consult interested parties, where appropriate, before adopting opinions, regulatory best practice or reports. The Rules of Procedure of the BEREC define the criteria under which the Board of Regulators shall decide to launch public consultations, leaving it up to the Board of Regulators to decide on a case-by-case basis about the need to consult interested parties.[102] Thus, it is at the BEREC's sole discretion when consultations shall be held and with whom, as no definition is provided of the terms 'interested parties'. In September 2010, general rules regarding procedures for carrying out consultations of draft BEREC documents were published.[103] Public consultation can be organized both as a written consultation or a public hearing,[104] with the timescale for responses being fifteen to twenty working days in principle.[105] Furthermore, the BEREC can publish a summary of all the contributions received and an explanation as to how the views expressed were taken into account in the final position.[106] The BEREC is obliged to adopt an annual programme.[107] It must consult on this and transmit it to the European Parliament, the Council, and the Commission as soon as it is adopted. During the first year of operation, the BEREC also held a number of public hearings in Brussels to supplement public consultations and debriefings following each plenary meeting.[108]

It appears that, apart from the specific reference to the annual work programme, which shall be subject to consultation, the BEREC shall, for the rest, decide which draft documents should be subject to public consultation as well as the relevant consultation deadlines. This mechanism is problematic as it does not guarantee full accountability of the body. Too much discretion is left to the Board of Regulators, to the extent that it is not even possible to provide a tentative assessment of the draft BEREC documents

---

100. *Ibid.*
101. Common Approach, section II, para. 11.
102. Art. 16, BEREC Rules of Procedure.
103. BEREC Procedures for Public Consultations held by BEREC, *BoR (10) 27* final
104. *Ibid.*, Art. 2.
105. Confronted with the criticism by some market players, the BEREC has defended the choice of a short timescale for responses on the ground that it is substantially in line with the common practice (30 days) applied by many NRAs at the national level and that, while the Rules of Procedure provide a general indication, the Board of Regulators may set different timescales, depending on the specific circumstances. See BEREC report of the consultation on the draft BEREC procedures for public consultations, *BoR (10) 27* Rev1b final, 3. In any case, the BEREC declared that the consultation period could be extended if circumstances require it, for instance to take account of holiday periods.
106. *Ibid.*, Art. 4.
107. The first work programme of the BEREC in 2010 was based on a draft work programme on which the ERG had previously consulted.
108. BEREC – Body of European Regulators for Electronic Communications, 'Annual Report 2010', 20.

that might eventually be subject to public consultation. Some indication is provided by the 'Explanatory Note to the BEREC Procedures for Public Consultations held by the BEREC'.[109] The outline only constitutes a tentative assessment of the BEREC documents which might eventually be subject to public consultation; the specific content and scope of the documents will drive each specific Board of Regulators' decision on whether to consult stakeholders. It is clear that the practices of the BEREC might attract, and indeed already attracted,[110] some criticism. In particular, it is striking that public consultation is not needed on the BEREC opinions on draft decisions, recommendations and guidelines of the Commission, to the Commission on national draft measures of NRAs, to the European Parliament and Council and to NRAs on cross-border disputes, which are probably the most important documents prepared by the BEREC. The BEREC's practice is however in line with Article 17 of the BEREC Regulation, which clearly provides room for discretion to the Board of Regulators in the evaluation of the need to hold public consultations when it states that 'where appropriate, BEREC shall, before adopting opinions, regulatory best practice or reports, consult interested parties (...)'.

Overall, in terms of transparency, the BEREC represents a significant improvement from the past practices: the loose cooperation behind closed doors, which existed in the ERG and which completely ignored transparency questions, is replaced by a more transparent approach, which appears to meet the reporting requirements set out by the Common Approach, at least with regard to the submission of an annual report to the EU institutions.[111] However, the BEREC's practices fall short of the Common Approach's recommendations in terms of relations with stakeholders, as the latter are neither represented in the Management Board of the BEREC nor are they involved in the BEREC's internal bodies and working groups. Overall, problems in terms of compliance with the principles of good governance appear to exist because of the nature of the BEREC, a body positioned in between two regimes: the EU on one hand and the national telecommunications regime on the other. The decisions adopted within the BEREC are likely to have impacts on both levels simultaneously due to the relationship between these two levels. In this complex scenario, the question remains where the main forum of accountability lies: at the EU, at the national level, or at both levels concurrently?

---

109. *BoR (10) 27 final.*
110. See the contributions by COLT, ETNO, Vodafone Romania and Wind on the draft BEREC procedures, available at < http://erg.eu.int/documents/cons/index_en.htm > .
111. A central concern of the Common Approach is that EU agencies should produce one single annual report including not only information on the implementation of their annual work programme, but also, *inter alia*, a budget and staff policy plan, management and internal control systems and audit findings. See Common Approach, section V, paras 46 et seq. See also House of Commons – European Scrutiny Committee, 'Fifth Report of Session 2010–2011' (2010), 43. See also the question asked by Lord Stoddart of Swindon on the EU Telecommunications Regulator and the answer provided by the Parliamentary Under-Secretary of State for Communications, Technology and Broadcasting Lord Carter of Barnes: '[BEREC]'s structure and operations accord with UK policy objectives which include independence, transparency, accountability and cost-effectiveness. We consequently support the creation of BEREC within the context of the framework review'. See < http://www.publications.parliament.uk/pa/ld 200809/ldhansrd/text/90428w0001.htm#column_WA28 > (accessed on 8 July 2013).

The two-tier institutional structure of the BEREC and the Office seems to complicate the accountability of these bodies. Network governance literature has extensively illustrated the negative effects of networks in terms of the accountability of the network members and of the policy they produce.[112] As observed by Cengiz, networks follow opaque procedures, involve actors from multiple levels, and tend to escape accountability mechanisms 'almost by their very nature'.[113] In the case of the BEREC and the Office, it remains unclear whether or not the Commission can be held accountable for decisions taken by the BEREC. Second, the European Courts will continue to have only a marginal voice on the regime, due to the reliance of the BEREC on soft law measures, which prevents the review of legality procedure under Article 263 Treaty on the Functioning of the European Union (TFEU). But this ultimately has two consequences: first, it results in the exclusion of judicial control over the decisions taken within the network as a safeguard for the parties involved. Second, it prevents the Courts from serving as a dispute resolution forum between the network members themselves in case of disputes.[114] Despite the formal institutional innovations, the establishment of the BEREC and the Office thus does not solve problems in terms of accountability. Had the EU telecom authority been designed as a true regulatory agency, compliant with the Common Approach, instead of a hybrid institutional model, this may have been a better solution for ensuring the respect of the principles of good governance.

§7.04   EVALUATION OF THE BEREC AND THE OFFICE: NEW MODEL OR COSMETIC EXERCISE?

It might be useful to compare the main features of the BEREC and the Office, looking in particular at the objectives, mandates and tasks defined in the founding Regulation. First, it is necessary to qualify the bodies concerned. For the Office, the analysis is rather straightforward: it is a small agency, featuring the essential characteristics of an EU agency as identified in the Common Approach. However, the BEREC has most of the characteristics of the ERG, which, as we concluded in the sections above, represented a genuine example of a network in the technical sense of the word. The new arrangements for the BEREC are thus a form of consolidation that builds on the existing structures, rather than being a clear break from the past. It could be argued that the BEREC and the Office together, given the identical composition of the Board of Regulators and the Management Committee, bear similarities with the model structure and governance identified in the Common Approach. But, at the same time, the BEREC alone possesses certain distinguishing elements. In this context, it is questionable

---

112. Y. Papadopoulos, 'Problems of Democratic Accountability in Network and Multilevel Governance', *European Law Journal* 13, no. 4 (2007); S. Lavrijssen-Heijmans & L. Hancher, 'Networks on Track: From European Regulatory Networks to European Regulatory "Network Agencies"', *Legal Issues of Economic Integration* 36, no. 1 (2009).
113. F. Cengiz, 'Multi-Level Governance in Competition Policy: The European Competition Network', *European Law Review* 35, no. 5 (2010): 8. See also C. Scott, 'The Governance of the European Union: The Potential for Multi-Level Control', *European Law Journal* 8, no. 1 (2002).
114. See, on the same line of reasoning: Cengiz, *supra* n. 113, at 673.

whether the group of regulators that sits in the BEREC can be deemed as an agency, a multi-level policy network or rather as a different entity. As for the agency, the answer is in the negative: the BEREC is very far away from a true internal market agency and does not include the competences which are usually reserved to European agencies.

The general characteristics of a network identified by the political science literature can be used once again when assessing the BEREC's features. First, a network generally emerges (naturally) between actors who need mutual cooperation in search of a common goal. This feature partially still holds true: the formation of the BEREC is not a break away from the past, but rather a formal recognition of the existing network. Only the Office has been designed centrally and largely to accommodate the desire of the European institutions. Second, a network can function effectively and can ultimately guarantee consistent policy enforcement only if there is harmony and homogeneity between the network members. In terms of powers and independence, to a large extent such harmony exists between the telecom regulators, mainly because of the influence of EU legislation in that field. Obviously there are authorities, the more experienced and resourceful ones, which are more active than others. But this is normal in the framework of a twenty-eight Member States Union. The BEREC is still a flat organization, lacking a hierarchical structure. Third, a network generally corresponds to an organization which produces policy outcomes based on agreement and consensus reached through extensive communication between network members. This is not true for the BEREC, where decisions are adopted by a two-thirds majority, unless provided otherwise.[115] This is a significant improvement from the ERG which, with its practice of working by consensus, had strong similarities with the traditional intergovernmental organizations. Fourth, the classical policy outcomes for networks are not binding decisions or soft law measures in general. This is only partially true for the BEREC. Although officially the BEREC is just providing opinions, advice and recommendations, there is an obligation for the Commission and the NRAs to take utmost account of the BEREC's output. This might eventually lead to a de facto binding power of that advice. The fifth feature of a network, namely the fact that the cooperation mechanisms of a network are not predetermined but rather they generally emerge naturally in time as the network continues to function, is also only partially true in the case of the BEREC. Indeed, specific and detailed cooperation mechanisms were predetermined by Regulation 1211/2009. The formal rules were only partially built on the tradition of cooperation and the common practices between the ERG members. In addition, one should not forget the creation of the Office which was set up next to the BEREC in order to support it.

This split personality and the fact that the Office is a small agency might hinder the performances of the BEREC. As observed by Hancher and Larouche:

> on the surface, BEREC is set up so as to comply with the *Meroni*[116] doctrine. (...) however, if [it] ends up with a sizeable expert staff and the Commission starts to rely increasingly on its advice, then BEREC will in practice be taking decisions

---

115. See the simple majority requirement in Art. 7a remedy proceedings.
116. Case 9/56, *Meroni & Co., Industrie Metallurgiche, S.p.a. v. High Authority of the ECSC*, 1957-58 ECR 133.

for the Commission, including some decisions going beyond mere implementation.[117]

In practice, BEREC's recommendations will likely affect the situation of market actors in the EU Member States, but the BEREC would exercise powers which are given to the NRAs and not to the Commission.[118] In this sense, on the one hand, there would not be any issue of non-compliance with the *Meroni* doctrine, but rather there would be a contribution of the BEREC in guaranteeing and fostering consistency among NRA's decisions, especially in the field of remedies. On the other hand, however, the BEREC's independence from the Commission may prove to be problematic in terms of success in completing the internal market through regulatory convergence. With a new actor in the regulatory process, the procedures seem to be more complex now. As observed by Rizzuto:

> it is not inconceivable that BEREC could become a vehicle for subtly protecting the regulatory autonomy of NRAs. On the other hand, it could develop into a vital source of assistance to the Commission in encouraging regulatory convergence and consistency if it puts in place a system of constant institutionalised dialogue, through the establishment of expert working groups(...).[119]

In light of the above, it can be concluded that the BEREC is not a new agency model but rather a hybrid institutional network model, possessing some, but not all, of the characteristics identified for policy networks by the political science literature. Its features clearly mirror the intention of the European institutions to institutionalize the pre-existing network of regulators and to confer a higher status upon it, with a strengthened and recognized position in the EU law framework. The BEREC is, in essence, a network which has been remodelled through an unusual institutionalization process. Basically, the network has become part of European law; it has been absorbed into the institutional framework of the EU. Through the formalization of its operations, it has become a hybrid network whose general compliance with the central require- ments of the recent Common Approach to agencies is problematic.[120]

The legal analysis of the evolution of the institutional bodies established in the field of EU telecom regulation leads to the conclusion that the turn to the BEREC represented little more than giving a new structure and a new appearance to the already existing network of regulatory authorities, to the extent that the adage 'everything must change so that everything can remain the same' seems to fit this picture. The establishment of an EU regulator with stronger powers and a structure aligned with that of EU agencies, as described in the Common Approach, would have

---

117. Hancher & Larouche, *supra* n. 17.
118. *Ibid.*
119. Rizzuto, *supra* n. 60, at 53.
120. Levi-Faur describes it as 'an agency disguised as a network', or an 'agencified network'. See Levi-Faur, *supra* n. 1, at 5. See also A. Saz-Carranza & F. Longo, 'The Evolution of the Governance of Regulatory Networks: The Case of the European Telecommunications Regula- tory Networks', Jerusalem Papers in Regulation & Governance, Working Paper No. 41, January 2012.

probably contributed better to a solution for the problems of the electronic communications single market. With the BEREC, the European dimension has an enhanced presence, when compared to that of the ERG. But the functioning of the BEREC is very intergovernmental in nature and risks are high that an overall European outlook will be missing in the operation of the new body.

§7.05 CONCLUSION

We have sought in this chapter to assess the legal features of the institutional design of European telecommunications policy and to assess the BEREC's legal status not only in comparison with its predecessors, from a historical perspective, but also in the light of the provisions of the Common Approach. The first models of governance of EU telecommunications recalled what Dehousse had called 'regulation by networks';[121] the networks (the IRG and the ERG) did not possess legal personality or autonomous powers normally associated with regulatory authorities. They were simply institutional settings where the national authorities could interact with each other and with the Commission on a variety of matters necessary for a successful exercise of their regulatory mandates. Despite many efforts, good intentions and undoubtedly some positive experiences, the networks faced many difficulties in ensuring the consistent implementation of the EU regulatory rules within the Member States. The networks also failed to address the problems related to accountability and transparency adequately, at a stage of great complexity for the European governance of telecoms.

Things have not changed with the creation of the BEREC: the latter may have a voice in several instances but it cannot legally impose its opinion. Therefore, its creation does not alter the hard law balance of regulatory competence laid down in the pre-existing regulatory framework. Moreover, the introduction of a two-tier institutional player in the regulatory process brings complexity to the existing consultative and consolidating mechanisms. The BEREC is the result of a European political compromise, reflecting on one hand the intergovernmental and not supranational character of EU telecommunications regulation, and on the other hand the desire to foster flexibility in the regulatory decision-making processes.

Certainly the BEREC replaces the loose cooperation behind closed doors of the ERG with a more transparent and more efficient approach; however, it does not seem to comply with the institutional and the operational criteria of EU agencies, as defined in the Common Approach. Rather, it shows a number of shortcomings, such as the anomalous two-tier structure and the lack of a member appointed by the European Parliament in the Management Board(s), which should be adjusted. Moreover, its accountability and openness to participation remain critical and far from the guidelines of the Common Approach. Lastly, the creation of the BEREC might foster cooperation at the EU level, but in practice regulation in the electronic communications sector remains to a large extent a national competence. In fact, at the EU level, despite the new

---

121. R. Dehousse, 'Regulation by Networks in the European Community: The role of European Agencies', *Journal of European Public Policy* 4 (1997).

institutional framework, the policy-making processes continue to be characterized by soft law tools. The dominant actor will be not the BEREC itself nor the Office, but the various national regulators sitting together in the BEREC's Board of Regulators. The recent institutional developments in the EU telecom regulatory field appear, in fact, to have been inspired and driven by the institutional self-interest of national regulators seeking to maintain (and possibly to extend) their influence in the EU regulatory processes and to strengthen their position vis-à-vis the EU institutions, despite the spirit of 'enhanced cooperation between Member States and the EU' which the Joint Statement accompanying the Common Approach requires EU agencies to pursue.

With the establishment of the BEREC, the national regulators have been empowered with a formal role in the EU. The institutional apparatus for the definition and the implementation of the new electronic communications legislative framework is definitely 'European' on paper, but the actual control over the functioning of the markets of the EU Member States is still dominated by national level interests. The picture that emerges is clearly one of coordination of national interests and policies rather than harmonization and convergence. All this leads to hesitations about the BEREC's future performance and on the point whether or not it will ensure consistency between the NRAs' approaches.

PART IV   Accountability and Democratic Control of European Agencies

CHAPTER 8

The Theory and Practice of EU Agency Autonomy and Accountability: Early Day Expectations, Today's Realities and Future Perspectives

Madalina Busuioc & Martijn Groenleer

§8.01   INTRODUCTION: FROM SOLUTION TO PROBLEM

During the 1990s and early 2000s, agencies were hailed as a solution to the many problems the EU was facing. Agencies could help increase the EU's effectiveness by providing high-quality expertise and problem-solving capacity, no longer solely relying on national institutes, centres, or agencies. They could at the same time boost the EU's legitimacy also given the manner in which such expertise would be rendered: open to public participation and transparent, particularly by comparison to the opaque (comitology) committee system, so as to ensure interest group monitoring, as well as independent from political and industry interference. All this at a time when the European Commission itself was grappling with a serious legitimacy crisis.

Whereas EU agencies have proliferated since then, with over thirty agencies currently in operation, their popularity has significantly declined in recent years. Initially created as part of a reform process, they have now often come to be perceived as a problem and are subject to reform themselves. Their non-majoritarian character, which does not sit comfortably with a traditional constitutional model, and perceived independence gave rise to growing anxiety about agencies becoming 'uncontrollable centres of arbitrary power'.[1] The haphazard creation of agencies led to calls of restraint from the European Parliament (EP) in particular where it concerned the delegation of

---

1. M. Everson, 'Independent Agencies: Hierarchy Beaters?', *European Law Journal* 1, no. 2 (1995):190.

autonomous powers to agencies and to vociferous concerns about their accountability and the need for increased oversight.[2] Interest groups have complained about their lack of transparency and openness and the gains in terms of public participation remain uncertain.[3]

In reaction, the Commission has proposed several reforms over the years to deal with the increasingly heterogeneous population of agencies, their autonomous role, and their alleged lack of accountability. While some have failed because of a lack of support from the Council and/or the Parliament – for example, the Draft inter-institutional agreement made no progress due to the Council's political opposition[4] – others have been somewhat more successful in that they brought about a level of institutional reflection with regard to agency creation. For instance, most recently, the Commission, the Parliament, and the Council have managed to agree on a 'Common Approach' towards agency governance, pledging to take it into account in the context of their future decisions concerning EU agencies.[5]

While two relatively weak agencies were founded in 1975, the creation of the European Environment Agency (EEA) in 1990 can be considered the real start of the 'agencification' process at the EU level, with a constant flow of new agencies being set up ever since. In the twenty years of practical experience with EU agencies that followed, it has become evident that the governance of these entities is not merely an administrative and technocratic matter, as initially argued or expected. It is an inherently political issue that gives rise to fierce inter-institutional struggles and heavy contestation in terms of its potential consequences for the distribution of resources and the balance of power in the EU. Ironically, the EU's non-majoritarian world is heavily politicized.

In this chapter, we address the perennial challenge that underlies agency governance[6] – as well as rendering it an inherently political issue: the balance between the autonomy of agencies, arguably the crucial ingredient for the effective operation of this model, and the accountability they must render, critical to their legitimacy (and

2. European Parliament, European Parliament resolution of 13 January 2004 on the Communication from the Commission: 'The operating framework for the European Regulatory Agencies', OJ C92 E/119, 16 April 2004, pp. 123–124 and European Parliament resolution of 21 October 2008 on a strategy for the future settlement of the institutional aspects of Regulatory Agencies (2008/2103(INI)) OJ C15 E/27, 21 January 2010.
3. M. Busuioc, *European Agencies: Law and Practices of Accountability* (Oxford: Oxford University Press, 2013).
4. Commission of the European Communities, Draft Interinstitutional Agreement on the operating framework for the European Regulatory Agencies, COM(2005) 59 final, 25 February 2005.
5. Council of the European Union, Evaluation of European Union agencies: Endorsement of the Joint Statement and Common Approach, 11450/12, 18 June 2012. See Annex 2 to this book.
6. A. Kreher, 'Agencies in the European Community – A Step Towards Administrative Integration in Europe', *Journal of European Public Policy* 4, no. 2 (1997): 225–245; E. Vos, 'Agencies and the European Union', in *Agencies in European and Comparative Law*, eds. L. Verhey & T. Zwart (Maastricht: Intersentia, 2003), 113–147; M. Groenleer, 'The Commission and Agencies', in *The European Commission*, ed. D. Spence (London: John Harper Publishing, 2006), 132–148; M. Busuioc, 'Accountability, Control and Independence: The Case of European Agencies', *European Law Journal* 15, no. 5 (2009): 599–615; M. Busuioc, D. Curtin & M. Groenleer, 'Agency Growth between Autonomy and Accountability: The European Police Office as a 'Living Institution', *Journal of European Public Policy* 18, no. 6 (2011): 848–867.

that of the EU more generally). We trace how, across the board, the autonomy and accountability of EU agencies has developed, to what extent early expectations have been matched or challenges have arisen.

The chapter proceeds as follows. First of all, we take stock of the debate on EU agencies and their autonomy and accountability. We have another look at the early day expectations of agencies as non-majoritarian institutions. Subsequently, we shift our focus to the realities of agencies today on the basis of extensive empirical research into the actual practice of autonomy and accountability. Finally, in the concluding section, we reflect on the findings, matching them to early day expectations, pinpointing the challenges ahead for the EU's agencification process.

§8.02 EARLY DAY EXPECTATIONS

[A] (Policy) Effectiveness through Independent Expertise

Much of the discourse surrounding the creation of EU agencies as well as the early years of agency creation emphasized agencies' independence, which would enable them to provide technical and scientific expertise, removed from political or industry interests. Indeed, as the Commission stated: 'the independence of their technical and/or scientific assessments is […] their real *raison d'être*.'[7] Agencies' independent expertise was supposed to increase the effectiveness of EU policy making, resolving functional as well as political problems, both in the preparatory and in the implementation phase.

[1] Improving Policy Advice

For a long time, the EU lacked its own experts to rely on for advice. The information available on which to base EU policy decisions was usually gathered at the Member State level by national agencies often lacking the necessary data collection capacities or using a variety of data gathering methodologies. This hindered the aggregation of data at the EU level. In the area of environmental protection, for instance, it proved difficult to gather comparable, reliable and objective data on environmental issues for the whole EU. At the end of the 1980s, the Commission, realizing that the Member States would probably not agree on expanding its services, therefore proposed the creation of an independent body, the EEA, to coordinate national resources and structures and amass EU data.[8]

---

7. Commission of the European Communities, Communication from the Commission. The Operating Framework for the European Regulatory Agencies, COM(2002) 718 final, 11 December 2002, p. 5.
8. A. Schout, 'The European Environment Agency (EEA): Heading Towards Maturity?', in *The Role of Specialised Agencies in Decentralising EU Governance. Report Presented to the Commission*, eds. M. Everson, G. Majone, L. Metcalfe & A. Schout (1999), 174–181; M. Groenleer, *The Autonomy of European Union Agencies: A Comparative Study of Institutional Development* (Delft: Eburon, 2009); M. Martens, 'Voice or Loyalty? The Evolution of the European Environment Agency (EEA)', *Journal of Common Market Studies* 48, no. 4 (2010): 881–901.

If expertise was available at the EU level, it was still often provided by national civil servants, for instance representing the Member States in comitology committees, or by experts in scientific committees that – while appointed by the Commission – were still nominated by the Member States. As a result, policy making was constrained by national interests, making it difficult to take informed decisions not driven by politics. This became particularly clear in the case of food safety regulation where scientists on the scientific committees for food and veterinary issues remained closely linked to national ministries of agriculture or economic affairs. Through these scientists, Member States frequently acted in defence of domestic industries, inhibiting the introduction of common regulatory measures to properly police the internal market for food. This allowed, for instance, the spread of Bovine Spongiform Encephalopathy (BSE) in the early 1990s. After the BSE crisis, the European Food Safety Authority (EFSA) was created to assess food risks independently, replacing or rather absorbing existing committees. Relying on scientific evidence in assisting the Commission and the Member States, EFSA was said to be in a better position to effectively manage such risks.[9]

[2]   *Enhancing the Enforcement of Policy Decisions*

Not only was comparable and reliable information and independent expertise lacking, the EU also did not have the capacity to police the implementation of policy decisions on the ground, this being the responsibility of the Member States. Frequently, Member States were unwilling to enforce EU rules because of national traditions, cultural differences and industry interests, or unable to do so because of lacking or failing regulatory enforcement structures and arrangements. After the sinking of the Erika oil tanker in 1999, legislation was adopted to improve maritime safety and prevent environmental pollution, the so-called Erika packages. The packages included the creation of a European Maritime Safety Agency (EMSA) to assist the Commission in monitoring the implementation of EU legislation in the Member States. Before the agency was established, however, the Prestige oil tanker sank, a disaster which according to the Commission could have been avoided if only Member States had applied and enforced the Erika packages fully.[10]

Even if Member States coordinated their actions, such as in European networks of regulatory or supervisory authorities, such coordination generally remained without binding effect, as a result of which Member States could still implement EU rules in

---

9. E. Vos, 'EU Food Safety Regulation in the Aftermath of the BSE Crisis', *Journal of Consumer Policy* 23, no. 3 (2000): 227–255; S. Krapohl & K. Zurek, 'The Perils of Committee Governance: Intergovernmental Bargaining during the BSE Scandal in the European Union', *European Integration Online Papers* 10, no. 2 (2006): 1–20; J. Lezaun & M. Groenleer, 'Food Control Emergencies and the Territorialization of the European Union', *Journal of European Integration* 28, no. 5 (2006): 437–455.

10. M. Groenleer, M. Kaeding & E. Versluis, 'Regulatory Governance through Agencies of the European Union? The Role of the European Agencies for Maritime and Aviation Safety in the Implementation of European Transport Legislation', *Journal of European Public Policy* 17, no. 8 (2010): 1212–1230.

different ways. From the point of view of the Commission, this resulted in undesirable differences among Member States and their businesses and citizens. For example, the European Regulators Group (ERG), a network in the area of telecoms, has been criticized in the past for being overly oriented towards consensus and, hence, eschewing tough measures on its members. It was therefore transformed, taking a more agency-like structure and being renamed the Body of European Regulators for Electronic Communications (BEREC), albeit after fierce opposition from national politicians and regulators, as well as lengthy negotiations with the European Parliament.[11]

[3] *Beyond Existing Institutional Solutions*

Agencies were thus presented as a solution to a set of functional and political problems because of their expected ability to provide expert based policy advice, to help enforce policy decisions and, importantly, to do so independently. Existing institutional solutions to the problems laid out above – the Commission, comitology committees, scientific committees and networks of national authorities – were not considered appropriate or desirable from both a functional and a political point of view.

The Commission was seen as already too big a bureaucratic organization and, hence, too rigid to respond dynamically to the problems with policy advice and implementation. Also, it was more focused on the process of decision making, being primarily made up of generalists, rather than on its specific scientific or technical contents. Even stronger, it was considered too politicized, being part of the political process and not the neutral administrator the Member States wished. Furthermore, the Commission, with the exception of its Competition Directorate General (DG), typically had no presence on the ground to ensure the application of EU law and most Member States were not willing to agree on the build-up of such capacity, fearing an even further loss of sovereignty to 'Brussels'.[12]

At the same time, the comitology committees, composed of Commission and Member State representatives, and especially the scientific committees were not perceived as the independent and transparent structures required to tackle the complex and uncertain regulatory issues at stake. Comitology is about Member State influence over the Commission's exercise of power,[13] and under certain circumstances also

---

11. M.L.P. Groenleer, 'Regulatory Governance in the European Union: The Political Struggle over Committees, Agencies and Networks', in *Handbook on the Politics of Regulation,* ed. D. Levi-Faur (Cheltenham: Edward Elgar, 2011), 548–560; D. Levi-Faur, 'Regulatory Networks and Regulatory Agencification: Towards a Single European Regulatory Space', *Journal of European Public Policy* 18, no. 6 (2011): 810–829; S. Simpson, '"New" Governance in European Union Policy-Making – Policy Innovation or Political Compromise in European Telecommunications', *West European Politics* 34, no. 5 (2011): 1114–1133.
12. R.D. Kelemen, 'The Politics of Eurocratic Structure and the New European Agencies', *West European Politics* 25, no. 4 (2002): 93–118.
13. M. Pollack, 'Control Mechanism or Deliberative Democracy? Two Images of Comitology', *Comparative Political Studies* 36, no. 1–2 (2003): 125–155.

about deliberation and deliberative supranationalism,[14] but it is not about unbiased and depoliticized decision making. Even if one considers the development of comitology, over the years, and at least until the BSE crisis, from a pure control mechanism of the Member States on the Commission to a more cooperative system between the Member States and the Commission, comitology still primarily concerns politics and not science.

Furthermore, in terms of sharing experiences and mutual learning, while the scientific committees perhaps contributed to regulatory convergence and consistent implementation, the same informal processes also made it possible for committees to be hijacked by Member States to advance their political interests.[15] In a similar manner, already existing networks of national agencies have, from the perspective of the Commission, often been considered too loose and voluntary. While created to discuss scientific or technical issues, there was always a risk of repoliticization whenever domestic concerns entered the debate, reducing the effectiveness of networks in terms of the uniform enforcement of policy decisions.[16]

[4]   The Assumption of Independence

An emphasis on agency 'independence' has subsequently structured the agency debate. What agency 'independence' precisely meant remained vague, however. The references to independence by early writers on EU agencies were often based on normative arguments, with 'independence' put forward as an important value in terms of impartiality, neutrality and objectivity.[17] Not many scholars empirically scrutinized EU agencies' constituent acts to examine whether 'independence' was provided for and, if so, in what way exactly. They simply assumed that agencies' founding regulations 'expressly stipulate that the agency will be completely independent from the makers of law and politics.'[18]

An analysis of agencies' constituent acts reveals that there is significant variation in the way in which constituent acts formally mention agencies independence, if their independence is stated at all.[19] Only in a few cases, including EFSA and the Fundamental Rights Agency (FRA), does the constituent regulation contain a separate article

---

14. C. Joerges & J. Neyer, 'Transforming Strategic Interaction into Deliberative Problem-solving: European Comitology in the Foodstuffs Sector', *Journal of European Public Policy* 4, no. 4 (1997): 609–625.
15. J. Grönvall, 'The Mad Cow Crisis, the Role of Experts and European Crisis Management', in *Managing Crises: Threats, Dilemmas, Opportunities,* eds. U. Rosenthal, R.A. Boin & L.K. Comfort (Springfield: Charles C. Thomas, 2001), 155–174.
16. B. Eberlein & E. Grande, 'Beyond Delegation: Transnational Regulatory Regimes and the EU Regulatory State', *Journal of European Public Policy* 12, no. 1 (2005): 89–112; D. Coen & M. Thatcher, 'Network Governance and Multi-level Delegation: European Networks of Regulatory Agencies', *Journal of Public Policy* 28, no. 1 (2008): 49–71.
17. Everson, *supra* n. 1. M. Shapiro, 'The Problems of Independent Agencies in the United States and the European Union', *Journal of European Public Policy* 4, no. 2 (1997): 276–291.
18. R.H. van Ooik, 'The Growing Importance of Agencies in the EU: Shifting Governance and the Institutional Balance', in *Good Governance and the European Union: Reflections on Concepts, Institutions and Substance,* eds. D.M. Curtin & R.A. Wessel (Antwerp: Intersentia, 2005), p. 145.
19. See for more details, Groenleer, *supra* n. 8.

on independence. In both the case of EFSA and FRA, the provision focuses on the independence of the agencies' employees and those individuals being part of their management boards and scientific committees. Exceptions to this are the newly established European financial supervisory authorities, whose constituent acts make extensive reference to independence.[20] Generally, however, the independence of EU agencies remains implicit and is not expounded upon in their constituent regulations.

Moreover, it often does not become clear from which actors exactly agencies' employees, boards and/or committees are intended to be independent: only from politicians or also from national ministries and agencies and/or perhaps also from industry and organized interests? Usually, constituent regulations do not answer these questions. In the case of the European Medicines Agency (EMA), it is explicitly stipulated that the agency is independent from industry, notably of pharmaceutical companies; explicit provisions on independence (vis-à-vis Union institutions or bodies, Member States or any other public or private body) are also laid down in the founding regulations of the financial supervisory authorities.

Most attention, however, has been paid to agencies as a solution in terms of their independence from 'politics', i.e., the Member States and the supranational EU institutions from which EU agencies have emanated (or their 'principals'), with the aim to ensure credible commitment.[21] Much like Ulysses facing the Sirens,[22] by delegating powers to an independent agency, political actors collectively bind their hands as a form of policy pre-commitment. Agency insulation thus aims to ensure policy effectiveness and continuity, which is considered imperative for policy credibility and, in the end, legitimacy.[23]

The very choice of the term 'independence' (rather than autonomy), however, has had an effect on expectations regarding agencies' relationships with other actors. Independence does not allow for degrees: one is either independent or not. In that sense 'independence' stresses the condition of being completely free from outside influence or interference.[24] The implication is therefore that when an agency is referred to as independent, it can decide for itself what to do instead of following what others tell it to do.

---

20. M. Busuioc, 'Rule-making by the European Financial Supervisory Authorities: Walking a Tight Rope', *European Law Journal* 19, no. 1 (2013): 111–125.
21. G. Majone, 'The New European Agencies: Regulation by Information', *Journal of European Public Policy* 4, no. 2 (1997): 262–275.
22. T. Gehring & S. Krapohl, 'Supranational Regulatory Agencies Between Independence and Control: the EMEA and the Authorization of Pharmaceuticals in the European Single Market', *Journal of European Public Policy* 14, no. 2 (2007): 208–226.
23. Majone, *supra* n. 21; E. Vos, 'Reforming the European Commission: What Role to Play for EU Agencies?', *Common Market Law Review* 37, no. 5 (2000): 1113–1134.
24. Groenleer, *supra* n. 8; M. Scholten, 'Independent, hence Unaccountable? The Need for a Broader Debate on Accountability of the Executive Union', *Review of Administrative Law* 4, no. 1 (2011): 5–44.

[B]   **Independent, Hence Unaccountable and Not (Democratically) Legitimate?**

As non-majoritarian institutions, not directly accountable to voters or their elected representatives, EU agencies are thus said to be insulated from the political process and its short-termism. This independence was, as mentioned above, expected to enhance the legitimacy of European policies and policy making through increased transparency and visibility as well as improved access for stakeholders.

At the same time, however, it was implicitly assumed that EU agencies, like other public organizations and even more so given their 'independence', would have a tendency to pursue their own goals and follow their own preferences, without taking into account the needs and interests of their principals. Whilst initially perceived as a solution to functional and political problems, the EU agencification process was a result increasingly seen as giving rise to new problems related to accountability.

[1]   Increasing Transparency, Visibility, and Accessibility

Especially in the early years of agency creation, agencies were said to improve transparency by transferring the task of scientific advice from opaque committees of national officials or Member State nominated experts to more visible European agencies, with individual constituent acts, legal personality, physical presence in the form of headquarters, a director and staff, own websites etc. By replacing such committees with agencies, transparency was thought to be enhanced as the European Parliament would be in a position to demand reports and hearings before it would release funds and citizens would be able to scrutinize agencies' publicly available decisions, thus encouraging well-argued decision making.

Moreover, as agencies were to be located throughout the EU Member States, from Lisbon to Warsaw, having their own buildings and staff, they were supposed to give increased visibility to EU decision making in the Member States, thereby bringing Europe closer to its citizens.

Agencies would also allow more easy access to stakeholders in the EU policy-making process. Before, stakeholders were essentially excluded from this process, as negotiation and bargaining occurred behind closed doors, without much participation from interested parties. The networks that agencies could create and coordinate would allow for more contacts with stakeholders.[25] The EEA, the European Drug Monitoring Centre (EMCDDA) and the EU Fundamental Rights Agency (before: European Monitoring Centre for Racism and Xenophobia, EUMC) have thus from the beginning

---

25. R. Dehousse, 'Regulation by Networks in the European Community: The Role of European Agencies', *Journal of European Public Policy* 4, no. 2 (1997): 246–261; Majone, *supra* n. 21.

connected research centres and institutes in the Member States, while EFSA and the European Aviation Safety Agency (EASA) have regularly consulted industry and consumer groups on the scientific opinions that they issue and the technical standards that they set.

[2] 'The Rise of the Unelected' and Its Risks

The 'independence' discourse strongly affected discussions of agency accountability. Given agencies' non-majoritarian character and the manner in which the debate on agency 'independence' developed and gained prevalence in academic and practitioner debates, the risks that 'the rise of the unelected'[26] posed to legitimacy and the democratic character of the Union were increasingly signalled. While originally welcomed for their functional benefits and separation from political organs, such as the Council and an increasingly politicized Commission, agencies subsequently came under attack, precisely due to their perceived independence and operation at a distance from the reach of well-established political controls.[27]

Initially an important legitimizing source of the agency model, their much-coveted independence became a liability in this context, particularly as agencies' numbers, the span of their powers and the sensitivity of their tasks increased. Some agencies were granted more significant powers, such as the power to adopt binding decisions on third parties and even (quasi-)rule-making powers. Even when agencies would 'only' gather information and perform analyses, their control over information could create significant informational asymmetries in their favour and become an important source of de facto power, not only vis-à-vis third parties or regulatees but also vis-à-vis their political overseers. Increasingly, agencies were perceived to be not that much more accountable and (democratically) legitimate than their institutional predecessors after all, especially because they would still rely on stealthy forms of governance, such as committees and networks, for their work.

Thus, the ability of agencies to act independently, presumably free of any checks, while being sources of power in their own right, whose decisions and measures can have direct repercussions for companies and citizens as well as EU institutions, Member States and national regulators, became the 'sore point' of the EU agencification process. Anxiety arose at the possibility of independent agencies escaping control. This 'independent, hence unaccountable causality'[28] also helps explain why accountability concerns surfaced in relation to agencies as opposed to one of the Commission's DGs, or one of the Council's working groups;[29] as independent entities, agencies would not be under the control of the Commission or the Council.

---

26. F. Vibert, *The Rise of the Unelected. Democracy and the New Separation of Powers* (Cambridge: Cambridge University Press, 2007).
27. Busuioc, *supra* n. 3.
28. Scholten, *supra* n. 24.
29. Busuioc, *supra* n. 6.

[3]   Towards a 'Catch 22'

Growing calls for increased control and supplementing existing arrangements for accountability were heard from both academics and EU institutions alike.[30] As pointed out by the Commission:

> the independence of these agencies goes hand in hand with an obligation to meet their responsibilities. In order to strengthen the legitimacy of Community action, it is important to establish and delimit the responsibilities of the institutions and agencies.[31]

The need for agency accountability became increasingly perceived as closely inter-linked to their legitimacy, and the lack thereof, as having a (potentially) delegitimizing effect on their work but also, more broadly, on the agencies themselves as organiza-tional entities.

In the prevailing (academic and institutional) discourse, such accountability checks would often come down to or be conflated with 'control', which entails an element of directing. 'Control' refers to a whole range of mechanisms employed by the controlling actor in order to steer and influence decision making and the behaviour of the controlled agents.[32] To illustrate: '[T]he principle of accountability requires that a clear system *of* controls be put in place.'[33] And again in 2008 the Commission observed: 'The need for clear lines of accountability to *govern* agencies' actions is at the core of the debate about agencies.'[34]

These demands for increased control, however, gave rise to a veritable 'Catch 22'.[35] As discussed above, agencies' independence was perceived and presented as the rationale for the choice of this institutional model. Yet, in order to maintain their

---

30. For example, Everson, *supra* n. 1; Shapiro, *supra* n. 17; Vos, *supra* n. 233; M. Flinders, 'Distributed Public Governance in the European Union', *Journal of European Public Policy* 11, no. 3 (2004): 520–544; D. Geradin, 'The Development of European Regulatory Agencies: Lessons from the American Experience', in *Regulation Through Agencies in the EU: A New Paradigm of European Governance*, eds. D. Geradin, R. Munoz & N. Petit (Cheltenham: Edward Elgar, 2005), 215–245; Commission of the European Communities, Draft Interinstitutional Agreement on the operating framework for the European Regulatory Agencies, COM(2005) 59 final, 25 February 2005, p. 2; Commission of the European Communities, Communication from the Commission to the European Parliament and Council, European Agencies – The Way Forward, COM(2008) 135 final, 11 March 2008, p. 2, p. 5; European Parliament, European Parliament resolution of 13 January 2004 on the Communication from the Commission: 'The operating framework for the European Regulatory Agencies', OJ C92 E/119, 16 April 2004, pp. 123–124; European Parliament resolution of 21 October 2008 on a strategy for the future settlement of the institutional aspects of Regulatory Agencies (2008/2103(INI)), OJ C15 E/27, 21 January 2010.
31. Commission of the European Communities, Draft Interinstitutional Agreement on the operating framework for the European Regulatory Agencies, COM(2005) 59 final, 25 February 2005, p. 2.
32. P.G. Roness, K. Rubecksen, K. Verhoest and M. MacCarthaigh, 'Autonomy and Regulation of State Agencies: Reinforcement, Indifference or Compensation', *Public Organisation Review* 8 (2008): 155–174.
33. Commission of the European Communities, Draft Interinstitutional Agreement on the operating framework for the European Regulatory Agencies, COM(2005) 59 final, 25 February 2005, p. 2.
34. Commission of the European Communities, Communication from the Commission to the European Parliament and Council, European Agencies – The Way Forward, COM(2008) 135 final, 11 March 2008, p. 5.
35. Busuioc, *supra* n. 6.

legitimacy credentials, these agencies required 'controls', which is 'difficult to reconcile with the previous observation that they should be more independent. Indeed, it is
sometimes considered that accountability and independence are conflicting concepts.'[36]

§8.03 TODAY'S REALITIES

[A] Autonomy

[1] From Independence to Autonomy

In reality, independent agencies do not exist and the term 'independent' is confusing,
if not misleading. Like other public organizations, EU agencies can never do entirely
what they want. An agency is granted a level of autonomy by other actors or will
attempt to ascertain a degree of control over its own affairs, but this does not mean that
it enjoys complete freedom, free from any control, without constraints and restrictions,
in fact being independent. EU agencies are not fully independent and political
authorities, most notably the Parliament, the Council and the Commission, can restrict
– in both formal and informal ways – agencies' ability to act or decide. If anything,
agencies are interdependent with these and other actors, relying on them to realize
their goals.

The term 'independence' is often used – in the academic as well as institutional
discourse – interchangeably with the term 'autonomy', as synonym for the same
concept. One may ask, given its actual meaning, whether 'independence' is the most
appropriate term to describe the empirical reality of EU agencies and whether 'autonomy' is perhaps not a more suitable term. Instead of being either independent or not
independent, EU agencies, like other public organizations, could be considered more or
less autonomous. Use of the term autonomy allows us to make a more fine-grained
assessment of EU agencies' relative position vis-à-vis other parties, both formally, as
granted by the agency's founders through design, and in actual practice, as acquired by
the agency through development.[37]

[2] Limited Formal Autonomy upon Creation

The exact amount of formal autonomy is determined by the scope and extent of the
formal rules, legal competences, and decision making procedures that govern the
organization's conduct. It is generally assessed along the following dimensions:[38]

---

36. Geradin, *supra* n. 300, at p. 231.
37. Groenleer, *supra* n. 8.
38. For example, G. Bouckaert & B.G. Peters, 'What is Missing and What is Available in the Study
    of Quangos?', in *Unbundled Government: A Critical Analysis of the Global Trend to Agencies,
    Quangos and Contractualisation,* eds. C. Pollitt & C. Talbot (London: Routledge, 2004), 22–49;
    K. Verhoest, B.G. Peters, G. Bouckaert & B. Verschuere, 'The Study of Organisational Autonomy:

- Policy autonomy: the extent to which agencies can decide on goals, prioritize tasks, choose clients or target audiences, determine working methods, and draw conclusions and opinions;
- Structural autonomy: the way by which those responsible for the management of the organization, in particular the director, are appointed and their appointment is renewed;
- Personnel autonomy: the extent to which they can recruit, train, promote and pay their staff (as well as fire them);
- Financial autonomy: the extent to which agencies can generate their own financial resources and decide on how to allocate them;
- Legal autonomy: the extent to which they can enter into agreements with or procure and provide goods and services from and to other organizations.

On the basis of a comparative assessment of EU agencies' design, it has been shown that agencies generally do not possess a high level of formal autonomy.[39] All agencies have legal autonomy, in the sense that they can procure and provide goods and services from other organizations, but this autonomy does not extend to the international plane. For formal permission to enter into negotiations or conclude agreements with, for instance, third countries or international organizations, agencies rely on the EU institutions.[40]

Moreover, the majority of agencies cannot generate their own funds but receive an EU subsidy. Since their funds are usually part of the Commission's budget, they depend on their 'parent' Commission DG to secure the required funding in the budget negotiations with the Council and the Parliament. Even if agencies acquire their own funding through fees for services they provide, such as product evaluation, registration, or certification, these fees are set by the Commission and the Council and they are generally only supposed to constitute a part of their income. Whereas agencies have some freedom to allocate funds, making transfers between budget items, they are generally bound by the EU's financial regulation, which does not allow them much room to manoeuvre. Agencies face a similar situation when it comes to staffing. In accordance with the EU's staff regulations, they rely on approval of their personnel policies by the Parliament and the Council. Agencies may decide who they select and how they train them but at what level they can recruit, what they can pay and whether

---

A Conceptual Review', *Public Administration and Development* 24 (2004): 101–118; F. Gilardi, *Delegation in the Regulatory State: Independent Regulatory Agencies in Western Europe* (Cheltenham: Edward Elgar, 2008).

39. Groenleer, *supra* n. 8.
40. M.L.P. Groenleer, 'Linking up Levels of Governance: Agencies of the European Union and their Interaction with International Institutions', in *The Influence of International Institutions on the European Union*, eds. O. Costa & K.-E. Joergensen (Basingstoke: Palgrave Macmillan, 2012), 135–154; M. Groenleer & S. Gabbi, 'EFSA in the International Arena: Caught in a Legal Straightjacket – or Performing an Autonomous Role?', in *New Directions in European Food Law and Policy: Ten Years of European Food Safety Authority*, eds. A. Alemanno & S. Gabbi (Farnham: Ashgate Publishing, forthcoming).

they can promote staff is usually fixed through their politically endorsed establishment plans.[41]

Budgeting and staffing is a key task of EU agencies' directors.[42] An important indicator of agencies' autonomy is therefore the way the director is appointed. Whereas the procedures vary considerably, directors depend on the Commission and the Council, and increasingly on the Parliament, for their appointment. This applies to a lesser extent for the way their appointments are renewed. A proposal to shift the decision making power on renewals from agencies' management boards to the Commission therefore evoked strong reactions, especially in the case of EFSA, which has a management board consisting of independent members. In most cases, however, agencies' management boards are primarily composed of representatives of the Member States which, in that way, remain in the driver's seat. Indeed, their representation in the boards of agencies has been, and still is, one of the key preconditions for Member States to agree upon the creation of EU agencies in the first place.[43]

While agencies generally do not possess a high level of formal autonomy, there is quite some variation between agencies in their levels of autonomy on the different dimensions, particularly the policy dimension. Clearly, in view of the rationale underlying agency creation, the extent to which agencies can decide on goals, prioritize tasks, choose clients or target audiences, determine working methods, and draw conclusions and opinions, serves as the most important sign of their autonomy. Agencies generally cannot decide on their objectives and tasks because these have been laid down in their constituent acts. Depending on the extent of formal coordination required with the Commission or the Council, they do have some leeway in prioritizing tasks, choosing clients or target audiences and determining their working methods through their work programmes. Variation is most significant in respect of agencies' powers of decision: some (regulatory) agencies can take decisions, albeit in individual cases, whereas other (information, coordination) agencies can 'merely' advise and support the EU institutions and its Member States.

There is no clear pattern when it comes to the variation across agencies in the levels of formal autonomy on the different dimensions. The so-called 'paradox of autonomization',[44] which has been identified at the national level and according to which agencies that score high on one dimension of autonomy (for example, policy autonomy) usually score low on another (for example, financial or personnel autonomy), only applies to a limited extent in the case of EU agencies. EU agencies that are highly autonomous with regard to, for instance, the sources of their funding do not necessarily have a low level of autonomy with regard to their objectives and tasks. If at

41. See also A. Schout & F. Pereyra, 'The Institutionalization of EU Agencies: Agencies as 'mini Commissions', *Public Administration* 89, no. 2 (2011): 418–432.
42. M. Busuioc & M.L.P. Groenleer, 'Wielders of Supranational Power? The Administrative Behaviour of the Heads of European Union Agencies', in *The Agency Phenomenon in the European Union: Emergence, Institutionalisation and Every-day Decision Making*, eds. M. Busuioc, M.L.P. Groenleer & J. Trondal (Manchester: Manchester University Press, 2012), 128–151.
43. R.D. Kelemen & A. Tarrant, 'The Political Foundations of the Eurocracy', *West European Politics* 34, no. 5 (2011): 922–947; Groenleer, *supra* n. 8.
44. A. Smullen, S. Van Thiel & C. Pollitt, 'Agentschappen en de Verzelfstandigingsparadox', *Beleid en Maatschappij* 28, no. 4 (2001): 190–201.

all a pattern could be distinguished it seems that this is not related to the different dimensions of autonomy but to the different actors from which agencies may be formally autonomous. EU agencies with a high degree of autonomy on a particular dimension, in relation to the Commission, often have a low level of autonomy on that dimension from the Member States and vice versa.

In recent years, we have witnessed a decrease of the variation in formal autonomy of existing agencies. As a result of the Lisbon Treaty, former third pillar agencies, such as Europol and EUROJUST, are now also part of the 'family' of EU agencies, which has led to changes in their institutional setup, notably in terms of financing and staffing, and has made them more similar to former Community agencies. In addition, revisions of various constituent acts have made agencies more alike. For instance, whereas Europol used to be based on an intergovernmental convention it is now based on a Council decision (soon to be replaced by a regulation), decreasing the influence of the Member States relative to the influence of the EU institutions. Finally, the recently adopted Common Approach may have a streamlining effect on agencies' constituent regulations with regard to the various dimensions, notably when it comes to structural autonomy.

At the same time, a number of new agencies has been created, notably in the financial area, that are much more powerful, at least on paper, than already existing agencies, and that for instance can take more generally binding decisions on financial market parties.[45]

[3]   Institutionalization: Variation in Actual Autonomy across Agencies and over Time

It remains unclear from their formally granted autonomy whether and to what extent EU agencies enjoy autonomy in practice. Because formal autonomy is designed into the structure of agencies, and thus is relatively static and fixed, the findings reported above do not tell us much about the degree of autonomy that they develop over time, often informally.[46]

Empirical research into the actual autonomy of agencies demonstrates that a narrow formal remit has not kept EU agencies from interpreting their mission and roles more broadly than their political masters may have liked, prioritizing those objectives and tasks that they prefer and giving shape to working methods in accordance with their wishes. The EEA engaged in the analysis of the effectiveness of EU environment policy, thereby going beyond its formal role as a 'mere' policy advisor; the EFSA spent considerable time 'self-tasking' instead of delivering opinions requested by the Commission; and the European Monitoring Centre for Racism and Xenophobia (now the

---

45. D. Curtin & R. Dehousse, 'EU Agencies: Tipping the Balance?', in *The Agency Phenomenon in the European Union: Emergence, Institutionalisation and Everyday Decision-making*, eds. M. Busuioc, M. Groenleer & J. Trondal (Manchester: Manchester University Press, 2012), 193–205; Busuioc, *supra* n. 200.
46. See also D.P. Carpenter, *Forging Bureaucratic Autonomy: Reputations, Networks, and Policy Innovation in Executive Agencies, 1862–1928* (Princeton: Princeton University Press, 2001).

FRA) actively campaigned against racism and discrimination, instead of solely focusing on its data collection tasks.[47]

None of the existing agencies appears to be fully autonomous from the Commission or the Member States however, neither on paper nor in practice, and the assertion that some EU agencies are 'out of control' or not under any control is therefore exaggerated.[48] At the same time, neither the Commission nor the Member States are always fully in control. While some agencies remain technical instruments for implementing legislation and regulating policy sectors, other agencies have achieved a level of actual autonomy which exceeds their formal autonomy and have developed in ways not foreseen at the time of their creation.

Agencies that have developed a level of actual autonomy appear to have undergone a process of institutionalization.[49] That is, they form a distinct identity on the basis of their unique and proven competences and, on that basis, generate high levels of legitimacy, or support, both from within the organization (staff, experts) and in networks outside the organization (EU institutions, Member States, national authorities, interest groups, media, etc.).

[4] Demonstrated Capacity

In order to maximize their autonomy, some agencies – such as EMA, EUROJUST, and EEA – have demonstrated that they add value to existing national, EU and international structures and arrangements. That is, they have shown that they are uniquely capable of performing the tasks that they have been delegated, and complement rather than duplicate existing structures and arrangements.

In a few instances, agencies, despite having an advisory function, have influenced the solutions to the problems on which they collect information, consequently 'regulating by information',[50] even when formal decisions on these solutions are made by others. The EMA is the most obvious example. Although the Commission has the legal authority to make final decisions on the approval of medicinal products, it has rarely, if ever, deviated from EMA's opinion.[51] The Commission not only lacks the scientific expertise required to determine whether EMA's advice is sound, but also realizes that questioning EMA opinions would put the credibility of the authorization system at risk.[52]

Other agencies with an advisory function have also had an influence on policy making, albeit a more limited one. Instead of relying on others to provide them with 'old' information and simply 'stapling' this information together, they generated 'new'

---

47. Groenleer, *supra* n. 8, at pp. 195–198, pp. 261–263.
48. Groenleer, *supra* n. 8, at p. 347.
49. P. Selznick, *Leadership in Administration: A Sociological Interpretation* (Berkeley: University of California Press, 1957); R.A. Boin, *Crafting Public Institutions: Leadership in Two Prison Systems* (Boulder: Lynne Rienner, 2001).
50. Majone, *supra* n. 21; Shapiro, *supra* n. 17.
51. Gehring & Krapohl, *supra* n. 22.
52. M. Everson, G. Majone, L. Metcalfe & A. Schout, *The Role of Specialised Agencies in Decentralising EU Governance*, Report Presented to the Commission (1999).

information, as the EU's body for judicial cooperation (EUROJUST) did, or they analysed information, drew trends and patterns from it and formulated conclusions at an aggregate (EU) level and made recommendations on the basis of their analyses, as the EEA did. They thus added value to the activities of the EU institutions and the Member States, and their distinct competence could not (easily) be denied.[53]

In terms of the implementation of policies, agencies such as EASA and EMSA, stimulated mutual learning processes among national regulatory authorities.[54] They for instance have organized inspections where a team of specialists from the agency and various Member States inspects the national authority of one Member State. In addition, EASA and EMSA serve as learning platforms for European and national stakeholders. By organizing workshops and trainings for national inspection professionals, agencies, as nodes in transnational networks, facilitate the diffusion of implementation practices across Europe, thereby contributing to the way rules are applied and enforced across the Union.

Of key importance thus seems to be that agencies demonstrate unique capacity and contribute to activities of EU and national bodies. They not only have to be effective in what they do, but also to build up a reputation for effectiveness. Such a reputation links agencies' actual performance with the perception and acceptance thereof among a variety of external actors.[55]

[5]   Networks of Support

Agencies cannot be autonomous in isolation, separate from external actors. Indeed, autonomous agencies have relied on others – not only when required by their founding regulations, but also by their own choosing – in order to demonstrate their unique capacity. This is a delicate balancing act. In order to get these other actors on board, agencies have included them in their activities, even though this sounds paradoxical and would certainly not fit with a strict interpretation of the term independence.

In spite of the conventional wisdom that it would reduce their autonomy, some agencies entered into partnerships with other organizations, whether Member State and third country agencies, other EU bodies or international organizations. Most EU agencies were not created in a vacuum. They came into being in an environment replete with other organizations on which they rely for professional expertise, such as EMA's relationship with national agencies,[56] and for the acceptance and credibility that relationships with such organizations confer upon them, as with the EEA's relations with the United Nations Environment Programme.

---

53. Groenleer, *supra* n. 8, at p. 352.
54. Groenleer, Kaeding & Versluis, *supra* n. 10; E. Versluis, 'Catalysts of Compliance? The Role of European Union Agencies in the Implementation of EU Legislation in Poland and Bulgaria', in *The Agency Phenomenon in the European Union: Emergence, Institutionalisation and Everyday Decision-making*, eds. M. Busuioc, M. Groenleer & J. Trondal (Manchester: Manchester University Press, 2012), 172–190.
55. See also Carpenter, *supra* n. 466. D.P. Carpenter, *Reputation and Power: Organizational Image and Pharmaceutical Regulation at the FDA* (Princeton: Princeton University Press, 2010).
56. L. Metcalfe, 'Linking Levels of Government: European Integration and Globalization.' *International Review of Administrative Sciences* 66, no. 1 (2000): 119–142.

EU agencies such as EMA, which incorporated national agencies in (transnational) networks, appeared more legitimate than those agencies that have sought to displace national agencies, as EASA initially tried, or adopt a command and control approach, as for instance the FRA did.[57] Some EU agencies thus developed a level of trust among actors that had, prior to their creation, mistrusted each other, while also becoming accepted as a trustworthy actor in the network themselves.[58] Cooperation and networking with and among national agencies thus resulted in gains in autonomy, rather than losses.

The support of national agencies has been heavily dependent on the reputation for effectiveness of EU agencies. The FRA and the European Police Office (Europol) did not deliver immediate results and even built up a reputation for ineffectiveness, for instance through the highly-politicized and publicized shelving of the FRA's anti-Semitism report in 2003 and the long delays, enormous cost overrun and fraud involved in setting up the Europol Information System. EMA and EUROJUST, by contrast, quickly developed reputations for effectiveness, showing a growing number of opinions and an increasing number of coordination meetings, thus distinguishing their products and services from those of other actors.[59]

In order to create networks of support, agencies have had to be modest. As the examples of EFSA and the FRA show, forcible demonstrations of autonomy proved to be counterproductive, alienated political actors and reinforced the negative expectation among external actors of agencies pursuing aims that might counter theirs. In the multi-actor setting in which EU agencies operate, they simply cannot be independent in the literal sense of the word; at most they can acquire a level of autonomy, vis-à-vis particular actors, and in regard of certain aspects of their functioning.

[B]   Accountability

[1]   *From Control to Accountability*

As with the distinction between 'independence' and 'autonomy', it is also important to differentiate between 'accountability' and 'control'. As mentioned above, the two concepts have been used interchangeably and equated with one another in the agency literature despite there being clear differences between the two. Although, indeed, mechanisms of accountability are mechanisms of control, the reverse is not true. In other words:

> "'control'' in the Anglo-Saxon sense is broader than accountability and can include both *ex ante* and *ex post* mechanisms of directing behaviour.[60] Control means "having power over" and can involve very proactive means of directing conduct, for example through straight orders, directives, financial incentives or regulations. But these hierarchical, financial or legal mechanisms are not

---

57. Groenleer, *supra* n. 8, at pp. 252–254, pp. 164–167.
58. Everson, Majone, Metcalfe & Schout, *supra* n. 52.
59. Groenleer, *supra* n. 8, at p. 362.
60. C. Scott, 'Accountability in the Regulatory State', *Journal of Law and Society* 27, no. 1 (2000): 39.

mechanisms of accountability *per se*, because they do not in themselves operate through procedures in which actors are to explain and justify their conduct to forums (...).[61]

Accountability precludes direct control on the part of the principal. The need for accountability and the introduction of accountability mechanisms is relevant precisely because the principal has delegated powers to an agent and thus renounced direct control. Following this line of reasoning, accountability is concerned with ex post oversight, with ascertaining after the fact, the extent to which the agent has lived up to its ex ante mandate and has acted within its zone of discretion. Accountability thus refers to 'a relationship between an actor and a forum, in which the actor has the obligation to explain and justify his or her conduct, the forum can pose questions and pass judgment, and the actor might face consequences'.[62] The process of accountability is a relationship between an actor and a forum, which is characterized by three main stages or elements: informing, debating, and possibility of consequences.

As in the case of autonomy, we can distinguish de jure and de facto accountability. De jure accountability refers to accountability arrangements as provided for by formal design. De facto accountability refers to practices of accountability and more explicitly, to how the various formal arrangements provided by design operate and are used in practice in the interaction between the actor and the forum, below or above formal requirements.

[2]   *Not Unaccountable: A Multiplicity of Accountability Obligations*

Contrary to early expectations, empirical research shows that agencies are not unaccountable. An examination of agencies' formal accountability arrangements reveals that agencies are enveloped in a complex web of accountability relations to a multiplicity of forums.[63] There is a large menu of accountability mechanisms in place; the sheer number is overwhelming if perhaps not always 'watertight.' Thus, in terms of the existence of accountability mechanisms on paper, there is no support for the claim that agencies operate as unaccountable agents.

On the basis of the type of accountability forum involved and/or the aspect of conduct subject to review i.e., to whom is account to be rendered and about what,[64] five major forms of accountability have been identified to which most EU agencies are formally subject:

- Managerial accountability: encompassing accountability obligations vis-à-vis the management board;
- Political accountability: encompassing accountability duties vis-à-vis political institutional actors (such as the European Parliament and the Council);

---

61. M. Bovens, 'Analysing and Assessing Accountability: A Conceptual Framework', *European Law Journal* 13, no. 4 (2007): 454.
62. Bovens, *supra* n. 611, at p. 450.
63. Busuioc, *supra* n. 3.
64. Bovens, *supra* n. 61.

- Judicial accountability: encompassing accountability arrangements vis-à-vis judicial forums such as the Court of Justice of the European Union (CJEU) or the Joint Supervisory Boards;
- Extra-judicial accountability: encompassing accountability towards a quasi-judicial forum such as the European Ombudsman;
- Financial accountability: encompassing accountability arrangements vis-à-vis financial forums (such as EP's budgetary committees, the Court of Auditors, the Commission's Internal Audit Service).

The five major forms of accountability laid out above are composed of a multitude of account-giving obligations – in the form of annual reports, activity reports, hearings, and evaluation reports – and are occasionally part of complex accountability cycles (for example, the discharge procedure).[65] They are clustered around various accountability forums as seen above, with each form of accountability taking place before a specific forum or set of forums.[66] The fully self-funded agencies (i.e., the Office for the Harmonization in the Internal Market (OHIM) and the Community Plant Variety Office (CPVO)) represent an exception to this, however, as their accountability mechanisms are rather sparse, constituted primarily by Member State structures (be it in the board or the Council) and lacking procedures for democratic accountability. The Common Approach aims for this issue to be taken up in the future in order to secure democratic accountability for these agencies.[67]

The major types of accountability identified in the case of EU agencies are generally also encountered in the case of national level agencies. Thus, a cross-agency study among national agencies[68] observed that 'in many countries, agencies have management boards', 'are subject to hierarchical oversight relations with one or (exceptionally) several ministries' and although 'ministerial responsibility for agencies is clearly prevailing at national level', 'some direct interactions between parliament and chief executives can be observed' in specific countries. Furthermore, 'agencies at national level issue annual reports and accounts', 'the possibility for judicial review of agency decisions is a general characteristic of national level agency governance' and that for auditing agencies, 'most countries have a specialized audit office which mainly focuses on financial management issues and proper use of public money.' In other words, instances of political, managerial, legal and financial accountability are in place for agencies at the national level, as is the case of EU agencies.

As such, EU agencies in general do not fare at all badly compared to their national level relatives in terms of the accountability structures formally in place. In fact, given the sheer magnitude of these procedures at the European level and the number of forums involved, compared to the administrative capacity of some of the agencies, the

---

65. See further Busuioc, *supra* n. 3.
66. Busuioc, *supra* n. 3.
67. Council of the European Union, Evaluation of European Union agencies: Endorsement of the Joint Statement and Common Approach, 11450/12, 18 June 2012, p. 14.
68. European Parliament, Directorate General Internal Policies of the Union, 'Best Practice in Governance of Agencies – A comparative study in view of identifying best practice for governing agencies carrying out activities on behalf of the European Union', Brussels, 30 January 2008.

level of accountability obligations to which EU agencies are subject is likely unparalleled in similar bodies at the national level.

These accountability obligations are reportedly complied with in practice. Accountability forums are generally satisfied with the level of informing and agency account-giving. With the exception of occasional informational delays or dissatisfaction on the part of the forums with the quality of some of the information supplied, which made follow-up necessary, agencies by and large have a good record in terms of complying with their accountability obligations. Furthermore, whereas some arrangements are more ad hoc in nature (for example, supervision by the management boards, hearings before the EP), others are well institutionalized with account-giving obligations being discharged at fixed times as part of broader accountability (or budgetary) cycles (for example, accountability vis-à-vis the Court of Auditors, discharge by the European Parliament).

These accountability mechanisms cover by and large different, major areas relevant to the agencies' work. The overall accountability system is intertwined, with accountability forums in their own right also serving as information providers or 'fire alarms' for other forums. Some mechanisms also tend to reinforce each other and are at times in a co-dependent relationship with one another, mirroring Scott's[69] 'interdependence model' of accountability, with respect to forums (rather than actors), however. For example, the expertise and audit reports of the European Court of Auditors help inform, enable and bolster oversight on financial matters by a political forum such as the European Parliament in its discharge role. Or, an institution such as the European Parliament can 'give teeth' to the findings of the European Ombudsman, which lacks the possibility to enact formal consequences. To this extent, the accountability regime of EU agencies can be described as a multi-centric, interconnected, and networked model, in which accountability is enacted towards different forums, for different purposes, generally on different (yet occasionally overlapping) matters,[70] with a certain level of interdependence in the operation of some of the forums.

There are also elements of 'redundancy' present, in line with Scott's other accountability model, with the presence of overlaps in the subject matter covered by different forums, particularly in the area of financial accountability between the internal audit capacity of the agency, the Commission's Internal Audit Service and the European Court of Auditors. Redundancy can be purposefully cultivated in an accountability regime as a 'failsafe' mechanism or it can be an unintended effect of particular institutional design choices.[71] For instance, agencies generally have two parallel internal audit capacities – each agency's internal audit capacity (IAC) as well as the Internal Service Audit of the Commission (IAS), which formally serves as most agencies' internal auditor. This set up was not purposefully designed as such. As the IAS only gained a mandate vis-à-vis agencies in 2003, some agencies had already set up an internal audit capacity. Additionally, since the IAS lacked resources in its early years

---

69. Scott, *supra* n. 600.
70. P. Barberis, 'The New Public Management and a New Accountability', *Public Administration* 76, no. 3 (1998): 464.
71. Scott, *supra* n. 60.

and was unable to comply with its obligations, other agencies had little choice but to establish their own internal audit capacity.[72] This led to the co-existence of two internal auditor systems for agencies.

[3]   A Lack of Tailored Accountability

This is not to say, however, that agencies' accountability procedures are 'foolproof'. Quite the contrary, challenges emerge and they come from unlikely places given earlier discussions in the literature of agency accountability. They have their origin for the most part in institutional design choices with respect to agency accountability, which impact upon their subsequent operation.

First of all, by and large, accountability arrangements provided for in agencies' constituent acts do not necessarily reflect differences in (de jure) autonomy. Although agencies were mostly granted limited formal autonomy, and none of the existing agencies appears to be fully autonomous either on paper or in practice, as mentioned above, they are nevertheless subject to extensive accountability obligations. For instance, in the case of Europol, its rather stunted autonomy in practice stands in contrast to the growth phenomenon that has been its accountability.[73] Whereas Europol was granted a limited degree of formal autonomy and was not subsequently able to harness the powers it was expected to be able to yield at its creation – i.e., in other words, its autonomy remained and remains rather 'limited', an expansion of accountability took place at the formal level which, depending on the eagerness of forums to use their powers, may also translate into an informal expansion.

Moreover, differences in agency powers have mostly not resulted in variations in the design of accountability obligations. Most agencies are subject to similar account-ability obligations as discussed above (for example, financial accountability to the European Court of Auditors, IAC/IAS, hearings to the European Parliament, manage-rial and (extra-)judicial accountability obligations etc.) regardless of the type of tasks and powers they exercise.[74]

In theory, accountability is closely linked to the exercise of power: 'the principle of accountability (...) concerns itself with power';[75] '[r]esponsibility should, indeed, be commensurate with the extent of the power possessed.'[76] In the case of EU agencies, however, accountability was not and is not linked to the level of formal autonomy and discretion granted and the type of powers and tasks exercised. It is also not linked to the size and administrative capacity of agencies. As a result, small agencies are subject to an identical set of accountability obligations as the overall agency population, with no exceptions (i.e., simplification of procedures or even exemptions) in light of their much

---

72. Busuioc, *supra* n. 3.
73. Busuioc, Curtin & Groenleer, *supra* n. 6.
74. The provisions for judicial review, which were initially only available for agencies explicitly provided with decision-making powers, are an exception to this.
75. S.B. Young, 'Reconceptualising Accountability in the Early Nineteenth Century: How The Tort of Negligence Appeared', *Connecticut Law Review* 21, no. 2 (1989): 202.
76. C. Turpin, 'Ministerial Responsibility', in *The Changing Constitution*, eds. J. Jowell & D. Oliver (Oxford: Clarendon, 1994), p. 111.

smaller capacity. Ironically however, the biggest agency, which also wields rather significant powers (as a decision making agency), OHIM, is one of the less accountable agencies from the overall population by virtue of its distinct, fully self-funded status.

Thus, accountability is not tailored to relevant agencies' specificities. When present, accountability variations are largely of the unwarranted kind, i.e., not related to rationales that would justify or warrant differences in the accountability regime. For instance, while the constituent acts of some agencies contain provisions for hearings of the director before the Parliament, in other cases (i.e., EASA) hearings are provided for both vis-à-vis the EP as well as the Council, while yet in other cases no hearings are provided for at all but nevertheless do take place de facto. There does not appear to be any underlying institutional logic for these differences but rather they seem to be a legacy of different waves of agencification, varying negotiation outcomes at the agency creation phase, different constellations of principals involved, subsequent revisions, and different powers of the EP at different phases of the EU agencification process.

[4]   Ensuing Overloads

As agency accountability arrangements are not tailored (to agency powers, size or accountability obligations already in place), in some cases we can speak of instances of 'accountability overloads.'[77] In the context of financial accountability procedures alone, for example agencies are accountable to four different financial accountability bodies: IAC, IAS, the Court of Auditors and the European Parliament as the discharge authority.

However, the issue of overloads is relevant beyond the financial accountability regime and permeates the system as a whole. The sheer number and complexity of some procedures can put a real strain on smaller scale bodies. The situation is exacerbated in the case of management boards alone, the meetings of which respondents reported as being attended by as many as 100–120 people (including management board representatives, their alternates and a handful of agency staff). In fact, in some cases the size of the management board is larger than the permanent staff of the agency (e.g., the European Agency for Safety and Health at Work (EU-OSHA), the European Police College (CEPOL)).

Whereas the larger agencies such as EMA or OHIM boast staffs of approximately 500 and respectively 700 employees, there are also agencies with a staff capacity of fifty (for example, the ENISA) or less (for example, CPVO or CEPOL). Yet, all of these bodies are subject to extensive accountability procedures for the most part similar to those encountered in the case of an institution like the European Commission,[78] which employs a staff of approximately 25,000 employees. This is due to the fact that accountability mechanisms applicable to (some of) the EU institutions – the discharge procedure by the European Parliament, external audit by Court of Auditors, internal audit by the IAS or annual activity reports (originally a reporting obligation of the

---

77. M. Bovens, T. Schillemans & P. 't Hart, 'Does Accountability Work? An Assessment Tool', *Public Administration* 86, no. 1 (2008): 227–230.
78. See further, Busuioc, *supra* n. 3.

Commission's Directors General) – were simply rendered applicable to agencies as well. Such extensive and cumbersome procedures risk paralyzing smaller scale agencies as the ones mentioned above and run counter to one of the central rationales for setting up agencies: their flexibility.[79] It risks turning accountability into their full-time business.

Whereas much of the literature on EU agency accountability has focused on the potential for agency deficits, overloads are equally problematic. From an accountability perspective, overloads, just as deficits, are failures of accountability, the 'negative externalities' of accountability. In the case of agencies, accountability procedures already in place for the main EU institutions were simply transplanted without much forethought as to the extent to which they were compatible with these smaller scale executive organisms. This has resulted, as observed above, in overloads and overlaps that affect the 'health' of the overall accountability system. The Common Approach adopted by the three institutions does not take up this crucial issue. As a result, agencies will most likely continue to lack accountability structures that are (better) aligned with their levels of autonomy, powers and administrative capacity for the foreseeable future.

[5]   *Yet Still Deficits: Underuse of Formal Accountability*

At the same time, paradoxically, 'accountability deficits' are also present and manifest themselves in the underuse of existing arrangements. Early literature focused on EU agencies as 'agents', on the extent to which they were accountable or, conversely, they were able to escape scrutiny. The 'accountability onus' was thus placed on agencies, with an emphasis on the presence of formal accountability obligations. Empirical investigation reveals, however, that problematic aspects intervene at the level of how the various arrangements are used in practice,[80] and particularly in the manner in which the 'principals' – referred to as 'forums' in the accountability literature – rather than the 'agents' discharge their responsibilities. Thus, the central issue relating to agency accountability is generally not the absence of such arrangements but the manner in which they operate and are enacted in practice by forums.

Forums possess a range of scrutinizing powers and the manner in which they avail themselves of these powers appears to be crucial to the functioning of accountability arrangements. An obligation to supply an annual report and an agency that complies with this obligation will have very little impact if the forum does not have the time, resources, or interest to read the report or enter into discussions with the agency. In practice, research shows that underuse of accountability arrangements is an issue of concern. There are significant differences among accountability forums in this regard, with highly active and even proactive forums but also poorly involved forums.

The Council, for instance, shows a predisposition towards scrutinizing more intensively the agencies that traditionally fell under its remit (for example, Europol,

---

79. Schout & Pereyra, *supra* n. 41.
80. Busuioc, *supra* n. 3.

EUROJUST), while all but ignoring some other former first pillar agencies (for example, EASA, OHIM), despite formal powers to engage. In the case of OHIM, the Council is the only EU principal foreseen in its contract design. As a result, there is no one to counteract the strong push for national interests and negative politicization in the OHIM board.[81] While some EP committees demonstrate interest and are involved with the agencies within their remit, others display a low level of involvement and low attendance during hearing meetings.

In relation to this, initiatives to improve parliamentary accountability, such as the one put forward in the Common Approach, which stipulates 'where appropriate' for the presence of EP nominees in the management boards,[82] will not necessarily improve these failures and lead to better practices of democratic accountability. In fact, such an approach might in fact detract from accountability as it amounts to involving the European Parliament, an external accountability forum, into internal agency decision making. It would lead to a blurring of responsibilities as the EP would become, to some extent, responsible for decisions that it simultaneously has the task of overseeing, thereby potentially jeopardizing its objectivity as an account-holder. Rather, to improve political accountability, better de facto involvement of these forums would need to be generated by raising awareness of agencies (the impact of) their work and their profiles within the EP's committees (as well as the Council's structures) in order to stimulate the better use of existing accountability arrangements.

'Failures of practice', where de jure powers do exist but the de facto use thereof is lacking, also apply to management boards in their roles as accountability forums. Boards suffer generic shortcomings, for example in terms of plethoric size and composition, and often lack time, resources, or simply interest and involvement. Some boards are dominated by strong conflicts of interests and a mindset not aligned with their supranational or European roles. The asymmetries of information inherent in any delegation process are exacerbated through failures of a large number of delegations to prepare for the meetings and participate in discussions. Furthermore, in the case of dissatisfaction with the performance of agency heads, board members are reluctant to resort to formal sanctions.[83]

The issue of underuse pertains not only to specific arrangements but also to the monitoring of particular aspects of agencies' functioning. An overwhelming number of board members lack knowledge and expertise in financial and managerial issues, which represent a significant part of their monitoring and steering responsibilities. Political accountability practices (vis-à-vis the EP or the Council) tend to be less intensive, incident-driven, focused on a limited number of issues and guided by political priorities and political saliency.[84]

---

81. See further, Busuioc, *supra* n. 3.
82. Council of the European Union, Evaluation of European Union agencies: Endorsement of the Joint Statement and Common Approach, 11450/12, 18 June 2012, p. 7.
83. Busuioc & Groenleer, *supra* n. 42.
84. M. Busuioc, 'European Agencies: Pockets of Accountability', in *The Real World of EU Accountability. What Deficit?* eds. M. Bovens, D. Curtin & P. 't Hart (Oxford: Oxford University Press, 2010), 87–116.

§8.04 CONCLUSION: FROM PROBLEM TO SOLUTION?

In this Chapter, we addressed the perennial challenge underlying EU agency governance: the balance between the autonomy of agencies, which is supposed to lead to more effective EU governance in their fields of operation, and the accountability they must render, which is to ensure their democratic legitimacy and that of the EU more generally. Striking this balance is an inherently political issue, which has frequently pitted the EU institutions, the Member States, and agencies against each other.

One of the first conclusions to be drawn is that, when assessing agency autonomy or accountability, it is important to move beyond a strictly formal analysis. While formal mandates are an important element of agencies' autonomy and accountability, they do not by any means convey the full post-creation picture. The concepts of autonomy and accountability only start to 'live' once agencies are in operation and drawing conclusions on the basis of formal arrangements can be misleading as observed in the case of EU agencies, where post-creation analysis reveals important divergences with early expectations based on formal design.

Another closely related conclusion is that, unlike 'independence' and 'control', 'autonomy' and 'accountability' can and do co-exist; they are not mutually exclusive but closely connected. Whereas independence stresses the condition of being politically and control-free, the term autonomy emphasizes the capacity to manage one's own affairs and does not preclude some form of (political) authority to scrutinize ex post the agency in its actions or decisions. Whereas control amounts to steering and can entail ongoing interference, accountability is concerned with ex post oversight, with assessing after the fact the behaviour of the agency. Thus, accountability is non-intrusive in the sense that it does not amount to a limitation of the agency's autonomy as laid down in its constituent act.

In terms of institutional design, we find that agencies' accountability obligations are not usually linked or tailored to agencies specificities, administrative capacity, and accountability arrangements already in place. Very importantly, they are also not linked to the level of agency autonomy (either de jure or de facto). A possible explanation for this is that, in reaction to agencies' perceived 'independence' (i.e., unqualified autonomy) and increased calls for enhanced agency accountability, the 'knee-jerk' institutional response was to simply add on accountability arrangements, irrespective of agencies' formal and/or actual autonomy.

Yet, the structure of accountability arrangements and their 'fit' with the agency, in light of its autonomy, is crucial. While accountability may reinforce autonomy, leading to enhanced trust and (democratic) legitimacy, it can also have the opposite effect, by stifling autonomous development. An overload of formal accountability arrangements can restrict actual autonomy, hampering performance. Overwhelming accountability arrangements can have a negative impact on an agency's expert capacity, one of the main reasons to create agencies in the first place, and its operational flexibility, another key reason for creation, thus undermining its credibility and effectiveness.

In spite of the often untailored accountability mechanisms, some agencies have become (political) players in their own right – more than just instruments to fulfil a particular job. They have done so by demonstrating their distinct capacity in a particular area and through active networking with other actors, most notably the EU institutions, the Member States and their national agencies, as a result of which the relationship between agencies and these actors has evolved and respective roles have been clarified. That does not mean that the agencies exert formal power and that this comes at the expense of other (political) actors; it certainly does not mean that agencies are unaccountable or, even stronger, out of control, as is sometimes claimed.

Many of the perceived problems with individual agencies in the past have resulted from the unfamiliarity with the agency phenomenon at the EU level and do not necessarily point to the failure of EU agencies as such. Over time, a lot of these problems have been resolved through incremental adaptations. But agencies do not and probably will never operate entirely without problems from the perspectives of the different actors involved in their creation, design, and development. There will always be debate over their governance, triggered by the enduring tension between autonomy and accountability.

It is unlikely that the Common Approach will silence this debate. Even if it actually materializes in institutional and legal follow-up – which remains to be seen given its non-binding nature – the Approach overlooks the crucial issue of the close link between agency autonomy and accountability and the need for an approach to accountability which is sensitive to its 'fit' with agency autonomy. A 'one-size-fits-all' approach is still dominating and thus, the much-coveted yet elusive balance between agency autonomy and accountability seems condemned to remain out of reach for now.

CHAPTER 9

EU Agencies and the European Parliament[*]

Francis Jacobs

§9.01 INTRODUCTION

The relationship between EU agencies and the European Parliament (EP) has become both increasingly complex and increasingly significant in recent years. There are three main reasons for this. First, the importance of these agencies has grown greatly in recent years, with the number of EU agencies of different types going up from eleven in 2000 to well over thirty in 2012, with their staff increasing from 1200 to 4800, their budget going up six fold, and with the power and autonomy at least of some of these agencies being very considerable. Second, the EP's own role and range of powers have evolved considerably in recent years, and this has affected its relations with agencies in a whole variety of ways. Finally, wider inter-institutional balances between the Parliament, the Council, and the Commission have also been modified, and this too has had impacts on the agencies.

The first section of this Chapter looks at why the EP is increasingly interested in the decentralized agencies, how its own evolving roles and powers have influenced its relations with these agencies, and why they have ensured that the EP has not had a homogeneous view towards agencies, but instead a number of different perspectives. This section also looks briefly at the opposite side of the coin, the perspectives of the agencies themselves towards the EP in its different roles, and some of the potential impacts on their wider relations with the Commission and Council.

The second section of the Chapter looks in more detail at the formal framework for EP involvement with the agencies, the various ways in which the Parliament has

---

[*] The opinions expressed in this document are the sole responsibility of the author and do not necessarily represent the official position of the European Parliament.

sought to help shape, to influence and to make use of the agencies, and the mechanisms used by the Parliament and its committees in these specific tasks. It also looks at some of the ways in which the agencies have sought to work more closely with the Parliament and its committees.

The final section of the Chapter begins by reviewing the attempts that have been made to provide a more standardized framework for agencies, culminating in July 2012 in a Joint Statement of the EP, Council and Commission on decentralized agencies, along with an accompanying Common Approach. The Chapter looks briefly at the effects that these might have on the EP's relations with the agencies.[1] It then seeks to make a number of concluding remarks about some of the distinguishing features as well as constraints in the EP's evolving relations with the agencies, and how these might further develop in the future.

One final word on the scope of this Chapter: any discussion of the EP's relations with agencies needs to start with a definition of what is covered by the term agencies in the first place and to take account of the great diversity of EU agencies, as there are very differing implications for democratic accountability and for EP involvement in their work. The definition of what is an agency has become an increasingly complex question, with decentralized agencies in many areas of EU activity as well as executive agencies with implementing powers in both community and more intergovernmental areas. The former are typically of a regulatory nature, and have their own and varying legal bases whereas the latter have a single legal basis, adopted in Council Regulation (EC) 58/2003 of 19 December 2002. Increasingly, there are also sui generis bodies and joint undertakings, such as ITER and the European Technology Institute. All of these have very differing implications for financial and other accountability. The present Chapter concentrates on the decentralized agencies in areas of classic Community competence.

§9.02   THE EUROPEAN PARLIAMENT'S INCREASING INVOLVEMENT WITH THE DECENTRALIZED AGENCIES

The first key question to ask is why the EP should be much more interested in, and closely involved with, the decentralized agencies than it was in the past. One obvious answer is that there are now far more agencies than before, many with regulatory and not just information-gathering powers and many which are highly relevant for the Parliament's work. A second answer is that the founding regulations of many of the more recent agencies have given the EP a much more direct role than was the case for earlier agencies. One of the reasons why this has been the case is related to the steady evolution of the EP's own roles and powers:

– In its legislative capacity. Where it now enjoys co-decision with the Council in the vast majority of areas, the Parliament has helped to adopt the EU legislation that has established individual agencies, set up their management structures, determined the scope of their activities, shaped their mechanisms

---

1. See also the Chapter on the Agencies and the Commission.

of accountability and, *inter alia*, determined the EP's own powers with regard to such agencies.

- In its budgetary capacity. Where Parliament now has analogous powers of co-decision over the vast majority of the budget, it has helped to decide how much money each agency should get and subject to what conditions.
- In its evolving role on nominations to EU posts, Parliament has had an uneven but growing role in choosing the leadership of and participating in the supervisory structures of individual agencies.
- In its equally evolving control functions, the EP has had a growing role in ensuring the appropriate oversight of EU agencies, especially in the more formal budgetary control context, signing off on their accounts and seeing whether they give value for money. It also has a wider role in the more informal context of monitoring their day-to-day performance and whether they are meeting their original objectives.
- Finally, in its role as a participant in EU institutional review and change, the EP has been involved in the debate as to whether there should be a more consistent overall institutional framework for the agencies and what specific forms this might take.

The above roles and powers often overlap, and complement each other. The legislative, budgetary, and nomination functions all help, for example, to shape the scope of EP oversight of individual agencies, and the EP is now confronted in several contexts with some broad strategic questions about the agencies, such as whether they should be set up in the first place or where they should be located.

The fact that the EP is now involved with these agencies in a number of different contexts has another important consequence, however, namely that there is not one homogeneous EP view on the agencies, but instead a number of different perspectives. There are at least three different perspectives:

- The Constitutional Affairs Committee (AFCO), with its say in the overall EU institutional architecture, has often expressed a preference for a more common framework for agencies, but has had little direct contact with individual agencies.
- The Budgets and Budgetary Control Committees, with their strong formal powers in providing money to agencies and giving budgetary discharge for the agencies, are forced both to take a regular and systematic interest in individual agencies. In addition, these Committees find themselves engaged with each and every agency established and have, therefore, developed a more comprehensive picture of agency operation within the EU.
- Finally the sectoral committees, some of which work together with a number of individual agencies, are usually more interested in the tasks that agencies perform, and in how their own committee works effectively with them, than in a common framework which might not respond to their particular circumstances. This is particularly the case when a committee is working with some of the more recent agencies where the EP has been given a stronger role in their

founding regulations. It should be noted, however, that there is no standard approach among these sectoral committees, whose individual stance depends both on the culture of that committee and on the presence in the committee of one or more members with a particular interest in, or expertise on, the agencies.

The different perspectives that evolved in each of the Committees are not, however, mutually exclusive. Powers exercised by the Budgets Committee, for example, can be deployed to support the concerns of sectoral committees. For example, funds to be dispersed to an agency may be placed in the reserve line of the budget, pending a positive report on an agency's activity by a sectoral committee.

In interacting with agencies, the EP thus has a number of separate, if often complementary agendas: trying to approve oversight and accountability of the agencies, asserting its own institutional position as well as its legislative and budgetary priorities and also, at the same time, seeking to harness the agencies expertise for the benefit of its own work.

This growing interaction has not just been at the initiative of the EP. Agencies have themselves also reached out to the Parliament, especially for support in their efforts to increase their own margin of manoeuvre, notably as regards their relations with the Commission.

There can, for example, be tension between the key role played by the Commission in setting up and monitoring the performance of an agency, and the understandable wish of a new, independent agency to assert its autonomy from the Commission. A good example of this was provided by the early days of the European Environment Agency (EEA) when there were tensions between its leadership and the Commission. At least partly as a result of this, the Agency was keen to build up its relationship with the EP, in order to help strengthen its independent status and be less under the sole supervision of the Commission. Another source of tension can be observed with certain agencies concerned about what they have interpreted to be the over-dominant position of the Commission in evaluating their performance and in the re-appointment of their Directors. They have also turned for support to the EP in these circumstances.

However, agencies have often been proactive in developing their relations with the EP, even where such tensions with the Commission have been absent, and have sought to obtain Parliament's goodwill by backing up the Parliament in its everyday work to ensure broad institutional support for their existence and to reinforce their own role within the overall EU institutional architecture. For these reasons, agencies have often been quick to supply input to Parliament committee work, including various forms of advice, studies, briefing notes, and scientific opinions, and also to seek EP input in their own work plans. The EP's relations with agencies have thus become richer and more varied over time and the establishment of independent agencies has also had wider impacts on inter-institutional relations.

§9.03 FORMAL FRAMEWORK FOR EUROPEAN PARLIAMENT INVOLVEMENT WITH THE AGENCIES

There are two main components to the formal framework for EP involvement with the decentralized agencies: first, the general references in the EU Treaties and in Inter-Institutional Agreements; second, the specific references to the EP in the founding regulations of the agencies; and finally, the references to the agencies in the EP's own internal rules of procedure, in the decisions of its leadership bodies, and in its own plenary resolutions.

[A] General References in the EU Treaties and in Inter-Institutional Agreements

Twenty-five of the agencies are either fully or partly funded by the EU budget on which the EP now co-decides pursuant to Article 314 of the TFEU. Moreover Articles 23 and 24 of the Financial Regulation permit the EP to keep part of the agencies proposed budget in reserve until the Commission submits a request for the release of the funds in question, and the EP's Budget Committee then agrees.

Article 319 TFEU also grants authority to the EP, on a recommendation of the Council, to give the Commission a discharge for the implementation of the EU budget. In addition, Point 47 of the Inter-Institutional Agreement on budgetary discipline and sound financial management[2] gives a central role to the EP, along with the Council, in examining the budgetary aspects of creating a new agency and in subsequently financing it. Point 47 of the IIA has since been reinforced by joint declarations in July 2007 and December 2009.

There is also a brief section on the relationship with regulatory agencies in the 2010 Framework Agreement on Relations between the EP and the Commission.[3] In point 32 of this Agreement it is stated that nominees for the post of Executive Director of regulatory agencies shall come to Parliamentary Committee hearings.

[B] Specific References to the European Parliament in the Founding Regulations of the Agencies

References to the EP in the founding regulations of the agencies were almost non-existent for the earlier agencies. They have, however, become more and more frequent since the introduction of EP-Council's co-decision has given the EP the chance to help introduce a much greater, if still uneven, say for itself in the structure and functioning of individual agencies.

---

2. OJ C139 of 14 June 2006.
3. See OJ L304/47 of 20 November 2010.

[C]   Appointment of Members of the Management Boards, the Executive Director and/or Other Organs

One of the less familiar aspects of the growing institutional role of the EP has been its increasing role in the EU appointments process. In line with this development, the EP has obtained a growing, but still varying, role with regard to appointments to the leadership positions within EU agencies. There are still a considerable number of agencies where the EP has no direct role, either in the choice of the Director or of the Management Board. Some of these are first generation agencies, such as CEDEFOP and EUROFOUND, where the EP was only consulted on their founding regulations. Others include more recent agencies, such as ETF, the CPVO, OHIM, OSHA, the Translation Centre, the Fisheries Control Agency and FRONTEX, where the EP was still only consulted on their founding regulations. More surprising, however, are those cases where the EP was involved in the founding regulation through co-decision, such as EASA and EMSA, but where the EP still has no direct role in the appointments process.

Even in some of these latter cases the EP has tried to obtain some kind of role for itself, such as the case of EASA, where the Transport Committee rapporteur sought EP consultation on the composition of the EASA Management Board or in the case of the Fisheries Control Agency, where the Fisheries Committee has asked to send a staff member or a Member of European Parliament (MEP) to the agency's Administrative Council; a request which has always been refused up to now.

Besides these cases where the EP has had no formal role in the appointments process, there are many other agencies where it does have such a role. These tend to fall into three main categories, as outlined below.

[1]   *Agencies Where the European Parliament Only Has the Right to Nominate Members of the Management Board*

One important means to link up with agencies is through the possibility foreseen in the founding regulations of a number of agencies to nominate members (one or two) as representatives of the EP on the Management Board. The first agency in which the EP was given the right to have nominees on its Management Board was the EEA in 1990, set up in 1990 on the basis of the then cooperation procedure, whereby the Parliament had two readings on the final legislation but did not have the same weight as in the co-decision procedure. In 1993 the EP also got two nominees on the Management Board of the European Monitoring Centre for Drugs and Drug Addiction, and in 1997 had one nominee on the MB of the European Monitoring Centre on Racism and Xenophobia. In a Decision of 5 March 1998 of the EP's Conference of Presidents, its key leadership body, consisting of the President and the leaders of the EP Political Groups, elaborated the essential framework for choosing these members and this is described below.

[2]   Agencies with an European Parliament Role in the Appointment of the Director but with No Nominees on the Management Board

The BSE crisis, which severely undermined trust in EU food standards if not in EU regulation more generally, sparked initiatives to depoliticize food safety standards which resulted in EFSA. Here an attempt was made to move beyond a purely intergovernmental board and towards one more based on specific expertise. The co-decision negotiations leading up to the establishment in 2002 of Council Regulation (EC)178/2002 thus explored the idea of a new type of agency model. The idea was that the EP be given a role for the first time in the appointment of the Agency's Director, that the Management Board be smaller than the number of Member States, and without nominees from the Parliament, but that the EP also be consulted on the nominees to the new-style Management Board.

The EFSA legislation provided for the nominee for the post of Director to appear before Parliament before being formally appointed. When this new model was implemented, it was interpreted as requiring a proper confirmation hearing before the responsible EP Committee, which then wrote a letter to the President of the Parliament giving its views on the capacity of the candidate. By analogy with the 1998 rules on choosing EP nominees to Management Boards, the final decision was then taken by the EP Conference of Presidents.

The other precedent in the EFSA case was the new EP role in the filtering of candidates to the reduced Management Board. The Commission drew up a list of possible nominees, which were then examined by a working group within the responsible EP Committee. They then put forward a recommended list of nominees for the approval of the full committee and subsequently of the Conference of Presidents.

No formal criteria were adopted by the working group, but they did agree on a number of informal principles, such as the need to avoid having heads of national food safety authorities on the Management Board, as they were better placed on the Advisory Committee on which all Member States were represented. The working group was also concerned about the limited number of consumer representatives on the list submitted by the Commission. They also, in a couple of cases, deliberately put forward two nominees from a single Member State, as these were both justified on the merit of the nominees and this also underlined the principle that the EU was moving away from the old model of one nominee per Member State. The final Council Decision, however, followed some but not all of the EP recommendations and tried to stay as close as possible to the old model of one representative per Member State. It became very clear that old habits die hard.

In light of this resistance from the Member States, it is perhaps not surprising that the proposed new model has had only limited success. The EP was also given a role in the choice of the Director of the European Network and Information Security Agency (ENISA), decided upon by co-decision in 2004. An attempt was also made to apply the new model in the far-reaching 2004 revision of the European Medicines Agency (EMEA), but the Member States insisted on keeping their national representatives on the Board, and the EP then ended up with the third model described below, namely having both a role in the appointment of the Director and with its own nominees on the

Management Board. This model, rather than the EFSA one, has been followed in a couple of other recent cases, as described below.

One important exception has been that of the European Fundamental Rights Agency (FRA), established in 2007.[4] Here the EP's role concentrates on the appointment of the Director. However, the EP has been given a more powerful formal say on the nomination of the FRA Director than for any other agency, in that it has formal equality in this process with the Council with hearings before both institutions and an order of preference established by both before the final formal decision by the Management Board (although concern has been expressed within the Parliament at the unsatisfactory manner in which this has been implemented). In another precedent, the EP is also consulted on nominations to the FRA Scientific Committee.

The full EFSA model has thus not been very durable. It has, however, had considerable subsequent influence, in that it has established the principle of an EP role in the appointment of Agency Directors, following on from a public hearing of the nominee before the responsible EP committee.

[3]   *Agencies Where European Parliament Has Both a Role in the Appointment of the Director and Has Its Own Nominees on the Management Board*

As pointed out above, this model was finally adopted when EMEA was being revised, with an additional innovation in that the EP was also to be consulted on representatives of patients, doctors, and vets on the Management Board. When this was first applied it was again on the basis of a filtering exercise by a working group in the responsible committee. The model was then again applied to the European Centre for Disease Protection and Control (ECDC) and to the European Chemicals Agency. The EP is thus continuing to hold confirmation hearings for new Directors and also choosing its own nominees for Management Boards. By analogy with the hearings for Directors, individual committees are now experimenting with hearings for its own nominees to such boards, with this being used, for example, in the cases of the EEA, ECDC and the European Chemicals Agency.

[4]   *Re-appointment of Directors or Other Officeholders*

A formal reference to the EP role in reappointment was first provided for in the penultimate paragraph of Article 15-3 of Council Regulation 168/2007 establishing the FRA. This states that:

> the Management Board shall inform the European Parliament and the Council about its intention to extend the Director's mandate. Within a delay of one month before the Management Board formally takes its decision to extend this mandate,

---

4. Council Regulation 168/2007 establishing a European Union Agency for Fundamental Rights, OJ L53/1–14 of 22 March 2007.

the Director may be asked to make a declaration before the competent committee of the European Parliament and to answer questions from its members.

Such a re-confirmation hearing is thus analogous to the initial EP role provided for in the appointment of many Agency Directors. Even where this is not formally provided for, some committees have been seeking to have a similar say in the process. This was the case, for example, when the Environment Committee held hearings with the outgoing Directors before agreeing to support the re-nominations of Mark Sprenger as the Executive Director of the ECDC (25 April 2010) and of Catherine Geslain-Laneelle (30 November 2010).[5]

The Regulation establishing a European Supervisory Authority (European Banking Authority)[6] gives an even stronger role to the EP as regards the Chairperson of the Authority in its Article 48-4 last paragraph. This states that 'the Board of Supervisors, taking into account the evaluation, may extend the term of the Chairperson once subject to confirmation by the EP.'

[5]   *Dismissal of Directors or Other Officeholders*

Until recently the EP has been given no formal role in this regard, but this has now changed with the adoption of Regulation 1093/2010 establishing a European Supervisory Authority (European Banking Authority)[7] which states, in its Article 48-5 'that the Chairperson may be removed from office only by the EP following a decision of the Board of Supervisors.'

§9.04   OTHER REFERENCES TO THE EUROPEAN PARLIAMENT

Besides the variable EP role in the choice of Agency Directors and Management Boards, the founding legal texts of the different agencies contain a wide range of other formal references to the role of the EP.

In view of its budgetary powers, there is a generalized reference to the role of the EP in the budgetary discharge process along with the related requirement to provide relevant information to the EP to carry out this task. Other references are less standardized but are still contained in the founding texts of a considerable number of agencies, for example the frequent reference to the EP receiving annual reports on an agency's activities (i.e., CEDEFOP, EEA, ERA, European Monitoring Centre on Racism and Xenophobia, ETF) or other evaluations of the functioning of an agency (Fisheries Agency, ECDC, EFSA, EMCDD ENISA, ERA). With the ERA there is a possibility of suggesting changes to the MB composition.

---

5. Midterm report of Environment Committee 2009–2014, Parliament.
6. Regulation 1093/2010 of the EP and Council establishing a European Supervisory Authority (European Banking Authority) amending Decision 716/2009/EC and repealing Commission Decision 2009/78/EC, *OJ* L331 of 15 December 2010.
7. *Ibid.*

Yet other references tend to be limited to just a few agencies or to even one agency. Examples of this are references to the EP receiving various assessments, data collection (EFSA), results of scientific reviews (EFSA), periodic reviews (for example, the annual report from ECDC on current and emerging health threats), rules of procedure (i.e., for OSHA) or the agency work programme (FRA, with formal consultation of EP specifically included). The regulations of a number of agencies similarly provide for the possibility of a hearing of the Director of the Agency at the request of the EP (for example, FRONTEX, EASA, and ENISA). In the regulation of certain agencies, the EP may also request scientific opinions (ECDC, EFSA), scientific research/surveys (European Monitoring Centre on Racism and Xenophobia) or may make other requests for advice and assistance (ENISA). EFSA provisions enable the EP to receive reasons why its requests for scientific opinions have been rejected or modified.

In spite of the increasing involvement of EP committee relations with agencies, they are only governed by a limited number of formal rules, guidelines, and resolutions.

The only explicit mention of agencies in the main body of the rules is in Rule 126 as described below. In addition to this, a number of agencies are referred to in Annex VII of the rules on the formal responsibility of committees for agencies. Otherwise the EP relations with agencies are provided for implicitly rather than explicitly in the EP rules.

The most detailed mention of EU agencies in the EP Rules is in Rule 126 on requests to European Agencies, a relatively new rule which was designed for one purpose only, namely to create a mechanism for MEPs to request scientific opinions from agencies. This is a right for MEPs which, as mentioned above, is only provided for in the founding regulations of a handful of recent EU agencies, notably the European Food Safety Authority (EFSA) and the European Centre for the Prevention and Control of Transmissible Diseases (ECDC).

The idea behind the rule is to provide for practical implementation of this new right, by ensuring that it is available to individual members while filtering out questions which have already been asked by another body, which are outside the remit of the agency or otherwise beyond its capacity to reply. Any member can thus submit their suggested question to the EP President, who then consults the responsible EP Committee (normally that is specifically mentioned as responsible for relations with the relevant agency in the list of committee competences). The committee staff checks with the agency staff to see, for example, whether the question can be responded to and in what time frame. Occasionally the agency may suggest that the question be reformulated, and this then has to be checked with its author. At the end of this process the committee informs the EP President, who then writes to the agency to confirm the content of the question and the timetable for the response. This rule has only been used on a few occasions.

Of greater strategic importance than Rule 126 have been the rules on the designation by the EP of members of the Management Boards of the Specialized Agencies and Bodies. These are not set down in the EP's Rules of Procedure but instead in a Decision of 5 March 1998 of the EP's Conference of Presidents, its key leadership body, consisting of the President and the leaders of the EP Political Groups. As outlined above, the founding regulations of a number of agencies provide for EP nominees or representatives on the Boards of the Agencies, and this decision provides the essential framework for choosing them. The responsible committee (normally designated in the annex to the EP Rules on the competences of standing committees) is given the central role in calling for and filtering candidates. Once the committee has decided on who it wishes to support, it then sends a letter with its recommendations to the Conference of Presidents, who then take the final decision for the EP. The decision also contains the key provision (in a footnote) that EP designees cannot be sitting MEPs, thus responding to one of the objections that have been made (see below) to the concept of EP nominees on the Board of an Agency.

The Decision of 5 May 1998 also sets out other guidelines governing EP contacts, not just with its own nominees but with the concerned agencies in general, including the need for regular information to be provided by the EP nominees, reimbursement for two annual visits from the nominees to the responsible EP committees, and the obligation for the responsible committees to send three member delegations to the concerned agency every two years.

A further set of guidance was provided by the Conference of Committee Chairmen guidelines of 14 July 1998 entitled Guidelines on cooperation between the committees with competence concerning the decentralized Community agencies. This stemmed from an initiative from the EP Budgets Committee. It encouraged the concerned committees to name standing rapporteurs on the agencies within their remit, to ensure an annual exchange of views with the relevant Agency Director on its Annual Work Programme, to carry out visits every two years, and to provide cooperation as regards the monitoring of agencies between the sectoral committees and the Budgets Committee, as well as exchange of information between all concerned committees.

The EP has also adopted a number of recent resolutions on the framework for EU agencies, including an EP resolution based on the Almeida Garrett report of December 2003 on the Commission's Communication on Agencies, and a further resolution of December 2005 on the basis of an oral question with debate on the draft Inter-Institutional Agreement proposed by the Commission.

§9.05 THE EUROPEAN PARLIAMENT AND AGENCIES AND THE EUROPEAN PARLIAMENT: THE MANAGEMENT OF MUTUAL RELATIONS

[A] Mechanisms for European Parliament Committee Engagement with the Agencies

The widening and deepening of agency interaction with the EP have meant that ever more EP committees have become involved with individual agencies. In turn, this has sparked discussions as to how such committees should work together with the agencies and for what purpose.

Around 1990 only five committees were involved with individual agencies. As shown in Table 9.1, this has increased to eleven in recent years, with six committees with explicit reference to individual agencies in their competences in Annex VII of the Rules of Procedure from 2009, and another five (and one subcommittee) with links with other agencies without such a specific reference in their competences. In addition, three EP Committees have horizontal responsibilities: the Budgets Committee, whose terms of reference in Annex VII of the EP Rules refer explicitly to the budgets of the decentralized bodies, the Budgetary Control Committee, with its responsibility for granting budgetary discharge to the vast majority of agencies for which this is envisaged, and the Constitutional Affairs Committee, with its responsibility for inter-institutional relations, and thus for the examination of the overall institutional framework for the agencies (see Table 9.1).

Table 9.1   European Parliament Committees with Responsibilities for Specific Agencies

Employment Committee	– European Foundation for the Improvement of Living and Working Conditions (EUROFOUND) – European Agency for Health and Safety at Work – European Training Foundation – the European Centre for the Development of Vocational Training (CEDEFOP)
Committee on Environment, Public Health and Food Safety	– European Centre for Disease Prevention and Control – European Environment Agency – European Food Safety Authority – The European Medicines Agency – The European Chemicals Agency
Agriculture Committee	– The Community Plant Variety Office
Legal Affairs Committee	– Office for Harmonization in the Internal Market – Trade Marks and Designs
Civil Liberties Committee	– The European Monitoring Centre for Drugs and Drug Addiction – European Fundamental Rights Agency (replacing European Monitoring Centre on Racism and Xenophobia) – European Agency for the Management of Operational Coordination at the External Borders of the Member States of the European Union - EUROJUST - EUROPOL – European Police College
Fisheries Committee	– Community Fisheries Control Agency

Industry, Energy, and Research Committee	– European GNSS Surveillance Authority (dealing with Global Navigation Satellite System)
	– European Network and Information Security Agency (ENISA)
	– European Agency for the Cooperation of Energy Regulators
	– Body of European Regulators for Electronic Communications
	– Euratom Supply Agency
Women's Committee	– European Institute for Gender Equality
Transport Committee	– European Maritime Safety Agency
	– European Aviation Safety Agency
	– European Railway Agency
Economic and Monetary Affairs Committee	– European Banking Authority
	– European Insurance and Occupational Pensions Authority
	– European Securities and Market Authority
Foreign Affairs Committee	– European Reconstruction Agency
Foreign Affairs Committee – Security and Defence Subcommittee	three CFSP Agencies (European Defence Agency, European Union Institute for Security Studies, European Union Satellite Centre)

Parliament Committees seeking to work more closely with the agencies are faced with a number of questions: how to bring agency information to the attention of the committee (and to the coordinators or political group spokesmen, in particular), how to liaise with the EP nominees on the Management Boards and the Directors of the Agencies, how to screen the work of the Management Board, how to follow agency budgetary issues, how to choose EP nominees to the Boards, how best to organize an Agency Director's confirmation and other hearings within the committee, and how to prepare and accompany committee delegations to the agency. Committees have used a variety of mechanisms to achieve these objectives.

[1]   Delegation Visits to Agencies

Following the updated Bureau decision of 14 January 2008, the latest version of the EP rules now allow committees to send, every two years, a three member delegation to agencies for which that committee is primarily responsible. Committees are given an annual quota for delegation visits (to prevent excessive travel and to reduce costs) but the above visits to agencies are outside this quota, and ensure greater continuity of contacts. This does not prevent other visits to agencies by committees, but they would have to be included within their normal annual quota of visits. Practice in this regard varies considerably between committees, and depends on the political interest of the agency. Some agencies with more technical remits are rarely visited by the concerned committee, whereas others are systematically visited every two years. For example, this has been the regular practice of the Environment Committee, which is now responsible for a considerable number of agencies but which tries, even if only for a short period, to go to each agency every other year.

The pattern of these visits tends to be quite similar, with an initial briefing of the delegation from the Agency Director, usually concentrating on the strategic direction of the agency and general staffing and management issues, followed by an exploration of specific policy points agreed upon by in advance by the committee and the agency.

[2]   Committee Contact Persons and Standing Rapporteurs

Another device for ensuring more systematic linkage between an EP committee and an agency is that of designating members to act as committee contact persons with such an agency or else as standing rapporteurs who follow the work of agencies over a longer period of time than just for a one-off report or opinion.

The aims of this procedure are to ensure an annual exchange of views with agencies within their formal area of responsibility, for example, to discuss the Annual Work Programme with the Agency Director, to carry out visits every two years, and to provide cooperation as regards the monitoring of agencies between the sectoral committees and the Budgets Committee, as well as exchange of information between all concerned committees. Two committees have been particularly associated with this: the Industry Committee which has appointed standing rapporteurs for certain agencies under its remit and the Environment Committee which has appointed contact persons.

The Environment Committee finally implemented this instrument of control in March 2007 with the nomination of six members of the committee to follow the agencies (as well as the European Food and Veterinary Office) within the committee's area of responsibility.

The contact persons of both the EP committee and the relevant agency should also hold a joint meeting at least twice a year, to exchange information and to discuss best practices. It is still too early to see how these interactions between EP and agencies will work. Among the practical problems that have been faced in the past has been the need to ensure that the contact persons can devote enough time to their tasks in addition to all their other responsibilities as MEPs. Other members of a committee, and notably the coordinators, have also expressed their concerns about relations with an agency being delegated to only one committee specialist. In order to give clearer guidance a set of guidelines for contact persons in charge of relations with the agencies (contained in Annex IV of the Environment Committee Activity report for 2004–2009) were adopted by the committee coordinators in December 2007. This sets out their role and tasks and provides for all the contact persons to meet together at least twice a year to exchange best practices and to prepare for input on the annual budgetary procedure.

[3]   *Dialogue with European Parliament Nominees on Management Boards*

In principle, the EP nominees need to provide regular feedback on the activities of the agencies in which they are involved and provide for reimbursement for two annual visits from the nominees to the responsible EP committees. This issue of feedback from the EP nominees to the EP committees has in the past appeared problematic for some agencies. For example, the representatives would have liked to have more instructions on the wishes of EP concerning the work programme of the agency. To address these critiques and the problems encountered in practice, the EP committees have tried to issue clearer remits to an EP nominee, *inter alia*, by means of a letter to the nominees from the committee chair outlining what the committee expects from them. However, with a view to respecting the distance EP needs to take from agencies, and due to difficulties in being involved in work programme decisions, the nominees from the EP on the board have remained rather independent in practice. The wider issue of whether the EP should have its own nominees on agency boards is still a controversial one and is discussed in more detail below.

[4]   *Exchange of Letters/Memoranda of Understanding between European Parliament Committee Chairs and Agency Directors*

The above relationships can often be on a rather 'ad hoc' basis. Therefore individual EP committee chairs have tried to develop them within a more structured context. A remarkable example of this was the exchange of letters between Caroline Jackson, the Chair of the EP Environment Committee between 1999 and 2004, and Jacqueline McGlade, the Director of the EEA. In the letter Caroline Jackson suggested a number of ways in which the EEA could assist the Committee in its endeavour to supervise the agency, including briefing notes for delegations and assessment of the impact of adopted EU environment legislation. Jacqueline McGlade replied by giving an indication of the ways in which the EEA could respond and where this might be more problematic. Caroline Jackson subsequently confirmed the arrangements that had been reached.

Such memoranda of understanding are important for the agencies with a view to building commitment for their work programme. With that, they also make themselves less dependent on the Commission. Hence, the actions of the EP have a wider impact on the institutional embedment of the agencies.

[5]   *The European Parliament and Agencies: Agencies as Information Providers*

The EP has traditionally had relatively limited in-house expertise. The need for more detailed and independent information, however, has become increasingly important, with Parliament's codecision powers being steadily extended to a variety of complex technical areas, and with other new demands on the Parliament such as the better regulation initiatives of the EU and the use of impact assessments to which the three rule-making institutions have committed themselves. Moreover, the Parliament has also sought to be not too dependent on the Commission whose proposals it is examining or on the interest groups who are seeking to influence it.

One way to compensate for the lack of specialized information has been the development of expertise budgets for committees. In addition, independent agencies can often be of great value in helping the EP carry out its own tasks through impartial and (relatively) rapid provision of expert advice.

Having cost-free advice from specialist agencies can thus be of great help for the EP. The EEA, for example, has provided the Environment Committee with briefing notes to prepare delegations, as well as committee member participation in international environment conferences, such as those on climate change or biodiversity. The EEA has also helped other EP committees such as those on Agriculture and Transport. Similarly, the ECDC has provided the Environment Committee with information notes on the spread of Asian flu in Turkey and elsewhere. Such notes have been produced at relatively short notice. The founding regulations of various agencies provide, moreover, for the possibilities of the EP to request scientific opinions (EFSA), scientific research/surveys (EUMC), or may make other requests for advice and assistance (ENISA). EFSA provisions enable the EP to receive reasons why its requests for scientific opinions have been rejected or modified that are instructed to provide scientific advice allow also the EP, in addition to the Commission and the Member States, to request scientific opinions from those agencies. Importantly, the EP has begun to make use of this possibility. Examples of this, again drawn from Environment Committee experience, include studies on the safety of farmed salmon, as well as what was provided in January 2007 on the health risks of feeding of ruminants with fishmeal in relation to the risk of TSE EFSA provisions, moreover enable the EP to receive reasons why its requests for scientific opinions have been rejected or modified (Article 38 1 9(g) Regulation 178/2002).

[6]   *The Budgets and Budgetary Discharge Instruments*

The EP codecides on the EU annual budget with the Council, and thus helps to take the decision on the grant provided for each agency which is within the EU budget which is generally the key source of an agency's income, apart from the handful of agencies that receive income from other sources. Agencies thus come to the EP Budgets Committee to plead their case and maintain regular contact with that committee. The Budgets Committee appoints a rapporteur to deal with the agencies, and there is an annual meeting of the Budgets Committee (held jointly with the Budgetary Control Committee) with agency heads to look at the follow-up of the previous budget, work programmes and staffing needs, and the next year's budget. Draftsmen of budgetary opinions from other committees are also invited to this meeting. Individual agencies also keep in close touch with the budgetary draftsmen of the EP committees with which they are particularly concerned.

The Parliament's powers of budgetary discharge are also crucial in ensuring open scrutiny of the management of EU funds by individual decentralized agencies as well as their overall political accountability. The ensuing close relationship between the Budgetary Control Committee, especially its rapporteur, and the agencies culminates in a series of votes in one of the Parliament's plenary sessions in which it adopts a decision on whether to give discharge in respect of the implementation of a budget of a specific agency, a second decision on the closure of accounts of that agency and finally an accompanying resolution with observations forming an integral part of its decision on the discharge. This latter resolution allows specific critical comments to be made on anything from problems of financial management to insufficient transparency, to problems of conflict of interest by an agency or inappropriate behaviour by its Director. If these critical comments are sufficiently serious the EP may postpone the granting of discharge for that agency until the latter has responded satisfactorily to the criticisms.

[B] Agency Mechanisms

From the side of agencies, the most obvious way to liaise with the relevant committees is through their Directors. The Directors of Agencies are now coming more frequently to address EP Committee meetings in Brussels, whether to update a committee on general developments at the agency, or to deal with a specific issue, such as avian flu or climate change. All or most of the Agency Directors also come to an annual meeting of the Budgets Committee. Agency Directors also brief committee delegations visiting their agency (see above) as well as meet more informally with committee chairmen or other individual members in Brussels or elsewhere.

A second standard way is for agencies to have their own designated contact persons with the EP who liaise with the relevant EP committees and their staff and follow developments within the EP that are of importance for the agency. One obvious way of doing this is through regular attendance at EP committee meetings where they can follow relevant debates, network with MEPs, and even answer questions that come up during the committee meetings. Conversely, the absence of agency staff at certain committee meetings has led at times to parliamentary criticism of the agency in question. Agency liaison officers have also been instituted to help to prepare EP committee delegations to the agency, have organized information seminars for EP staff, channel requests from EP committees for scientific opinions and briefing notes, and handle the involvement of MEPs in evaluations of agency management plans and work programmes. The liaison officers perform similar functions in relation to the Commission with a view to streamlining the work planning and drafting of the work programmes.

Agencies have also tried to facilitate the work of EP nominees on agency Management Boards. The EEA held a management seminar, for example, at the agency at which agency staff, EP nominees and their alternates as well as EP committee staff all got to exchange views on topical issues and got to know each other better.

Agencies are also beginning to involve the EP in other aspects of an agency's work. Besides the involvement of EP nominees on Management Boards in agency working parties (as in EMEA), MEPs are also being asked to take part in certain agency activities. For example, agencies such as the ECDC, have invited MEPs to participate in internal working groups on disease surveillance networks and on evaluation of the agency's work.

§9.06   EUROPEAN PARLIAMENT'S POSITION AS REGARDS GENERAL STRATEGIC QUESTIONS CONCERNING AGENCIES

The next section of this Chapter explores a number of strategic questions with which the EP is confronted when working with the agencies, such as whether an individual agency should be set up in the first place, where it should be located, the EP's role in the appointment and reappointment of an agency's Director or Management Board, and budgetary issues.

[A]   Need to Create an Agency

The EP's essential role in the creation of agencies, increasingly now through co-decision, has been mentioned above. The EP has established some general criteria to govern the establishment of new agencies, for example, in its resolution on agencies of 1 December 2005 when it called for the setting up of agencies to come under the normal legislative procedure of co-decision, and in which it also stated that:

> any proposal for setting up an agency should be accompanied by a cost-benefit assessment and by a thorough impact assessment showing that the agency option is more cost-effective than having the relevant tasks performed by the Commission departments themselves.

There should also be an ex-ante evaluation of the likely costs of monitoring and coordination and the impact on human resources and administrative expenditure.

In this context, a draft report by Ms De Castillo Vera from the EP Industry Committee expressed major reservations about the Commission's proposal for a new European Electronic Communications Market Authority on the grounds that it would be cumbersome and remote from the markets it would be called upon to regulate. The rapporteur proposed, instead, a lighter coordinating body of European Telecommunications Regulators. The final outcome, adopted as part of an overall telecoms package in 2009, was much closer to this vision.

[B]   Location

The question of the geographical seat of a new agency is a highly political question and is often part of a political package deal between European leaders. The EP has no formal say in these specific decisions, and even its informal say has been limited.

The EP has, however, expressed its concerns about the general danger of creating new agencies in order to be able to locate them in as many Member States as possible and about the need for objective criteria to govern the question of their location. The EP resolution based on the Almeida Garrett report of December 2003 stated, for example, in its paragraph 6, that:

> decisions on the location of any future regulatory agencies should form an integral and vital part of the basic instruments establishing them and that, in accordance with criteria on transparency, efficiency and scrutiny of costs, the seats of the agencies should be near those of the authorities which are to supervise them.

Finally the EP has taken a considerable interest in the 'ex-post' implications of establishing agencies in particular locations. Individual EP committees have looked at the consequences of impractical locations on staff recruitment or on other matters likely to slow up the establishment of an agency or to undercut its likely effectiveness. The Environment Committee, for example, has taken a particular interest in the problems relating to difficult access to the location of the EFSA in Parma due to its distance from an international airport (Milan). This is a problem, notably for members of its scientific advisory committees, who have to visit it on a regular basis.

[C]   Experience of the European Parliament Nominees on the Board, and Is Their Presence Justified?

Some have argued, even within the EP, that the EP should not have nominees on boards of agencies that it is trying to scrutinize, primarily because of a potential conflict of roles. In the past the Commission has also expressed its reserve on this matter because this would cast doubt on the Parliament's ability to perform external controls objectively.[8]

The EP Conference of President's Decision of 5 May 1998 already addresses this critique to some extent as it stipulates that EP designees cannot be sitting MEPs, precisely to avoid such a conflict. Moreover, the EP nominees are not formal representatives of the EP (unlike the Member States and Commission representatives). In addition, the EP has now linked the issue of its own nominations to Agency Management Boards with that of the size of those boards. If they are greatly downsized (as currently appears unlikely) Parliament's position might then be re-evaluated.

So what has been Parliament's experience with its nominees? The Environment Committee is the committee which has been most involved. This experience appears to indicate that such nominees can play a very important role in ensuring adequate links between the EP and the agency in question. The EP nominees cannot, as pointed out above, be sitting MEPs. Being dedicated specialists, often university professors, they often have certain advantages in following the technical work of agencies as compared to EP committee members. They tend to have higher levels of scientific expertise and often more time to follow the work of the agency. They can attend all Board meetings,

---

8. Commission text of 25 February 2005.

receive all the relevant documentation, and are sometimes given additional responsi-bilities. Individual EP nominees have become Vice-Chairman of their Board (for example, Minerva Malliori at ECDC), have been on Board Bureaux, co-chaired a steering group advising upon the independent evaluation of an Agency's impact and effectiveness (for example, Michael Scoullos at the EEA), and have been seconded to working parties on specific problems (such as the EP nominees to EMEA), as well as having been given other tasks. They have sometimes also helped to ensure a continuity of contacts that would otherwise not occur. Michael Scoullos, for example, has been one of the EP nominees for eighteen years ever since 1994.

EP nominees can thus carry out a variety of useful roles. Perhaps the most obvious is to provide regular feedback and documentation on Management Board agendas and later on the decisions when the meetings have taken place (this now occurs systematically, for example, by means of letters to the committee from the EP nominees to the EEA). They can also provide early warning on new issues arising at the agency and help to prepare committee visits to an agency (as with ECDC nominee briefings to delegation members in Brussels on the day before a visit) and/or accom-pany the MEPs on the delegation when they visit the agency (as has happened at EMEA, EEA, and ECDC). They can attend EP committee meetings, on their own or when the Agency Director is being heard by the committee, and can provide formal or informal information on these occasions to the members of the committee. They can brief the EP committee on the selection process for a new Agency Director (as happened at the EEA where the EP has no formal role in the choice of the Director, and the EP nominees both informally discussed the shortlisted candidates and listened to the committee coordinators views on the criteria which they should take into account).

They can also defend EP points of view at the agency and call for them to be taken into account in the work programme of the agency. A good example of this was Nigel Haigh's and Michael Scoullos's insistence that the EEA become more involved in work on the effectiveness of adopted EU environment policies, in spite of concerns being expressed by the European Commission that this would lead the EEA into tasks falling more within the areas of competence of the Commission.

If EP's use of these nominees is to be most effective, however, they need to be both well chosen and also be given a clear remit from the committee. Parliament has been learning-by-doing in both these respects and better practice is gradually being developed. In the context of choice of EP nominees, hearings of the candidates have now been introduced, to examine their experience and qualities, and to review their understanding of Parliament's needs and concerns. Also several former MEPs have emerged well from this exercise, being both known by their former colleagues, but also often having a better understanding of EP political concerns. With a view to prevent the types of problems related to lack of transparency and overlapping loyalties that characterized the BSE crisis, possible conflict of interest criteria that may occur are also being examined for all candidates.

The practice of independent experts being chosen to represent the EP in the Board proved to have an important influence on the functioning of the Board as a whole. As remarked by Schout, both the Commission and the Member States have particular interests to defend, whereas the scientists appointed by the EP may have a more neutral perspective on, for example, the work programme of the agency compared to the Member States.

[D]   Role of the European Parliament in the Appointment and Reappointment of Agency Directors

As the text above shows, the EP has carved out a significant role for itself as regards the initial appointment of Agency Directors and, to a much lesser extent, as regards their re-appointment. In most cases the formal power is not a strong one, with no right for the EP to veto an appointment but merely to invite the nominee to a meeting of the responsible EP committee and to pose questions to him or her. In practice, however, and while falling short of the Parliament's powers as regards the Commission (because of the leverage given by Parliament's power to reject the Commission as a whole) the committee meetings with the nominees to head the concerned agencies have increasingly taken on the character of de facto confirmation hearings.

What has this meant for the process of choosing agency heads, especially because no nominee has yet been given a negative assessment by a committee and because the consequences of doing so are still unclear? Certainly a negative assessment and even one in which committee support was heavily qualified would seriously damage a nominee. Moreover, hearings of nominees tend to set an important benchmark for the future relationship between the nominee and the Parliamentary committee, and thus on the wider relationships between the EP and the agency. Such hearings also give an important opportunity for a committee to express its concerns and obtain a reaction from the nominee about the future direction and policies of the agency, as well as on its administrative and organizational structures.

A related question is the procedure to be followed in the case of the reappointment of Agency Directors and the nature of the EP's involvement in such a decision. There has been concern expressed in recent years, both within individual agencies and in the EP, that the Commission has been proposing too much of a role for itself in this regard, that this was inappropriate for an allegedly independent agency, and that the final decision should be left to the Management Board of the agency concerned. A dominant position of the Commission in the re-appointment would render the Director virtually dependent on the Commission. The December 2005 resolution of the EP on the Inter-Institutional Agreement on Agencies, made the EP's position clear in this respect: 'A decision to extend the term of office of a director should be taken solely by the board of directors, on the basis of an evaluation of the director's first term of office'.

The role of the EP itself in the reappointment process has not yet been clarified, but it is to be expected that it will be seeking a stronger involvement in the future. A very important precedent in this respect has been set in the case of the FRA where, as described above, the EP is given the possibility of a reconfirmation hearing in the relevant committee in the case of reappointment of the sitting Director.

The nature of the EP's role in these matters remains an unsettled question. The EP has continued to argue forcefully for a more systematic role in the choice of all Agency Directors, and for better internal procedures to implement its own new powers in this respect. This was restated in paragraph 60 of the EP resolution of 12 December 2007 on the Commission legislative and work programme for 2008 which read:

> Calls on the Commission to reform without delay its procedures and to involve more closely the Parliament and its competent committees during the process for the selection and appointment of Agency Directors; will take the necessary measures to allow for a more in-depth process for the selection of Agency Directors.

All of this was under discussion in the context of the proposed Joint Statement on the decentralized agencies being examined by the Parliament, Commission, and Council as described below, but there was no formal reference to the EP role in the final text. Existing procedures are thus likely to remain, but there is uncertainty as to how these may further develop in other cases.

[E]   Budgetary Issues

There are a number of strategic budgetary issues concerning the EP and include questions such as which agencies should be covered, how much money should they get, and do they give good value for money?

The budgets of agencies have been a problem for different reasons. In view of ever-expanding work programmes, in combination with agencies trying to solidify their existence and prove their added value, agencies have generally overstretched themselves. In addition, agencies have suffered from annual budgets whereas their work requires multi-annual planning, for example, because projects need to be phased in and require a longer breadth. Moreover, setting up new agencies demanded funds that cannot always easily be found in the existing EU's multi-annual Financial Perspective. Realism, feasibility and reliability have therefore been major issues for the agencies and their budgets. For example, the creation of the Aviation Safety Agency demanded substantial funding involving an agency expanding towards 600 employees and more that resulted in major deficits in its first years that could have been easily foreseen.

The Inter-Institutional Agreement of 17 May 2006 on Budgetary discipline and sound financial management states, in its paragraph 47, that:

> when drawing up its proposal for the creation of any new agency, the Commission will assess the budgetary implications for the expenditure heading concerned. On the basis of that information and without prejudice to the legislative procedures governing the setting up of the agency, the two arms of the budgetary authority commit themselves, in the framework of budgetary cooperation, to arrive at a timely agreement on the financing of the agency.

This phrase was included, on the insistence of the EP, to ensure that the financing of each agency should not automatically come out of the Financial Perspective and might require fresh money. The process of implementing Article 47 is still underway and, as a result, issues related to agencies have been on the agenda of many recent budgetary trilogues between the three institutions, not least because of the ongoing problem of agency budgets clashing with other EU expenditure under the broad headings of the financial perspective.

Even without final agreement on such implementing procedures, and as described above, the EP already plays a key role in determining the budget of most EU agencies.

The EP's work in the budgetary area is, of course, also backed up by the Commission. The Commission has thus provided the EP, for example, with two evaluation reports in the context of the 2008 budgetary process: one summarizing the state of play and planning concerning evaluation of agencies and the other the actual evaluations that have been carried out.

In addition to the setting of the overall budget for agencies, the EP is also working towards answering the question of the value added by agencies. The annual budgetary discharge procedure already helps to keep agencies on their toes at least as far as the legality of expenses. The Budgets Committee has also recently tried to get specialized committees to evaluate performance of agencies through putting part (10%) of the budget of each agency in the reserve until they had provided the Budgets Committee with a positive evaluation of the work of each agency, on the basis of their work programme.

The Budgetary Control Committee has also sought to encourage such evaluation, by calling for agencies to be governed, for example, by a yearly performance agreement containing its main objectives for the year and clear indicators to measure performance. To date, however, relatively little cost-effectiveness analysis has been carried out within the individual committees, but this may change in the future.

In the meantime, the budgetary discharge exercise has continued to raise key questions of transparency, independence and potential conflicts of interest with regard to individual agencies. The Parliament's important role in these respects again came sharply to the fore in 2012. On 10 May 2012 the EP postponed its decisions on granting discharge in respect of the implementation of the budget of three agencies for their 2010 budget in the light of critical comments on all three agencies. These were the EEA, the EMEA and the EFSA.

All three were then forced to respond to the Budgetary Control Committee and on 26 September 2012 the Committee voted to recommend the approval of the accounts of the EMEA and of the EFSA in view of the reactions of those agencies. This was subsequently confirmed by the full parliament plenary on 23 October 2012.

At its 26 September meeting, however, the Budgetary Control Committee was still dissatisfied with the response of the EEA, including its replies on the relationship between its Director and an environment NGO. The Committee thus voted again (by sixteen votes to twelve with one abstention) to refuse discharge for the EEA's 2010 accounts. This then became a hotly-contested item at the October plenary but on 23 October the full Parliament voted to overturn the Budgetary Control Committees recommendation and to grant discharge to the EEA on a relatively close vote of 326–288 with twenty abstentions. A number of key amendments in the accompanying resolution were also adopted by narrow margins. Although the resolution was modified in a less harshly critical direction, a number of critical comments did remain. The whole episode was thus again a reminder that the Parliament's budgetary discharge powers can have real teeth.

§9.07   THE SEARCH FOR A GENERAL FRAMEWORK

A final strategic question that has emerged on several occasions in recent years is directly related to the great variety of agency structures and procedures that have been mentioned on numerous occasions throughout this chapter. This has led to calls for a more uniform overall framework for the agencies. An important catalyst for this debate was a communication submitted by the Commission[9] on 'the operating framework for the European regulatory agencies', which was then the subject of a report in December 2003 by the EP Constitutional Affairs Committee, for which Ms Almeida Garrett was the rapporteur.[10]

The report regretted the multitude of different forms taken by the agencies and considered that it was 'essential to rationalize and standardize the structure of the present and future agencies in the interests of clarity, transparency and legal security'. It then went on to call for a number of criteria to be applied to all agencies, including the need for them to be established by a normal legislative procedure involving co-decision rather than by use of Article 308 (the flexibility article currently requiring unanimity and simple consultation of the EP), for all agencies to be monitored politically by the EP through its specialized committees, for the choice of creating an agency to be subject to cost-benefit assessment, for decisions on location of an agency to be based on transparency, efficiency and cost criteria and to be part of the initial decision, and for sunset clauses where appropriate. As mentioned above, it also called for an EP role in the appointment of the Director and for a small administrative board without EP members (but only 'if a structure designed according to this model is adopted').

The Commission subsequently presented a draft Inter-Institutional Agreement on the operational framework for the European regulatory agencies,[11] which was itself the subject of a new EP resolution that was adopted in plenary on 1 December 2005. The adopted text welcomed the presentation of a draft IIA by the Commission and went on to reaffirm many of the key principles from the earlier report. On the issue of EP members of Management Boards, however, it took a different stance (for the reasons mentioned before), and considered that the EP should continue to have two members of a Board as long as each Member State had a member on the Board.

The EP has thus consistently expressed concerns about the ways in which agencies have proliferated, on the legal bases by which they have been created, on the lack of adequate criteria for their location, and for the need for them to be subject to a proper framework of political accountability. All these points are shared both by the EP committees with a horizontal interest in the agencies and by the various specialized committees. The main difference of emphasis between them would be on the issue of

---

9.   COM(2002) 718 fin. Of 11 December 2002.
10. Adopted in plenary on 13 January 2004.
11. COM(2005) 0059 of 25 February 2005.

standardization of agency models, which the specialized committees would tend to consider to be a matter of lesser importance than the other principles mentioned above.

In spite of support from the Parliament, the draft IIA was not backed by the Council and, as outlined in other chapters, the Commission adopted a new Communication on 'European Agencies – The way forward' in March 2008,[12] in which it announced its intention to withdraw its proposal for an IIA. It also recognized that 'the varied roles of agencies today show that there will never be a single model for what an agency should do …' but that 'a clear explanation of these different types of function would improve clarity and understanding about their role.' It then went on to call for an inter-institutional working group in which the EP, Commission, and Council could make a 'collective political assessment of experience of agencies', and 'develop a common understanding of what should be the shape of regulatory agencies and define clearly the responsibilities of each institution vis-à-vis the agencies.'

This shift in focus matched the efforts of the Commission to come up with a meta-evaluation Pending a political understanding on the way forward for agencies, the Commission would, over the next couple of years, carry out a thorough evaluation of their functioning and would not make proposals for any new regulatory agencies until the conclusion of this evaluation process. However, pressing problems, such as the financial crisis of 2008–2009, later led to calls for new agencies such as credit rating agencies.

The EP drew up a new resolution on this strategy, on the basis of a report from the Constitutional Affairs Committee by Mr Papastamkos. Moreover, on 18 December 2008, the EP Conference of Presidents nominated five members of the EP (Mr Papastamkos, Ms Haug, Mr Deprez, Mr Czarnecki, and Ms Hassi) to be its representatives on the Inter-Institutional Working Party on the role of regulatory agencies. An Inter-Institutional Working Group was then set up in March 2009.

Given continuing Council opposition to a binding text, the emphasis then shifted to a looser, non-legally binding declaration of political will. It subsequently proved difficult to conclude negotiations even on this more limited objective but agreement was finally reached in July 2012 in the form of a draft Joint Statement of the EP, Council, and Commission on decentralized agencies. Annexed to this was a draft Common Approach to be taken into account when considering any future decisions on EU decentralized agencies (executive agencies are excluded from this remit, as are agencies operating in the field of Foreign and Security Policy). Both texts are legally non-binding, and respect the legal and budgetary prerogatives of the institutions. Any decisions would still have to follow case-by-case analysis. The Commission was also requested to present a roadmap on the follow-up to the Common Approach by the end of 2012, including concrete timetables for any planned initiatives.

The Common Approach is a detailed document covering a wide range of matters, the establishment and ending of agencies (including mandatory sunset or review clauses and the possibility of closing down an already established agency), the agencies' seat and role of the host country, the structure and governance of agencies

---

12. COM(2008) 135 final of 11 March 2008.

(Management Board, Director and other internal bodies), the operation of agencies, the programming of activities and resources (work programmes, staffing, budgets, etc.), and accountability, controls and transparency and relations with shareholders, reporting requirements, internal and external audits, discharge, warning systems, prevention of fraud and ensuring openness.

The role of the EP is covered in a number of places in the draft text.

The Management Board should consist of one representative from each Member State (the EFSA model has clearly not prevailed) and an appropriate number of representatives from the Commission. There had been extensive debate, however, on the role of the EP, whether there should be an explicit reference to EP designated members and, if so, how many (an appropriate number as supported by the Commission, just one or some other formula). The final text provides instead for, where appropriate, one member designated by the EP, without prejudice to relevant arrangements for existing agencies.

There was also debate over the EP role in the choice of the Agency Director, with disagreement about whether to stick to the most common current formula (the candidate selected by the Management Board may be invited to make a statement before the competent EP committee and to answer questions put by its/their members) or else to include a more explicit reference to a formal hearing in the Parliament, either before or after the decision of the Management Board. In the final text the issue was completely sidestepped, with reference only to the Director being appointed by a Management Board on the basis of a shortlist drawn up by the Commission and without an explicit reference to the EP role.

As regards multi-annual work programmes of agencies, the EP should be consulted, provided that the purpose is for an exchange of views and that the outcome is not binding on the agency. The current practice of Agency Directors presenting their annual work programmes to the relevant EP committee should also continue. Agency Annual Reports and the assessment of the Management Board should be transmitted to all relevant institutions, including the EP, by 1 July.

A further reference is in the context of discharge where an Agency Director is made accountable to the EP and the Council for the use of the EU contribution through the annual discharge procedure. The EP would be one of the institutions to which an Agency's annual report on the execution of their budget would have to be submitted. Agencies might also have to consider any request or recommendation issued by the EP or the Council.

Another important point concerns the democratic accountability of fully self-financed agencies, which are Union bodies in charge of implementing EU policies but not subject to a discharge within the meaning of the TFEU. The possibilities for this are to be explored. One such possibility that is mooted in the text could be that the agencies in question, submit to the EP, to the Council and to the Commission an annual report on the execution of the budget and to any request or recommendation issued by the President and Council.

If the Commission activates a proposed alert or early warning system about the behaviour of an agency, there is a conflict with the Management Board and the board sets aside the relevant Commission request, the EP would have to be formally informed, so that the EP, Commission and Council could then 'react quickly'. The Commission would also have to provide the EP and Council with other information on the evaluation of agencies if so requested.

Finally the introduction of any new provisions on classified information should not be detrimental to the EP's current right of access to agencies' information nor imply the multiplication of bilateral agreements between the EP and EU bodies or agencies.

The EP has thus been closely involved in an ongoing inter-institutional dialogue over the future of EU agencies. This has neither led to a binding set of guidelines nor to a homogeneous framework for decentralized agencies but is likely to give greater clarity than in the past, especially as regards new agencies. Even in these cases, however, their final shape will depend on the outcome of specific EP-Council negotiations which will have to take the joint statement and common approach into account but will not necessarily be bound by them. The situation as regards the thirty-plus existing agencies with their very differing structures is even less certain.

In the meantime, and in parallel with the Commission's own promised review of its own internal systems governing its relations with agencies, the EP is likely to continue to examine its own internal procedures and guidelines, through initiatives by the Conference of Presidents, the Conference of Committee Chairmen or even by individual committees, such as the Budgets Committee.

§9.08 CONCLUDING REMARKS

This Chapter has sought to show the increasing extent to which the EP is now engaging with the developing phenomenon of decentralized EU agencies, the formal and informal framework that is being established by the founding regulations of the agencies, by the forthcoming Joint Statement and Common Approach, and by rules and evolving practice within the EP itself. It seems highly likely that this trend will continue in the future.

The Parliament's relationships with agencies are not, however, without a number of constraints. With the exception of Parliament's budget and budgetary control powers, and its initial but time-limited co-decision powers on an agency's founding regulation, the EP's formal powers vis-à-vis agencies are rather limited. With so many competing demands on MEPs time, and with many having an understandable emphasis on policy making rather than on administrative process, it is often easier for them to concentrate on the exercise of Parliament's formal powers rather than the more informal and discretionary powers involved in ensuring oversight and accountability of the agencies. Such oversight is often dependent on individual MEPs and is often further complicated by high MEP turnover (typically 50% at each election) as well as staff mobility. It takes time and often technical expertise to build up the knowledge and experience to hold an agency to proper account. Yet another factor is the very different EP perspectives on agencies, be they budgetary, sectoral or more broadly institutional, that were noted at the beginning of this Chapter.

All this should not, however, make Parliament's role towards agencies a less important one. The growth in the number of agencies, their increasing budgets, the regulatory and other tasks that they carry out, the links between their work and Parliament's own responsibilities, and the strategic questions they pose, all underline the need for the EP to be more involved than ever.

So far, Parliament's role of scrutiny has only been unevenly exercised but it has already shown that it is capable of being innovative and flexible. Ironically, in some cases, agencies have been the subject of greater scrutiny than individual directorates-general of the Commission who do not receive individual committee delegation visits every two years and are not directly monitored by designated contact persons within a committee.

A key challenge for the future will be for this scrutiny and oversight to become even more systematic and thorough, ensuring proper implementation of the new inter-institutional common approach to agencies, while not attempting a one-size fits all approach and still permitting creative new solutions to oversight and accountability.

PART V   Conclusion

CHAPTER 10

What Is the Future of European Agencies?

Michelle Everson, Cosimo Monda & Ellen Vos

§10.01 THE EXTRAORDINARY AGENCY PHENOMENON

Madalina Busuioc and Martijn Groenleer make extensive reference in their contribution to this Volume (Chapter 8) to a 'founding EU literature' on the then emerging European agencies of the 1990s. In no small part driven by the efficient regulatory pre-occupations of writers such Giandomenico Majone,[1] academic analysis of the 1990s was largely favourable to this non-majoritarian form of governance, arguing that independent – or 'autonomous' agencies (Busuioc and Groenleer) – would represent a vital increase in the expert regulatory capacity of the EU. At the same time, they would also further integration goals by isolating technical regulatory tasks from political interests that might disrupt the efficiency of EU regulation. Favourable and optimistic as this literature was, however, we can now safely assume that these proponents of the 'fourth-branch of government' (Busuioc and Groenleer) would not, in their wildest of dreams, have envisaged the quite extraordinary number and variety of agency vehicles that have emerged at EU level in the short intervening period of twenty years.

The inquiry into the upsurge of agencies in the EU's institutional landscape (Ellen Vos, Chapter 2) shows that where broadly defined 'as bodies governed by European public law that are institutionally separate from the EU institutions' which 'have their own legal personality', European agencies – currently named 'decentralized agencies' by EU institutions – now number well over thirty. This mass of decentralized institutions deal with manifold tasks as diverse as provision of information or decision-making in various policy fields, such as food and air safety, medicines, environment, telecommunications, disease prevention, border control, fundamental rights, trademarks, and banking. The diversity of tasks assigned the plethora of

---

1. See, in particular, G. Majone (ed.), *Regulating Europe* (London: Routledge, 1996).

decentralized agencies is similarly matched by their striking degree of institutional heterogeneity; a multiplicity, which has created its own academic industry, dedicated to the many and various legal, functional and structural categorizations of the agency vehicle currently deployed at EU level.

If we consciously review the extraordinary agency phenomenon from a two decade distance – that is from the perspective of 1990s literature – the number and diversity of EU agencies now operative accordingly raises its own immediate point of interest. Although not wholly unexpectedly, decentralized European agencies have evolved far beyond the ideal model of the fourth-branch of government envisaged by Majone. In other words, they have sprung the strict confines of a technical regulatory blueprint. Above all, where agencies such as the European Union Agency for Fundamental Rights (FRA), are drawn into the equation, the agency vehicle at EU level would seem to be far less about efficient completion of strictly defined regulatory tasks, and far more about broader policy initiation and implementation within the Union. The FRA, after all, would appear to be evolving its own independent normative mission to create equality of opportunity for all European citizens (Busuioc and Groenleer); a task far removed from the technical regulation of the internal market.

Set in the broader historical context of the creation of a plethora of independent Commissions, Authorities and Agencies, not only in the United States, but also within European national states, such diversity of function and structure is indeed far from unusual.[2] Government, after all, has always needed to reach to ad hoc institutions to aid it in technical, novel and unexpected tasks. Nonetheless, within the very particular context of the EU, and, above all, in view of the continuing relevance of the *Meroni* doctrine,[3] any departure from the ideal-type form of agency operation proposed in the 1990s cannot but raise concerns in the realm of EU institutional politics and their legitimation. With its own very particular normative base, the propounded theory of a fourth-branch of government within Europe drew its persuasive power from an economy of reasoning, which, in particular, argued that independent policy-making and implementation need not pose any legitimacy concerns where – but only where – the tasks conferred upon agencies are founded in a clear mandate, strictly technical in nature and wholly neutral in distributive or redistributive terms.[4] As the *Meroni* doctrine forcefully reminds us, deployment of agencies at EU level would represent a potential assault upon the 'institutional balance of powers' established within the Union, not simply as regards the potential abuse of powers by agencies vis-à-vis individual citizens of the Union, but also in relation to disguised transfers of powers between the various institutions of the EU (Everson, Chapter 3). By stark contrast, however, an efficiency-based model of agency operation would inevitably ameliorate these particular concerns, restricting agency competences to operations that are wholly distinct from political decision-making. Within the latter constellation, the primary

---

2. See, once again, G. Majone, 'Independence v accountability: European non-majoritarian institutions and democratic government in Europe', EUI Working Papers (SPS) 1993/09.
3. Cases 9/56 and 10/56 *Meroni v. High Authority* [1957-1958] ECR 133.
4. See, in particular, M. Everson, 'Independent Agencies: Hierarchy Beaters?', *European Law Journal* 1, no. 2 (1995): 180.

legitimacy concern would accordingly simply be one of ensuring that agencies are competent and technically capable of fulfilling their limited functions. This would be achieved through multi-institutional oversight of their budgets, working plans and achieved results.[5]

Clearly, the simplicity of such arguments and models is highly attractive but is rather deceptive. For, above all, the view that technical regulatory tasks may be distinguished from policy-making or politics appears wholly chimeric, particularly in view of the fact that much supposedly technical, EU market regulation concerns the management of 'risk'; a matter that inexorably raises ethical and cultural concerns, and demands constant political oversight.[6] Yet, for all that efficiency-based regulatory concepts may be intrinsically doubted, the underlying strengths of their aspirational prescriptions have just as surely become apparent as the proliferation of so very many and so very varied decentralized agencies has been accompanied by a greatly increased degree of institutional and academic concern about their appropriateness within the governance structures of the EU. Suffice it to note in this regard, only, the very particular constellation of the delegation of powers principle established within the new Articles 290 and 291 TFEU; as well as, the tortuous path from the 2007 White Paper on Governance, the draft Inter-Institutional Agreement on Agencies and the 'Way Forward for Agencies', or Communication initially withdrawing the draft Inter-institutional Agreement,[7] to the recent 'Joint Statement and Common Approach of the European Parliament, the Council of the EU and the European Commission on decentralized agencies' (Common Approach).[8] As agencies have multiplied, as their tasks have proliferated and their structures have diversified, it has grown increasingly difficult to reconcile their operations with often conflicting interests of Council, Parliament, Commission, and Member States within the principle of the institutional balance of powers of the EU.

In short, beyond any ideal-type regulatory model, European agencies continue to present great problems of accountability, control, and institutional coordination. These problems are discussed in great details throughout the contributions to this volume and will be referred to again below. However, prior to any such discussion, a vital question becomes one of why exactly the EU has placed so much of its governing faith in so very many and so very varied decentralized agencies. The question is pressing, not least since a recent edited volume on the agency phenomenon – although almost as an afterthought – has begun to point to growing concerns about the 'efficiency' of European agencies.[9] In other words, and perhaps somewhat surprisingly, recent

---

5. See, Majone, *supra* n. 2.
6. See, M. Everson & E. Vos (eds.), *Uncertain Risks Regulated* (London: Routledge, 2009).
7. Parliament had rejected a proposed Institutional Agreement on a common operating framework for EU agencies (COM(2005) 59 final) creating a factual moratorium on their establishment by demanding that the Commission undertake further review of the operations of such bodies already operating at EU level; see 'European Agencies – the Way Forward', COM(2008) 159 final.
8. Available at: < http://europa.eu/agencies/documents/joint_statement_and_common_approach _2012_en.pdf > and in Annex 2 to this book.
9. D. Curtin & R. Dehousse, 'European Agencies: Tipping the Balance', in *The Agency Phenomenon in the European Union*, eds. M. Busuioc, M. Groenleer & J. Trondal (Manchester: Manchester University Press, 2013), 193-205.

queries about the agency phenomenon in the EU include worries that agencies are not adequate to the tasks endowed upon them, or indeed are not always the appropriate vehicle for European policy-making and regulation. Such concerns are also very much present within this volume. Thus, Michael Kaeding and Esther Versluis (Chapter 4) point with concern to the lack of a comprehensive vision of just how agencies might act in order to improve implementation of EU regulation at national level. Similarly, both Annetje Ottow (Chapter 6) and Michelle Everson (Chapter 3) concern themselves with the efficiency of new agencies within financial markets, as well as within banking and insurance sectors. Michelle Everson thus highlights sectoral concerns that European regulators will not possess the local knowledge necessary to respond quickly and effectively to points of risk pressure within the system whilst Annetje Ottow underlines the continuing obscurities within the overall system for protection against systemic risk that now mark an (unclear) division of functions within the European Central Bank (ECB), as well as between the ECB and the European Banking Authority (EBA). Equally, and perhaps most intriguingly, Marco Zinzani's Chapter on developments within the field of telecommunications regulation (Chapter 7) cannot but raise doubts with regard to a two-tiered model of agency and regulatory network operation which was imposed upon the sector as a result of continuing divergence in national regulatory philosophies and interests, but which is, at the same time, perhaps not perfectly placed to overcome these difficulties.

Confirmation that growing efficiency concerns about the agency model at EU level should not, in any case be underestimated, however, comes from a very important source. In a forthcoming book, Giandomenico Majone – 'Godfather' of the EU agency model in the 1990s – highlights, with frightening clarity, a fundamental break within processes of European integration.[10] Post financial crisis, and, above all, in view of the continuing failure to comprehensively control and combat sovereign debt crisis, Europe can no longer continue – in a spirit of 'blind optimism' – to posit the total success of harmonization strategies. Crisis has not only taught us, that European projects can and do fail, but has also required us to review the famous 'Community Method' of total harmonization without our once somewhat rose-tinted, integration spectacles. Majone points to a series of problems that characterize that method: first, the European tendency, most apparent in relation to the construction of Economic and Monetary Union to disguise precarious political projects as technical exercises, and thus to obscure the fact that such projects are contentious and might fail; second, the focusing of integration processes upon a goal of total harmonization, which again obscures the fact that Member State interests can and do differ, also endangering the success of harmonization per se; and third, a European obsession with process, rather than results, which determines that the success of European integration processes are measured solely in line with the yardstick of 'legitimate decision-making', with concomitantly very little regard for the quality of European 'outputs' – a quality, which post-crisis is now of far greater interest to European public than was once the case.

---

10. *The EU in Comparative Context: Regional Integration and Political Transaction Costs* (Cambridge: Cambridge University Press, forthcoming 2014).

Although Majone's observations are global in nature, concerning the state of European integration *grosso mondo*, they provide constructive guidance also for this volume's more limited remit of evaluating the development of the EU agency model. More particularly, they prompt examination of the question of whether in its headlong rush to deploy 'the' agency model, the EU is likewise obfuscating political projects and increasing potential for failure through application of technical instruments where (a lack of) political will is instead determinative. Whether it is engaging in totalizing harmonization strategies without thought for continuing divergence in national interests; and once again, whether it is placing far too much emphasis upon process rather than outputs. In this regard then, although the contributions to this volume do not provide us with a comprehensive overview, they still hint explicitly and implicitly at the variety of motivations behind the recent growth in the use of agencies at EU level. They thus also – and prior to any discussion about the operational and legitimacy problems posed by agency operations – allow us to take pre-emptive stock, asking whether motivations for agency operation really are persuasive.

In reviewing the broad historical sweep of agency design, Busuioc and Groenleer identify a particularly interesting adjunct to the most commonly cited advantages of agency operation within the EU. Agencies are not merely useful to the EU in terms of the role that they can play in improving policy advice, more specifically by radically increasing the EU's expert and technical capacity. Neither are they simply an aid in policy implementation, providing vital coordination between the varied (national) implementation authorities within Europe. Instead, exactly by virtue of their ad hoc nature, agencies provide for solutions beyond technical and political impasses which have arisen within the existing institutional structures of the EU (Chapter 8). As Busuioc and Groenleer indicate, a crucial problem here is one of the status, function, and composition of the Commission; but not simply because of its lack of technical expertise or administrative capacities. Instead, agencies have been established within the Union, because it was felt that it would not be politically appropriate to entrust certain tasks to this institution. In other words, a lack of political faith in the Commission which arises by virtue of its own 'politicized', 'generalist', or 'bureaucratic' nature, as well as its – in the ambit of comitology proceedings – vulnerability to the renewed assertion of Member State interests, has greatly facilitated the rise of agencies within EU structures.

This finding at once raises certain alarm bells within the context of the critique made of the Community Method by Giandomenico Majone. Certainly, depoliticized operation is the hallmark of the agency model; and, to the degree that the Commission is expected also to play a role in policy initiation, certain technical tasks might be better undertaken in isolation from it. However, where autonomous administration is proposed in order to circumvent still existing and serious political divisions – within the Commission, amongst the Member States, or between Union institutions – technical depoliticization is highly illusive. Within such a scenario, European agencies are not simply fulfilling clear mandates; instead, they are negotiating between a host of complex and conflicting interests to pursue rather open-ended mandates – which in itself is a paradoxically political task, prone to failure.

This proposition finds some support in further contributions to this volume. To be sure, agencies have developed new tasks and new rationales, which do and would continue to justify their intensified deployment at EU level, far beyond any traditional justifications. Kaeding and Versluis (Chapter 4), for example, point to the vital role that networked agencies can play in increasing the regulatory and implementing capacity within old and, in particular, new Member States. Similarly, Ott, Vos, and Coman-Kund (Chapter 5) also make important note of the manner in which EU agencies such as the European Food Safety Authority (EFSA) have vitally increased capacity for EU action at international level. For example, within the *Codex Alimentarius*, this agency has provided the Commission with significant support, in particular with regard to information gathering.[11] Likewise, Francis Jacobs (Chapter 9) similarly highlights the new role which agencies play in supporting the work of the European Parliament, furnishing vital technical information and assistance to parliamentary committees. Nevertheless, contributions also hint at a paradox of 'politicized depoliticization' within the EU agency model. The rationale that agencies will help to improve implementation of EU policies throughout the Union, is, after all, closely allied with the Community Method, which has so often conceived of European integration as a unitary harmonizing process, which can be achieved in a technical manner, despite and contrary to the strong interests of the Member States in continuing diversity. To this degree, the unusual two-tiered model of agency operation adopted in the European telecommunications sector to overcome divergence may also be argued to appear as its own hostage to fortune. Even more strikingly, however, the three new agencies introduced to regulate banking, insurance and financial markets (EBA, EIOPA, and ESMA) have been endowed with a particularly onerous regulatory task of setting harmonized standards across Europe; a precarious enterprise, not least because of explicit and continuing conflict about the evolution of a single European financial regime in a Europe which is split between Member States who are, and who are not, members of the Eurozone.

§10.02   LEGITIMATING 'POLITICIZED' AUTONOMY?

An immediate lesson to be drawn from the conclusion that agencies may be used to move European policy and integration strategies beyond current institutional impasses and political conflicts, is thus the following. Where the EU is moving increasingly beyond giving an efficiency-based regulatory mandate to agencies and is asking agencies to engage in political process and the pursuit of political projects, it must similarly be prepared for the potential inability of these autonomous bodies to complete their open-ended mandates. This potential for failure similarly raises its own points of concern. Therefore a broad observation on the European agency debate might be one that it has to date paid far too little regard to this particular problem of the paradox of politicized depoliticized administration. Where potential failings in the activities or

---

11. See e.g., M. Masson-Matthee, *The Codex Alimentarius Commission and Its Standards* (The Hague: TMC Asser Press, 2007).

operations of European agencies might also be characterized, as shortcomings caused by the broader politics, policy formation, and integration strategy pursued by the Union as a whole and not as failings in the agency model per se, we argue that academic debate also needs to move beyond its very particular concerns with the process of agency formation and design, to question – at a fundamental level – whether the posited efficiency-gains of agency operation are real, or whether we are asking simply too much of technical bodies which have been catapulted into the awkward politics of EU institutional impasse.

This volume cannot and would not want to pre-empt the outcomes of such a 'post-crisis' debate on European agencies. After all, contributions to the volume also hint at the great advantages which a flexible approach to the use of the agency model, including a political role for agencies, may bring to the EU (see below). Nevertheless, as contributions also demonstrate, such issues are becoming increasingly important. Broader issues of institutional politics within the EU are already impacting heavily upon the question of the institutional design of European agencies, and, in particular, also help to explain some of the problems which might now be discerned with regard to the perceived legitimacy deficit of the EU's fourth-branch of government. Thus, most strikingly, although various contributions demonstrate that European agencies might be said to pose the same problems that have long been observed with regard to agency operation at national level; others, also point to the very particular difficulties which have arisen with regard to the legitimation of a politicized administration.

In the former group, Busuioc and Groenleer (Chapter 8) capture the prime conundrum posed by all agency operation, and demonstrate that this is also a topic within the EU. Where agencies are conceived of as standing in a principal-agent relationship with a mandating power, the perceived danger is always one that the agency will act in an ultra vires manner. The problem, as noted by Ott, Vos, and Coman-Kund (Chapter 5) is certainly highlighted within an increasingly post-national context of regulatory co-ordination, whereby agencies may even commit their principals to new legal obligations; yet, the core concern is similarly one which might be described as a 'catch 22', whereby the underlying rationale of 'autonomous' agency operation will always conflict with the desire of the principal to ensure the 'accountability' of administration. By contrast, however, both Everson (Chapter 3) and Vos (Chapter 2) move beyond the general problems of legitimacy posed by agency operation to concern themselves with the very particular problem of the legality and/or constitutionality of European agencies within the specific structures of the Union.

At one level, this latter pre-occupation is a very old one indeed. The *Meroni* doctrine continues to preclude the full independence of European agencies.[12] Similarly, writings have long abounded, urging a reconfiguration of EU legal principles in order to facilitate necessary agency operation within the EU.[13] So far, so familiar: What is

---

12. See *supra* n. 3.
13. Exemplary, D. Geradin & N. Petit, 'The Development of Agencies at EU and National Levels: Conceptual Analysis and Proposal for Reform', Jean Monnet Working Paper 1/2004, New York (2004); D. Geradin, N. Petit & R. Munoz (eds.), *Regulation through Agencies: A New Paradigm for EC Governance* (Cheltenham: Edward Elgar, 2005).

new, however, is the situation as of 2012, and the seeming conclusion of institutional efforts to ensure that, whilst agencies may not be independent, their autonomy might be still assured within a scheme of accountability suited to the current structures of the Union. As noted above, the Common Approach caps a long process of negotiation around this issue which also includes the revision of the Treaties, and, more specifically, Articles 290 and 291 TFEU. The time that it has taken to complete this process, is – in and of itself – an indication of the extremely politicized nature of the institutional debate on European agencies; with, in particular, all EU institutions jockeying for a position from which they might oversee agency operation. Nevertheless, the potentially very damaging degree of continuing discord in relation to EU agency operation is most readily apparent in the 'alert/warning system' proposed by the European Commission, which allows it to alert Council and Parliament to malfunctions in agency Management Boards (paragraph 59).[14]

The provision is extraordinary, reflecting a lack of trust within the Commission of the action and powers of bodies that are – nominally at least – still operating under its own umbrella. Yet, the Commission's logic is similarly impeccable. Agencies operating within the new financial services regime, for example, can, in practice exercise powers without reference to the Commission, which will be held responsible for them.[15] As Vos notes, this situation may likewise be of the Commission's own making particularly in view of the Commission's unwillingness to allow for the explicit nomination of agencies within the EU treaties. Nevertheless, when taken together with the Council and the Parliament's efforts to increase their own direct influence over agencies, through mechanisms such as sunset clauses (Article 290 TFEU), the measure bears potential for extraordinary conflict as each institution seeks to exercise its own influence over a supposedly autonomous administration in mutual games of threat, protest, and confusion.[16] As Busuioc and Groenleer note, under these circumstances, the real measure of the autonomy of European agencies will be their political refinement; their ability to satisfy all EU institutions at all times (Chapter 8). Equally, however, where the public concern is one for the output legitimacy of European agencies, or the results that they furnish, the very real danger must be one of the establishment of 'supervisory black hole' (Ottow, Chapter 6); of a lack of regulatory response – especially in cases of systemic risk within the financial sector – where EU institutions are engaged in political infighting rather than responding in a unitary manner to crisis.

§10.03   A FUTURE UNDER NEGOTIATION

Returning to the thesis of Giandomenico Majone, the institutional reform of agencies encapsulated within the final Common Approach, as well as treaty revisions, might thus also be argued to be – potentially – a triumph of process over result. Certainly, the

---

14. See, in particular Vos in this Volume.
15. See, in particular, Everson in this Volume.
16. See, in particular, Everson in this Volume.

legitimacy or accountability concerns of all EU institutions might be represented within its provisions. Nonetheless, the establishment of this scheme of accountability for 'depoliticized' yet political agencies presents very real dangers of regulatory failure. What then is the future for European agencies? In this regard, however, a more positive assessment is possible. Although this volume does point to some very real problems besetting a proliferation of agencies within the EU, in many cases, their utility simply cannot be doubted. Perhaps most striking in this regard is the contribution made by Francis Jacobs (Chapter 9). The European Parliament has not always been supportive of the development of agencies at EU level. Yet, as Jacobs demonstrates, the European Parliament is currently evolving a set of intense relations with agencies, especially as regards areas of individual sectoral regulation. Relations are mutually beneficial, with the agencies providing Parliament with vital information and, in turn, gaining in overall (accountability-derived) legitimacy through their exposure to the views of the representatives of European citizens.

The most interesting point to note within this positive constellation, however, is also one that agencies are, and necessarily must be regarded as, political creatures. There is nothing new in this finding: US agencies have only been able to rise to their prominent positions as they have won and harnessed the political support of the institutions of the US government and the US public.[17] A similar future is conceivable for EU agencies. Nevertheless, care must be taken not to implicate agencies in political controversies within which they – as results-driven institutions – might 'drown'. Therefore, processes of executive 'depoliticization' resorting to agencies should never be used to obscure continuing political conflict. To do so is to create a great potential for failures with regard to the output legitimacy of agencies. Certainly, the EU might be better advised to work with the motto 'less is more' and to no longer create agencies where efficiency-gains are threatened by ongoing political conflict. At the same time however, the legitimacy of European agencies is to be found in negotiation with their utility. After all, if agencies cannot provide results (also in terms of better regulation or implementation), we should not make recourse to them.

Seen in this light, a positive future for European agencies might then be argued to reside in a renewed political honesty within the EU. Such honesty, however, must be a double-headed phenomenon. On the one hand, the political character of agencies should be recognized within their design; in particular, agencies should be given requisite room to develop their own missions in an autonomous manner. On the other hand, however, the EU Institutions – Commission, Parliament, Council as well as the Member States, must also develop a willingness to reassess their own political relations and integration ambitions. This honesty requires however at the same time that in both ways the hybrid and sui generis character of EU agencies, typified by the interaction with their national counterparts, should be taken account of and acknowledged. Hereby it is of utmost importance that they are seen to belong to, and confirm, the

---

17. See, Majone, *supra* n. 2.

composite character of the EU executive. For clearly EU agencies are not solely 'pure' EU agencies but similarly assist and connect with Member States, acting also on behalf of the Member States, for instance to fulfil global obligations. Critically, as the title of this volume indicates, EU agencies are thus to be found in between EU institutions and Member States.

ANNEX I

Overview of European Agencies

EU DECENTRALIZED AGENCIES

Name	Legal Basis of Founding Regulation Article	Founding Regulation	Seat	Type of Task	Revenue according to Founding Regulation
ACER Agency for the Cooperation of Energy Regulators	114 TFEU (ex 95 TEC)	Reg. 713/2009 (OJ 2009, L 211/1)	Ljubljana	To create European network rules, taking binding individual decisions on conditions for access and operational security for cross-border infrastructure if NRAs cannot agree, giving advice on various energy related issues to the EU institutions and monitoring and reporting to the EP and the Council.	• EU subsidy • fees • voluntary contributions from MS or from regulatory authorities • legacies, donations or grants

Name	Legal Basis of Founding Regulation Article	Founding Regulation	Seat	Type of Task	Revenue according to Founding Regulation
BEREC Body of European Regulators for Electronic Communications	114 TFEU (ex 95 TEC)	Reg. 1211/2009 (OJ 2009, L 337/1)	Riga	To provide administrative and professional support services to BEREC, collect information from NRAs, disseminate regulatory best practices among NRAs, to monitor and report on the electronic communications sector.	• EU subsidy • voluntary financial contributions from Member States or from their NRAs
CdT Translation Centre for the Bodies of the European Union	352(1)TFEU (ex 308 TEC)	Reg. 2965/94 (OJ 1994 L 314/1)	Luxembourg	To provide the translation services required by the institutions, bodies and decentralized agencies of the European Union.	• Own resources (transfers from agencies, offices and institutions in exchange for service provided)

Name	Legal Basis of Founding Regulation Article	Founding Regulation	Seat	Type of Task	Revenue according to Founding Regulation
CEDEFOP European Centre for the Development of Vocational Training	352(1)TFEU (ex 308 TEC)	Reg. 337/75 (OJ 1975, L 39/1)	Thessaloniki	To promote a European area of lifelong learning throughout an enlarged EU, by providing information on and analyses of vocational education and training systems, policies, research and practice.	• EU subsidy
CEPOL European Police College	87, 88 TFEU (ex 30(1)(c), 34(2)(c) (repealed) TEU)	Council Decision 2005/681/JHA (OJ 2005, L 256/63)	Bramshill	To encourage cross-border cooperation in the fight against crime, maintenance of public security and law and order by developing and providing training for police officers from across Europe.	• EU subsidy
CPVO Community Plant Variety Office	352(1)TFEU (ex 308 TEC)	Reg. 2100/94 (OJ 1994, L 227/1)	Angers	To implement and apply a system of EU plant variety rights, allowing for intellectual property rights to be granted for plant varieties.	• fees • EU subsidy, if necessary

Name	Legal Basis of Founding Regulation Article	Founding Regulation	Seat	Type of Task	Revenue according to Founding Regulation
EASA European Aviation Safety Agency	100(2) TFEU (ex 80 (2) TEC)	Reg. 1592/2002 (OJ 2002, L 240/1) replaced by: Reg. 216/08/EC (OJ 2008, L 79/1)	Cologne	To provide technical expertise to the European Commission by assisting in the drafting of rules for aviation safety, to carry out certification tasks regarding aeronautical products and organizations involved in their design, production and maintenance, which help to ensure compliance with airworthiness and environmental protection standards, conduct inspections and investigations	• EU contribution • contributions from European third countries participating in the work of the Agency • fees • charges for publications, trainings, other services • voluntary financial contributions from MS, third countries or other entities

Name	Legal Basis of Founding Regulation Article	Founding Regulation	Seat	Type of Task	Revenue according to Founding Regulation
EASO European Asylum Support Office	74, 78(1)(2) TFEU (ex 66, 63 TEC)	Reg. 439/2010 (OJ 2010, L 132/11)	Valetta Harbour	To gather information on emergency measures, identify and analyse information about asylum cases and capacities in MS, analyse date on arrivals of large groups of TCNs, upon request, support MS by coordinating their asylum support teams and the rapid set up of reception facilities	• EU subsidy • voluntary contributions from MS • charges for publications and services • contributions from associate countries
EBA European Banking Authority	114 TFEU (ex 95 TEC)	Reg. 1093/2010 (OJ 2010, L 331/12)	London	To preventing regulatory arbitrage, guaranteeing a level playing field, strengthening international supervisory coordination, promoting supervisory convergence, and providing advice to the	• EU subsidy • obligatory contributions from MS public authorities competent for supervision of financial institutions • fees

Name	Legal Basis of Founding Regulation Article	Founding Regulation	Seat	Type of Task	Revenue according to Founding Regulation
				EU institutions in the areas of banking, payments and e-money regulation as well as on issues related to corporate governance, auditing and financial reporting.	
ECDC European Centre for Disease Prevention and Control	168 TFEU (ex 152 (4) TEC)	Reg. 851/04 (OJ 2004/L 142/1)	Solna	To enhance the capacity of the EU and the Member States to protect human health through the prevention and control of human disease, to act on its own initiative when outbreaks of contagious illness of unknown origin threaten the EU, and to ensure complementary and coherent action in the field of public health by bringing together the MS, the EU institutions and the relevant international organizations	• EU subsidy • payments for services rendered • any financial contributions from the competent bodies recognized by MS • any voluntary contribution from the MS

Name	Legal Basis of Founding Regulation Article	Founding Regulation	Seat	Type of Task	Revenue according to Founding Regulation
ECHA European Chemicals Agency	114 TFEU (ex 95 TEC)	Reg. 1907/2006 (OJ 2006, L 396/1)	Helsinki	To manage the registration, evaluation, authorization and restriction processes for chemical substances, to ensure consistency in chemicals management across the EU and to provide technical and scientific advice, guidance and information on chemicals.	• EU subsidy • fees paid by undertakings • any voluntary contribution from the MS
EEA European Environment Agency	192 TFEU (ex 175 TEC)	Reg. 1210/90 (OJ 1990, L 120/1) replaced by Reg. 401/2009 (OJ 2009, L 126/13)	Copenhagen	To provide sound and independent information on the environment and environmental policies and to develop and coordinate the European environment information and observation network (Eionet).	• EU subsidy • payment for services

247

Name	Legal Basis of Founding Regulation Article	Founding Regulation	Seat	Type of Task	Revenue according to Founding Regulation
EFCA European Fisheries Control Agency	43 TFEU (ex 37 TEC)	Reg. 768/2005 (OJ 2005, L 128/1)	Vigo	To organize operational coordination of fisheries control and inspection activities by Member States and to assist them to cooperate so and to comply with the rules of the Common EU Fisheries Policy in order to ensure its effective and uniform application.	• EU subsidy • charges for services provided to MS • charges for publications, training and/or any other services provided
EFSA European Food Safety Authority	43, 114, 207 and 168 (4)(b) TFEU (ex 37, 95, 133 and 152 (4)(b) TEC)	Reg. 178/2002/EC (OJ 2002, L 31/1)	Parma	To collect and analyze scientific date, identify emerging risks and provide independent scientific advice on all matters with a direct or indirect impact on food safety, including animal health and welfare and plant protection.	• EU subsidy • contributions from third countries with which the EU has concluded relevant agreements • charges for publications, conferences, training and any other similar activities • possibility of fees (under discussion)

Name	Legal Basis of Founding Regulation Article	Founding Regulation	Seat	Type of Task	Revenue according to Founding Regulation
EIGE European Institute for Gender Equality	19 (2), 157 (3) TFEU (ex 13(2), 141(3) TEC)	Reg. 1922/2006 (OJ 2006, L 403/9)	Vilnius	To contribute to and strengthen the promotion of gender equality and the fight against discrimination based on sex, to collect, analyze and disseminate relevant, objective, comparable and reliable information as regards gender equality, to raise EU citizens' awareness of gender equality and to set up and coordinate a European Network on Gender Equality	• EU subsidy • payments received for services rendered • contributions from organizations or third countries • any voluntary contribution from the MS
EIOPA European Insurance and Occupational Pensions Authority	114 TFEU (ex 95 TEC)	Reg. 1094/2010 (OJ 2010, L 331/48)	Frankfurt	Protecting consumers, monitoring and identifying trends, potential risks and vulnerabilities stemming from the microprudential level, ensuring a high, effective and	• EU subsidy • obligatory contributions from MS public authorities competent for supervision of financial institutions • fees

Name	Legal Basis of Founding Regulation Article	Founding Regulation	Seat	Type of Task	Revenue according to Founding Regulation
				consistent level of regulation and supervision, promoting a coordinated EU supervisory response, achieving greater harmonization and coherent application of rules for financial institutions.	
EMA European Medicines Agency	114, 168 (4) (c)T-FEU (ex 95, 152 (4) (b) TEC)	Reg. 726/2004 (OJ 2004, L 136/1)	London	To perform the scientific evaluation of applications for European marketing authorization for medicinal products for human and veterinary use.	• EU subsidy • fees
EMCDDA European Monitoring Centre for Drugs and Drug Addiction	352(1) TFEU (ex 308 TEC) According to Reg 1920/2006 the legal basis is 168 TFEU (ex 152 TEC)	Reg. 302/93 (OJ 1993, L 36/1) replaced by Reg. 1920/2006 (OJ 2006, L 376/1)	Lisbon	To gather, analyze and disseminate objective, reliable and comparable information on drugs and drug addiction and, in doing so provide its audience with a sound and	• EU subsidy • payment for services • financial contributions from organizations, bodies and third countries

Name	Legal Basis of Founding Regulation Article	Founding Regulation	Seat	Type of Task	Revenue according to Founding Regulation
				evidence-based picture of the drug phenomenon at European level, coordination of the European Information Network on Drugs and Drug Addiction (Reitox).	
EMSA European Maritime Safety Agency	100(2) TFEU (ex 80 (2) TEC)	Reg. 1406/2002 (OJ 2002, L 208/1)	Lisbon	To assist the EU and national authorities in matters of maritime safety, security and the prevention of pollution caused by ships, to control the proper application of EU law in this field and to promote cooperation between national authorities.	• EU contribution • possible contributions of third countries • charges for publications, trainings, other services
ENISA European Network and Information Security Agency	114 TFEU (ex 95 TEC)	Reg. 460/2004 (OJ 2004, L 77/1)	Heraklion	To advise and assist the Commission and the MS on information security and to address security-related problems in	• EU subsidy • contributions from third countries participating in work of ENISA

Name	Legal Basis of Founding Regulation Article	Founding Regulation	Seat	Type of Task	Revenue according to Founding Regulation
				hardware and software products in dialogue with industry, to collect and analyze data on security incidents in Europe and emerging risks, to promote risk assessment and risk management methods to enhance the capability to deal with information security threats, to exchange best practices and to track development of standards for products and services on network and information society.	
ERA European Railway Agency	91 TFEU (ex 71(1) TEC)	Reg. 881/2004 (OJ 2004, L 164/1)	Valenciennes	To reinforce safety and interoperability of railways throughout Europe	• EU subsidy • contributions by third countries participating in the work of the agency • charges for publication, training and any other services provided

Name	Legal Basis of Founding Regulation Article	Founding Regulation	Seat	Type of Task	Revenue according to Founding Regulation
ESMA European Securities and Markets Authority	114 TFEU (ex 95 TEC)	Reg. 1095/2010 (OJ 2010, L 331/84)	Paris	Improving the functioning of the internal market, in particular by ensuring a high, effective and consistent level of regulation and supervision, guarantee a level playing field, and strengthen international supervisory coordination, providing advice to the Union institutions.	• EU subsidy • obligatory contributions from MS supervisory authorities • fees
ETF European Training Foundation	352(1) TFEU (ex 308 TEC) According to Reg 1339/2008 the legal basis is 166 TFEU (ex 150 TEC)	Reg. 1360/90 (OJ 1990, L 131/1) replaced by Reg. 1339/2008 (OJ 2008, L 354/82)	Turin	To contribute to the development and vocational training systems in partner countries and to facilitate dialogue amongst stakeholders by developing international, national and local networks.	• EU subsidy • payment for services • other resources

Name	Legal Basis of Founding Regulation Article	Founding Regulation	Seat	Type of Task	Revenue according to Founding Regulation
EU-OSHA European Agency for Safety and Health at Work	352(1) TFEU (ex 308 TEC)	Reg. 2062/94 (OJ 1994, L 216/1)	Bilbao	To develop, analyze and disseminate information to improve occupational safety and health in Europe and to develop a comprehensive network with national focus points, European institutions, European social partners, and international organizations.	• EU subsidy • payment for services
Eurofound European Foundation for the Improvement of Living and Working Conditions	352(1) TFEU (ex 308 TEC)	Reg. 1365/75 (OJ 1975, L 139/1)	Dublin	To provide information, advice and expertise – on living and working conditions, industrial relations and managing change in Europe – for key actors in the field of EU social policy on the basis of comparative information, research and analysis.	• EU subsidy

Name	Legal Basis of Founding Regulation Article	Founding Regulation	Seat	Type of Task	Revenue according to Founding Regulation
Eurojust European Union's Judicial Cooperation Unit	82, 83, 85 TFEU (ex 31(2), 34(2)(c) (repealed) TEU)	Council Decision 2002/187/JHA (OJ 2002, L 63/1)	The Hague	To enhance the effectiveness of the competent authorities within MS when they are dealing with serious cross-border and organized crime, to stimulate and improve the coordination of investigations and prosecutions and to support the MS in order to render their investigations and prosecutions more effective.	• EU subsidy • other sources (Subsidy from participating in Criminal Justice Program?)
Europol European Police Office	87, 88 TFEU (ex 30(1)(b), 30(2), 34(2)(c) (repealed) TEU)	Council Decision 2009/371/JHA (OJ 2009, L 121/37)	The Hague	To help MS co-operate more closely and effectively in preventing and combating organized international crime by facilitating the exchange of information between Europol and Europol Liaison Officers, providing	• EU subsidy • other types of income possible

Name	Legal Basis of Founding Regulation Article	Founding Regulation	Seat	Type of Task	Revenue according to Founding Regulation
				operational analysis and supporting MS' organizations, providing expertise and technical support for investigations and operations carried out within the EU and generating strategic reports and crime analysis in the basis of information and intelligence supplied by MS or gathered from other sources.	
FRA European Union Agency for Fundamental Rights	352(1) TFEU (ex 308 TEC)	Reg. 168/2007 (OJ 2007, L 53/1)	Vienna	To provide EU institutions and Member States with information, assistance and expertise on fundamental rights when implementing community law, and to support them in taking measures and formulating appropriate courses of action.	• EU subsidy • other sources possible

Name	Legal Basis of Founding Regulation Article	Founding Regulation	Seat	Type of Task	Revenue according to Founding Regulation
FRONTEX European Agency for the Management of Operational Cooperation at the External Borders of the Member States of the European Union	77(2)(a), 74 TFEU (ex 62(2)(a), 66 TEC)	Reg. 2007/2004 (OJ 2004, L 349/1)	Warsaw	To coordinate operational cooperation between Member States in the field of management of external borders, to assist Member States in the training of national border guards, to strengthen border security by ensuring the coordination of MS' actions in the implementation of EU measures relating to the management of external borders, and to promote overall cohesion by liasing with other EU partners responsible for the security of the external border.	• EU subsidy • contribution from the countries associated with the implementation application and development of the Schengen aquis • fees for services provided • any voluntary contribution from the MS

Name	Legal Basis of Founding Regulation Article	Founding Regulation	Seat	Type of Task	Revenue according to Founding Regulation
GSA European GNSS Agency	352(1) TFEU (ex 308 TEC) According to Reg 912/2010 the legal basis is 188 TFEU (ex 172 TEC)	Reg. 1321/2004 (OJ 2004, L 246/1) Replaced by: Reg. 912/2010 (OJ 2010, L 276/11)	Prague	To manage the European satellite navigation programmes	• EU subsidy • other resources and dues (yet to be defined!) possible
IT-Agency European Agency for the operational management of large-scale IT systems in the area of freedom, security and justice	74, 77(2)(a) and (b), 78(2)(e), 79(2)(c), 82(1)(d), 85(1), 87(2)(a), and 88(2) TFEU	Reg. 1077/2011 (OJ 2011 L 286/1)	Tallin	To keep the IT systems under its responsibility functioning 24 hours a day, seven days a week, ensuring the continuous, uninterrupted exchange of data between national authorities, to adopt and implement security measures, to organise training for IT experts on the systems under its management, and reporting, publishing statistics and monitoring research activities.	• EU subsidy • contribution from the countries associated with the implementation, application and development of the Schengen *acquis* and Eurodac-related measures; • any financial contribution from the Member States

Name	Legal Basis of Founding Regulation Article	Founding Regulation	Seat	Type of Task	Revenue according to Founding Regulation
OHIM Office for Harmonisation in the Internal Market	352(1) TFEU (ex 308 TEC)	Reg. 40/94 (OJ 1994, L 11/1) replaced by Reg. 207/2009 (OJ 2009, L 78/1	Alicante	To register and manage the applications for the Community trade mark and Community registered design.	• fees • EU subsidy if necessary • other types of income possible

EU EXECUTIVE AGENCIES

Name	Legal Basis of Founding Regulation Article	Founding Regulation	Seat	Type of Task	Revenue according to Founding Regulation
EACEA Education, Audiovisual and Culture Executive Agency	3(1) Reg. 58/2003/EC	Dec. 2005/56/EC (OJ 2005, L 24/35) Replaced by: Dec. 2009/336/EC (OJ 2009, L 101/26)	Brussels	To implement the EU funded programs and actions in the fields of education and training, active citizenship, youth, audiovisual and culture	• EU subsidy (general budget + EDF) • other revenue possible
EACI Executive Agency for Competitiveness and Innovation	3(1) Reg. 58/2003/EC	Dec. 2004/20/EC (IEEA) (OJ 2004, L 5/85) amended by Dec. 2007/372/EC (OJ 2007, L 140/52)	Brussels	To manage the projects and events funded under Intelligent Energy-Energy Europe program and to disseminate the resulting know-how and best practice.	• EU subsidy

EAHC Executive Agency for Health and Consumers	3(1) Reg. 58/2003/EC	Dec. 2004/858/EC (OJ 2004, L 369/73)	Luxembourg	To manage and support actions to improve and protect human health in the EU	• EU subsidy
ERCEA European Research Council Executive Agency	3(1) Reg. 58/2003/EC	Dec. 2008/37/EC (OJ 2008, L 9/15)	Brussels	To stimulate scientific excellence in Europe by supporting and encouraging the very best, truly creative scientists, scholars and engineers.	• EU subsidy
REA Research Executive Agency	3(1) Reg. 58/2003/EC	Dec. 2008/46/EC (OJ 2008, L 11/9)	Brussels	To manage large parts of the seventh framework programme for research	• EU subsidy
TEN-T EA Trans-European Transport Network Executive Agency	3(1) Reg. 58/2003/EC	Dec. 2007/60/EC (OJ 2007, L 32/88)	Brussels	To manage the projects and events for the promotion of the Trans-European Transport Network (TEN-T)programme	• EU subsidy

AGENCIES SET UP UNDER THE EU'S COMMON SECURITY AND DEFENCE POLICY

EDA European Defence Agency	28 TEU (ex 14 TEU) 42 and 45 TEU according to Council Decision 2011/411/CFSP	Council Joint Action 2004/551/CFSP (OJ 2004, L 245/17) replaced by Council Decision 2011/411/CFSP (OJ 2011, L 183/223)	Brussels	To improve the EU's defence capabilities, especially in the field of crisis management, to promote EU armament cooperations, to assist in the development and overall restructuring of the European defence-related research and technology.	• MS contributions based on GNI • other revenue • for specific purposes: EU subsidy, Member State, third country or other third party contributions
EUISS European Union Institute for Security Studies	28 TEU (ex 14 TEU)	Council Joint Action 2001/554/CFSP (OJ 2001, L 200/1)	Paris	To help create a common European security culture, to support the strategic debate by organizing research and debate on security and defense issues that are of importance to the EU, and to create a network of academics, officials, experts and decision-makers in order to provide a forward-looking analysis on security and defense issues	• MS contributions based on GNI scale • additional contributions from individual Member States or from other sources for specific activities

| EUSC European Union Satellite Centre | 28 TEU (ex 14 TEU) | Council Joint Action 2001/555/CFSP (OJ 2001, L 200/5) | Torrejón de Ardoz | To support the decision-making of the EU by providing analysis of satellite imagery and collateral data. | • MS contributions (except Denmark) based on GNI
• remuneration for services rendered
• miscellaneous income |

Joint Statement and Common Approach of the European Parliament, the Council of the EU and the European Commission on Decentralized Agencies of 19 July 2012

As in many Member States, EU decentralized agencies have become an established part of the way the EU operates. In 2011, thirty one decentralized agencies perform a wide range of important tasks, using a significant amount of resources: they contribute to the implementation of important Union policies, thus helping all the institutions, in particular the Commission, to concentrate on core policy-making tasks. Agencies also have a role in supporting the decision-making process by pooling the technical or specialist expertise available at European and national level and thereby help enhance the cooperation between Member States and the EU in important policy areas. Moreover, the spread of agencies beyond Brussels and Luxembourg adds to the visibility of the Union in the different Member States.

The establishment of agencies was done on a case by case basis and has not been accompanied by an overall vision of their role and place in the Union. Following the Commission Communication entitled 'European agencies: the way forward',[1] addressed to the European Parliament and to the Council in March 2008, the three Institutions have recognised the important role of decentralized agencies in implementing the policies of the EU as independent legal entities and the need to make them a more effective tool in this respect. With a view to assessing the existing situation, specifically the coherence, effectiveness, accountability and transparency of these agencies, and finding common ground on how to improve their work, the European Parliament, the Council of the European Union and the European Commission have

---

1. See COM(2008) 135.

agreed to launch an inter-institutional dialogue on decentralized agencies leading to the creation of an Inter-Institutional Working Group (IIWG) in March 2009.

The IIWG has addressed a number of key issues put forward by the participating institutions, including the role and position of the agencies in the EU's institutional landscape, the creation, structure and operation of these agencies, together with funding, budgetary, supervision and management issues.

The Common Approach in the annex is based on the conclusions reached by the IIWG on decentralized agencies. This Common Approach relates neither to agencies operating in the field of Foreign and Security Policy, nor to executive agencies.

The European Parliament, the Council of the European Union and the European Commission will refer to the Common Approach set out in the annex to this document. While fully acknowledging the legally non-binding character of this Joint Statement and of the Common Approach in its annex, and without prejudice to their attributions in the legislative and annual budgetary procedures, the institutions will take this Common Approach into account in the context of all their future decisions concerning EU decentralized agencies, following a case by case analysis.

In a political and economic context that is driven by the concern for efficiency gains, the three institutions urge decentralized agencies to pursue their efforts to streamline their activities and increase their performance by implementing those principles set out in the Common Approach which are within their remit.

Member States are also invited to create the conditions for decentralized agencies to operate as efficiently as possible by taking into account the elements of the Common Approach that relate to them.

Taking into account the specificities of each agency, the Commission should present a roadmap on the follow-up to the Common Approach with concrete timetables for the planned initiatives by the end of 2012 at the latest. The implementation of the roadmap should be done in cooperation with agencies whenever relevant. The Commission should inform the European Parliament and the Council regularly, and for the first time by the end of 2013, about progress on the implementation of the roadmap.

Annex

Common Approach

I.   Role and position of agencies in the EU's institutional landscape

Definition and classification of agencies

    1. To avoid confusion among citizens and stakeholders:

- a standard term should be used for future agencies, "European Union agency for …"

- aligning the names of existing agencies should be explored; however the costs that this would entail and the already established image of the agency should be taken into account.

Establishment and ending of agencies

2. The decision to create a new agency should be based on objective impact assessments of all relevant options. Models for standard provisions to be used in any founding act could be developed by the Commission in order to streamline the process.
3. It is important to manage in the best possible way the start-up phase of agencies, for which the Commission is responsible. To this end, the Commission should be empowered to take management measures, including the appointment, for a limited period, of seconded staff and of the interim Director (in principle a Commission official, although justified exceptions can be made).
4. Agencies' founding acts should contain either a sunset or a review clause. Whether a sunset clause or a review clause is the better solution should be decided on a case-by-case basis, taking into account the specificities of each agency. Any sunset clause must be accompanied by the concomitant provisions for disbanding the agency, addressing in particular issues related to staff contracts and budget arrangements.
5. Common and objective criteria should be used to assess both the opportunity to disband agencies or the possibility to merge them:

   - merging agencies should be considered in cases where their respective tasks are overlapping, where synergies can be contemplated or when agencies would be more efficient if inserted in a bigger structure.
   - closing down an agency could be a solution for dealing with underperforming agencies unless the agency is still the most relevant policy option, in which case the Agency should be reformed.

Agencies' seat and role of the host country

6. Without prejudice to the political decision on an agency's seat taken by common agreement between the representatives of the Member States meeting at Head of State or government level or by the Council, to the desirability of geographical spread, and to the objective set in December 2003 by the representatives of the Member States, meeting at head of State or government level (when deciding the seat of new agencies, priority should be given to new Member States):

- the decision on the agency's seat should be taken before the end of the legislative process, in order to allow the agency to be set up directly in the location of its seat.
- objective criteria to be taken into account in order to contribute to the decision making process for choosing an agency's seat may include:

  - the assurance that the agency can be set up on site upon the entry into force of its founding act,
  - the accessibility of the location,
  - the existence of adequate education facilities for the children of staff members,
  - appropriate access to the labour market, social security and medical care for both children and spouses,

- Member States should address those criteria in a transparent way when presenting their offers to host an agency. The Commission is available to help assess the offers of the Member States, if necessary.

7. Concerning the specific criteria of accessibility:

- Member States currently hosting an agency could consider if and how accessibility can be improved in order to increase agencies' overall efficiency and ensure an even better interaction with stakeholders
- during agencies' regular evaluations, the accessibility to the agency could also be assessed.

8. The host State should make a formal commitment at the time of the adoption of the agency's founding act to ensure that all conditions necessary for the operation of the agency are in place by the time the agency starts its operational phase. In addition, it should commit itself to continue to respond to the agency's needs and provide the necessary conditions for the smooth operation of the agency, also after the latter has been set up.

9. All agencies should have headquarters agreements, which should be concluded before the agency starts its operational phase. Agencies still lacking headquarters agreement and the host country in question should reach an agreement in accordance with the legal order of the relevant Member State. The Commission will put together a set of provisions on the basis of existing best practices, to serve as a good orientation tool for future headquarters agreements.

II. Structure and governance of agencies

Management Board

10. To improve the performance of agencies' boards and reinforce their capacity to supervise the administrative, operational and budgetary management of agencies, while guaranteeing full participation of the Member States and of the Commission:

   - the composition of the board should be:

     - one representative from each Member State,
     - two representatives from the Commission without prejudice to the relevant arrangements for existing agencies,
     - where appropriate, one member designated by the European Parliament, without prejudice to the relevant arrangements for existing agencies,
     - where appropriate, a fairly limited number of stakeholders' representatives.

   - members of the boards should be appointed in light of their knowledge of the agency's core business, taking into account relevant managerial, administrative and budgetary skills.
   - the duration of the term of office of board members should be four years (renewable); all parties should increase efforts to limit turnover of their representatives in the boards, in order to ensure continuity of the boards' work.
   - in order to streamline the decision making process in the agency and contribute to enhancing efficiency and effectiveness, a two-level governance structure should be introduced, when this promises more efficiency: in addition to the Management Board, giving general orientations for the agency's activities, a small-sized Executive Board, with the presence of a Commission representative, should operate and be more closely involved in the monitoring of the agency's activities, with a view to reinforcing supervision of administrative and budgetary management, in particular on audit matters.

11. A coherent policy on preventing and managing conflict of interests concerning members of the Management Board, whether or not they sit in personal capacity, should be developed and applied in all agencies.

12. In order to align it with the situation within the Institutions, the agency's Management Board should be given the powers of the Appointing Authority, not only for the Director but also for the rest of the staff. Except for the appointment of the Director, these competences should, however, be delegated to the Director and the board should only become involved on a case by case basis in exceptional circumstances.

13. For the sake of consistency, agencies' boards should in principle take decisions with the same voting rules:

   - absolute majority voting for current business matters
   - 2/3 majority for the appointment and dismissal of the director, the designation of the chairperson of the board, adoption of the annual budget and of the work programme. Exceptions to this approach can be foreseen, if justified in specific cases.

Director

14. Given the wide tasks attributed to Agencies' Directors by agencies' constituent acts, their role is crucial for agencies' governance, notably as regards the overall agencies' management and relationship towards EU institutions. They are responsible for the administrative management of the agencies, and for the implementation of the duties assigned to the agencies. In this framework, they are in particular in charge of the implementation of work programmes, budget and decisions taken by the Management Board and are a full management power concerning financial and staff matters. They are the legal representatives of the agencies.

15. Agencies' Directors are, first and foremost, accountable to their Management Board, to which they submit an annual report, including accounts. They are also accountable to the European Parliament and the Council for the use of the EU contribution through the annual discharge procedure. However, the discharge procedure focuses on accountability and regulatory compliance, rather than on performance per se. This is due, inter alia, to the lack of performance indicators. Agencies' Directors should therefore be more clearly accountable for performance. To this end, tailored performance indicators should be introduced allowing for effective assessment of the results achieved in terms of objectives.

16. To respect the autonomy of the agencies, it is up to the Management Board to appoint Directors on the basis of a shortlist drawn up by the Commission following an open and transparent selection procedure that guarantees a rigorous evaluation of candidates and a high level of independence. Exceptions to this approach can be foreseen if justified in specific cases.

17. Directors' terms of office are defined in Agencies' constituent acts. In those cases where the Director has performed well, the Management Board, acting as appointing authority, may decide to extend once his/her mandate. The opportunity is assessed against the evaluation of the Director's first mandate which takes into account both annual appraisal reports and foreseen requirements of the Agency for the next years. A director whose term of office has been extended should not participate in another selection procedure for the same post at the end of the overall period.

18. A coherent policy on preventing and managing conflict of interests concerning the Director should be developed and applied in all agencies. The Commission should examine, together with the agencies, whether there is scope for a harmonised approach.

19. A procedure should be foreseen for dismissing the Director in the event of misconduct, unsatisfactory performance or recurring / serious irregularities; it should mirror the appointment procedure.

Other internal bodies:

20. The functioning of scientific committees should be improved:

- Agencies should exchange information on their experience with scientific committees and possibly contribute to developing a coordinated approach to common problems in this area. The Commission will provide support, as appropriate.
- Selection procedures should be periodically reviewed, notably in the context of the agency's evaluations. The following elements should be assessed: their degree of transparency, their cost-effectiveness, and their suitability to ensure independence and competence of members of scientific committees and to prevent conflicts of interests.
- The independence of the scientific experts should be fully ensured, inter alia by promoting the highest standards, setting sound selection criteria and promoting best practices. The Commission will provide guidelines on standards, criteria and best practice, including on how EU agencies' national counterparts should be involved. In addition, this issue should also be covered by the regular external evaluations of the agencies.

21. For Boards of appeal, the same measures as for scientific committees, notably in terms of exchange of best practice and assessment of selection procedures, should apply. The impartiality and independence of their members should continue to be guaranteed, on the basis of transparent and objectively verifiable criteria to be defined by agencies. In this context, recruitment of Board of Appeal's members from among the staff of the agency and/or the agency's Management Board should be taken with great care and should not put into question the above-mentioned principles of impartiality and independence.

22. Taking into account the importance of their contributions to the work of agencies' internal bodies, it is advisable that Member States regularly review the adequacy of resources/staff they assign for this purpose and take appropriate actions to remedy possible weaknesses. In addition, it is important that they ensure information flows between the different authorities concerned at national level in relation to agencies' activities, inter alia by appointing contact points in their national administrations for relations with the given

agency. This contact point should be in principle the representative of the Member State sitting in the management board.

III. Operation of agencies

23. In order to deliver the administrative support that agencies need to operate in the most efficient manner, the following three options can be envisaged:

    - improving or extending the services provided by the Commission
    - merging smaller agencies to achieve economies of scale based on an impact assessment
    - sharing services between agencies, either by proximity of locations or by policy area.

24. Concerning the creation or handling of EU classified information, agencies should apply a level of protection equivalent to that afforded by the security rules of the Council or the Commission, as appropriate:

    - relevant provisions should be introduced in the founding acts. For existing agencies, agencies' Management Boards should adopt appropriate decisions as soon as possible, even before the founding acts are formally amended.
    - the introduction of any new provisions on classified information should not be detrimental to the European Parliament's current right of access to agencies' information, nor imply the multiplication of bilateral agreements between the EP and EU bodies and agencies

25. Agencies' international relations should be streamlined:

    - Agencies whose mandate or work programme foresees cooperation with third countries and/or international organisations should have a clear strategy for those activities. This strategy should, in principle, be embedded in the annual and/or multi-annual work programme(s), with a specification of associated resources, and should lay down a number of principles and modalities for international cooperation.
    - This strategy and appropriate working arrangements with partner DGs in the Commission should ensure that the agencies operate within their mandate and the existing institutional framework, and that they are not seen as representing the EU position to an outside audience or as committing the EU to international obligations.
    - The strategy and specific initiatives with an international dimension (e.g. administrative arrangements with third countries) should be subject to approval by the Management Board.
    - An early exchange of information should take place on respective international activities between agencies, the Commission and the relevant EU Delegations, to ensure the consistency of EU policy.

26. Agencies should be entitled to engage in communication activities, within the following framework:

- the content and implementation of an agency's communication strategy should be coherent, relevant and coordinated with the strategies and activities of the Commission and the other institutions in order to take into consideration the broader EU image.
- ground rules for agencies' communication strategies will be developed by the Commission, in cooperation with the agencies.
- Communication activities should not be detrimental to agencies' core tasks.
- Agencies' access to central communication tools and coordination structures should be facilitated. Agencies should also be able to make use of Commission's framework contracts.

IV. Programming of activities and resources

Annual and multiannual work programmes

27. As far as possible, annual work programmes could be based on a template, in order to ease comparisons.
28. In addition to annual work programmes, agencies should draw up multiannual strategic programmes or guidelines, tailored to the specificities of their activities. Such multiannual activity planning should be linked with multiannual resource planning (budget and staff in particular).
29. The Commission should always be consulted and issue a formal advice on both documents. The European Parliament should be consulted on the multiannual work programmes of agencies, provided that the purpose of the consultations is an exchange of views and the outcome is not binding on the agency. For the annual work programme, the actual practice of the agency's Director presenting it to the relevant EP committee should continue.
30. Multi-annual work programmes should include the actions necessary to respond to the outcome of overall evaluations.
31. Key performance indicators should be developed by the agencies and the Commission and be adapted to agencies' specificities. Furthermore, the link between financial and human resources and each specific action to be carried out should be reinforced and become systematic. The link between successive annual work programmes and the multiannual programme should be enhanced.
32. The Director should report to the Management Board on the agency's progress in implementing the multiannual work programme. This reporting should take place prior to setting the objectives of the following annual work programme and be integrated in the reporting cycle on the annual work programme.

Human resources

33. While fully guaranteeing the respect of the principles of accountability and transparency, an effort should be made to simplify Agencies' human resources procedures and to better take into account their specificities in this field, to the extent necessary for ensuring their smooth functioning.

34. Agencies' Staff Policy Plans (SPP) should provide a full picture of their staff needs and therefore include comprehensive and detailed information on the number of all types of external staff, including interim staff and service providers; information on promotions, as well as gender and geographical balance should continue to be reflected. The smallest agencies should not be requested to provide the number of estimated promotions per grade, but only an overall figure, so as to avoid the early identification of individual promotions. The Commission, in cooperation with agencies, should make the necessary adjustments to the SPP template and consider potential other improvements to the SPP format.

35. Agencies' human resources programming as presented in the SPP and the preparation of the Draft Budget of the Union need to be consistent. The respective calendars of the presentation of the establishment plans and SPPs should therefore be aligned. The agencies should submit their draft SPPs and establishment plans to the Commission (and for information to the Management Board) by 31 January. Taking into account the Commission's reasoned opinion on the draft SPPs, agencies should adopt their final SPPs and submit them to the budgetary authority and the Commission by end May. For transparency purposes, agencies need to provide adequate explanations if they decide not to fully take into account the Commission's opinion on their draft SPP.

Funding, management of budgetary resources and budgetary procedure

36. Agencies should improve their internal planning and general revenue forecasting in order to reduce their high carry over and cancellation rates. The Commission will provide guidance in this regard. In addition, agencies should improve their management of commitments in order to align them with real needs.

37. For agencies fully financed from the EU budget, the surplus should continue to be recovered in the usual manner, i.e. unused funds from year n are deducted from the EU subsidy for year n+2, after recovery in year n+1.

38. For self-financed agencies, fees should be set at a realistic level to avoid the accumulation of significant surpluses.

39. For partially self-financed agencies, the clients should pay for the full cost of the services provided to them by those agencies, including the employer's prorata contribution to the pension scheme. Concerning the issue of how to deal with a possible shortfall against forecast of fee revenue from the clients and the need to ensure the availability of necessary funding to agencies, the Commission will investigate the necessity and possible modalities of creating a limited ring-fenced reserve fund to be operated in a transparent way.

40. All agencies should apply, more systematically than at present, a system of activity based budgeting / activity based management (ABB/ABM). The available ABB/ABM tools (i.e. to plan, monitor, report and evaluate activities) should be adapted to the reality of agencies. In this context, agencies should be encouraged to exchange best practice and their idea to develop an ABB/ABM toolbox is to be welcomed. The Commission will provide assistance in this regard, for instance by giving a general ABB training to agencies.

41. In order to avoid automatisms, all relevant actors should respect their duty, within the budgetary procedure, to provide adequate justification for their requests with regard to each agency's budget (initial budget request, increases, decreases).

42. In order to justify the need for additional (financial and/or human) resources in the case of agencies being in their "start-up phase" or agencies being entrusted with new tasks, a legislative financial statement should be presented to the legislative and budgetary authorities.

43. Should the legislative authority decide to assign additional tasks to agencies as compared to the initial Commission proposal, the reprioritization of their activities should always be considered as an alternative besides granting additional resources. In the latter case, the Commission will update previous legislative financial statements, so as to clarify the additional resources required by the agency in question to carry out such additional tasks. Subsequently, the revised legislative financial statement would be presented to a budgetary trilogue. The same procedure should apply to new agency's tasks which do not derive from a modification of the basic act of the agency.

44. Any modification to agencies' budgets which does not require the budget authority's approval should be communicated to the latter, together with adequate justification.

45. While respecting the principles of transparency, accountability and sound financial management, an effort should be made to simplify the implementation of the Financial Regulation rules by the Agencies, to the extent necessary for ensuring their smooth functioning.

V. Accountability, controls and transparency and relations with stakeholders

Reporting requirements

46. Agencies reporting obligations need to be streamlined and harmonized. In principle, agencies should produce one single Annual Report; exceptions should however be possible.

47. The single Annual Report should include information on the implementation of their annual work programme, budget and staff policy plan, management and internal control systems, internal /external audit findings, the follow-up to the audit recommendations and to the discharge recommendation, as well as the statement of assurance of the Executive Director. The single Annual Report could also include the information resulting from the Financial Statements and from the report on budgetary and financial management foreseen in the context of the discharge procedure, provided the time constraints of the preparation of the EU annual consolidated accounts are respected.

48. As far as possible, the structure of the single Annual Report should include a number of common elements based on best practice across agencies, with a view to easing comparison. The Commission should develop an indicative template in cooperation with agencies.

49. This single Annual Report should be drawn by the agency's Director, who should present it to the agency's Management Board for assessment. The Director or the Board itself should then transmit the Report and the assessment of the Management Board to the Court of Auditors, to the Parliament and Council and to the Commission by 1st July.

Internal audit

50. The costs of basic Internal Audit Service (IAS) work should remain to be covered by the Commission. As basic audit work, IAS will undertake a risk assessment to maximise its coverage of major risks over a three-year cycle, maintaining, as far as possible, the current practice of one audit per year in each agency.

51. Internal audits have a clear added value and agencies need to accept the burden associated to them. To facilitate this acceptance, IAS should discuss its audit planning with agencies' management, in order to avoid an overlap of audit topics or calendar with audits from the Internal Audit Capabilities (IACs), when they exist, or from the European Court of Auditors (ECA).

52. The internal auditor shall continue to report to the executive director and to the management board. The appropriate follow-up of IAS audit conclusions should be organised at board level, possibly by the Executive Board if there is one. This should not increase administrative expenses.

53. Concerning the internal audit architecture of agencies, agencies should have the possibility to set up internal audit services to complement the work of the IAS. Therefore, Agencies (Executive Directors and Boards) may decide to set up an Internal Audit Capability (IAC) that follows internationally recognised standards of internal auditing and coordinate audit work and exchange information with IAS. If this is not cost-effective or possible, agencies may decide to contribute resources and share a full-fledged IAC with another agency. IACs should also be required to coordinate audit plans with the IAS.

External audit

54. Without prejudice to the competences of the European Court of Auditors (ECA), private sector auditors might have to be involved in the external audit of agencies accounts in order to remedy the lack of resources of the ECA. Should this be the case, the appointment of those private sector auditors should be done in conformity with the applicable rules and appropriate control mechanisms should be put in place, in order to ensure that work on the legality and regularity of revenue and expenditure and the reliability of an agency's accounts is carried out in accordance with the required standards. All aspects of such outsourced external audits, including the reported audit findings, remain under the full responsibility of the ECA, which manages all administrative and procurement procedures required and finances these, as well as any other costs associated with outsourced external audits, from its own budget.

55. Cooperation should continue to be promoted between all audit bodies involved, bearing in mind their respective mandate, purposes as well as their legal or regulatory bases.

Discharge

56. Agencies should systematically inform their partner Directorate General and the Directorate General for the Budget within the Commission of the results of the audit of the European Court of Auditors (at the earliest stage possible), as well as of the measures taken to meet the recommendations of the discharge authority and those of the Court.

57. A more rigorous differentiation between the responsibilities of the Commission and those of the agencies would be appropriate in discharge decisions and resolutions. Council's recommendations on the discharge of each agency should be fully taken into consideration.

58. The possibilities for securing democratic accountability for fully self-financed agencies (i.e. financed by their clients) should be explored, as they are Union bodies in charge of implementing EU policies but not subject to a discharge within the meaning of the TFUE. A possibility could be that the agencies in question, submit to the European Parliament, to the Council and to the

Commission an annual report on the execution of their budget and consider requests or recommendations issued by the Parliament and Council.

Alert/warning system

59. An alert/warning system will be activated by the Commission if it has serious reasons for concern that an agency's Management Board is about to take decisions which may not comply with the mandate of the agency, may violate EU law or be in manifest contradiction with EU policy objectives. In these cases, the Commission will raise formally the question in the Management Board and request it to refrain from adopting the relevant decision. Should the Management Board set aside the request, the Commission will formally inform the European Parliament and the Council, with a view to allow the three institutions to react quickly. The Commission may request the Management Board to refrain from implementing the contentious decision while the representatives of the three institutions are still discussing the issue.

Evaluation of the agencies

60. Each agency's founding act should provide for a periodic overall evaluation, to be commissioned by the Commission. The first evaluation should take place five years after the agency has started its operational phase. Subsequent evaluations should be conducted every five years and on the occasion of every second evaluation the sunset/review clause should be applied. Evaluations should be conducted in a manner that provides solid grounds for a decision to continue or discontinue the agency's mandate. The feasibility of a common template for agencies' evaluation should be explored.

61. Ex-ante evaluation of agencies' activities/programmes should be either made mandatory for programmes/activities of a significant budget, or done at the request of the Management board or the executive board, if deemed necessary. Ex-post evaluation should be mandatory for all programmes/activities.

62. Agencies should prepare a roadmap with a follow-up action plan regarding the conclusions of retrospective evaluations, and report on progress bi-annually to the Commission. Follow-up to evaluations should be a task of the Management Board, and of the Executive Board if there is one.

63. In addition to the performance information presented in agencies' annual reports, the Commission should provide Parliament and Council with any other information on the evaluation of agencies if requested.

Transparency and relations with stakeholders

64. Agencies' websites should be made as multilingual as possible, in order to facilitate their consultation by citizens of all Member States. Agencies should provide, via their websites, information necessary to ensure transparency, including financial transparency.

65. Agencies' relations with stakeholders should be coherent with their mandate, the institutional division of tasks in international relations, EU policies and priorities and Commission's actions. Agencies should exercise their functions in coordination with the different actors charged with the definition and implementation of the given policy. Agencies should also clarify the sharing of roles between them and their national counterparts. When relevant stakeholders are not represented in management boards, they should be involved in agencies' internal bodies and/or advisory groups/working groups, if appropriate.

Prevention, detection and investigation of fraud, corruption, irregularities and other illegal activities

66. OLAF's role vis-à-vis agencies should be formalised, enhanced and made more visible. In order to preserve evidence and/or to avoid inadvertently alerting persons concerned, agencies should refrain from carrying out investigations on facts liable to lead to an investigation by OLAF, in conformity with relevant EU legislation. In addition, agencies should be more active in relation to fraud prevention and should also better communicate on those activities.

EUROPEAN MONOGRAPH SERIES

1. Lammy Betten (ed.), *The Future of European Social Policy*, 1991 (ISBN 90-654-4585-4).
2. Annemarie Loman, Kamiel Mortelmans, Harry H.G. Post & Stewart Watson, *Culture and Common Law: Before and After Maastricht*, 1992 (ISBN 90-654-4638-9).
3. John A.E. Vervaele, *Fraud against the Community: The Need for European Fraud Legislation*, 1994 (ISBN 90-654-4634-6).
4. Philip Raworth, *The Legislative Process in the European Community*, 1993 (ISBN 90-654-4690-7).
5. Jules Stuyck, *Financial and Monetary Integration in the European Economic Community*, 1993 (ISBN 90-654-4718-0).
6. Jules Stuyck & A.J. Vossestein (eds), *State Entrepreneurship, National Monopolies and European Community Law*, 1993 (ISBN 90-654-4773-3).
7. Jules Stuyck & A. Looijestijn-Clearie (eds), *The European Economic Area EC-EFTA*, 1994 (ISBN 90-654-4815-2).
8. Rosita B. Bouterse, *Competition and Integration: What Goals Count?*, 1995 (ISBN 90-654-4816-0).
9. René Barents, *The Agricultural Law of the EC: An Inquiry into the Administrative Law*, 1994 (ISBN 90-654-4867-5).
10. Nicholas Emiliou, *Principles of Proportionality in European Law: A Comparative Study*, 1996 (ISBN 90-411-0866-1).
11. Eivind Smith, *National Parliaments as Cornerstones of European Integration*, 1996 (ISBN 90-411-0898-X).
12. Jan H. Jans, *European Environmental Law*, 1996 (ISBN 90-411-0877-7).
13. Síofra O'Leary, *The Evolving Concept of Community Citizenship: From the Free Movement of Persons to Union Citizenship*, 1997 (ISBN 90-411-0878-5).
14. Laurence W. Gormley (ed.), *Current and Future Perspectives on EC Competition Law*, 1983 (ISBN 90-411-0691-X).
15. Simone White, *Protection of the Financial Interests of the European Communities: The Fight against Fraud and Corruption*, 1998 (ISBN 90-411-9647-1).
16. Morten P. Broberg, *Broberg on the European Commission's Jurisdiction to Scrutinise Mergers*, 4th Edition, 2013 (ISBN 978-90-411-3339-7).
17. Doris Hildebrand, *The Role of Economic Analysis in the EC Competition Rules: The European School*, 2nd Edition, 2002 (ISBN 90-411-1706-7).
18. Christof R.A. Swaak, *European Community Law and the Automobile Industry*, 1999 (ISBN 90-411-1140-9).

19. Dorthe Dahlgaard Dingel, *Public Procurement: A Harmonization of the National Judicial Review of the Application of European Community Law*, 1999 (ISBN 90-411-1161-1).
20. John A.E. Vervaele (ed.), *Compliance and Enforcement of European Community Law*, 1999 (ISBN 90-411-1151-4).
21. Martin Trybus, *European Defence Procurement Law: International and National Procurement Systems as Models for a Liberalized Defence Procurement Market in Europe*, 1999 (ISBN 90-411-1167-0).
22. Helen Staples, *The Legal Status of Third Country Nationals Resident in the European Union*, 1999 (ISBN 90-411-1277-4).
23. Damien Geradin (ed.), *The Liberalization of State Monopolies in the European Union and Beyond*, 1999 (ISBN 90-411-1264-2).
24. Katja Heede, *European Ombudsman: Redress and Control at Union Level*, 2000 (ISBN 90-411-1413-0).
25. Ulf Bernitz & Joakim Nergelius (eds), *General Principles of European Community Law*, 2000 (ISBN 90-411-1402-5).
26. Michaela Drahos, *Convergence of Competition Laws and Policies in the European Community*, 2002 (ISBN 90-411-1562-5).
27. Damien Geradin (ed.), *The Liberalization of Electricity and Natural Gas in the European Union*, 2001 (ISBN 90-411-1560-9).
28. Gisella Gori, *Towards an EU Right to Education*, 2001 (ISBN 90-411-1670-2).
29. Brendan P.G. Smith, *Constitution Building in the European Union*, 2001 (ISBN 90-411-1695-8).
30. Friedl Weiss & Frank Wooldridge, *Free Movement of Persons within the European Community*, 2nd Edition, 2007 (ISBN 978-90-411-2545-3).
31. Ingrid Boccardi, *Europe and Refugees: Towards an EU Asylum Policy*, 2002 (ISBN 90-411-1709-1).
32. John A.E. Vervaele & André Klip (eds), *European Cooperation Between Tax, Customs and Judicial Authorities*, 2001 (ISBN 90-411-1747-4).
33. Wouter P.J. Wils, *The Optimal Enforcement of EC Antitrust Law: Essays in Law and Economics*, 2002 (ISBN 90-411-1757-1).
34. Damien Geradin (ed.), *The Liberalization of Postal Services in the European Union*, 2002 (ISBN 90-411-1780-6).
35. Nick Bernard, *Multilevel Governance in the European Union*, 2002 (ISBN 90-411-1812-8).
36. Jill Wakefield, *Judicial Protection through the Use of Article 288(2) EC*, 2002 (ISBN 90-411-1823-3).
37. Sebastiaan Princen, *EU Regulation and Transatlantic Trade*, 2002 (ISBN 90-411-1871-3).

38. Amaryllis Verhoeven, *The European Union in Search of a Democratic and Constitutional Theory*, 2002 (ISBN 90-411-1872-1).
39. Paul L.C. Torremans, *Cross Border Insolvencies in EU, English and Belgian Law*, 2002 (ISBN 90-411-1888-8).
40. Malcolm Anderson & Joanna Apap (eds), *Police and Justice Cooperation and the New European Borders*, 2002 (ISBN 90-411-1893-4).
41. Christin M. Forstinger, *Takeover Law in EU and USA: A Comparative Analysis*, 2002 (ISBN 90-411-1919-1).
42. Antonio Bavasso, *Communications in EU Antitrust Law: Market Power and Public Interest*, 2003 (ISBN 90-411-1974-4).
43. Fiona G. Wishlade, *Regional State Aid and Competition Policy in the European Union*, 2003 (ISBN 90-411-1975-2).
44. Gareth Davies, *Nationality Discrimination in the European Internal Market*, 2003 (ISBN 90-411-1998-1).
45. René Barents, *The Autonomy of Community Law*, 2003 (ISBN 90-411-2251-6).
46. Gerhard Dannecker & Oswald Jansen (eds), *Competition Law Sanctioning in the European Union*, 2004 (ISBN 90-411-2100-5).
47. Nauta Dutilh (ed.), *Dealing with Dominance: The Experience of National Competition Authorities*, 2004 (ISBN 90-411-2211-7).
48. Stefaan van den Bogaert, *Practical Regulation of the Mobility of Sportsmen in the EU Post Bosman*, 2005 (ISBN 90-411-2327-X).
49. Katalin Judit Cseres, *Competition Law and Consumer Protection*, 2005 (ISBN 90-411-2380-6).
50. Philipp Kiiver, *The National Parliaments in the European Union: A Critical View on EU Constitution Building*, 2006 (ISBN 978-90-411-2452-4).
51. Alexander Turk, *The Concept of Legislation in European Community Law*, 2006 (ISBN 978-90-411-2472-2).
52. Dimitrios Sinaniotis, *The Interim Protection of Individuals before the European and National Courts*, 2006 (ISBN 978-90-411-2498-2).
53. M. Holoubek & D. Damjanovic, M. Traimer (eds), *Regulating Content: The European Regulatory Framework for the Media and Related Creative Sectors*, 2006 (ISBN 978-90-411-2597-2).
54. Anneli Albi & Jacques Ziller (eds), *The European Constitution and National Constitutions: Ratification and Beyond*, 2006 (ISBN 978-90-411-2524-8).
55. Gustavo E. Luengo, *Regulation of Subsidies and State Aids in WTO and EC Law: Conflicts in International Trade Law*, 2007 (ISBN 978-90-411-2547-7).
56. Eniko Horvath, *Mandating Identity: Citizenship, Kinship Laws and Plural Nationality in the European Union*, 2007 (ISBN 978-90-411-2662-7).

57. Rass Holdgaard, *External Relations Law of the European Community: Legal Reasoning and Legal Discourses*, 2007 (ISBN 978-90-411-2604-7).
58. Jill Wakefield, *The Right to Good Administration*, 2007 (ISBN 978-90-411-2697-9).
59. Dimitry Kochenov, *EU Enlargement and the Failure of Conditionality: Pre- accession Conditionality in the Fields of Democracy and the Rule of Law*, 2008 (ISBN 978-90-411-2696-2).
60. Despina Mavromati, *The Law of Payment Services in the EU: The EC Directive on Payment Services in the Internal Market*, 2008 (ISBN 978-90-411-2700-6).
61. Anne Meuwese, *Impact Assessment in EU Lawmaking*, 2008 (ISBN 978-90-411-2720-4).
62. Ulf Bernitz, Joakim Nergelius & Cecilia Cardner (eds), *General Principles of EC Law in a Process of Development*, 2008 (ISBN 978-90-411-2705-1).
63. Johan van de Gronden (ed.), *The EU and WTO Law on Services: Limits to the Realisation of General Interest Policies within the Services Markets?*, 2008 (ISBN 978-90-411-2809-6).
64. Alina Tryfonidou, *Reverse Discrimination in EC Law*, 2009 (ISBN 978-90-411-2751-8).
65. Mikael Berglund, *Cross-Border Enforcement of Claims in the EU: History Present Time and Future*, 2009 (ISBN 978-90-411-2861-4).
66. Theodore Konstadinides, *Division of Powers in European Union Law: The Delimitation of Internal Competence between the EU and the Member States*, 2009 (ISBN 978-90-411-2615-3).
67. Mattias Derlén, *Multilingual Interpretation of European Union Law*, 2009 (ISBN 978-90-411-2853-9).
68. René Barents, *Directory of EU Case Law on the Preliminary Ruling Procedure*, 2009 (ISBN 978-90-411-3150-8).
69. Yan Luo, *Anti-dumping in the WTO, the EU and China: The Rise of Legalization in the Trade Regime and its Consequences*, 2010 (ISBN 978-90-411-3207-9).
70. Patrick Birkinshaw & Mike Varney (eds), *The European Union Legal Order after Lisbon*, 2010 (ISBN 978-90-411-3152-2).
71. Thomas Gr. Papadopoulos, *EU Law and Harmonization of Takeovers in the Internal Market*, 2010 (978-90-411-3340-3).
72. Bas van Bockel, *The* Ne Bis In Idem *Principle in EU Law*, 2010 (978-90-411-3156-0).
73. Veljko Milutinović, *The 'Right to Damages' under EU Competition Law: From* Courage v. Crehan *to the White Paper and Beyond*, 2010 (978-90-411-3235-2).

74. Amandine Garde, *EU Law and Obesity Prevention*, 2010 (978-90-411-2706-8).
75. Leonard Besselink, Frans Pennings & Sacha Prechal (eds), *The Eclipse of the Legality Principle in the European Union*, 2011 (978-90-411-3262-8).
76. Sacha Garben, *EU Higher Education Law: The Bologna Process and Harmonization by Stealth*, 2011 (978-90-411-3365-6).
77. Dimitry Kochenov (ed.), *EU Law of the Overseas: Outermost Regions, Associated Overseas Countries and Territories, Territories Sui Generis*, 2011 (978-90-411-3445-5).
78. Pablo Ibáñez Colomo, *European Communications Law and Technological Convergence: Deregulation, Re-regulation and Regulatory Convergence in Television and Telecommunications*, 2012 (978-90-411-3829-3).
79. Elise Muir, *EU Regulation of Access to Labour Markets: A Case Study of EU Constraints on Member State Competences*, 2012 (978-90-411-3823-1).
80. Tim Corthaut, *EU Ordre Public*, 2012 (978-90-411-3232-1).
81. Oana Ştefan, *Soft Law in Court: Competition Law, State Aid and the Court of Justice of the European Union*, 2013 (978-90-411-3997-9).
82. Francesco Rossi dal Pozzo, *Citizenship Rights and Freedom of Movement in the European Union*, 2013 (978-90-411-4660-1).
83. Jens Hartig Danielsen, *EU Agricultural Law*, 2013 (978-90-411-3280-2).
84. Ulf Bernitz, Xavier Groussot & Felix Schulyok (eds), *General Principles of EU Law and European Private Law*, 2013 (978-90-411-4683-0).
85. Michelle Everson, Cosimo Monda & Ellen Vos (eds), European Agencies in between Institutions and Member States, 2014 (978-90-411-2843-0).

Ingram Content Group UK Ltd.
Milton Keynes UK
UKHW022036140323
418579UK00005B/133

9 789041 128430